About this book

Accelerated population ageing is a global trend. It has long been a significant issue for developed countries, and it is now becoming one in the developing world. There is a tendency to depict population ageing as a threat to the future. Rather, it should be recognised as one of the great achievements of the past century – albeit one which also generates a range of social, economic, political and cultural challenges. The wellbeing and quality of life of older people are strongly conditioned by their capacity to manage opportunities and risks. Social protection, both formal and informal, can play a key role in mediating these processes. This book examines relationships between the wellbeing of older people and processes of development, taking examples from a diverse range of low-, middle- and high-income countries. A key message is the danger of generalisation: older people are an extremely heterogeneous group, with varying needs, capabilities and expectations.

The book is divided into three sections. The first explores the wellbeing of older people in selected, very different development contexts – the UK, Brazil, Ukraine and China. The second section focuses on formal social protection for older people. It includes evaluations of pension schemes in four middle-income countries, an assessment of Japan's new long-term care insurance fund, and a comparison of health care financing for pensioners in the USA and Argentina. The third section considers informal social protection and the care economy. This is explored with reference to intergenerational relationships in Ghana, informal care in Mexico, the impact of HIV/AIDS on older people in Thailand, and a wider philosophical discussion of care and social justice.

Taken together, these chapters highlight the complexity of relationships between development and the way later life is experienced. They identify key priorities for policymakers, and map out an urgent research agenda.

About UNRISD

The United Nations Research Institute for Social Development (UNRISD) is an autonomous agency engaging in multidisciplinary research on the social dimensions of contemporary problems affecting development. Its work is guided by the conviction that, for effective development policies to be formulated, an understanding of the social and political context is crucial. The Institute attempts to provide governments, development agencies, grassroots organisations and scholars with a better understanding of how development policies and processes of economic, social and environmental change affect different social groups. Working through an extensive network of national research centres, UNRISD aims to promote original research and strengthen research capacity in developing countries.

Current research programmes include: Civil Society and Social Movements; Democracy, Governance and Human Rights; Identities, Conflict and Cohesion; Social Policy and Development; and Technology, Business and Society.

A list of UNRISD's free and priced publications can be obtained by contacting the Reference Centre, UNRISD, Palais des Nations, 1211 Geneva 10, Switzerland; Phone: (4122) 917 3020; Fax: (4122) 917 0650; E-mail: info@unrisd.org; Internet: http://www.unrisd.org

UNRISD thanks the governments of Denmark, Finland, Mexico, the Netherlands, Norway, Sweden, Switzerland and the United Kingdom for their core funding.

Living Longer

Ageing, Development and Social Protection

edited by
Peter Lloyd-Sherlock

UNRISD

UNITED NATIONS RESEARCH INSTITUTE
FOR SOCIAL DEVELOPMENT

Zed Books

LONDON & NEW YORK

Living Longer: Ageing, Development and Social Protection
was first published in 2004 by
Zed Books Ltd, 7 Cynthia Street, London N1 9JF, UK and
Room 400, 175 Fifth Avenue, New York, NY 10010, USA

www.zedbooks.co.uk

On behalf of the United Nations Research Institute for Social Development
(UNRISD), Palais des Nations, 1211 Geneva 10, Switzerland

Cover designed by Andrew Corbett
Set in 10½/12 pt Bembo
by Long House, Cumbria, UK
Printed and bound in Malta
by Gutenberg Ltd

Distributed exclusively in the USA by Palgrave Macmillan, a division of
St Martin's Press, LLC, 175 Fifth Avenue, New York, NY 10010

A catalogue record for this book
is available from the British Library

US Cataloging-in-Publication Data
is available from the Library of Congress

ISBN   1 84277 356 9 Hb
        1 84277 357 7 Pb

ACKNOWLEDGEMENTS

This book was largely derived from an UNRISD workshop on Ageing, Development and Social Protection held in Madrid in April 2002 as part of the Second World Assembly on Ageing. UNRISD provided full financial and organisational support for this event. The editor would like to extend his appreciation to the chapter contributors who always responded positively to the numerous rounds of revision that were requested. In particular, he would like to thank Caroline Danloy and Shahra Razavi of UNRISD for their support and encouragement throughout this project.

CONTENTS

Tables

ACRONYMS

AIDS	Acquired Immunity Deficiency Syndrome
ART	Antiretroviral therapy
CNCOA	China National Committee on Ageing
DALY	Disability Adjusted Life Year
FEMEBA	Medical Federation of the Province of Buenos Aires
GDP	gross domestic product
HDI	Human Development Index
HIPC	heavily indebted poor countries
HIV	human immunodeficiency virus
IDEA	Individuals with Disabilities Education Act (US)
IDA	International Development Association (of the World Bank)
IEP	Individualized Education Plan
ILO	International Labour Organisation
INSSJP	National Institute of Social Services for Retirees and Pensioners (Argentina)
JPY	Japanese Yen
KIDS	KwaZulu–Natal Income Dynamics Study
LSMS	Living Standards Measurement Survey (Japan)
NGO	nongovernmental organisation
NIS	newly independent states (of Europe)
NPS	National People's Congress
OECD	Organisation for Economic Cooperation and Development
PAMI	El Programa de Atencíon Médica Integral (Argentina)
PDS	person who dies from AIDS
PHC	primary health care
PRSP	poverty reduction strategy paper
SERPS	State Earnings Related Pension Scheme
SHI	social health insurance
SOE	state-owned enterprise
TFR	total fertility rate
UK	United Kingdom
UN	United Nations
UNDP	United Nations Development Programme
UNFPA	United Nations Population Fund
UNRISD	United Nations Research Institute for Social Development
US	United States of America
WHO	World Health Organisation

PREFACE

In contribution to the United Nations Second World Assembly on Ageing, the United Nations Research Institute for Social Development (UNRISD) carried out, under the umbrella of its Special Events programme, a two-year (2001–3) research project addressing the dynamics and challenges of population ageing in contexts of rapid social change, as well as in situations of social crisis. The project also examined policy responses to population ageing, whether through formal social protection, or through informal care and intergenerational exchange.

Concern over a population's age structure as a social and economic phenomenon has largely been confined to its effect on the dependency ratio (calculated as the number of individuals aged under 15 or over 64 divided by the number of individuals aged between 15 and 64, and expressed as a percentage). In the developing countries, attention has focused on the young, while in the industrialised countries the focus has been on the aged. In the former, there has been particular interest in how the dependency ratio affects development via savings rates, costs of provision of child care and education. In the latter group of countries, demographic shifts have been seen as a threat to the sustainability of a number of welfare activities and systems – including elder care and pensions. It is partly because of this perception of the dependency ratio as driven by different age groups in developing and industrialised countries, respectively, that one finds a limited amount of research on ageing in developing countries.

There are, however, certain features of ageing in the developing countries that call for special attention and justify increased research. First, there are the sheer numbers to contend with: the majority of the world's older people live in the developing countries. Second, demographic transformation in the developing countries is occurring more rapidly than in the industrialised ones, spurred by much faster rates of decline in fertility and mortality. Third, there are new patterns of mortality among various age groups that are likely to create serious and unprecedented problems. In some countries, for example, the scourge of HIV/AIDS is likely to cause a sudden rise in the relative size of the dependent population by reducing the size of the economically active population. We have yet to understand the full implications of such demographic transition. And finally, in any prudent society, the challenges raised by an ageing population should be addressed before they actually set in. Thus the questions of pension systems and infrastructure for the care of the aged in the future must be the concerns of society today. It also bears mentioning that for developing countries, the savings generated in the process of preparing for the future can be a major contributor to the development process itself. How a society thinks about ageing will affect how it mobilises current resources for the future and how it intertemporarily and intergenerationally allocates burdens and gains.

The paradox of the dependency ratio is that it is the result of some great achievements of the twentieth century – sharply reduced infant mortality rates and longer life expectancy, both of which have created new challenges and opportunities that can only be met or captured by well-informed policy measures. Research in these areas is, therefore, vital.

Most of the commissioned chapters appearing in this volume were presented and discussed at an UNRISD conference on Ageing, Development and Social Protection, held in Madrid on 8–9 April 2002 to coincide with the Second World Assembly on Ageing. Thirteen members of the research team and the editor of the volume presented their work at the conference, and a report was subsequently prepared highlighting the issues raised in the presentations and during the discussion. The report was published as an issue of *UNRISD Conference News*.

I would like to express my gratitude to Peter Lloyd-Sherlock, external coordinator of this project, and to Caroline Danloy and Shahra Razavi for in-house coordination. I would also like to thank the United Nations Department of Economic and Social Affairs (UN-DESA), and UNRISD's core funders (the governments of Denmark, Finland, Mexico, the Netherlands, Norway, Sweden, Switzerland and the United Kingdom) for financial assistance that allowed the preparation of this volume and the UNRISD conference in Madrid. My thanks also go to the government of Spain for logistical support during the conference.

Thandika Mkandawire

CHAPTER 1

Ageing, Development and Social Protection: Generalisations, Myths and Stereotypes

PETER LLOYD-SHERLOCK

Population ageing (defined as an increase in the percentage of a population aged 65 years or older) is a global trend. It is long-established in developed countries and is now occurring in many poorer parts of the world. There is a tendency to portray population ageing as a threat to the future. Rather, it should be recognised as one of the great achievements of the past century, albeit one which generates a range of social, economic, political and cultural challenges. Population ageing is both part of and influenced by wider processes of development and transformation. The wellbeing and quality of life of elderly populations are strongly conditioned by their capacity to manage opportunities and risks associated with rapid and complex change. Social protection, both formal and informal, can play a key role in mediating these relationships.

This edited volume maps out current knowledge about academic research and debate on core issues related to ageing and development as they affect different (including non-elderly) social groups, countries and regions. To date, research about population ageing, particularly in low- and middle-income countries, remains underdeveloped and patchy. There is an urgent need for a stronger knowledge base, and for coherent policy frameworks which address the effects of ageing and the needs of older people. This book examines the opportunities, problems and challenges of effective social protection for older people. These include formal public policies, along with strategies derived from informal agency, such as household support systems.

Setting out a general analytical framework for such a book is not an easy task, given the lack of an obvious organising framework for a discussion of ageing and development. In many ways, thinking about ageing and development is still in its infancy. This can be seen in the small volume of published research, compared to fields such as gender studies. Much current thinking is closely derived from other fields of enquiry. These include Northern gerontology, traditional debates about social policy and, increasingly, work on gender and development. To some extent, these varied influences have helped make ageing and development a rich, eclectic and exciting field to work in. However, they have also served to inhibit the emergence of a set of research concerns that are particular to ageing and development. Partly because of this, policy debates have been pervaded by a number of generalisations, stereotypes and myths. This introduction examines some of the misconceptions that underlie current thinking. Other chapters in the book go further in challenging narrow policy agendas, and demonstrate the potential contribution of comparative research to these debates.

I will now go on to examine four sets of issues, each of which relates to a commonly held misconception. These are that:

▶ population ageing is mainly a northern phenomenon;

▶ *inevitably*, older people are unproductive, are high consumers, and represent a brake on economic development;

▶ *inevitably*, population ageing will place unsustainable pressures on formal social protection;

▶ the care economy can care for itself.

Population ageing is mainly a northern phenomenon

There is no universally accepted definition of what constitutes old age. While there is general dissatisfaction with defining old age in purely chronological terms, there would appear to be no better alternative. Old age is perceived and understood in a multitude of different ways, often with important cultural variations (Midwinter 1991; Keith *et al.* 1994). These may refer to biological processes and physical appearance, key life events (for example retirement or some other form of disengagement), or social roles (grandparenthood or ceremonial duties). Since old age can cover a span of over three decades, most cultures distinguish between the 'old old' and the 'young old', and it is usually more meaningful to think in terms of a gradual change, rather than a sharp cut-off between adulthood and later life.

Tables 1.1 and 1.2 show that although the oldest population structures tend to be found in richer countries, the majority of the world's elderly people live in the South. This has been the case since the early 1980s, and by 2030 there will be nearly three times as many people aged 60 or more in the South than the North. In fact, these figures

Table 1.1 Population ageing and *per capita* wealth for selected countries

	Population aged 60+, 1995 (%)	GDP *per capita* (US$ ppp) 1998
Japan	20.5	23,257
USA	16.4	29,605
Brazil	7.1	6,625
India	7.2	2,077
Uganda	3.6	867
Burkina Faso	4.3	870

Sources: UN Population Division (1999); UNDP (2000).

Table 1.2 Population ageing in more and less developed regions

		1990	2030
More developed regions*	Total population (000s)	1,147,980	1,209,507
	Population aged 60+ (%)	17.7	29.2
	Population aged 60+ (000s)	203,192	353,175
Less developed regions**	Total population (000s)	4,188,462	6,902,473
	Population aged 60+ (%)	6.9	14.6
	Population aged 60+ (000s)	284,174	1,007,761

* North America, Japan, Europe, Australia and New Zealand
** The rest of the world
Source: UN Population Division (1999).

understate the ageing gap, given that in poorer countries effective old age is likely to set in long before a person reaches 60 or 65 years of age.

Population ageing is usually associated with the final stage of demographic transition, which involves sustained falls in fertility and hence smaller numbers of younger age groups (Chesnais 1992). The timing and intensity of demographic transition and population ageing vary. Some countries have experienced ageing since the early twentieth century: by 1950, 7 per cent of Argentina's population was already aged 60 or more. By contrast, in a small number of poor countries, persistently high fertility continues to lower the average age of the population: in Pakistan the over-60s' share of total population fell from 6.3 to 4.7 per cent between 1960 and 1990. In most of the South, demographic transition has been much more abrupt than in established industrialised economies. It took about a century for the proportion of elders in Western Europe to double. In many developing countries, including India, China and Brazil, this is expected to occur in less than 20 years.

Demographic transition is associated with broader processes of modernisation and development. However, it should not be assumed that countries ultimately reach an equilibrium state where fertility is sufficient to sustain a fixed population size (and hence a stable age structure) (Demeny 1997). In over 60 countries fertility has already reached replacement level or fallen below it, which may lead to significant long-term population declines. This makes it difficult to predict the point at which population ageing may tail off in the future. Current projections show that 36 per cent of Japanese will be aged over 65 by 2050. However, we should not assume that this figure represents a high water mark for future trends.

As their fertility rates drop, it is to be expected that poorer countries will follow the course of Japan and the North, although the timing of this trend is difficult to gauge. The relative size of the elderly cohorts of many sub-Saharan African countries is not yet rising. Nevertheless, a context of rapid population growth means that absolute numbers of older people are increasing. Because of accelerated lifecycle transitions, standard chronological thresholds of old age understate the true importance of the ageing process in the region (Apt 1997). Also, high rates of mortality from HIV/AIDS among younger groups are likely to cause a sudden rise in the relative size of the elderly population in the near future.

Table 1.3 Subnational variations of population ageing (population aged 65 or over), circa 1991

	Region with highest %		Region with lowest %	
Argentina (1991)	Federal capital	16.3	Formosa	4.7
India (1991)	Kerala	6.2	Assam	3.1
Thailand (1990)	Ang Thong	12.9	Udon Thani	5.1
Brazil (1991)	Paraíba	6.5	Roraima	2.2

Sources: Gulati and Rajan 1999; INDEC 1998; Government of Thailand 1995; IBGE 1991.

Misleading generalisations about global ageing trends are paralleled by a tendency to aggregate demographic data at the national level. This can mask important subnational variations. Disparities may occur between different subregions (Table 1.3) and socio-economic groupings, and by gender as well as other criteria. Europe and North America contain disproportionate numbers of female elders, especially among the very old. This has led some to refer to the 'feminisation of old age'

(Arber and Ginn 1991). In other regions, such as South Asia, this relationship is less clear, often reflecting a masculine bias in the population as a whole.

Inevitably, older people are unproductive, are high consumers, and represent a brake on economic development

> Global ageing could trigger a crisis that engulfs the world economy. This crisis may even threaten democracy itself. (Petersen 1999: 55)

According to this view, ageing may be desirable from the point of view of an individual, but is bad for society as a whole. While few people would go as far as Petersen, much of the policy debate is tinged with alarmism. In an influential report, the World Bank observes that:

> The world is approaching an old age crisis.... The proportion of the population that is old is expanding rapidly, swelling the potential economic burden on the young. (World Bank 1994)

Debates about the impact of ageing are shot through with what might be called a negative paradigm of population ageing and later life. In this paradigm, later life is associated with dependency, vulnerability, an inherent lack of capability and, of course, a poor quality of life. With reference to economic development, it is claimed that older people use up savings, sell off assets, are unproductive and have expensive needs whose cost reduces the resource base of the economy as a whole. These sorts of ideas sometimes translate into specific policy agendas. For example, the main cost effectiveness tool used by the World Bank in allocating health care resources gives a lower social value to health improvements for those aged 60 and over than it does for younger groups (Paalman *et al.* 1998). The Bank justifies this on the grounds that younger people are productive, but older people are not. This represents a blatant form of discrimination against older people, and may be based on misguided assumptions about the contributions they make.

Slowly, a number of challenges are being made to the negative paradigm. According to HelpAge International, the leading NGO working in this area:

> The substantial productive contribution of older people … is largely unrecognised by policy makers. Too often older people are stereotyped as passive or helpless – the realities of their lives unobserved' (HelpAge International 1999: xiii).

It is clear that older people are not all inherently incapable. What we call 'old age' can span more than 40 years of a person's life. Older people are a diverse group, living in very different circumstances. Examples of economic contributions include the care of grandchildren (including AIDS orphans), pension sharing, continued economic activity, and the provision of accommodation (which they may have built or paid for) to other household members (Kaiser 1994; Sagner and Mtati 1999; Saengtienchai and Knodel 2001). More general contributions include involvement in household and community decision making, and the transmission of cultural values and wisdom. According to this view, policy should seek to promote the capacity of older people to make contributions, and should increase the opportunities for them to do so. This would contribute to healthy, active and meaningful ageing experiences (Troisi 1995). These new ideas have come together under the general label of 'active ageing' (WHO 2002).

The emergence of active ageing is to be welcomed, since it provides a refreshing alternative to the old, negative paradigm. However, this new agenda may sometimes go too far to the other extreme, playing down the real needs and vulnerabilities of many older people. For many of the aged, active ageing may remain a distant ideal. For example, how can the concept of active ageing be put into practice for a sick, impoverished older person with severe cognitive and physical impairments?

It is important to recognise the dangers of generalising about later life experiences from either a negative or a positive perspective. There is some truth in both of these generalisations: some older people have high levels of vulnerability and dependence, others may be making more social and economic contributions than at any previous time in their lives, and the great majority are both dependent and depended-upon.[1] The main shortcoming of these opposed viewpoints is that they portray later life as a common experience. A more balanced perspective requires an appreciation of later life as a fluid, complex and heterogeneous phenomenon. All the chapters in this volume are sensitive to the complexity of ageing experiences. They recognise that the diverse characteristics of older people influence the degree to which they can manage opportunities and risks.

Given this diversity of experience, claims that elders represent a dead weight on economies and societies are over-generalised and likely to distort policy. Nevertheless, the links between processes of demographic transition and economic development are seen as inevitable. According to the United Nations Population Fund (UNPA):

> A growing working age population compared with older and younger dependants opens up a window of opportunity for developing countries.... Wise use of the 'demographic bonus' can lighten the burden of a rising older population in later years. (UNFPA 1998: 14)

UNFPA observes that many East Asian countries have obtained short-run development dividends from rapid falls in fertility. However, it argues that there may be a price to pay in the medium run as smaller cohorts of young adults are subsequently required to support expanded cohorts of elders. If younger generations are not prepared to provide this support on a personal basis, then the cost may be passed on to the state, such as in the form of publicly financed residential care. On a more alarmist note, a recent European Commission report predicts that population ageing represents 'a significant factor in holding economic growth [in the EU] down to less than half that in the US, where the [dependency] ratio will be lower' (*Financial Times*, 14 December 2002).

The above scenarios may be mitigated by changing patterns of capability and functioning among elders. The current economic contribution of some older people may be understated, and there may be ways to promote participation through effective policies such as lifelong training and access to credit. In many countries a combination of economic necessity, changing social attitudes, and the improving health profiles of elders, may weaken the link between ageing and a shrinking workforce. Richer countries may be able to sustain the total size of their workforces by attracting large influxes of replacement migration (UN Population Division 2000).

The debate about ageing and development draws heavily on the view that the middle years of the life course are characterised by high savings rates, and that later life sees a decline in assets. It is argued that population ageing will therefore lead to reduced aggregate savings rates, a view apparently borne out by international comparisons (OECD 1998). However, micro-economic research has challenged this finding, observing that many elders continue to save, albeit at a lower rate than previously (Disney 1996). One reason for this may be that sustaining the size of future bequests increases the likelihood that younger family members will take an interest in their wellbeing. Conversely, a consumption boom among older Japanese has been a key factor in mitigating the country's economic problems of recent years. A key stimulus for the 'grey yen' has been the introduction of a hefty inheritance tax, which reduces the incentive to sustain savings and assets in old age.

There is similar uncertainty about the relationship between an ageing workforce and levels of productivity. On the one hand, older workers may have accumulated a higher stock of human capital and experience. On the other, it is sometimes claimed that older workforces tend to be less entrepreneurial, ambitious and flexible. Both of these views can be linked to the positive and negative characterisations of the ageing experience outlined earlier. A key factor will be the overall structure of the economy, as older people may have more comparative advantage in

some areas of activity than in others. Where opportunities for employment are scarce, the scope for utilising the productive potential of all age
groups, not just older workers, may be limited (Messkoub 1999). One
key issue is whether old age pensioners should be permitted to continue
in salaried employment. Several developed countries, including the
United Kingdom (UK), are now actively pursuing more flexible retirement policies.

Another conventional wisdom is that ageing holds back development because investment is lost to the mounting costs of social
provision. Again this process is not inevitable, and will be heavily
influenced by the ways in which people experience later life. The cost
of supporting an elderly population with high levels of protracted
chronic disease and general dependence will be greater than that for a
healthy, active population. There are other problems with demographic
determinism: the US spends twice as much of its economic output on
health care as the UK does, but contains a similar proportion of elders.
The gap is mainly due to inefficiencies in the US private health
insurance market. This suggests that the impact of ageing on social
spending is mediated by the ways in which the social sectors are
structured. In poorer countries the social sectors currently fail to meet
the basic needs of many people, old and young. In these cases, it is
meaningless to project the impact of population ageing on expenditure
based on the experiences of other countries.

Debates about ageing and development may be able to learn from
long-running controversies about population growth. These have
ranged from pessimistic neo-Malthusian predictions of a population
'time-bomb', to the claims of optimists such as Julian Simon that
population growth is an essential component for economic development (Stanford 1972; Simon 1977). Empirical research has often
favoured a more nuanced view: that the relationship is context-specific
and includes different long-run and short-run effects (Ahlburg 1998).
Parallels may be drawn with apocalyptic claims that the world is now
facing an 'old age crisis'. With time and a more robust empirical basis,
debates about ageing and development may take on a less extreme hue.

Inevitably, population ageing will place unsustainable pressures on formal social protection

A key part of the relationship between development and the wellbeing
of older people relates to the creation of formal social protection
programmes. As the chapters in this book demonstrate, it is dangerous
to assume a direct association between general levels of prosperity and
the strength of formal social protection. In the liberal welfare regimes of

some Asian countries, the state makes little formal provision for older people. Conversely, Cuba's generous welfare services belie a context of economic stagnation. Ideology, institutional path dependency and social choices can be as significant as economic growth in determining the scale of formal social protection in a country.

Nevertheless, it is possible to identify some general differences in formal social protection between high-, middle- and low-income countries. Developed countries tend to spend larger amounts on formal social protection, and a high share of this is devoted to programmes of direct relevance to older people. These programmes range from the provision of pensions to health care, institutional care and other forms of social service. Such programmes tend to be based on a dependency view of older people. These programmes are expensive, and are often viewed as beyond the financial and institutional means of many developing and, increasingly, developed countries. This has led to concerns that pressures on public policy caused by population ageing are likely to cause a global 'old age crisis' (World Bank 1994).

In most low-income countries, social policies have tended to focus on the needs of other age groups, such as mothers, children and 'workers'. Instead of sustaining existing programmes, the main challenge for such countries will be to factor older people into social policies for the first time. In many cases, this will occur against a backdrop of severe resource constraints and generalised hardship. In these cases, a shift in the priorities of external donors and NGOs will be required. For some countries, meeting the needs of older people may be overshadowed by the HIV/AIDS pandemic. Several chapters in this book show how older people are directly and indirectly affected by HIV/AIDS, and that they can play key roles in surviving communities.

Across middle-income countries, the scale of formal social protection for older people is extremely varied, ranging from minimal intervention to schemes which rival those of the North (Lloyd-Sherlock 2002a). There is a tendency to focus on income support programmes, particularly contributory pensions, rather than dedicated health programmes or social services. Typically, access to services and benefits is restricted to relatively privileged socio-economic groups, raising concerns about equity and the social exclusion of poor older people. In many middle-income countries, social protection for all groups has been threatened by structural adjustment, by abrupt transitions from socialist welfare models, and by the rapid growth of private sector welfare agencies, in what is often a very weak regulatory setting. The effectiveness and sustainability of social policies will depend on institutional structures as much as ageing. In a context of poor governance and anarchic private provision, the chances are that social policies will be exclusionary, inefficient and expensive.

Debates about public policy for older people are strongly derived from the experiences of the North, and have been dominated by controversies about pension reform (Lloyd-Sherlock 2000b). Recent reforms have mainly sought to replace unitary public sector pension funds with more pluralistic arrangements, including a significant private sector component. The arguments in favour of this arrangement are that it promotes competition (and hence efficiency), stimulates capital markets and relieves the public sector of an activity it was not well-suited to perform. Some of these contentions have been challenged by studies of reformed systems in countries such as Chile and the UK.

However, debates about pension reform overlook several key issues. The first is that the majority of the world's older people do not receive a pension, be it publicly or privately managed, and are unlikely to do so in the foreseeable future. Those who do receive pensions may share this income with other family members, and may supplement it with other sources. As such, the relationship between old age pension policy and the economic welfare of older people is not always direct and should not be overstated. Secondly, the debate has tended to overlook the existence of successful pension programmes which do not fit within the parameters of the new neoliberal model: examples include publicly administered provident funds in Singapore and Malaysia, and non-contributory schemes in a number of countries (Charlton and McKinnon 2001). These call into doubt the 'one size fits all' approach to pensions of some international agencies. It is possible that these experiences might be applied to other contexts.

While it may be debatable whether poor countries should undertake to establish large-scale pension programmes, it is accepted that all governments have some responsibility for the health of their populations, including elders. Older people are usually associated with chronic conditions that are expensive to treat. This has two consequences. First, it has provoked fears of an ageing-related health care cost explosion in the North. Second, it has promoted the view that, as with pensions, comprehensive geriatric care is beyond the financial means of most developing countries.

Prophets of a cost explosion overlook the fact that any impact of ageing on health spending is strongly mediated by a range of other factors, including how services are organised and financed (van der Gaag and Preker 1997). As such, the ambitious health sector reforms being applied in many countries are likely to have a large effect on their capacity to service elders efficiently (Cassels 1995). The growing literature on new public management, cost recovery, private insurance and decentralisation makes scant reference to their impacts on elders. However, there are indications that the growing role of private insurance may both increase the overall costs of old age provision, as well as promoting inequity and exclusion (Lloyd-Sherlock 2000a).

The view that health care for older people is inherently expensive ignores the potential contributions of appropriate primary health care (PHC) programmes to older people. As initially conceived, PHC places a strong emphasis on mother and child health, to the exclusion of groups such as elders (Rifkin and Walt 1986). However, research from the European Union has found that appropriate strategies of health education and promotion can have major benefits for older people (Fletcher et al. 1998). In developing countries where many elders lack access to basic services, the potential benefits of extending PHC to meet their specific needs may be even greater. Other strengths of the PHC approach are its holistic nature (which allows for linkages with informal carers) and its capacity to promote active, healthy ageing, whilst not excluding the most frail and vulnerable. As such, it embraces the heterogeneity of needs and experiences of older people.

Even less attention has been paid to the impact of education on the wellbeing of elders. Elderly cohorts in poorer countries usually suffer from disproportionately high levels of illiteracy. As societies age, and as workplace skill requirements become increasingly prone to sudden change, there is a greater need to take a life-long approach to education and training. This would promote opportunities for older people and reduce pressures on dependency-oriented public policies. Appropriate programmes of education may also increase the capacity of other groups to meet the challenges of population ageing. For example, in low- and middle-income countries there is an urgent need to sensitise health professionals, social workers and informal carers to the specific needs and concerns of elders.

The care economy can care for itself

Divisions between formal social protection and informal means of support for elders are often blurred, and increasing attention is now being paid to the interface between them. This is particularly significant in the area of long-term care for vulnerable elders. As the numbers of people surviving to very old ages increase, the demand for care services is projected to soar. Estimates for the US show that the number of older people using nursing homes will rise from 2.2 to 3.8 million between 1993 and 2018. Over the same period, the number of users of in-home services is projected to more than double, reaching 10.74 million (Weiner et al. 1994). In the UK it has been estimated that around 14 per cent of women and 7 per cent of men aged 65 years or more require daily help to maintain independent living. This includes services ranging from home cleaning to full-time, intensive nursing care. In many countries of the North, the state only finances or provides a small part of care services. Most are being met by either the private sector or informal carers. As such, a burning issue is how to effectively combine the state, family and private sector in order to ensure care provision is adequate (Walker 1992). In the private sector there are problems of regulation (not least concerns about elder abuse); of equity (for many older people private care is simply not an option), and of supply (the total number of places in UK residential care has fallen by about 9 per cent since 1996). Recent research from the UK calculated the cost of paying informal carers at market rates to be £8 billion a year (*British Medical Journal* editorial, 3 October 1998). There is an urgent need to recognise the contribution of informal carers, support them and compensate them. This is not just an issue of social justice. We need to pay more attention to informal caring for more instrumental reasons – we rely on informal caring so much that we cannot afford to take it for granted. Also, more should be done to develop innovative approaches to combining informal care with state support, such as respite programmes.

In the South it is widely assumed that care and social services are not a policy priority, since traditional household and community structures are still able to play this role. In most developing countries the great majority of older people continue to live with children or other family members (Sokolovsky 2000). However, this in itself does not guarantee satisfactory care. Contexts of poverty and rapid change put families under strain and reduce their capacity to meet these needs. Increased female participation in the salaried labour force is likely to constrain the supply of informal care, regardless of household structure. Rapid rises in the numbers of very old are likely to stimulate demand for residential care, but these services remain very underdeveloped in the South. Widespread publicly funded care may not be an affordable option for poorer countries, but little is being done to examine how the roles of households as informal carers might be complemented and bolstered by relatively inexpensive policy interventions.

The issues of care for and care by elderly people contain strong gender dimensions. Although cultural attitudes to supporting the aged vary, women are almost always the main providers of care, whether the responsibility falls to youngest daughters, daughters-in-law, sisters or some other relation. Women also predominate as paid carers, either in institutions or working in private households. In poorer, three-generation households, this may add to the multiple responsibilities of employment, domestic chores and child care. Where older people are themselves the providers of care, women also tend to predominate. Grand-parenting often represents an extension of a woman's previous domestic responsibilities. Studies from Latin America and South Africa have found cases where older women, increasingly weary from the continued domestic obligations placed on them, expressed a strong preference to live alone (Sagner and Mtati 1999; Varley and Blasco 2000). Since women are more likely to survive their male spouses, they are more likely to provide care to their spouses, rather than receive it. Women are also more likely to be widowed, which reduces their access to informal care, particularly in cultures that discriminate against widowhood.

Patterns of care are strongly influenced by intergenerational exchange and reciprocity. Even when they have little current income, many older people still own houses and other valuable assets, such as land. Research has found that both explicit and implicit contracts about inheritance and asset transfer may have an important effect on current care arrangements. A study from Thailand found that older people often transferred land and housing to children well in advance of their deaths, on the understanding that this was an 'up-front' payment for care provision (Chayovan and Knodel 1997). However, it should not be assumed that inheritance and similar forms of intergenerational exchange accord with a perfect moral economy, in which care giving is matched by subsequent bequests. Possessing inheritance goods does not guarantee that an older person will receive good care: equally, the principal carer may go unrewarded. Also, it may be simplistic to reduce such relations to an economic rationale, ignoring cultural norms of filial duty. Practices and traditions of inheritance and exchange vary around the world. In India, for example, inheritance is usually patrilineal, increasing the vulnerability of elderly widows (Agnes 1999). There is a need to explore how these practices might be reinforced or modified through the application of appropriate legal codes or other public policy interventions.

Exchange between generations may be deferred as well as immediate, often in unintended ways. As adults enter later life, their position of authority within households may be replaced by one of dependence, leading to unforeseen consequences. In Mexico the quality of care provided by daughters-in-law to older women is sometimes mediated by past situations in which the older women dominated (even to the point of abuse) the younger ones (Varley and Blasco 2000). Elderly men are particularly vulnerable to paying the price for poor past relations with younger family members, and this may result in neglect and abandonment (Aboderin 2001). Similarly, patterns and expectations of intergenerational relations may be influenced by historical experiences.

For the first time, many developed countries are seeing large numbers of older people, especially women, who have already experienced the role of long-term carer for an elderly parent. By contrast, few older people in poor countries saw their own parents or grandparents experience a protracted old age, and therefore they are less inclined to foresee that this will be their own fate, or to appreciate the care that may be required from younger relatives.

More attention should be given to the impact of public policy on intergenerational exchange. There is still controversy about whether public pension programmes crowd out transfers within families. The World Bank argues that this is the case, but the limited empirical evidence is less conclusive (World Bank 1994). Where exchange is based on a notion of reciprocity, it may be bolstered by the provision of pensions to elders. Less has been said about the impacts of privatising health care and education on intergenerational exchange. These transfer the arena of exchange from the public domain and society as a whole to the domain of financial decision-making within the private household. This could make intergenerational conflicts starker, as, for example, households are faced with a trade-off between continuing to pay for the education of a child or paying for the health care of an older person.

Concluding comments

Any general discussion of population ageing and older people begs one very important question: in what way are elders (or later life) significantly different from younger age groups (or earlier stages in the life course)? This is not an easy question to answer for several reasons. First, there is no obvious cut-off between later life and earlier life, nor is there a satisfactory definition of old age. Second, as has been seen, older people are a heterogeneous group, living in very different circumstances. The problems faced by elders in low-income countries may have much more in common with those of younger generations than with those of elders living in the rich North.

Nevertheless, it is possible to make at least some generalisations about older people. As a group, they are less likely to be engaged in salaried economic activity. They are more exposed to age-related risks, such as physical decline and some kinds of chronic disease. Older people are also exposed to the general stereotypes and prejudices of society at large: attitudes which may become self-fulfilling prophecies. Taken together, these mean that the capabilities of older people tend to be restricted, and become increasingly so as they progress through later life to death. These common characteristics go some way towards justifying the emerging academic interest and policy focus on older people around the world. However, they do not justify the portrayal of older people as a special interest group, whose interests are separate from, and possibly in conflict with, those of other generations. Elders do not exist in isolation (despite the best efforts of some societies to promote this), and so their wellbeing is intimately bound in with that of society as a whole. Many of the concerns raised in this discussion relate to wider issues, such as poverty reduction and gender equity. As with gender, policy needs to recognise both difference and interdependence.

Population ageing is accelerating, and can now be considered a global phenomenon. However, it is unwise to generalise about what this may mean, either for older people or for the societies in which they live. There is a prevailing negative paradigm that labels older people as inherently incapable, as well as representing a brake on development and a burden on public policy and informal carers. Yet these views are more often based on supposition than hard evidence, and there are increasing calls for a more up-beat, 'active ageing' approach. Population ageing requires a dynamic response from public policy and social attitudes, a key challenge being the need to reduce the exclusion of elders from salaried economic activity. This process of adaptation has been slow, uncertain and imperfect, and is likely to continue to be so.

Population ageing poses particular challenges for developing countries. International debates are almost exclusively drawn from Northern gerontology and neoliberal political economy. While these may provide some useful insights, they have very little to say about the situation of many older people in many parts of the world. There is a manifest gap in current knowledge about policies and frames of reference which may be of relevance to the South. If the needs of older people in such countries are not addressed, population ageing may simply constitute an extension of privation and misery, rather than an enrichment of lifetime opportunities.

NOTE

1 For theoretical discussion of the diversity of older people's capabilities and functionings, see Lloyd-Sherlock (2003).

REFERENCES

Aboderin, I. (2000) 'Social change and the decline in family support for older people in Ghana: an investigation of the nature and causes of shifts in support', PhD dissertation, School for Policy Studies, University of Bristol.
Agnes, F. (1999) 'Law and women of age. a short note', *Economic and Political Weekly*, 30 October, pp. 51–4.
Ahlburg, D. (1998) 'Julian Simon and the population growth debate', *Population and Development Review*, 24 (2): 317–27.

16 LIVING LONGER

Apt, N. (1997) *Ageing in Africa*, Geneva: World Health Organisation.

Arber, S. and Ginn, J. (1991) *Gender and Later Life – a Sociological Analysis of Resources and Constraints*, Sage, London.

Cassels, A. (1995) 'Health sector reform: key issues in less developed countries', *Journal of International Development*, 7(3): 329–48.

Charlton, R. and R. McKinnon (2001) *Pensions in Development*, Ashgate, London.

Chayovan, N. and J. Knodel (1997) 'A report on the survey of the welfare of the elderly in Thailand', unpublished paper, Institute of Population Studies, Chulalongkorn University, Bangkok.

Chesnais, J. (1992) *The Demographic Transition. Stages, Patterns and Economic Implications*, Oxford University Press, Oxford.

Da Vanzo, J. and D. Adamson (1997) 'Russia's demographic crisis: how real is it?', Rand Center for Russian and Eurasian Studies [www.rand.org/publications].

Demeny, P. (1997) 'Replacement-level fertility: the implausible endpoint of demographic transition', in G. Jones et al. (eds.), *The Continuing Demographic Transition*, Clarendon, Oxford.

Disney, R. (1996) *Can We Afford to Grow Old?*, MIT Press, London.

Fletcher, A., E. Breeze and R. Walters (1998) 'Health promotion for elderly people: recommendations for the European Union', London School of Hygiene and Tropical Medicine, London.

Government of Thailand, National Statistics Office (1995) *1990 Population and Housing Census of Thailand*, Bangkok.

Gulati, L. and S. Rajan (1999) 'The added years: elderly in India and Kerala', *Economic and Political Weekly*, 30 October, pp. 46–51.

HelpAge International (1999) 'Ageing and development: the message', in HelpAge International (ed.), *The Ageing and Development Report. Poverty, Independence and the World's Older People*, Earthscan, London.

Instituto Brasileiro de Geografia e Estatística (IBGE) (1991) *Censo Demográfico 1991. Número 1. Brasil*, IBGE, Rio de Janiero.

Instituto Nacional de Estadística y Censos (INDEC) (1998) *Statistical Yearbook of the Argentine Republic 1998*, INDEC, Buenos Aires.

Kaiser, M. (1994) 'Economic activities of the elderly in developing countries: myths and realities', *UN Bulletin on Ageing*, Vol. 2/3.

Keith, J., C. Fry, A. Glascock, C. Ikels, J. Dickerson-Putman, H. Harpending and P. Draper (1994) *The Aging Experience. Diversity and Commonality Across Cultures*, Sage, London.

Knodel, J., N. Chayovan, S. Graiurapong and C. Suraratolecha (1999) 'Aging in Thailand: an overview of formal and informal support', Report No. 99–53, Comparative Study of the Elderly in Asia Research Reports, Population Studies Center, University of Michigan.

Lloyd-Sherlock, P. (2000a) 'Population ageing in developed and developing regions: implications for health policy', *Social Science and Medicine*, 51 (6): 887–98.

—— (2000b) 'Old age and poverty in developing countries: new policy challenges', *World Development*, 18 (12): 2157–68.

—— (2002a) 'Formal social protection for older people in developing countries: three different approaches', *Journal of Social Policy*, 31 (4): 695–714.

—— (2002b) 'Nussbaum, capabilities and older people', *Journal of International Development*, 14 (3): 1163–73.

Messkoub, M. (1999) 'Crisis of ageing in less-developed countries: too much consumption or too little production?', *Development and Change*, 30 (2): 217–35.

Midwinter, E. (1991) *The British Gas Report on Attitudes to Ageing 1991*, Burson-Marstellar, London.

Organisation for Economic Cooperation and Development (OECD) (1998) *Maintaining*

Prosperity in an Ageing Society, OECD, Paris.

Paalman, M., H. Bekedam, L. Hawken and D. Nyheim (1998) 'A critical review of policy setting in the health sector: the methodology of the 1993 World Development Report', *Health Policy and Planning*, 13 (1): 13–31.

Petersen, P. (1999) 'Gray dawn: the global aging crisis', *Foreign Affairs*, 78 (1): 42–55.

Rifkin S. and G. Walt (1986) 'Why health improves: defining the issues concerning "comprehensive primary health care" and "selective primary health care"', *Social Science and Medicine*, 23 (6): 559–66.

Saengtienchai, C. and J. Knodel (2001) 'Parental caregiving to adult children with AIDS: a qualitative analysis of circumstances and consequences in Thailand', Research Report 01-481, Population Studies Center, University of Michigan.

Sagner, A. and R. Mtati (1999) 'Politics of pension sharing in urban South Africa', *Ageing and Society*, 19 (4): 393–416.

Simon, J. (1977) *The Economics of Population Growth*, Princeton University Press, Princeton.

Sokolovsky, J. (2000) 'Living arrangements of older persons and family support in less developed countries', UN Population Division Technical Meeting on Population Ageing and Living Arrangements of Older Persons, New York, February.

Stanford, Q. (1972) *The World's Population. Problems of Growth*, Oxford University Press, Oxford.

Troisi, J. (1995) 'Ageing in a changing world: older persons as a resource', in J. Calleja (ed.), *Meeting the Challenges of Ageing Populations in the Developing World. Proceedings of an Experts' Group Meeting, 23–25 October 1995*, United Nations International Institute on Ageing, Malta.

United Nations Development Programme (UNDP) (1999) *Poland National Human Development Report 1999: Towards Active Dignified Old Age*, UNDP, Warsaw.

—— (2000) *Human Development Report 2000*, UNDP, New York.

UN Population Division (1999) *World Population Prospects. The 1998 Revision*, UN Population Division, New York.

—— (2000) 'The United Nations population division on replacement migration', *Population and Development Review*, 26 (2).

United Nations Population Fund (UNFPA) (1998) *The State of World Population. The New Generations*, United Nations Population Fund, New York.

Van der Gaag, J. and A. Precker (1997) 'Health care for aging populations: issues and options', in N. Prescott (ed.), *Choices in Financing Health Care and Old Age Security: Proceedings of a Conference Sponsored by the Institute of Policy Studies, Singapore, and the World Bank, November 8, 1997*, World Bank, Washington DC.

Varley, A. and M. Blasco (2000) 'Reaping what you sow? Older women, housing and family dynamics in urban Mexico', in United Nations International Research and Training Institute for the Advancement of Women (INSTRAW) (ed.), *Women's Life-cycle and Ageing*, INSTRAW, Santo Domingo.

Walker, A. (1992) 'The Care for Elderly People in Industrial Society: a Conflict Between the Family and the State', in P. Krishnan and K. Mahadevan (eds.), *The Elderly Population in the Developed and Developing Worlds*, B.R. Publishing Co., New Delhi.

Weiner, J., L. Ilston and R. Handley (1994) *Sharing the Burden: Strategies for Public and Private Long-term Care Insurance*, Brookings Institution, Washington DC.

World Bank (1994) *Averting the Old Age Crisis. Policies to Protect the Old and Promote Growth*, Oxford University Press, Oxford.

WHO (2002) *Active Ageing: A Policy Framework*, World Health Organisation, Geneva.

PART I

Development Trajectories, Social Change and Wellbeing in Later Life

As seen in Chapter 1, whether population ageing is 'bad' for development remains a matter of controversy. Much of the current debate is informed more by anecdote and prejudice than by reliable empirical evidence. This section examines four very different experiences of development. The UK, taken as roughly representative of advanced industrial nations, provides a long-run historical perspective on development and the wellbeing of older people. In Brazil, where accelerated population ageing has set in more recently, a shift from protectionist industrialisation to market opening has coincided with faltering economic performance. The Ukraine exemplifies many of the problems being faced by formerly socialist economies, including sharp economic contraction and the retrenchment of social welfare programmes. These problems have influenced population trends: low fertility, rising mortality and out-migration are leading to a rapid population decline. China's 'economic miracle' has been matched by a demographic one. A combination of radical family planning policies and rapid modernisation have pulled the country back from the brink of a potentially disastrous crisis of overpopulation. One side-effect of population policy has been a surge in demographic ageing: China now contains the largest number of older people in the world.

None of these country chapters seeks to analyse the impact of population ageing on historical patterns of development: in every case it is apparent that other factors have had a much more significant effect. This does not mean that ageing had no influence over their development experiences, but any effect is difficult to isolate and therefore demographic determinism should be avoided. The chapters pay more attention to the future consequences of population change. Of particular interest is the effect of population ageing on the rising 'burden' of demographic dependency: the share of population aged under 15 or over 65 to those of working age. This crude ratio is based on a number of increasingly dubious generalisations about age and economic activity. Growing numbers of people aged between 15 and 65 may not be active, due to continued study, unemployment or some other reason. Likewise, as seen in these chapters, many older people continue in economic activity or make other forms of contribution. Recent debates about raising the retirement age in OECD countries are a clear indication of the blurred association between age and economic status.

The chapters in this section also explore the other side of the relationship: how processes of development and change influence the wellbeing of elders. It is sometimes argued that rapid modernisation has a particularly unfavourable effect on elderly people (Cowgill 1976). According to this view, older people's abilities become less relevant to modern needs, such as intensive farming or skilled industrial employment. With development, household structures change from three to two generations, isolating elders. The growing participation of women in salaried labour reduces their capacity to provide informal care. High levels of rural to urban migration, as well as international population movements are also likely to separate older people from children and other family members. These issues are particularly evident in developing countries, where processes of change have usually occurred more abruptly than in the West. However, as with many debates in ageing and development, such claims are largely unevidenced, and empirical research suggests a more complex picture. The chapters in this section reveal a variety of experience, both within countries and across them. The discussions of Brazil and China find strong regional variations in the impact of development on elders' wellbeing. Likewise, the chapters on Ukraine and the UK identify relative winners and losers among different groups of older people.

Formal social protection programmes may be able to do much to reduce potential associations between old age and vulnerability. Economic development influences the capacity of societies to pay for such programmes, although there is also an important element of public choice about where and to whom to allocate resources. The countries examined in this section provide useful perspectives about different stages in the evolution of such programmes: a case where relatively inclusive welfare schemes are long-established (the UK), an example of recent, rapid extension (Brazil), a country where provision has been cut back (Ukraine), and one where services are at an incipient stage of development (China). Social welfare programmes have sometimes been criticised for socially constructing old age, by, for example, obliging people to withdraw from mainstream economic activity once they have reached an officially determined retirement age. Some critics argue that these policies reinforce later-life dependency, and have increased the social and economic exclusion of elders (Walker 1990; Graebner 1980). While there may be some truth in this argument, the evidence presented here emphasises the importance of a strong commitment to welfare programmes. This is especially apparent in Brazil, where upgrading pension provision brought about a demonstrable improvement in the economic and social status of older people in a short space of time. In the UK old age may not have been socially constructed before the twentieth century, but to be old and out of work was an effective guarantee of destitution.

Relationships between development and the wellbeing of older people are also mediated by political participation. The chapters on the UK and the Ukraine provide some useful insights into this under-researched issue. The historical emergence of pension programmes has usually responded to the concerns of organised labour (that is, those of working age), rather than older people. However, as growing numbers survive to retirement age, and as the costs of meeting these commitments mount, the importance of pensioner politics has grown, particularly, though not exclusively, in the North. In the increasingly democratised contexts of many developing countries, older people account for a growing proportion of voters. In some countries there are signs that the 'grey agenda' is being set by richer and better-educated elders, and may exclude less privileged groups. There are some examples of successful grassroots-led efforts to promote the social and political participation of poor older people, but these usually require a high level of external support, and have not been replicated on a larger scale.

The four chapters in this section go some way towards exploring the diversity and complexity of relationships between ageing and development. They make a significant contribution to what remains a grossly under-researched field. Even so, many key issues are not directly addressed here, including the experiences of very poor countries or the possible effects of culture. Some of these themes re-emerge later in the book.

REFERENCES

Cowgill, D. (1976) 'Aging and Modernization: a Revision of the Theory' in J. Gubrum (ed.) *Late Life: Communities and Environmental Policy,* Springfield, Ill.: Charles C. Thomas.

Graebner, W. (1980) *A History of Retirement. The Meaning and Function of an American Institution, 1885–1978,* New Haven: Yale University Press.

Walker, A. (1990) 'The Social Construction of Dependency in Old Age', in M. Loney, J. Clarke, A. Cochrane, P. Graham and M. Wilson (eds.), *The State or the Market. Politics and Welfare in Contemporary Britain,* London: Sage.

CHAPTER 2

Long-term Historical Changes in the Status of Elders: the United Kingdom as an Exemplar of Advanced Industrial Economies

PAUL JOHNSON

This chapter examines the interaction between long-term economic and social change and the status of older people in the UK, and uses this case study to illuminate more general patterns that are common to advanced industrial economies. The study of older people and of population ageing in past times cannot generate any simple 'lessons from history', because the enormous variety in the social, economic and cultural context of ageing in different times and places precludes direct comparison across geographical or temporal boundaries. Yet the past *is* important for today's policy makers. History directly impinges on the contemporary process of policy making for an ageing world in at least two different ways.

First, history determines the context, and so sets the parameters, within which today's debate occurs. One hundred years ago it was perfectly acceptable – and normal – for governments in Europe to declare that they had no direct responsibility for the welfare of their older citizens. Germany had introduced an insurance-based pension system for some manual workers in 1881, but the great majority of European elders had to rely on family, charity, savings or employment to pay for their old age. A century of social security development means that all industrialised countries now have comprehensive public pension systems. The ideological and substantive context in which today's debate about old age and ageing takes place has been shaped by this process of long-run institutional change.

Second, history matters because it is directly imprinted on the life experiences of each birth cohort. A typical French or German or British or Belgian man now in his early eighties was a young adult trying to get a job during the inter-war economic depression, was conscripted during five years of total war, and throughout the later 1940s and early 1950s lived in an economy characterised by shortages and rationing. Contrast this experience with a 60-year-old compatriot, who entered the labour market during the boom of the later 1950s and who then enjoyed for five decades the most sustained rise in real wages ever recorded. The 60-year-old is from a 'lucky', and the 80-year-old from an 'unlucky' generation. The historical experiences that different birth cohorts have lived through are significant determinants of their current characteristics.

This chapter will survey the way in which historical context, and the historical experiences of different generations of elders, has changed in the UK over time, particularly over the course of the twentieth century. The aim is to show how the status of older people has been affected by (but has also had an impact on) these historical developments. Status is, of course, a loose concept – perhaps too loose to permit descriptive precision or analytical rigour. It can refer to a wide range of social, economic, political and cultural attributes. I have therefore chosen to focus on three separate aspects which together have been primary determinants of change in the socio–economic position of older persons in Britain over the last hundred years.

1 *Participation* refers not only to the presence of older people in the labour market, but also to their informal (household or communal) activities, relating to both production and consumption. It broadly connotes the active involvement of older persons in civil society.

2 *Wellbeing* refers to economic wellbeing (or lack thereof) and the provision of welfare support by family and by formal and informal public systems, together with the physical wellbeing of older people and their care and treatment when ill. It broadly relates to the passive treatment of older persons by civil society.

3 *Social status* refers to the social position of older individuals and of the elderly as a group, as determined by political, legal, medical, and cultural rules and customs. It broadly relates to the construction of categories about and by older people in civil society.

The historical record displays few linearities, but it is very different from a popular perception that there existed some previous golden age of old age, when older people were respected and valued *because of* their age. This chapter will attempt to dispel such historical myths, and to challenge a number of historical assumptions about the nature of ageing and social protection in the modern world. Before turning to the specific issues of participation, well-being and social status, this chapter first reviews the demographic history of Britain in order to dispel one of the most enduring myths – that it was exceptional for any individual to reach old age in a pre-modern society.

Demographic background

It is often presumed that older people were few and far between in earlier centuries, because life expectancy was so low. In the 1840s, when the first comprehensive demographic data were collected for England, it was revealed that average life expectancy at birth for the country as a whole was only 41.7 years, while in the rapidly growing industrial city of Manchester it was a mere 25.3 years (Wrigley *et al.* 1997: 614; Szreter and Mooney 1998: 93). However, in pre-modern times life expectancy at birth was dominated by the very high rates of infant and early child mortality: once an individual reached his or her teens, survival to old age was much more likely. In fact in late nineteenth-century Britain the majority of 20-year-olds could expect to survive at least to age 60 (with women, then as now, having better survival rates than men).

Thus if we look at overall population shares, we see that older people were far from invisible. Between the sixteenth and the early twentieth centuries, the proportion of the English population aged 60 and above varied between 7 and 10 per cent of the total, with the higher figure being reached in the 1720s and 1910s, and the lower figure in the 1580s and 1810s (Wrigley and Schofield 1989: 528–9). This fluctuation in the relative size of the older population was driven almost entirely by changes in fertility, which were themselves a function of variation in the age of first marriage. But since the beginning of the twentieth century fluctuation has been replaced by unbroken trend as the share of older people in the population has risen without interruption to reach over 18 per cent by the 1990s. However, as a proportion of the *adult* population, the change has been less dramatic.

Prior to the twentieth century, children accounted for a very large share of the population, typically 40 per cent, and in the mid-nineteenth century almost half. Thus people over 60 must have constituted something between 10 and 18 per cent of the adult population. Today, the adult population is proportionately much larger than in the past, with 11.7 million children accounting for little more than one fifth of the total British population. As a result, the 10.5 million pensioners in Britain in 2001 accounted for just over 22 per cent of an adult population of 46.6 million (UK Government 2000)

These figures are striking. They show that although there has been massive demographic change over the past four centuries, the relative share of older people within the changing adult population has grown only slowly. There was never a time when older people were so few and far between as to be almost invisible. Nor is it the case that recent demographic change has massively increased their physical presence in society. If we wish to explain changes in the participation, well-being and status of older people in recent times, then we need to appeal to forces other than simple weight of numbers.

Participation

What does a reading of historical evidence tell us about the active involvement of older persons in past societies? The discourse on the socio-economic position of older people in modern society embodies a strong belief that the twentieth century has witnessed a significant marginalisation of the aged. This is most clearly articulated in arguments about the declining economic standing of older workers in the labour market as retirement has become formalised and routinised (Jacobs et al. 1991). Yet similar views also emerge in discussion of modern consumer society – that its emphasis on youthful purchasers, products and images serves to denigrate the interests of older people with older bodies (Featherstone and Hepworth 1991).

Implicit in these modern beliefs is a strong assumption that older people were in some ways more active and more valued participants in civil society in the past. There are some striking instances in the historical record of people retaining, or even extending, their political, social or economic role as they aged. Lanfranc was appointed Archbishop of Canterbury by William the Conqueror when he was 65, and died in office in 1089, aged 84. The average age of death of the nine seventeenth-century Archbishops of Canterbury was 73, and their average age of appointment was 60 (Thane 2000: 4). Towards the end of the nineteenth century the British government was led by an octogenarian Prime Minister, Gladstone, who reported to an octogenarian head of state, Queen Victoria.

When we turn from well-known but exceptional cases of active and powerful older persons to seek more representative details, the historical record is less clear-cut. This is partly because very little evidence exists for the medieval or early modern periods about the participation of the majority of older persons who were neither literate, nor wealthy nor powerful. However, some clear inferences can be drawn from an important and extensive body of evidence – the administrative records of England's early form of public welfare system, the Poor Law. A study of the pension histories of seventeenth-century manual workers and their wives shows that around 40 per cent of those over the age of 60 were likely to require financial assistance from the Poor Law for some period prior to death (Smith 1998). Thus in old age they were characterised as much by dependency as by economic independence. Yet even frail older female recipients of public assistance were expected to contribute to their own upkeep through domestic work. It is far from clear that this sort of labour force participation was a positive or liberating experience; the administrative presumption appears to have been that poor elders should continue to work until prevented by complete physical or mental incapacity.

It is the twentieth century that has witnessed a transformation in the active labour force participation of older people. In the 1880s almost 75 per cent of men aged 65 and above were in some form of employment, a figure that had probably not changed much over the preceding several centuries. Those who could work did work. But over the past hundred years retirement has shifted from being an exception to being the norm; by 1951 only 31 per cent of men in this age group were in work, a figure which had fallen to a mere 8 per cent by 1991. The causes of this secular decline in labour force participation rates for older men and rise in retirement are still not fully understood.

Most of the fall in participation rates between 1881 and 1921 was a result of sectoral shifts in the economy. In the UK, as in other countries, employment opportunities for older workers were much higher in agriculture than in industry or commerce, and the contraction of the agricultural sector from the late-nineteenth century had a dispropor-tionate impact on the participation rates of older men (Johnson 1994). In the inter-war period, however, there was an unambiguous decline in participation rates for men over 65, irrespective of changes in the sectoral composition of the workforce.

Although public pensions became available at age 65 to some manual workers from 1928, this does not seem to be the primary cause of declining labour force participation at older ages. The pension was worth less than 20 per cent of an average manual worker's wage, and stood well below contemporary estimates of the poverty line (Rowntree 1941: 502).

Far from older workers being lured from the labour force by the attraction of high public pensions, they instead appear increasingly to have been forced out by the policy of employers. Analysis of a survey conducted in London in 1931 of almost 27,000 working–class house-holds indicates that the labour market options for older workers were severely constrained. There was almost no opportunity for older workers to 'trade-down' by moving to a less-demanding, lower-paid job over time; they were required either to maintain labour effort and productivity at the same rate as younger workers or to withdraw from work entirely (Baines and Johnson 1999).

In fact even when older men were able and willing to maintain their effort and productivity, this was no guarantee that they would keep their jobs. Unemployment in the inter-war period was particularly concentrated among older industrial workers; employers and trade unions conspired to preserve jobs for younger workers with family responsibilities. As if this age bias were not enough, age discrimination was widely advocated as a potentially beneficial workplace practice. The trade union leader Ernest Bevin was just one of a number of socialists who advocated the use of the public pension system to promote higher levels of retirement in order to create more employment opportunities for the young (Macnicol and Blaikie 1989: 31).

Labour shortage during the Second World War temporarily reversed the downward trend in employment among older men, although the introduction in 1948 of a public pension that was conditional on retirement from full-time employment must have had some negative impact on participation. More important in accounting for the collapse of employment at higher ages over the last five decades are two other factors: the desire of many employers to replace older staff with younger workers, and the accumulation by many older workers of sufficient savings to allow them to give up full-time work.

Age discrimination in the workplace is certainly not a creation of the post-war period. In the 1890s trade unionists were arguing that older men were finding it increasingly difficult to retain their jobs because of growing levels of workplace stress, and in recognition of this fact several craft unions established independent superannuation funds in the last decades of the nineteenth century (Fukasawa 1996). Yet since the 1960s employers appear to have become increasingly youth-oriented in their hiring policy, so that many jobs are now effectively barred to applicants over 40 or 45. The problem for the older worker is not that he (or, in the expanded female labour market of the post-war period, she) suffers a much higher risk of becoming unemployed, but rather that, once out of work, the older person finds it much more difficult to re-enter the workforce (Laczko and Phillipson 1991: Chapter 3).

Discriminatory recruitment policies are in part determined by economics, since in the seniority wage systems operated by many large employers, pay is positively related to age, and therefore for any given task an older employee costs more than a younger one. But ageism in the workplace is also the result of deep-seated, but quite erroneous, beliefs that the productivity of workers declines after age 40. Detailed laboratory and workplace tests of capacity reveal that, for the great majority of manual and non-manual tasks, there is on average no appreciable age-related decrement in performance for people until they reach their mid-60s (Warr 1992). Nevertheless, age discrimination has acted to push older workers out of employment, and at increasingly young ages. In 1961, 97 per cent of British men aged 55–59, and 91 per cent of those aged 60–64, were active in the labour force; by 1991 these rates had fallen to 77 and 53 per cent respectively. The pattern is similar for female workers: although female labour force participation at all ages has risen since 1950, the rate at which working women aged 55 and above have withdrawn from the workforce has increased over time (Johnson 1993).

This negative account of the declining fortunes of older workers over the course of the twentieth century is, however, only one part of the complex history of work and retirement in twentieth-century Britain. Not all older people wish to work, and over time more of them have been able to choose to leave the workforce because they have accumulated sufficient savings, the most important of which have been pension entitlements in company pension schemes. About 5 per cent of workers were enrolled in company pension schemes around 1900, rising to 13 per cent in 1936, 35 per cent in 1956, and 53 per cent in 1967, since when coverage has stabilised at around half the total workforce (Hannah 1985: 40, 125). However, the time lag between joining a pension scheme and receiving benefits means that it was not until 1985 that the proportion of pensioners in receipt of a company pension crept above 50 per cent, up from 34 per cent in 1970 (Dawson and Evans 1987).

Whether older workers have been pushed unwillingly into retirement or have deliberately sought to exchange work for leisure is difficult to determine. Most workers seem to be pushed at age 65 (few companies permit employees to stay on after this age) but at earlier ages the retirement decision has owed much more to individual circumstances that are largely a function of (poor) health and (good) pension savings (Johnson 1989b; Laczko *et al.* 1988). Recent evidence indicates that no more than one third of early retirees aged 50 and above left the labour force voluntarily, and only 12 per cent had planned for their retirement (UK Government, Cabinet Office 2000).

Some idea of the relative importance of these push-and-pull factors, and how this may have changed over time, can be gleaned from Table 2.1, which shows how the composition of UK pensioner incomes has changed over the past 60 years. The share of social security benefits in average pensioner income has risen over time from more than 40 to over 50 per cent. However, even as early as 1929–31 state benefits were the dominant source of pensioner income, and it seems implausible that the relatively small increase in their proportionate share since then could account for the massive fall in participation rates. Income from savings and investments has remained stable, but the contribution of occupational pensions has increased significantly. Comparing 1993 with 1929–31, private sources of non-employment income in retirement (from pensions and investments) have doubled their relative share. At

Table 2.1 Main components of UK pensioner incomes (%)

	Earnings	State benefits	Occupational pension	Investment income
1929–31	35	44	5	14
1951	27	42	15	15
1961	22	48	16	15
1971	18	48	21	10
1981	10	59	21	10
1993	6	56	23	16

Source: Johnson (1989a: 70); Johnson and Stears (1995: 73).

the same time, employment income has changed over sixty years from being a major to a minor source of pensioner income.

This illustrates just how important the twentieth-century evolution of the British labour market has been to the economic status of older people in the UK. It also demonstrates why the enormous expansion of public income support for older people has failed to achieve the expected improvement in pensioners' relative incomes. The rise in public provision has done little more than compensate for the loss of employment income. As the welfare state has expanded, so more demands have been placed on it by autonomous changes in the economy and the labour market; the achievements have consistently fallen short of the ever-widening objectives. Meanwhile the proportion of people entering retirement with substantial assets and large occupational pension entitlements has increased, and this has created a gap, ever more visible, between rich and poor retirees.

The twentieth-century history of retirees is a history of changing fortunes. At the beginning of the century to be old and out of work was synonymous with being poor for all but a very small minority of middle- and upper-class people. Today for a growing proportion of retirees (though by no means all), the end of work heralds not poverty and economic dependency but instead a new life-course stage of active and well-resourced leisure. A key determinant of fortune in old age is now the individual's earlier labour force history. If this is a history of continuous employment in a pensionable job at average or above-average wages, then retirement is likely to be financially secure. But if the previous work history involved long earnings gaps, or part-time work, or below-average pay and a non-pensionable job (all of which are more common for women than for men), then retirement will almost inevitably be a time of reduced financial capacity and dependency on public welfare. The type of work you do now determines the type of retirement you live. Twentieth-century labour market changes in the UK have enormously improved the retirement experience of many people – the 'core' workers in well-paid, stable jobs – but have done little to enhance living conditions in old age for 'peripheral' workers. It is this group who comprise today's impoverished retirees, unable to obtain employment, but unable to thrive on their meagre assets.

Participation in the formal labour market is the most important mechanism for the accumulation of pension assets, and these assets are a key determinant of the ability of retired persons to participate in society as consumers. In our consumerist age, active citizenship is as much a function of consumption as of productive activity, so poor retirees are doubly excluded – from both producer and consumer activities. In the last twenty years the range of leisure and recreational activities targeted at older persons in the UK has grown enormously, and their relative cost has declined, so more retired persons now participate in forms of active ageing than ever before. On the other hand, the social exclusion of impoverished elders (who tend to be disproportionately female and aged over 80 years) has, if anything, become more acute.

It may be thought that the emphasis here on pension assets ignores one of most important resources of retired persons – time. Even if an older person is income- and asset-poor, she is likely to be time-rich, and thus can participate in a wide variety of non-market activity such as caring for spouse or grandchild, or engaging in voluntary work. For example, in 1981 42 per cent of people over 65 in Britain reported giving regular help to other older people – most often a close relative, but in 11 per cent of cases a neighbour (UK Government 1984, tables 11.4 and 11.6). Moreover, the UK National Survey of Volunteering found that the proportion of people aged 65–74 who engaged in some form of voluntary work which benefited people other than close relatives had risen from 34 per cent in 1991 to 45 per cent in 1997 (Davis Smith 1998). Although this sort of activity is largely invisible in terms of a country's measured national income, it is nevertheless an important – some would say vital – aspect of civil society (Putnam 2000). Yet being a voluntary hospital worker, or an active grandparent, is not costless, so the opportunity that retired persons have to use their time in non-market participation is constrained or facilitated by access to financial resources. Thus an individual's personal history of formal labour market participation, and the associated accumulation of pension and other assets, is a major determinant even of their non-waged participation in civil society after retirement.

Wellbeing

At the end of the twentieth century, many more elders in Britain enjoyed a reasonably well-resourced period of retirement than was the case in 1900. But general trends conceal the considerable heterogeneity of experience, and divergence of outcomes, that have in fact occurred. The historian's eye can as easily locate stories of enduring inadequacy as of progressive achievement. Take the case of poverty. Just over 100 years ago the British parliament received a report from a Royal Commission that had been appointed to investigate the economic and social circumstances of the aged poor. The Commission concluded that although the great majority of working people were 'fairly provident, fairly thrifty, fairly industrious and fairly temperate' throughout their working lives, well over a third of them became abjectly poor in old age and had to rely on Poor Law financial assistance to prevent absolute destitution (UK Government 1895: xv). Almost a century later, in 1992, the second national report on the United Kingdom for the European Commission Observatory on Ageing and Older People noted that 30 per cent of all pensioners had incomes at or below the national poverty level, and that elders constituted a large proportion of the 'socially excluded' (Walker 1992: 64). To be sure, conceptions of poverty have changed enormously over the intervening years, but this constancy in the proportion of older people living below some socially acceptable standard is a profoundly depressing outcome after decades of social reform and welfare state expansion.

In 1908 the British government introduced a national noncontributory old age pension for all citizens of good character aged 70 years and above, whose annual income was less than £21. This pioneering piece of legislation was the first time that central government had acknowledged and assumed direct responsibility for the financial welfare of British people in old age, and it has, therefore, been seen as a 'tentative and halting step' along a path towards the comprehensive 'cradle to grave' welfare state established after the Second World War (Ogus 1982: 178–9). The expansion of public financial provision for old age and retirement has involved incremental extension of coverage to an ever larger proportion of the population, and on an ever more comprehensive basis. In 1925 a contributory national insurance pension payable to manual workers at age 65 was grafted on to the original non-contributory scheme. In 1940 the eligibility age for female pensioners was reduced from 65 to 60. In 1948 this contributory insurance pension was extended, as part of the Beveridge social insurance system, to include all citizens and not just manual workers. In 1959 graduated contributions were introduced for higher earners, who in return received a higher state pension, and in 1975 a supplementary state earnings-related pension scheme (SERPS) was launched to provide additional income in old age to workers who were not members of an employer pension scheme.

Simultaneously with this widening public involvement in pension provision has come a significant increase in the size of the older population. The combination of policy extension and demographic change has increased the proportion of the population eligible for pensions from little more than 3 per cent of the total before the First World War to almost 20 per cent today, and public expenditure on pensions has grown to become the largest single item in the government's budget (see Table 2.2).

Table 2.2 State pension payments in the UK, 1910–1993

	Pension payments (£m)	Payments as a percentage of		UK population over pension age (%)
		GNP	Government expenditure	
1910	10	0.4	4.3	3.1
1930	54	1.2	5.0	9.6
1950	305	2.6	7.8	13.4
1970	1,896	4.3	11.3	16.1
1993	31,500	5.2	13.0	18.7

Source: Johnson and Falkingham (1988: 141); Department of Social Security (1993: 6–10).

Has this expansion of public involvement in the provision of income security in old age been driven by an enduring and broad-based political commitment to enhance the wellbeing of older citizens? Historians have identified many causal factors behind the initial 1908 pension – political pressures from organised labour, an attempt by the predominantly middle-class Liberal party to win working-class votes, an evolving ideology of state intervention for the public good, and a conscious attempt by capitalists to shift some of the costs of the reproduction of labour from themselves to the state (Freeden 1988; Hay 1975; Hennock 1987). Each of these interpretations is valid, but none of them alone is convincing in explaining why this first piece of pension legislation was introduced. For the thirty years before the introduction of the 1908 Old Age Pension Act there was an ongoing debate about the need for a public pension, its mode of finance, who should be eligible and at what level it should be paid (Thane 1978). The breadth of ideas aired, opinions advanced and positions taken means that there is no shortage of alternative historical readings. Much depends on whether greater weight is placed on the influence of long-term economic and social forces or that of short-term political expediency.

Simple explanations also fail to account for the course of subsequent pension system development. The Conservative Party was responsible for introducing insurance pensions in 1925 and graduated pensions in 1959, the Labour Party for extending pension coverage beyond the manual working population in 1948, and for inaugurating the supplementary SERPS pension in 1975, although over this legislation there was conspicuous all-party support (Shragge 1984; Lowe 1993). However, neither party has ever made pension policy a major campaign issue in the run-up to a general election, nor has the trade union movement prioritised pension issues over more overtly employment-related concerns. In the post-war period politicians have found pension policy easy to promise, but hard to deliver. In the late 1950s a Labour Party study group chaired by Richard Crossman developed a radical proposal for a comprehensive national superannuation scheme, but it was shelved during the 1964–70 Labour government (Fawcett 1996). The Conservative government in the 1990s indicated that it would radically reform the state pension, but no proposals were forthcoming until two months before the party was voted out of office in May 1997. The Labour opposition throughout the 1980s promised to restore cuts made in 1980 to the basic state pension, but this pledge was dropped before the 1997 election campaign.

When looking at the political record of pensions policy in Britain since 1908, it is clear that pensioners have consistently been viewed by all main political parties as worthy of legislative attention and deserving of public financial support. Yet the proportion of pensioners deemed to be living in or on the margins of poverty remains around the 30 per cent level. The gap between the political rhetoric of a 'fair deal for pensioners' and the reality of public policy is striking. The reason for this lies not in the latent venality of politicians, but in the practical constraints of financial expediency. Although the 1908 pension was the first incursion of central government into the field of old age income support, local government had long been supporting infirm and penurious elders through the Poor Law. By the end of the nineteenth century the Poor Law provided pensions in fact, if not in name, to the majority of people who survived to 70 years of age (Thomson 1984). The 1908 legislation transferred much of the cost of this income support from local ratepayers (that is, property owners) to the national exchequer, and part of this cost was immediately switched back onto manual workers through an increase in excise duties on alcohol and tobacco. The extension of pensions to people aged 65 to 70 in 1925 was based entirely on an insurance model, with pensioners earning their entitlements through contributions made by themselves and their employers, because the non-contributory basis of the initial old age pension was considered too expensive to develop (Macnicol 1998). In these early excursions into the provision of public pensions, politicians were well aware that they could not afford, for reasons of fiscal propriety, to give pensioners a blank cheque.

William Beveridge was also concerned about the cost of pensions when he was conducting his review of social insurance in Britain during the Second World War. He recognised that 'the problem of the nature and extent of the provision to be made for old age is the most important, and in some ways the most difficult, of all the problems of social security' because of the growing number of older people and the very high cost involved in providing them all with a pension income (UK Government 1942: 90). The 1948 pension system finessed this problem by using current workers' national insurance contributions to pay for current pensions. This pay-as-you-go pension system effectively created a direct trade-off between the income of pensioners and the contributions of workers. In this competition, the interests of workers – well-organised, vocal and electorally dominant – were always likely to dominate the interests of pensioners, even if the public debate was seldom posed in these starkly confrontational terms.

By the mid-1980s, however, public discussion of pension policy was explicitly cast in terms of a zero-sum trade-off between workers and pensioners. The Conservative government's proposals for the reform of social security focused heavily on the projected future cost of the public pension, particularly the supplementary SERPS pension (UK Government 1985). Although motivated to some degree by an ideological desire to reduce the scope and cost of the welfare state, the proposal to abolish SERPS was also in part a response to independent estimates that the long-run cost would be far higher than originally intended (Hemming and Kay 1982). A compromise decision was taken to reduce the level of public pension benefits in order to allow personal tax rates to fall (or to prevent them rising) and to encourage private provision for old age. The inevitable result of the 1980s pension reforms was to make current pensioners worse-off in order to reduce the tax liability on future workers. Since 1997 the Labour government has done little to mitigate the effects of these prior reforms: British public pensions remain among the lowest in Europe.

It is clear that throughout the twentieth century financial considerations have been a consistent impediment to the scope of public old age income support. When the Royal Commission investigated the condition of the aged poor in the 1890s their financial need was plain for all to see, and there was widespread agreement that some form of public support for elders was morally justified. What delayed government action was the cost – in 1895 the Royal Commission balked at the financial burden on property and industrial enterprise that would be imposed by tax-financed pensions (UK Government 1895: lxix). It was concern over cost that constrained Beveridge's ambitions for pensions after the Second World War, and the enormous fiscal implications of raising the real value of pensions in a universal pay-as-you-go public pension system continue to undermine calls for more generous pensions. The twentieth-century history of public policy towards retirement and pensions in Britain is, therefore, curiously polarised. On the one hand there is the story of popular and successful institutional innovation which has led to the comprehensive incorporation of older people within the welfare state in a role as 'pensioners', and to the allocation of a large share of public revenue to this group via the state pension. On the other hand there is a consistent history of cross-party inability or unwillingness ever to provide adequate resources to meet expectations or to provide a pension income above a low subsistence level.

Social status

As well as being an element of public policy intervention and labour market change, the history of retirement has also been an important part of the re-conceptualisation of the lifecourse that has occurred in the twentieth century. People's expectations of old age, how they plan for it and experience it, have altered enormously over the past 100 years. One very simple reason for this is that most people can now expect not only to survive into retirement, but to do so in good health for well over a decade. Retirement has, therefore, changed from being a residual phase of life, experienced by a minority, to being a normal part of the life course, of equal or longer duration than childhood and adolescence.

With this demographic change has come a revolution in personal expectations. During the inter-war depression the novelist J. B. Priestley described the life course of the workers of Bradford as 'a brief childhood at one end and a few sinking weary years at the other end, and between them these five solid decades of work: that is their record' (Priestley 1934: 194). This negative view of old age was widely held, and with good reason. Old age and retirement appeared to the outside observer as a postscript to working life, a brief and insignificant interlude between the end of economic activity and the end of physical existence. How it was viewed by older people themselves is much more difficult to determine. As Thane (2000: Chapter 18) has noted, the majority of social investigations of older people in the post–1945 period problematised elders because of their perceived social or economic dependency. This was equally true for earlier periods, when official interest focused on the demands that the dependent aged poor might place on public authorities. Since investigators were primed to address the problems of old age it is little wonder that they conspicuously failed to ask questions about capacity and achievement. And since there are few diaries or autobiographies for the pre–1945 period that give more than passing treatment to the experience of ageing and the condition of being a retiree or pensioner, it is difficult, perhaps impossible, to discover how people negotiated their own ageing. Did they see the later part of their life course as just 'a few sinking weary years', or did it provide opportunities for personal fulfilment?

If the historical record is almost silent on this question, then we might draw inferences from more recent experience. Rising life expectancy, better health and, for some at least, significantly higher real incomes have made retirement into something positive; a new chapter rather than a postscript. Instead of using the word 'retired', with all its negative connotations of economic redundancy, older people in Britain increasingly use the term 'third age' to describe their phase of the life course, and 'senior citizen' to describe their status. To quote Peter Laslett, the leading advocate of this reconceptualisation of the life course, 'First comes an era of dependence, socialisation, immaturity and education; second an era of independence, maturity and responsibility, of earning and saving; third an era of personal fulfilment' (Laslett 1989:4). Personal fulfilment involves older people taking a much more active role in political affairs, being more assertive in their demands for equal access to employment opportunities, and being central rather than marginal to the social activities of civil society. Instead of a monochrome old age of general dependency and poverty there is opportunity for colourful, active diversity.

Popular images of retirement have also become much more diverse and fragmented, reflecting the enormous diversity of capacity and experience amongst older people. Stories of impoverished pensioners dying of hypothermia in unheated apartments vie with accounts of thousands of British retirees who over-winter in the sunshine of Spain or Florida. For each media tale of hardship in old age there is one of wayward abandon – the bungee-jumping octogenarian, the parachuting granny. But these are, of course, no more than images, views from without. They give little indication of whether the experience of old age has changed from within, from the perspective of the ageing individual.

The cultural history of old age in twentieth-century Britain has yet to be written, and the paucity of source material on the mass of working-class elders means that any future account will at best be partial. Instead we can look to contemporary studies. Paul Thompson has used the methodology of the oral historian to investigate the experience of old age in the 1980s among a cross-section of older women and men (Thompson *et al.* 1990). The central finding of this sympathetic and evocative study is summed up in the title: *I Don't Feel Old*. For Thompson's respondents, old age was some 'other', to which they did not belong. They certainly did not regard themselves as being in a liminal state between a meaningful world of work and the oblivion of death. For these people retirement had its own challenges, achievements and disappointments, just like other phases of life – childhood, adolescence, marriage, parenthood.

International comparisons

How does the historical evolution of participation, wellbeing and social status of older people in other industrialised countries compare with that of the UK? Is the story one of universal trends and common responses, or is it instead one of national exceptionalism?

If we look first at participation, then the most striking feature is the similarity of long-run trends. Labour force participation rates for older men have fallen almost without interruption over the course of the twentieth century throughout Europe and North America, and since the 1960s in Japan as well. This behavioural trend is not confined simply to men above the normal retirement age: as Figure 2.1 shows, over the last thirty years the participation rate for men aged 60-64 has also been on a consistent downward course in Europe. On the other hand, Figure 2.1 also shows considerable national variation in the *level* of participation among this age group. In 1999, for example, a male aged 60–64 in Britain had double the chance of being in paid employment when compared with a male of similar age in France or the Netherlands. This demonstrates that, despite many similarities between countries, national conditions – such as early retirement rules, employment laws, employer attitudes and social expectations – still matter.

This long-run decline in labour force participation rates among older people coincides with the introduction and expansion of public pension systems in the industrialised economies, and it seems likely that public policy has contributed to this decline. In addition to the standard public pension entitlements, the 1970s and 1980s saw the invention of many other pathways out of the labour force for older workers who could demonstrate some loss of functionality due to illness, disability or redundancy (Jacobs *et al.* 1991). There is now a very large literature that considers how the labour supply of older workers may be affected by

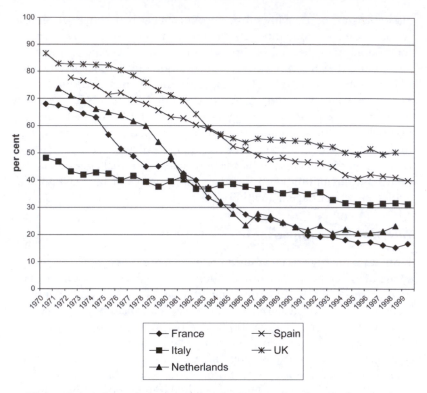

Figure 2.1 Labour force participation rates of males aged 60–64 in some European countries   *Source:* OECD 1998.

social security incentives relating to replacement rates, earnings tests, taxes, wealth accrual, etcetera (for a recent survey, see the essays in Gruber and Wise 1999). However, it has not yet produced a convincing evaluation of the relative contribution of public policy to the secular rise in retirement in the developed economies.

There is considerable dispute about the quantitative significance, or leverage, of public pension systems on participation. Gruber and Wise (1999) have conducted a major cross-country study of public pension systems and find a strong relationship between retirement rules (which determine pension wealth) and the average male age of retirement, particularly for early retirement in the age range 60–64. They demonstrate that there is a clear relationship between discontinuities in the accrual rate of social security wealth and spikes in the distribution of retirement by age. Blöndal and Scarpetta (1998) have similarly found that public old age pension systems discourage work at older ages in virtually all OECD countries, and Börsch-Supan (2000) has found the same for Germany. However, a recent study by Richard Johnson (2000) which models the retirement incentive created by public pension rules for a panel of 13 countries from 1880 to 1990 finds that while public pensions have a negative impact on participation, this effect is modest, with the pension variables explaining only 11 per cent of the decline in average participation rates of men aged 60–64 in 1920–90. Johnson speculates that the participation declines not attributable to the expansion of public pensions or other public programmes may result from higher private wealth. This is certainly the view of Costa (1999), who ascribes the long–run rise of retirement in the US to increasing private wealth and the declining relative price of leisure.

For countries with less developed public pension systems than are typical within the OECD, it really matters whether declining participation is driven by public pension entitlements or by increasing private wealth. If the former, then productive labour supply (and thus long–run economic growth) can be maximised by curtailing the scope and generosity of public pensions. If, on the other hand, retirement is mainly a response to increasing wealth at older ages, then it is largely an automatic and inevitable concomitant of economic growth, and a curtailment of public pension entitlements may have little impact on overall labour supply, yet may significantly reduce the welfare of poorer older persons.

What about the wellbeing of older persons in other industrialised countries? The general pattern is similar to that in the UK, but the earnings–related nature of public pensions in most OECD countries,

Table 2.3 The cost of public pensions as % of GDP in selected OECD countries in 2000 and 2050 (projected)

	2000	2050
Australia	3.0	4.6
Canada	5.1	10.9
Denmark	6.1	8.8
France	12.1	16.0
Germany	11.8	16.8
Italy	14.2	13.9
Japan	7.9	8.5
Korea	2.1	10.1
Spain	9.4	17.4
Sweden	9.2	10.8
UK	4.3	3.6
USA	4.4	6.2

Source: Visco, 2001.

compared with the flat-rate basis in Britain, means that on average pensions are higher relative to average earnings. This can be seen in Table 2.3, which reports the cost of current public old age pensions as a proportion of gross domestic product, and provides projections of this cost ratio over the next half-century.

The UK currently devotes only a third as much of its national income to public pensions as France, Germany or Italy, despite similar population age structures. Furthermore, this expenditure share in Britain is projected to decline as the value of the public pension relative to average wages continues to fall, whereas in most countries an increasing pensioner population, combined with fairly static real pension levels implies a rising expenditure share. This is good news for future pensioner welfare, but it does raise important questions about the affordability and political sustainability of public pension systems, an issue discussed in other chapters.

As for social status, the long-run trends are difficult to identify with any precision. There can be no doubt that the voice of older people is now articulated and heard in the political arena. In the US the American Association of Retired Persons is one of the largest membership organisations in the country, and maintains a full-time presence in Washington to monitor federal government activity and lobby for the rights of older people. In Italy in the 1990s pensioner groups were active in mobilising demonstrations against proposed public pension reductions. The United Nations designated 1999 as the International Year of Older Persons and supported a number of initiatives to promote active ageing and social inclusion. On the other hand, negative attitudes towards older people persist. In television they are usually invisible in advertisements, and stereotyped as inadequate, dependent or curmudgeonly in drama and comedy programmes

In truth, the attitudes and behaviour of older people, and the way they are viewed by others in society, are as diverse as for any other age group. What twentieth-century social and economic development in the UK and other industrialised countries has done is give many more people, whether old or young, the time and resources to develop their individual interests and capabilities. Thus we see an older population today that is characterised by much greater economic and social heterogeneity than was the case a hundred years ago. This has important implications for public policy. It means that age alone has become a less useful identifier for inclusion or exclusion from any particular policy initiative. Indeed, when the population of seventy-year-olds includes both the physically fit and active and the bedridden, the very wealthy and the abjectly poor, the socially connected and the socially excluded, the family figurehead and the isolated singleton, then it is no longer evident that age should be regarded as a meaningful social or economic category. Developments in the participation, wellbeing and social status of older people in advanced industrial societies over the course of the twentieth century have fundamentally transformed the conditions of life for the majority of older people, and have gone a long way to undermine the rationale for age-based public policy.

REFERENCES

Baines, Dudley and Paul Johnson (1999) 'Did they jump or were they pushed? The exit of older men from the London labour market, 1929 to 1931', *Journal of Economic History*, 59: 949–71.

Blöndal, S. and S. Scarpetta (1998) 'The retirement decision in OECD countries', *OECD Working Paper AWP 1.4*, Paris: OECD.

Börsch-Supan, A. (2000) 'Incentive effects of social security on labor force participation: evidence in Germany and across Europe', *Journal of Public Economics* 78: 25–49.

Costa, D. (1998) *The Evolution of Retirement: an American History 1880–1999*, Chicago: University of Chicago Press.

Dawson, A. and G. Evans (1987) 'Pensioners' incomes and expenditure, 1970–1985', *Employment Gazette*, May, pp. 243–52.

Davis Smith, J. (1998) *National Survey of Volunteering in the UK*, Institute for Volunteering Research, London.

Fawcett, Helen (1996) 'The Beveridge strait-jacket: policy formation and the problem of poverty in old age', *Contemporary British History*, 10 (1): 20–42.

Featherstone, M. and M. Hepworth (1991) 'The mask of ageing and the postmodern lifecourse', in M. Featherstone, M. Hepworth and B. S. Turner (eds.), *The Body*, London: Sage.

Freeden, Michael (1978) *The New Liberalism*, Oxford: Oxford University Press.

Fukasawa, K. (1996) 'Voluntary provision for old age by trade unions in Britain before the coming of the Welfare State', unpublished PhD thesis, University of London.

Gruber, J. and D. Wise (1999) *Social Security and Retirement Around the World*, NBER/ University of Chicago Press, Chicago.

Hannah, Leslie (1985) *Inventing Retirement*, Cambridge, Cambridge University Press.

Hay, J. R. (1975) *The Origins of the Liberal Welfare Reforms, 1906–1914*, Macmillan, London.

Hemming, R. and J. Kay (1982) 'The costs of the state earnings related pension scheme', *Economic Journal*, 92 (June): 300–19.

Hennock, E. P. (1987) *British Social Reform and German Precedents. The Case of Social Insurance 1880–1914*, Oxford: Clarendon.

Jacobs, Klaus, Martin Kohli and Martin Rein (1991) 'The evolution of early exit: a comparative analysis of labor force participation patterns', in Martin Kohli, Martin Rein, Anne-Marie Guillemard and Herman van Gunsteren (eds.), *Time for Retirement*, Cambridge: Cambridge University Press.

Johnson, Paul (1989a) 'The structured dependency of the elderly: a critical note', in Margot Jefferys (ed.), *Growing Old in the Twentieth Century*, London: Routledge.

—— (1989b) 'The labour force participation of older men in Britain, 1951–81', *Work, Employment and Society*, 3: 351–68.

—— (1993) 'Older workers and the British labour market: analysing long-run trends', in G. D. Snooks (ed.), *Historical Analysis in Economics*, London: Routledge.

—— (1994) 'The employment and retirement of older men in England and Wales, 1881–1981', *Economic History Review*, 47: 106-28.

—— and Jane Falkingham (1988) 'Intergenerational transfers and public expenditure on the elderly in modern Britain', *Ageing and Society*, 8: 129–46.

—— and Jane Falkingham (1992) *Ageing and Economic Welfare*, London: Sage.

—— and G. Stears (1995) 'Pensioner income inequality', *Fiscal Studies*, 16 (4): 69–93.

Johnson, Richard (2000) 'The effect of old-age insurance on male retirement: evidence from historical cross-country data', *Working Paper RWP 00-09*, Federal Reserve Bank of Kansas City.

Laczko, F., A. Dale, S. Arber and N. Gilbert (1988) 'Early retirement in a period of high unemployment', *Journal of Social Policy*, 17: 313–33.

Laczko, Frank, and Chris Phillipson (1991) *Changing Work and Retirement*, Buckingham: Open University Press.

Laslett, Peter (1989) *A Fresh Map of Life*, London: Harvard University Press.

Lowe, Rodney (1993) *The Welfare State in Britain since 1945*, Basingstoke: Macmillan.

Macnicol, John (1998) *The Politics of Retirement in Britain, 1878–1948*, Cambridge: Cambridge University Press.

—— and Andrew Blaikie (1989) 'The politics of retirement, 1908-1948', in Margot Jefferys (ed.) *Growing Old in the Twentieth Century*, Routledge, London.

Offe, C. (1984) *Contradictions of the Welfare State*, MIT Press, Cambridge, Mass.

Ogus, A. I. (1982) 'Great Britain', in P. A. Kohler, H. F. Zacher and M. Partington (eds.), *The Evolution of Social Insurance, 1881–1981*, St Martin's Press, London.

Organisation for Economic Cooperation and Development (OECD) (1998) *Maintaining Prosperity in an Ageing Society*, Paris: Organisation for Economic Cooperation and Development.

Priestley, J. B. (1934) *English Journey*, London.

Putnam, Robert (2001) *Bowling Alone*, New York: Simon & Schuster.

Rowntree, B. S. (1941) *Poverty and Progress. A Second Social Survey of York*, New York: Longman.

Shragge, Eric (1984) *Pensions Policy in Britain*, London: Routledge.

Smith, Richard (1998) 'Ageing and well-being in early modern England: pension trends and gender preferences under the English Old Poor Law c. 1650–1800', in Paul Johnson and Pat Thane (eds.), *Old Age from Antiquity to Post-modernity*, London: Routledge.

Szreter, S. and G. Mooney (1998) 'Urbanisation, mortality and the standard of living debate: new estimates of the expectation of life at birth in nineteenth-century British cities', *Economic History Review,* 51 (1): 84–112.

Thane, Pat (1978) 'Non–contributory versus insurance pensions, 1878–1908', in Pat Thane (ed.), *The Origins of British Social Policy*, London: Croom Helm.

—— (2000) *Old Age in English History*, Oxford: Oxford University Press.

Thompson, Paul, Catherine Itzin and Michelle Abendstern (1990) *I Don't Feel Old: The Experience of Later Life*, Oxford: Oxford University Press.

Thomson, David (1984) 'The decline of social welfare; falling state support for the elderly since early Victorian times', *Ageing and Society*, 4: 451-82.

Tinker, Anthea (1992) *Elderly People in Modern Society,* London: Longman.

UK Government (1895) *Royal Commission on the Aged Poor,* London.

—— (1942) *Social Insurance and Allied Services* (The Beveridge Report), Cmd. 6404, HMSO, London, p. 90.

—— (Central Statistical Office) (1984) *Social Trends*, Vol. 14, London.

—— (Department of Health and Social Security) (1985) *Reform of Social Security*, Cmd. 9517, London: HMSO.

—— (Cabinet Office) (2000) *Winning the Generation Game,* Performance and Innovation Unit, Cabinet Office, London.

—— (Department of Social Security) (2000) *The Changing Welfare State: Social Security Spending*, London.

Visco, I. (2001) 'Fiscal implications of ageing: projections of age-related spending', *OECD Economic Outlook*, 69 (June).

Walker, Alan (1992) 'Social and economic policies and older people in the UK', mimeo, University of Sheffield, p. 64.

Warr, Peter (1992) 'Age and employment', in M. Dunnette, L. Hough and H. Triandis (eds.), *Handbook of Industrial and Organisational Psychology*, vol. 4, Palo Alto: Consulting Psychologists Press.

Wrigley, E. A., R. S. Davies, J. E. Oeppen and R. S. Schofield (1997) *English Population History from Family Reconstitution*, Cambridge: Cambridge University Press.

Wrigley, E. A., and R. Schofield (1989) *The Population History of England, 1541–1871: A Reconstruction,* Cambridge University Press, Cambridge.

CHAPTER 3

Social Policy and the Wellbeing of Older People at a Time of Economic Slowdown: the Case of Brazil

ANA AMÉLIA CAMARANO

In Brazil the share of population aged 60 and over increased from 4 to 9 per cent between 1940 and 2000. Over the next 20 years this age group will expand from approximately 14 to 25.5 million people; and in 2001 at least one older person was found in 26 per cent of families (IBGE 2000). Population ageing is, in general, to be welcomed. Nevertheless, it has led to concerns about resource transfers and about pressures on society, the state and the productive sectors.

Much current debate still assumes that we can divide the population into two groups: the productive and the dependent, and that the elderly population constitutes a homogeneous group, composed only by vulnerable people. Dependency in later life results from a loss of labour capacity, along with poor health status and disability. The former means a potential lack of income and the latter means a lack of autonomy. This chapter shows that this association between age and dependency can be weakened by social policy.

It also shows that not all older people have similar levels of vulnerability. In fact, a large proportion of Brazilian elders play important social roles, such as continued economic activity and caring for grandchildren. Financially, many older people are better off than other age groups, and many share their income with younger family members.

This chapter examines relationships between ageing and well-being over the past 20 years, making particular reference to differences between rural and urban areas and richer and poorer regions. Four dimensions of older peoples' lives are considered: health conditions, income, economic activities and family arrangements. These changes are located within the country's general development experience and social policy structures.

Regional disparities and development trends

Brazil is characterised by large regional, demographic and socio-economic variations, and is usually divided into five major regions for the purposes of social and economic description (see Figure 3.1). This chapter focuses on two of these regions: the South-east, which is relatively wealthy, urban and industrial, and the relatively poor and rural North-east. As Table 3.1 shows, these regions represent the two extremes of wealth and poverty in Brazil. The South-east is the most populous region in Brazil, containing 42 per cent of the total population

REGIONS
- North
- North-East
- South-East
- South
- Mid-West

Figure 3.1 Map of Brazilian regions

Table 3.1 Some economic characteristics of Brazilian regions

Regions	Population 2000	Area %	% Pop. 60+	Life expectancy* At birth	At 60	GNP (%) 2000	Per capita income 1999†
North	12,919,949	45.3	5.5	64.19	15.47	6	183.63
North-east	47,679,381	18.2	8.4	63.93	16.75	16	141.03
South-east	72,262,411	10.9	9.3	67.87	17.84	54	322.34
South	25,070,380	6.8	8.0	69.53	17.67	17	290.62
Mid-west	11,611,491	18.9	6.6	66.13	16.01	7	274.58
Brazil	169,543,612	100.0	8.6	67.05	17.31	100	254.73

Sources: IBGE, *Censo Demográfico de 2000*; PNAD of 1999, Health Ministry, Mortality Information System and Silva and IPEADATA.
Note: ★ 1998 figures   † In reais, monthly

in 2000. Although it occupies only 11 per cent of the total land mass, it includes the three most important industrial centres: São Paulo, Rio de Janeiro and Belo Horizonte. This region dominates Brazil economically in all sectors, including agriculture. Furthermore, *per capita* income is almost three times as high as that of the North-east.

In a very broad sense, it is possible to distinguish two general periods in Brazil's economic performance since the Second World War. From 1945 to 1980, GDP expanded at a rate of over 7 per cent a year. Since then, annual growth rates have been much less impressive, roughly averaging three per cent (OECD 2001).

The first period was characterised by protectionist state-driven industrialisation. Both manufacturing and state bureaucracy grew rapidly, and there was a substantial transfer of population away from rural areas and agriculture (Baer 1995). The national population increased from 70 million in 1960 to 119 million in 1980 as a result of high fertility and declining mortality. The gross national product grew more than fourfold over the same time period. Nevertheless, these economic results were not accompanied by general gains in wellbeing. The pre-existing regional disparities in wealth and development were reinforced, with the relatively urban and industrial South-east out-performing the less dynamic rural economy of the North-east. At the same time, the income distribution became more skewed. In 1960, the incomes of the richest 10 per cent of Brazilians were 34 times greater than for the poorest 10 per cent. By 1980 this ratio had reached 47 to 1.

The 1930s saw the initial development of a modern welfare state system, which included social security, health, education and housing provision. By the 1970s, social security covered all workers engaged in the formal sector of the economy. However, rather than serve as a tool of redistribution, these policies largely reproduced existing inequalities in Brazilian society. As part of a wider, corporatist system of 'regulated citizenship', welfare entitlements and social spending were skewed towards politically powerful occupational groups, while unskilled rural workers and those in the informal sector were largely excluded from protection (Santos 1979).[1] This concept of citizenship was not rooted in a code of political values, but rather in a system of occupational stratification (Draibe 1990).

One element of welfare policy in this period which is of particular importance for the wellbeing of today's older people was the creation of the National Housing Bank in 1964. This Bank financed the construction of 4.5 million new houses between 1964 and 1986 through subsidised loans, repayable over a 25-year period. It is claimed that almost 40 per cent of the new houses benefited poorer social strata

(Azevedo 1996). This explains the high levels of home ownership among the current cohort of older people (85 per cent in 2001).

Another important feature of this period was the great dynamism of the urban labour market, especially between 1960 and 1980. During this period, industrial employment grew at 6.8 per cent a year, and most of the new jobs were in the formal sector (Oliveira 1998). Industrial development was accompanied by a diversification of the urban labour market, and employment in the modern tertiary sector also grew dramatically. These labour market trends occurred at a time when the current cohort of older people were at their prime working ages, and are likely to have had a major impact on their wellbeing in later life.

Since 1980 Brazil's development trajectory has been associated with the impact of the debt crisis and a stalling of the inward-oriented industrial model. Between 1986 and 1994 different governments implemented a series of failed stabilisation plans. Only in 1994 did the Real Plan achieve a measure of economic stability. By pegging the domestic currency to the US dollar, the Real Plan led to a significant over-valuation of the terms of trade. The Plan was accompanied by policies to 'flexibilise' the labour market (Cano 1998). Consequences have included an increase in interest rates, a deterioration of employment conditions, and a surge in joblessness. Economic activity rates for men, especially younger ones, have declined. This reflects difficulties in getting a first job, as well as the low quality of many newly created jobs (Wanjman et al. 1999). Although poverty levels fell immediately after the Real Plan,[2] measures of inequalities point to little change. Disparities between rural and urban areas are particularly striking: in 1999 29.7 per cent of the rural population were below the official poverty line, compared to 18.8 per cent of the urban population. Brazil continues to have one of the worst income distributions in the world (Camarano 2002b).

Until recently, population ageing was not particularly marked in Brazil (Table 3.2). This was due to the continuation of high fertility

Table 3.2 Brazilian demographic trends, 1995–2000

Period	Total fertility rate	Population age 60+ (%)
1965–1970	5.75	5.1
1975–1980	4.17	6.1
1985–1990	2.82	7.3
1995–2000	2.38	8.6

Source: IBGE/Demographic Census 1970, 1980, 1991 and 2000.

rates through to the late 1960s. Since then, the fertility decline has been sharp, responding to a complex array of indirect socio-economic and cultural stimuli. While family planning programmes were not officially adopted on a large scale in Brazil, it is thought that various aspects of public policy may have been influential. One of these was the rapid extension of pension schemes for formal and, later, informal sector workers, which may have reduced the 'old age security' motivation for having large families (Martine 1996).

It would seem unlikely that demographic ageing has had an important effect on Brazil's development trajectory to date. Nevertheless, concern with social security costs is a frequent theme in literature since the 1980s and has remained a prominent issue on the policy agenda. Beltrão and Oliveira (1999) point to a breakdown of the Brazilian social security system in the medium run if present conditions are left unchanged. In fact, it would be more accurate to view this as a pensions, or even a labour market, crisis rather than an ageing one. As in Europe, Brazil's social security system assumed full employment conditions, and an unbroken work career followed by relatively few years of retirement prior to death. These assumptions clearly no longer pertain to Brazil. Changes to the labour market have resulted in significant reductions in contributions to the social security system. The Brazilian social security system has a long tradition of allowing people to retire on the basis of years in employment (or years of pension contribution), rather than chronological age. This has resulted in large numbers of formal sector workers retiring well in advance of reaching old age, some even in their forties.[3] This kind of benefit is responsible for the largest share of the current social security budget. Thus, the link between population ageing and sustainability of the pensions system is tenuous.

The crisis of the Brazilian economy in the 1980s coincided with a return to democratic rule. A key political event was the agreement of a new national constitution in 1988. This constitution genuinely sought to reduce the social exclusion of poorer and less powerful groups and shift the country towards a social-democratic model of governance. One important part of this change was the extension of formal social protection to those older people who had been ignored by the previous corporatist model (Draibe 1990). As will be seen, these changes have had major implications for the wellbeing of older people and their families.

Ageing and wellbeing in later life

The process of ageing in Brazil is heterogeneous and complex, with important differences between rural and urban areas. Although fertility and mortality are higher in rural areas, population ageing is more marked there, due to the out-migration of younger age groups (Camarano and Abramovay 1998). The majority of these rural migrants are young women, so gender ratios vary between rural and urban areas. This may have implications for how the care needs of older people are met. Despite this rural bias, population ageing is more advanced in the South-east, reflecting lower fertility and higher life expectancy at old age (see Table 3.3).

Table 3.3 Some characteristics of Brazilians aged 60+

Some characteristics	Urban		Rural	
	1981	2001	1981	2001
% Population	6.51	8.88	6.24	9.95
Sex ratio	80.61	74.58	116.2	104.99
Mean age	68.75	69.61	68.55	69.55
% Heads of family	60.32	64.17	64.36	63.13
% Spouses	20.03	21.42	21.51	25.08
% Other relatives	18.61	13.39	13.62	10.48
% Living alone	8.76	12.44	8.72	10.51
Years of schooling	2.58	3.75	0.71	1.31
% No income	20.4	12.63	28.95	6.04
% Poor families	28.06	16.33	52.37	25.28
% Working	21.7	24.28	38.4	57.83
% House owner	64.4	85.23	66.3	85.49
% Good health*	—	73.26	—	87.18
% Handicapped	6.3	4.00**	6.7	3.70**
Difficulty with feeding (%)**		13.31		17.14
Walking more than 100 m (%)**		16.81		16.61
Walking more than 1 km (%)**		36.27		44.29

Source: IBGE. PNADs 1981 and 2001.
Notes: * This is a self reported response and refers to 1998.
** Data refer to 1991.

Concerns about the consequences of rural–urban migration on familial arrangements and the wellbeing of older people are a key theme in the Brazilian literature on ageing. It is recognised that this can result in the isolation and abandonment of older people in rural areas. This highlights the need for comparative analysis of social support for older people in rural and urban settings (Saad 1999; Camarano et al. 1999).

Analysis by time-period

Brazil's older people are now living longer and better than in previous decades. Life expectancy at the age of 60 increased from 10.7 years in 1981 to 13.1 in 1998 for males, and from 12.7 to 15.4 for females (Camarano 2002a). Older people are experiencing lower levels of physical and mental disability. This improvement has been especially marked for people in rural areas, although their health status is slightly behind their urban counterparts (Table 3.3). For example, in 1998 about 84 per cent of older people living in urban areas reported being in good health, compared to 81 per cent in rural areas.

Whilst overall self-reported health in later life is good, access to the health care system is highly differentiated according to social classes. The new constitution guaranteed the entitlements of all citizens to public health care. Also, there were attempts to reduce disparities in access by focusing on public provision at the municipal level. However, private health insurance has grown rapidly for those Brazilians who can afford it. Thus, it is not surprising that Romero (2002) found that older people who lived in a family with monthly *per capita* income lower than half the minimum wage (about US$37) were 51 per cent more likely to report bad health status than ones who lived in a family with a *per capita* income higher than five minimum wages. Gender differences are also apparent. Although women live longer than men, they experience a higher incidence of chronic diseases and reduced autonomy (Nogales 1998). Table 3.4 shows that women are more prone to experience all the most important diseases associated with later life. Women also make more use of health services than men do, regardless of their age. To conclude, ageing and the sex-compositional effect have resulted in an increased demand for health services.

Table 3.3 also gives information about disability in later life and the capacity of older people to engage in activities of daily living. This includes the proportion of older people who reported difficulty in (1) feeding, taking a shower and going to the bathroom; (2) walking more than 100 metres; and (3) walking more than one kilometre. Respondents displayed a good level of functional ability and over half were able to perform relatively demanding tasks, such as walking more than a kilometre. Difficulties with basic activities such as feeding, showering or bathing affected about 15 per cent of respondents. There is some empirical evidence that functional difficulties affect the living arrangements of older people. As institutional care is not widespread in Brazil, families have to take over the responsibility of care for older people who need it. This is reflected in data from 1998 which shows that about a quarter of the older people who experienced some kind of disability lived in relatives' households as 'other relatives'.

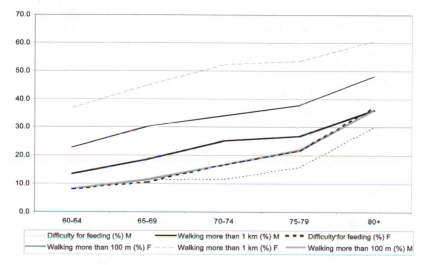

**Figure 3.2 Proportion of people aged 60+
with difficulties in daily functioning, Brazil**

Source: IBGE, PNAD, 1998.

As expected, health conditions and disabilities get worse for the very old (Figure 3.2). The largest impact is on being able to perform basic activities such as feeding, showering or bathing and walking more than 100 metres. Women experience a higher proportion of disability than

Table 3.4 Self-reported health problems of people aged 60+, 1998 (%)

	Men		Women	
	Urban	Rural	Urban	Rural
Back problems	39.3	50.6	47.6	50.3
Arthritis	27.1	39.3	41.9	50.8
Cancer	1.6	0.7	1.0	0.4
Diabetes	9.1	4.3	12.8	8.8
Respiratory diseases	7.9	7.6	7.7	7.7
Blood pressure	38.2	31.6	50.2	47.5
Heart diseases	17.8	12.8	22.3	15.3
Kidney disease	6.5	8.6	6.6	7.1
Depression	8.7	5.9	16.3	10.7
Difficulty in feeding	13.1	14.1	16.9	18.0
Walking more than 100m	15.1	11.7	24.9	21.5
Walking more than 1 km	34.4	35.5	52.3	55.3

Source: IBGE, 1998 Household Survey.

men, and gender differences increase with age, especially with regard to difficulties in walking more than 100 metres. Nevertheless, at the age of 80, about 40 per cent of older women can still walk more than one kilometre. These indicators also suggest that Brazil's older population enjoys a relative high degree of autonomy and independence.

Assessing the wellbeing of older people through income data is methodologically complex, especially in rural areas, and thus findings should be treated with caution. If we consider older people without any earnings, and the proportion considered poor, it would appear that older people made substantial gains over the last 20 years. These findings were especially marked for people living in rural areas, especially older women, although overall rates of poverty remain higher than in the cities (Table 3.3 and Figure 3.3).

In rural areas, the proportion of women without any income whatsoever declined sharply (from 45 to 10 per cent, 1981 to 2001). The decline in urban areas was also large, albeit from a lower baseline (35 to 14 per cent). Barros, Mendonça and Santos (1999) found that for the non-elderly population, poverty is higher among women. This situation was reversed when older people were considered. One reason for this is that Brazilian legislation allows women simultaneously to receive retirement benefits, widow's pensions and earnings from employment.

A large proportion of older people's earnings come from the social security system. By 2001 in rural areas, 85 per cent of older people received some kind of social benefit, reaching 34 per cent of all households. In urban areas, the figures were 76 and 28 per cent, respectively. Pension benefits have served to reduce the potential association between old age and economic vulnerability. Nevertheless, earnings from work are still an important source of wealth for older people, accounting for around 30 per cent of their total income (Camarano 2001).

In Brazil it is quite common for retired people to continue participating in the labour market, since pension legislation allows for this. The National Policy for Older People, adopted in 1994, makes provision for training programmes for older people who want to keep up with changes in the labour market. While the scale of this initiative may not be large, it indicates a progressive attitude towards the potential contribution of older people on the part of policy makers. Even though the proportion of retired older people increased sharply from 1981 to 1998, their economic activity rate remained stable at around 27 per cent (Camarano 2001). This is particularly notable given the general slowdown of job creation over the past two decades. For older women, participation in the labour market has actually increased. This is

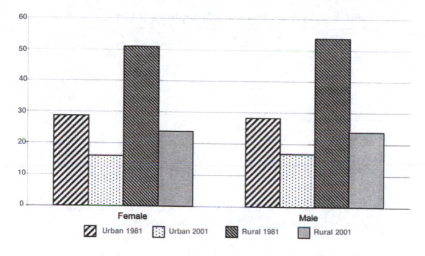

Source: IBGE, PNADs 1981 and 2001.

Figure 3.3 Proportion of people aged 60+ living in poverty in Brazil

probably a cohort effect, reflecting a large overall rise in female participation in the labour market in the recent past. However, access to the
labour market remains highly gendered in later life: about 70 per cent of
older men in work have a full-time job, compared to only 37 per cent
of women (Camarano 2001).

Certain labour market characteristics may act as incentives for
economic participation in later life. For example, federal legislation
obliges firms to pay the transport costs of their employees. As people
aged over 64 are entitled to free urban transport, this means lower costs
for employers. Traditionally in Brazil, general clerical tasks were done
by 'office boys', but these are now being replaced by 'office oldies'.
Research in metropolitan areas found that older people who were more
dependent on labour income (men, heads of household, the poor, and
unskilled workers) made particular efforts to obtain work, but that they
had less chance of staying in economic activity than was the case for
skilled workers (Wajnman, Oliveira and Oliveira 1999).

Table 3.5 gives data for reported income according to different
sources. Large gender disparities can be seen, and women are worse off
in all areas with the unsurprising exception of widows' pensions. The
importance of economic activity is apparent, as those older people who
both work and receive a pension are substantially better off than those
who just work, and somewhat wealthier than those who just receive a

Table 3.5 Average income of people aged 60+, by source

	Male	Female	Total
Only work	546.61	357.02	469.31
Retired working	814.41	310.19	666.21
Only retired	472.79	228.74	352.39
Net survivor's pension	213.10	345.54	343.63
Others*	838.37	250.70	356.39

Source: IBGE 1999 Household Survey.
*Includes rents, interest and gifts.

pension. Part of this variation may occur because non-working older people were rather older (on average 3.5 years more) than those who have a job.

It is likely that improvements in health conditions have allowed older people to stay in work until advanced ages. Although activity rates decline rapidly with age, in 1998 about 20 per cent of men aged 80 and over were still working (Camarano 2001). To be working is an indicator of autonomy, as well as one of need. For older people, it also suggests good health and physical and mental capability and results in an advantageous economic situation for the retired worker.

Another indication of the relatively better situation of older people has been a rise in home ownership. This has taken place in both rural and urban areas (see Table 3.6). Home ownership is highest for the oldest old, revealing that assets continue to be accumulated throughout the life cycle (Camarano *et al.* 1999). Many older people benefited from the National Housing Programme during the 1960s, 1970s and early 1980s, which coincided with their prime working years. This trend contrasts with declining acquisition rates among the younger generation (Neri, Nascimento and Pinto 1999).

In most countries, economic exchange between older people and other family members is a major determinant of their material wellbeing. It is possible to gain some idea about the status of older people within households by the way their relationship to the household head is categorised. Brazil's General Household Survey identifies five categories of relationships: head, spouse, child, 'other relatives' and non-relative members. Table 3.6 points to an increase in the proportion of older heads and spouses, and to a reduction in the proportion of 'other relatives'. This suggests that either older people's status in families has gained ground, or more are living alone.

As will be seen later, relationships between co-residence and inter-generational support are complex and difficult to predict. Nevertheless,

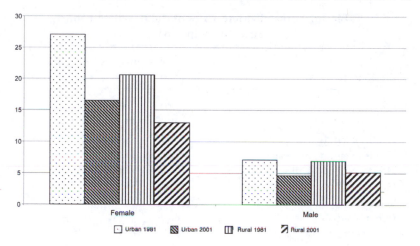

Legend: Urban 1981 | Urban 2001 | Rural 1981 | Rural 2001

Figure 3.4 Proportion of people aged 60+ classified as 'other relatives' in Brazil

numerous aspects of older people's living arrangements are worthy of comment. The probability of living with other relatives is higher for older women and for people in urban areas (Figure 3.4). Although women live longer than men, they experience greater disability and may have stronger psychological ties with their relatives. This partly explains why they tend to spend more time as dependants. Also, for this generation of women, dependence may be a reflection of low social status and low participation in the labour market in the past, rather than ageing itself. Generally, the proportion of older people living alone is increasing and this is more common for women. The gender gap reflects patterns of widowhood, which affected about 41 per cent of older women in 2000, compared to 12.6 per cent of men. This disparity is partly caused by higher female life expectancy. Also, women face more difficulties than men do in remarrying, as it is quite common for men to marry younger women.

Comparing 1981 with 2001, changes in family dependence were more notable for women than men regardless of whether they were living in rural or urban areas (Figure 3.4). Also, the reduction of poverty was more marked for women, especially in rural areas (Figure 3.3). These two trends are interconnected and are closely associated with the extension of rural social security pensions to women after 1991.

Analysis by cohort
Some characteristics of older populations at any particular moment in time are more a reflection of the cohort they were born into and of the

Table 3.6 Some characteristics of the Brazilian cohort
aged 40–59 in 1981

| Some characteristics | Urban | | Rural | |
of the cohort	1981	2001	1981	2001
% Population	16.01	7.82	14.35	8.76
Sex ratio	92.84	77.23	107.02	107.95
% Heads of family	55.18	65.05	54.23	63.08
% Heads of family living alone	2.73	11.88	2.28	9.60
% Heads of family with spouses	76.23	52.65	83.91	64.40
% Heads of family with children	85.47	54.34	88.27	53.63
% Spouses	33.21	23.21	34.57	27.37
% Other relatives	8.63	10.76	8.43	8.22
% No income	29.04	13.66	36.56	24.42
% Poor families	27.7	15.96	62.95	23.33
% Working	57.90	26.73	65.31	62.34
% House owner	71.71	93.78	70.22	85.91
% Contributed to social security	40.73	7.86	11.36	3.93
% Receiving some social security benefit	15.63	74.21	5.80	83.52

Source: IBGE 1981 and 2001 Household Surveys.

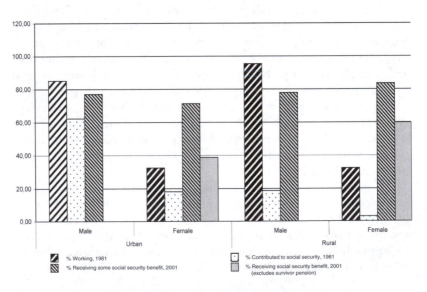

Source: IBGE 1981 and 2001 Household Surveys.

Figure 3.5 Some characteristics of the Brazilian cohort
aged 40–59 in 1981

way they spent their adult lives than of old age itself. However, there are reasons to believe that ageing in Brazil brings certain compensations, at least from the point of view of income. In order to separate out these two effects, a cohort analysis was undertaken comparing the population aged 40–59 in 1981 to the population aged 60–79 in 2001. This assumes that these age groups constitute a single cohort.

In a typical situation, it might be expected that people would experience a decline in economic status, and would become more dependent on family support when they reach old age. The cohort study finds that these generalisations do not match the Brazilian experience. It finds gains in economic wellbeing for the older cohort (Table 3.6). These gains can be measured by a decline in both the proportion of the population without any earnings and the proportion of older people in poverty. A high proportion of this cohort has access to social security benefits, especially in rural areas and among females in 2001 (Figure 3.5). This is greater for women than for men, as it includes survival pensions. These proportions were much higher than those of working people or people contributing to social security in 1981, especially in rural areas and among elderly females.[4]

In terms of family dependence, the findings of the cohort study are more mixed and less easily interpreted. There are some signs that the status of the older cohort had improved. For example, the proportion of older people who lived in their own homes, which was already high for the younger cohort, increased. The proportion who were categorised as household heads (which might signify their status and economic contribution to households) had also risen with age. However, this was also a reflection of the rising number of older people who lived alone, which may be equally a sign of greater autonomy or abandonment. Indications of elderly dependence were the rising proportion of the urban cohort living as 'other relatives' of the head of the household. Not surprisingly, the proportion of couples declined over time, as did the share of households containing children.

Regional differences

The situation of older people is not homogeneous throughout Brazil. Table 3.7 compares some aspects of their wellbeing for the North-east and South-east in 1981 and 2001. Older people are healthier in the South-east and these differences are more marked when the ability to perform activities of daily living is taken into account. By contrast, regional disparities in serious disability in later life have almost disappeared, resulting from a large decline for the country as a whole.

Patterns of family dependence for the two regions do not diverge substantially from national trends. Despite higher levels of poverty in

Table 3.7 Some characteristics of the 60+ population by region and rural/urban location, Brazil

Some characteristics	North-east				South-east			
	Urban		Rural		Urban		Rural	
	1981	2001	1981	2001	1981	2001	1981	2001
% Population	6.60	8.30	6.82	8.69	6.88	9.34	5.89	8.81
Sex ratio	78.86	72.93	111.81	102.67	80.60	73.89	121.98	110.35
% Heads of family	62.50	66.06	65.76	66.33	59.79	63.77	65.04	66.58
% Spouses	18.63	21.34	21.36	24.08	24.44	22.37	20.17	22.83
% Other relatives	17.58	11.97	12.53	9.25	18.83	13.35	14.06	10.13
% Living alone	9.06	10.32	8.58	11.51	9.17	11.71	9.78	10.68
Years of schooling	1.71	2.48	0.40	0.73	3.00	4.07	0.93	1.45
% Poor families	54.33	35.10	64.66	35.36	18.73	12.44	38.01	21.17
% Working	24.10	21.90	37.45	43.49	20.40	18.51	38.27	38.31
★ Receiving SS benefit	64.30	80.23	55.20	88.8	69.30	86.90	49.80	76.4
% Good health★		77.27		79.12		87.56		84.93
% Handicapped	6.90	3.81[†]	7.40	3.99[†]	6.20	3.41[†]	6.70	3.66[†]
Difficulty in feeding (%)[†]		19.5		16.5		13.7		15.1
Walking more than 100 m (%)[†]		23.5		18.6		20.7		15.2
Walking more than 1 km (%)[†]		50.6				42.9		42.7

Note: ★ Data refer to 1998
        † Data refer to 1991
Source: IBGE 1981 and 2001 Household Surveys.

the North-east, family dependence does not appear to be greater there than in the South-east. In both regions, dependence would seem to be higher in urban areas, perhaps reflecting a larger share of very old people and a higher proportion of women living there. For both regions, the proportion of older people defined as 'other relatives' fell, while there were rises in likelihood of older people living alone and in the proportion of household heads. Taken together, this suggests an overall decline in dependence on family support.

As for Brazil as a whole, the most important changes in the wellbeing of older people were related to income. The proportion of poor older people declined dramatically in both regions, particularly in rural areas. This is a reflection of a marked increase in the proportion of older people receiving social security benefits (Table 3.7). In the North-east, this was much higher in rural areas than in urban ones. The speed of the decline of overall poverty was approximately the same in the North–east and in the South–east, and was more marked in rural areas. The relative regional differences in poverty did not change; they have been kept at very high levels and remain unfavourable for the North-east.

Social policies for older people

The previous sections reveal a number of surprising trends. Despite a lack of dynamism in Brazil's economy over the past 20 years, there have been notable advances in many aspects of older people's wellbeing. The preceding analysis suggests that social policy, particularly pensions policy, has played a leading role in these gains. Also, work experience during adult life and the accumulation of assets are important for later life wellbeing. Although it is recognised that advances in medical technology and access to health services have had an important effect on older peoples' lives, this section concentrates on the policy most specifically concerned with later life: social security.

During the 1930s, Brazil was one of the first countries in Latin America to adopt some kind of formal social protection. As mentioned above, these policies were not equitable, benefiting workers in urban formal sectors and excluding large segments of society. Among the excluded groups were rural workers (who then accounted for the majority of the labour force), the self-employed and domestic servants. Santos (1979, quoted by Draibe 1990) refers to this process as 'regulated citizenship', observing that it was not rooted in a code of general

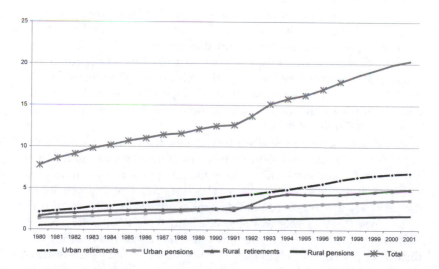

Source: AEPS Infologo/MPAS.

Figure 3.6 Social security benefits paid to older people, Brazil (million)

solidarity values, but in a system of occupational stratification. During the 1960s and 1970s, the coverage of all existing social policies expanded dramatically. At the same time, social assistance programmes for non-insured older people and the disabled were created and a new social security scheme for the rural population was established, although coverage remained fragmentary and modest through the 1970s and 1980s.

The critical turning point in Brazilian social policy occurred with the new constitution of 1988, which introduced a more inclusive concept of social security, increasing rural social protection. This has resulted in changes to benefit eligibility and the minimal benefit value was set at the minimum wage in both rural and urban areas, reducing inequalities between them. In rural areas, the beneficiary unit changed from the household to the individual. These changes have dramatically affected the situation of older people, especially women, who are now allowed to apply for social security benefits regardless of their position in the household. In addition, the new constitution reduced the age requirement for the rural old age benefit by five years for men and ten for women.

The results can be seen in Figure 3.6, which shows benefit payments from 1980 to 2000. Payments increased throughout this period, but there was a step-change in 1992. In 1980 rural payments to women were only 18 per cent of the total. Since 1992, 60 per cent of new rural benefits have been paid to women, which explains the degree of poverty reduction among them.

In 1974 a lifetime monthly-income benefit was created for those aged 70 and over who had no other form of social security benefit and who were proved unable to support themselves. In 1993 the value of this benefit was increased from 50 per cent per cent of the minimum wage to 100 per cent, and in 1998 the minimum age requirement for this benefit was reduced from 70 to 67. Figure 3.7 gives data for the number of these benefits paid out. These rose from 88,085 to 206,261 between 1997 and 1998.

Brazil has a separate social security system for civil servants and the military. The former contribute 11 per cent of their salaries and the latter 8 per cent. In both cases, the value of the pension is equivalent to their full wage at the time of retirement. This is supposed to compensate for the relatively low wages of public sector workers compared to private sector ones. Private sector workers contribute 8 per cent of their salaries (but only for 10 months of the year) and the employer contributes a further 11 per cent. In contrast to the upgrading of the basic assistance schemes, there has been a retrenchment in the value of benefits for private sector workers. In 1994 the maximum private sector pension was capped at 8.3 minimum wages, but this had fallen to 7.8 by 2002.

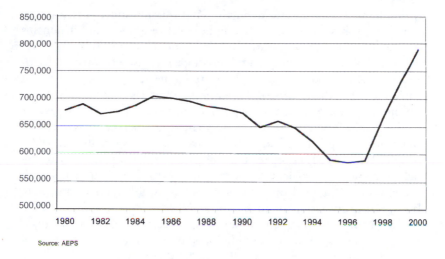

Source: AEPS

**Figure 3.7 Number of social assistance benefits
paid to older people, Brazil**

In the light of Brazil's worsening economic performance, it is not
surprising that there have been vocal calls to significantly reform the
social policy system. Rising unemployment and informality have
reduced the contribution base, exacerbating pension fund deficits
(Baltar 1998; Fagnani 1999). To date, pension reforms have mainly
been targeted at reducing the value of the benefit and extending the
contribution time. There has not been a sustained campaign to reassess
the commitment to extending coverage to previously excluded groups.
Particular attention has been given to the notorious 'length-of-service
pensions', which enabled some groups of workers to retire after just 25
(women) and 30 (men) years of employment or contribution.

Despite strong opposition, important changes were introduced for
private sector workers in 1998. These reforms have sought to link
benefit entitlements more closely to contributions. The new rules of
the social security system require at least 30 years of contributions for a
retirement pension and 15 years for a minimum old age benefit.
Oliveira, Guerra and Cardoso (2000) estimate that the new formula will
reduce future average benefit values by 34 per cent for men and 44 per
cent for women, as compared to the present situation. There are
concerns that stricter eligibility criteria will limit access to the system for
those in the informal sector, as it will be difficult for them to contribute
for a sufficiently long time period. The current government is seeking

to implement similar reforms in the civil servant and military funds. However, it has encountered strong political resistance, and it remains unclear whether these measures will be adopted.

Brazilians rely on both government and, increasingly, private health systems. The 1988 constitution enshrined health care as a right of citizenship, but the quality of the services still varies considerably. Long waiting times for treatment have been identified as a particular weakness of the public health system. Consequently, an increasing number of Brazilians use private plans that are expensive, especially for older people. Reis (2000) estimates that spending on private health care by older people is equivalent to 8 per cent of total government health expenditure. Regional differences in public health services are quite large and are always unfavourable to the North-east.

The National Policy for Older People sees families as the main providers of long-term care to older people. As a result, the coverage of public institutional care is very low. In 2001 these services provided care for around 300,000 older people, less than 2 per cent of the elderly population (Brazil 2002). In general, institutional care is required for the very old who lose their physical and mental autonomy and whose families or who themselves do not have income to cover their living expenses. Also, families may not have the time or the physical and emotional resources to look after frail older people. Greater attention is now being placed on the role of day centres as an alternative form of support for older people and their carers. To date, there is no information about how many public day centres are already working.

The impact of social policy on family arrangements, poverty and economic activity

This section provides an analysis of the impact of the pension pro- gramme on older peoples' lives and wellbeing. It examines how families are organising themselves in order to make the most of older people's pension income. By 2001 at least one older person could be found in 26 per cent of urban households and 28 per cent of rural ones. Thus, the resource base of many households does not just depend on labour market opportunities; it is also affected by state transfers and by the location of each member in his or her life cycle.

Rather than a reduction in older people's dependence on the family, it is more apt to talk of a change in the direction of this dependence. As mentioned above, families containing older people are better off than other ones. The contribution of the social security system to these families is substantial: in 2001, 54 per cent of urban families and 40 per cent of rural families containing older people derived their income

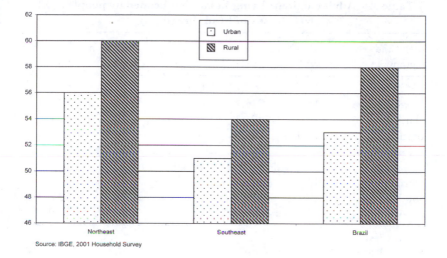

Source: IBGE, 2001 Household Survey

Figure 3.8 Contribution of people aged 60+ to family budgets in Brazil, 2001 (%)

solely from pensions. This raised the status of older people: in 2001 older people headed around 85 per cent of families in which they were living. Their contribution to household budgets was 58 and 53 per cent in rural and urban areas, respectively. This contribution was particularly important in the relatively poor North-east (Figure 3.8).

The presence of adult children aged 21 and older in families headed by older people may represent another form of contribution on the part of older people. This has become more widespread, as seen in Table 3.8. The largest increase was among families living in the urban North-east. For all regions, the proportion of families with adult children is greater among families headed by women. Although the majority of these children are single, a significant proportion had already formed their own families. A survey undertaken in Fortaleza found that co-residence of generations is more associated with the needs of offspring than with those of older people. Requests for support from divorced daughters were particularly frequent. The survey found that 53 per cent of older people interviewed had already helped their children, two thirds being adult offspring (Saad 1999).

These patterns of co-residence and intergenerational support are associated with a reduction of economic opportunities for younger people over the last 20 years. For instance, the unemployment rate for people aged between 15 and 24 increased from 6 to 19 per cent between 1981 and 1999 (Camarano et al. 2003). Furthermore, teenage

Table 3.8 Adult children* living in families headed by people aged 60+, by sex of head, Brazil (%)

Brazil and	Male			Female	
regions	1981	2001		1981	2001
			Urban		
North-east	14.3	19.7		20.8	28.3
South-east	19.0	21.3		26.1	30.5
Brazil	17.0	19.9		23.7	28.8
			Rural		
North-east	13.0	15.8		19.8	23.1
South-east	19.8	19.3		27.0	32.8
Brazil	14.9	16.9		22.4	26.9

Note: * Over 21.
Source: IBGE, 1981 and 2001 Household Surveys.

Table 3.9 Other relatives under 14 years living in families headed by people 60+, by sex of head, Brazil (%)

Brazil and	Male			Female	
regions	1981	2001		1981	2001
			Urban		
North-east	5.1	6.9		12.0	15.4
South-east	2.1	3.8		5.3	10.9
Brazil	3.2	4.4		8.2	12.8
			Rural		
North-east	5.8	6.9		12.0	16.8
South-east	3.3	2.5		5.9	10.3
Brazil	4.4	5.1		7.3	12.9

Source: IBGE 1981 and 2001 Household Survey.

pregnancy is increasing, as well as divorces and separations among the young population. Difficulties in getting a first job and in leaving the parental home have encouraged growing numbers of teenage girls to see motherhood as an important social role, regardless of marital status (Medeiros 1998; Camarano 1998). This has increased demand for support from parents, including elderly ones.

The proportion of 'other relatives' aged 14 and under living with older people has also increased in both rural and urban families,

Table 3.10 Poverty prevalence data, 1981 and 2001, Brazil (%)

	Male		Female	
	1981	2001	1981	2001
Poor elderly				
Urban	28.2	19.1	28.7	18.4
Rural	53.9	29.9	51.0	25.4
Poor non-elderly				
Urban	33.9	34.9	34.7	36.7
Rural	69.4	65.6	72.6	68.1

Source: IBGE, 1981 and 2001 Household Surveys. Special tabulations, IPEA.

especially among those headed by older women (Table 3.9). In almost all cases, it can be assumed that 'other relatives' refers to grandchildren. The presence of grandchildren is particularly high among families in the rural North-east. In 2001, children aged under 14 accounted for about 13 per cent of members of households containing older people. There are numerous indications that when young children live with a pensioner, their wellbeing is improved in various ways. For example, De Carvalho Filho (2000) found that the rural pension was significantly associated with increased school enrolment, particularly for girls aged 12 to 14; the effect was particularly strong when they were living with female pensioners. Taken together, these different findings suggest that families containing older people cannot be called 'empty nests'. In truth, what seems to be taking place in Brazil is a re-filling of these nests.

A key issue for policy makers is the impact of social security benefits on poverty, both for older people and their households. In 1981, the distribution of household poverty was not greatly affected by the presence of an older member. In 2001, the situation had dramatically changed. It has been calculated that if no rural families were to contain older people, 49 per cent would be in poverty, compared to the actual figure of 30 per cent. Throughout the past 20 years, there has been much progress in reducing poverty among older people and the rural population in general. By contrast, poverty increased for the urban population aged 25 to 59 (Table 3.10). There are indications that extending pension benefits to rural women aged 55 and over was a major factor in the general decline in rural poverty. Gender comparisons also reveal the impact of the pensions system. Among younger groups, poverty is higher for women than men, but the situation is reversed for older people.

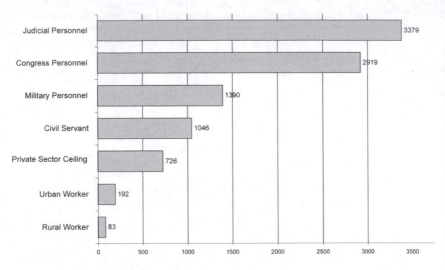

Source: Boletim Estatstico de Pessoal/ MP e AEPS Infologo / MPAS.

**Figure 3.9 Average monthly value of Brazilian
social security benefits, 2000 (US$)**

Delgado and Cardoso Júnior (2000) report similar findings from fieldwork undertaken in the South and the North-east of Brazil. They also claim that pension benefits may have stimulated local economies in numerous ways. First, in 61 per cent of municipal districts, social security transfers exceeded federal government transfers. Moreover, around 40 per cent of pension income in rural households was being used to fund agricultural activities. In households containing older couples, both are entitled to benefits, and so the 'extra' benefit can be invested in productive activities (on average, households received 1.78 pensions). One characteristic feature of Brazilian small town trading is commerce based on trust, whereby people are able to defer payment for purchases until they have access to cash. It has been shown that entitlement to a social security benefit does much to sustain these flexible arrangements. Based on these findings, Delgado and Cardoso Júnior (2000) conclude that the rural benefit plays three important roles: life insurance, family budget support and agricultural insurance, which generates additional income.

The improvements to the lives of women and rural workers resulting from the social security system are undeniable. Being a beneficiary means at least being less poor. Nevertheless, the distribution of benefits among the various groups of beneficiaries is quite unequal (Figure 3.9).

It can be seen that in 2000 the average benefit of urban workers was 2.3 times greater than that of rural workers, retired civil servants received 5.4 times more than urban workers, and benefits for people previously employed in the judicial system were about 41 times larger than those of rural workers. This partly explains why, although rural poverty has fallen, Brazil continues to have one of the most inequitable income distributions in the world. Were the pensions system organised on a more equitable basis, its potential for improving the lives of vulnerable older people and their families would be even greater.

Final considerations

Population ageing in Brazil has been accompanied by important processes such as the spread of social security coverage, improved health conditions, the development of new technologies, wider access to education, especially for women, and changes in gender relations, such as increased participation of women in labour. Some of these changes have been more important for younger people (that is, future cohorts of older people) than for older people themselves.

In Brazil the traditional role of older people as 'dependants' has been replaced by that of provider. Overall, older people in Brazil are in a better financial position than younger age groups. Part of this reflects recent policy developments, but it is also important to consider other conditions, which have shaped the life course of the present cohort of older people. Today's older people are more likely to have experienced a long period of stable employment at a time of national economic buoyancy. Affective relationships, especially marriages, were also more stable. During the 1960s and 1970s, access to private housing was easier since household income was more stable and large public programmes subsidised the purchase of homes. The universalisation of social security rights in both rural and urban areas built on these existing advantages.

Older peoples' improved living conditions contrast with the effects of entrenched economic crisis on the young population. This can be seen in different ways, including unemployment, rising violence and drug abuse, teenage pregnancy and marital disruption. These have tended to increase the amount of time adult children spend as dependants of their parents. The plight of younger generations raises concerns about future cohorts of older people. It is very likely that current generations of workers will fail to meet the new contribution requirements and will thus be excluded from formal social protection. Thus, history may view today's generation of older people as a fortunate exception, when their wellbeing is compared to those who preceded them and those who followed.

It is often argued that better living standards for older people have meant marked rises in expenditure on social security benefits and health policies (Beltrão and Oliveira 1999). It is true that the social security system as a whole absorbs large amounts of public spending and contribution levies may, arguably, reduce the international competitiveness of Brazilian workers. However, those aspects of the system which have done most to benefit poor older people have been comparatively cheap. Likewise, mounting expenditure on health care may have more to do with the extension of private financing and systemic failings than with demographic change.

Like Europe's, Brazil's social security system assumed full employment conditions, involving an unbroken work career followed by a short period of retirement prior to death. However, formal employment is declining rapidly. This means a departure from secure employment relationships towards more precarious and temporary contracts and greater wage differentiation. This poses problems for entitlements to retirement benefits and for funding the social security system as a whole. Existing ways of funding social security will not be able to meet the needs of future generations of older people. Thus, while Brazil's model of social protection may appear to be a great success in the present circumstances, there is a need to rethink the role of pension financing and other aspects of social policy for future cohorts.

At the micro-level, it is apparent that older people's level of dependency is largely determined by social security income. This depends on previous contributions, state funding and social legislation. Older people account for an important share of household income, and so these households are exposed to any change in pension policy. It is estimated that 13 million households, many of them vulnerable, currently benefit from the social security system. Any changes to pension policy must consider potential impacts on such a large swathe of the population.

The Brazilian experience shows that relationships between population ageing and dependency are complex. To consider ageing as a 'problem' is to assume an inelastic resource distribution. Globally, over the last two centuries the supply of resources has kept pace with increases in population. Increasing world poverty has been much more a consequence of defective resource distribution than of a lack of resources per se. Population ageing, like any other change in age composition, is neither intrinsically good nor bad. Whether it becomes a problem depends on the way society chooses to deal with it.

NOTES

The author wishes to thank Peter Lloyd-Sherlock, Kaizo Beltrão and Maria Tereza Pazianto for their comments and Solange Kanso and Ana Roberta Pati Pascom for all the data tabulation.

1 Quoted by Brumer (2002: 5).
2 The proportion of the population living below the official poverty line declined from 20.1 per cent in 1994 to 16.7 per cent in 1995. This proportion was kept approximately constant till 2001 (Camarano *et al.* 2003).
3 In 1998, according to Beltrão and Oliveira, 75 per cent of men retired before reaching 55 years. The comparable proportion for women is 83 per cent (see Beltrão and Oliveira 1999).
4 The proportion of contributors to social security does not have the same meaning in urban as in rural areas. Rural earnings are very different from urban ones with regard to timing, source (monetary or not) and the different ways of insertion in the labour market. The largest proportion of rural employees works on small farms that are more vulnerable with regard to income generation. The contribution consists of a percentage of the value of the production sold (2.2 per cent). The purchaser is personally responsible for paying it (Brumer 2002).

REFERENCES

Azevedo, Sérgio (1996) 'A crise da política habitacional: dilemas e perspectivas', in Luís César Queiroz (ed.), *A Crise da Moradia nas Grandes Cidades*, editora da UFRJ, Rio de Janeiro.

Baer, W. (1995) *The Brazilian Economy: Growth and Development*, London: Praeger.

Baltar, P. E. (1998) 'A crise contemporânea e mercado de trabalho no Brasil', in M. A. Oliveira *et al.* (eds.), *Economia e Trabalho – Textos Básicos*, Campinas: Instituto de Economia, Universidade de Campinas.

Barros, R. P. de, R. Mendonça and D, Santos (1999) 'Incidência e natureza da pobreza entre idosos no Brasil', in A. A. Camarano (ed.), *Muito Além dos 60: Os Novos Idosos Brasileiros*, Rio de Janeiro: Instituto de Pesquisa Econômica Aplicada, IPEA.

Beltrão, K. I. and F. E. B. de Oliveira (1999) 'O idoso e a previdência social', in A. A. Camarano (ed.), *Muito Além dos 60: Os Novos Idosos Brasileiros*, IPEA, Rio de Janeiro.

Brazil (2002) *Informe Nacional Brasileño*, issued for the Second World Assembly on Ageing, Madrid, Spain.

Brumer, A. (2002) 'Gender relations and rural social security in Brazil', in Christopher Abel and Colin M. Lewis (eds.), *Exclusion and Engagement, social policy in Latin America*, The Brookings Institute, London.

Cano, Wilson (1998) 'Políticas econômicas e de ajuste na América Latina', in M. A. Oliveira *et al.* (eds.), *Economia e Trabalho – Textos Básicos*, Campinas: Instituto de Economia, Universidade de Campinas.

Camarano, A. A. (1998) 'Fecundidade e anticoncepção da população de 15–19 anos', in E. M. Vieira, M. E. L. Fernandes, P. Bailey and A. McKay (eds.), *Seminário Gravidez na Adolescência*, Ministério da Saúde/Family Health International/Associação Saúde Família, Rio de Janeiro.

—— (2001) 'O idoso brasileiro no mercado de trabalho', *Texto para Discussão No. 830*, IPEA, Rio de Janeiro.

—— (2002a) 'Envelhecimento da população brasileira: uma contribuição demográfica', in Elizabete Viana de Freitas, Ligia Py, Anita Liberalesso Neri, Flávio Aluizio Xavier Cançado, Milton Luiz Gorzoni and Sônia Maria da Rocha (eds.), *Tratado de Geriatria e Gerontologia*, Guanabara Koogan, Rio de Janeiro.

—— (2002b) 'Brazilian population ageing: differences in wellbeing by rural and urban areas', *Texto para Discussão No. 878*, IPEA, Rio de Janeiro.

Camarano, A. A. and R. Abramovay (1998) 'Êxodo rural, envelhecimento e masculinização no Brasil: panorama dos últimos 50 anos', *Revista Brasileira de Estudos Populacionais*, 15 (2): 45–66.

Camarano, A. A., K. I. Beltrão, A. R. P. Pascom, M. Medeiros and A. M. Goldani (1999) 'Como vive o idoso brasileiro?', in A. A. Camarano (ed.), *Muito além dos 60: os novos idosos brasileiros*, IPEA, Rio de Janeiro.

Camarano, A. A. and S. K. El Ghaouri (1999) 'Idosos brasileiros: que dependência é essa?', in A. A. Camarano (ed.) *Muito além dos 60: os novos idosos brasileiros*, IPEA, Rio de Janeiro.

Camarano, A. A., Maria Tereza Pasinato, Marcela Arruda and Nicolas Lovisolo (2003) 'Os jovens Brasileiros no mercado de trabalho', in *Mercado de Trabalho: Conjuntura e Análise*, 6 (November), IPEA/Ministério da Saúde, Rio de Janeiro.

De Carvalho Filho, I. (2000) 'Household income as a determinant of child labour and school enrolment in Brazil: evidence from a social security reform', mimeo, MIT.

Delgado, G. C. and J. C. Cardoso Júnior (eds.) (2000) *A Universalização dos Direitos Sociais no Brasil: a Previdência Rural nos Anos 90: a Experiência Recente da Universalização*, IPEA, Rio de Janeiro.

Deud, C. A. F. and R. V. P. Malvar (1993) *A Mulher e a Previdência. A previdência social e a revisão constitucional*, Brasília: MPS/CEPAL, vol. III.

Draibe, S. M. (1990) 'As políticas sociais brasileiras: diagnósticos e perspectivas', in IPEA, *Para a década de 90 – prioridades e perspectivas de políticas públicas*, IPEA, Rio de Janeiro.

Fagnani, Eduardo (1999) 'Ajuste econômico e financiamento da política social Brasileira: notas sobre o período 1993/98', in *Economia e Sociedade*, No. 13, UNICAMP.

Instituto Brasileiro de Geografia e Estadística (IBGE) (2000) *Projeção da população do Brasil por sexo e idade para o período 1980–2050*, Diretoria de Pesquisas, Departamento de População e Indicadores Sociais, Divisão de Estudos e Análises da Dinâmica Demográfica, revised.

Martine, G. (1996) 'Brazil's fertility decline, 1965–95: a fresh look at key factors', *Population and Development Review*, 22 (1): 47–75.

Medeiros, M. C. de S. (1998) 'A maternidade nas mulheres de 15 a 19 anos como desvantagem social', in E. M Vieira, M. E. L. Fernandes, P. Bailey and A. McKay (eds.), *Seminário Gravidez na Adolescência*, Rio de Janeiro: Ministério da Saúde/Family Health International/ Associação Saúde Família.

Neri M., M. Nascimiento and A. Pinto (1999) 'O acesso ao capital dos idosos Brasileiros: uma perspectiva do ciclo da vida', in A. A. Camarano (ed.), *Muito além dos 60: os novos idosos brasileiros*, IPEA, Rio de Janeiro.

Nogales, A. M. V. (1998) 'A mortalidade da população idosa no Brasil', in *Como vai? População brasileira*. IPEA, Rio de Janeiro, 3 (3), pp. 24–32.

OECD (2001) *OECD Economic Surveys 2000–2001. Brazil*, OECD, Paris.

Oliveira, Carlos Alonso Barbosa de (1998) 'Formação do mercado de trabalho no Brasil', in M. A. Oliveira *et al.* (eds.), *Economia e Trabalho – Textos Básicos*. Campinas: Universidade de Campinas, Instituto de Economia.

Oliveira, F. E. B. de, M. Guerra and F. P. Cardoso (2000) 'Uma avaliação das reformas recentes do regime de previdência', in *Anais do XII Encontro da Abep*, Minas Gerais.

Reis, Carlos Otávio (2000) 'O Gasto de Saúde dos Idosos: Sinal dos Tempos', in *Como vai? População brasileira*, 5 (1), March: 41–50, IPEA, Rio de Janeiro.

Romero, D.E. (2002) 'Variações de Gênero na Relação entre arranjo familiar e status de saúde dos idosos Brasileiros', paper presented to the XIII Encontro Nacional de Estudos da Associação Brasileira de Estudos Populacionais, November, Ouro Preto-MG.

Saad, P. M. (1999) 'Transferências de apoio entre gerações no Brasil: um estudo para São Paulo e Fortaleza', in A. A. Camarano (ed.), *Muito além dos 60: os novos idosos brasileiros*, IPEA, Rio de Janeiro.

Wanjman, S., A. M. H. C. Oliveira and E. L. de Oliveira (1999) 'A atividade econômica dos idosos no Brasil', in A. A. Camarano (ed.), *Muito Além dos 60: os Novos Idosos Brasileiros*, IPEA, Rio de Janeiro.

CHAPTER 4

The Impact of Transition
on Older People in Ukraine:
Looking to the Future with Hope

VLADISLAV V. BEZRUKOV
& NATALIA A. FOIGT

In some newly independent states (NISs), the transition from centrally planned to market-oriented economies is progressing more or less smoothly; in others it has been a shock therapy; and in others a shock without therapy. The crisis of transition has had severe socio-economic consequences such as unemployment, economic inequality and poverty. It has also had a worrying impact on demographic trends, including an unprecedented fall of birthrates, rising mortality and population ageing. In turn, the growing share of dependent older people in society, who consume considerable material resources for their subsistence, has seriously challenged the social transition linked to the new economic order.

Political instability and economic crisis in the post-communist NISs has led to a change of social policy priorities and to the destruction of the former social protection system. The decentralisation of control over social protection and central governments' shifting of responsibilities to local governments, as well as non-governmental and private sectors, have made additional inroads on the wellbeing of older people. As a result, elders find themselves extremely unprotected in all spheres of life, including income security, health care and living arrangements. The most significant consequences include increasing impoverishment of many older people, unemployment worsened by discrimination against older workers, worsening health status in old age due to an impaired health care system, and increasing inequalities and inter-generational tensions in society. Compared to other European NISs, these effects have been particularly significant in Ukraine.

It follows that the surge in population ageing has not been accompanied by an increase of quality of life for older people. This is reinforced by social attitudes. Efforts taken by older people themselves to earn their own living are not perceived by society as a contribution to development. Current patterns of family composition suggest that the older generation plays a leading role in supporting young family formation, but this is not widely perceived as a contribution to the construction of a new society.

To find positive solutions, it is essential to analyse both the difficulties related to economic transition, and the negative effects of inappropriate social and economic policy decisions. Such analysis will help reveal hidden reserves for improving the economic status and strengthening social protection of older people, as well as increasing their integration into a modern Ukrainian community.

Socio-economic transition in Ukraine and other European NISs: must it really be so hard?

The present economic status of Ukraine is characterised by declines in production, falling GDP and a decrease of living standards. Between 1990 and 1998 GDP fell by 40.9 per cent (State Statistics Committee of Ukraine 1999b). This unprecedented fall in production has been accompanied by rising inflation, creating serious consequences for social protection. Across the NISs, over 100 million people are below the poverty line, and still greater numbers of people can hardly earn a subsistence wage (UNDP 1999a). There have been national variations in performance, reflecting different economic and social strategies, and the relative success of reforms (Table 4.1 and Figure 4.1). Ukraine performed particularly badly, with a significant rise in poverty (by 2000 estimates of family poverty ranged from 70 to 90 per cent). Although the share of people who could not afford a basket of the 22 most important food

Table 4.1 Economic performance in the European NIS

	GDP per capita (PPP US$)	GDP per capita annual growth rate, %		Average annual change in consumer price index, %	
	1999	1975–99	1990–99	1990–99	1998–99
Estonia	8,355	−1.3	−0.3	25.3	3.3
Latvia	6,264	−0.9	−3.7	34.6	2.4
Lithuania	6,656	−3.6	−3.9	40.2	0.8
Belarus	6,876	−2.7	−2.9	383.7	293.7
Russia	7,473	−1.2	−5.9	116.1	85.7
Ukraine	3,458	−9.2	−10.3	413.4	119.2
Moldova	2,037	...	−10.8	16.0	45.9

Note: PPP = purchasing power parity
Source: UNDP 2001.

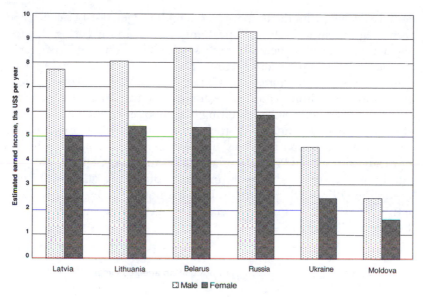

Source: UNDP 2001.

**Figure 4.1 Estimated earned income (PPP US$) in the
European NISs by gender, 1999**

items fell from 22 per cent in 1995 to 16 per cent in 1998, it still remains
very high.

There are several reasons why Ukraine's economic crisis has been
especially severe compared to other formerly socialist countries.
Ukraine's economy is particularly dependent on heavy industry which
does not easily lend itself to short-term restructuring. Unlike Russia,
the country lacks significant natural resources, such as oil or gas, which
could generate foreign revenue earnings. Also, the Ukrainian state has
grown increasingly weak, and has shown little stomach for consistent,
radical economic reform.

Demographic ageing and epidemiological problems of older
people related to the economic crisis

Population ageing has a long history in Ukraine: in 1959 the proportion
of persons aged 65 or more was already 6.3 per cent, rising to 11.7 per
cent in 1989. In recent years, population ageing has accelerated (in
2000, the population aged 65 or more reached 14.1 per cent). This has
been particularly marked in rural areas: 19 per cent, compared to 12 per
cent in urban ones. This acceleration has responded to numerous
effects. The transitional period has seen unprecedentedly high rates of

fertility decline, with the proportion of children aged 0–14 years falling from 22 per cent in 1989 to 19 per cent in 1998. In rural areas, due to the decrease in births, there was not a single child born in 10.7 per cent of villages, and 25 per cent contained no youths under 28 years of age (State Statistics Committee of Ukraine 2001a). The working-age population has shrunk due to a disproportionate rise of mortality among this particular group, resulting from poor environmental conditions and socio-psychological stress related to failed reforms. Also, recent years have seen the entry into old age of those larger cohorts born after the Second World War, and the completion of passage to old age of smaller cohorts born during years of famine (1932–34) and repression (1937– 39). As a result, Ukraine now has one of the lowest fertility rates and the highest level of demographic ageing among the European NISs (Figure 4.2).

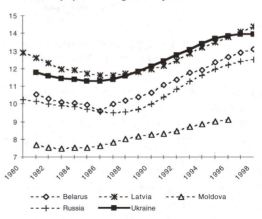

**Figure 4.2
The proportions of
population aged
65+ and birthrates
in the European
NISs, 1980–98**

Source: HFA Data Base
(WHO 2001).

One important socio-economic consequence of population ageing is a loading of non-working individuals onto the working population. According to data from the State Statistics Committee of Ukraine (1999b), the overall dependency ratio remained almost unchanged between 1989 and 1998. However, this reflected falling numbers of children, and the ratio of elders to working-age groups rose from 0.38 to 0.41. The most worrying situation was observed in the rural population, where by the beginning of 2001 the dependency ratio was 961 non-working to 1000 working persons. In some regions the number of persons in the non-working-age groups now exceeds that in working ones. This implies a reduction in the population who are potential providers of material and social support for elders (Table 4.2).

Table 4.2 Population age structure and potential support ratio by generation in Ukraine, 1989 and 1998 (average length of generation = 26 years)

Generations	Age structure, (%)		Potential support ratio per generations (number of supporters per 100 supportees)		
	1989	1998		1989	1998
Children (persons at age 0–26)	38.0	36.6	Children/parents	105	102
Parents (persons at age 27–52)	36.1	35.8	Parents/grandparents	155	143
Grandparents (persons at age 53–78)	23.3	25.0	Grandparents/great-grandparents	868	961
Great-grandparents (persons at age 79+)	2.7	2.6			

Sources: Ministry for Statistics (1991); State Statistical Committee (1999a).

Forecasts for 2026 show that, according to the most probable scenario, the total population of Ukraine will decrease to 42 million, while the share aged 60 or more will reach 24.6 per cent (Steshenko *et al.* 1999). At the same time, it is predicted that the ratio of older people to people of working age will reach 0.51.

Population ageing has not been driven by improved health in old age. Since the beginning of transition, there has been a marked rise in mortality rates, particularly among elders (Figure 4.3). As a result, life expectancy at 65 fell from 15 to 14 years between 1989 and 1998 (WHO 2001). With regard to the overall mortality rate by major cause,

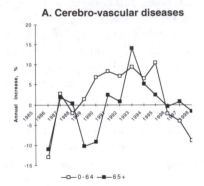

A. Cerebro-vascular diseases

—□—0-64 —■—65+

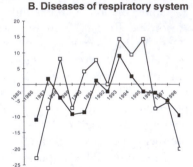

B. Diseases of respiratory system

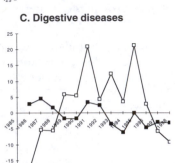

C. Digestive diseases

Fig. 4.3 Annual changes in mortality rates at age 0–64 and 65+ in Ukraine, 1990–98

Source: Estimates of the Laboratory of Demography, Institute of Gerontology.

cardiovascular pathologies remain the leading cause of death for older people, followed by cancers. High cardiovascular mortality is linked to stressful conditions of life and the collapse of public health care. This effect has crowded out deaths from cancer. In the Baltic states, where the socio-economic situation is better, mortality among the population aged 65+ is lower. The negative effects of transition on health status and longevity in Ukraine are also seen in the accelerated biological ageing of the population, with an increasing prevalence of age-dependent illnesses among younger ages.

The spread of the AIDS epidemic now represents the most urgent health problem for Ukraine. Among the European NISs, Ukraine has the greatest proportion of people aged 15–49 years living with HIV/AIDS (UNDP 2001). Between 1987 and 1999 relatively few people aged 50 years and over died of AIDS (Figure 4.4). However the epidemic's indirect impacts on older people are likely to be significant. According to estimates by Barnett *et al.* (1998), if one assumes that a third of the HIV-infected population (in 1997 this figure was 60,000 people) give material support to one of their parents, and if half of these

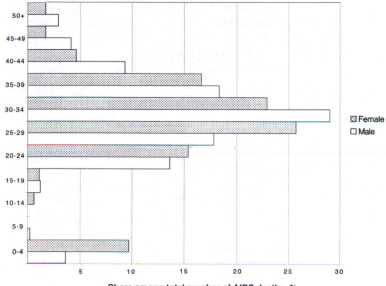

Source: UNDP 2000.

**Figure 4.4 Age structure of deaths
from AIDS in Ukraine by gender, 1987–99**

supporters have a brother or a sister who shares this care burden, around 30,000 elderly persons will soon find themselves without any family support. Another indirect effect will be the rising numbers of HIV-infected children and AIDS orphans, whose care needs may be provided by grandparents.

Changes of formal social protection of older people under conditions of socio-economic crisis

Before the transition, financing for the protection of older people was derived from two sources: generalised public expenditures (public consumption funds) and the personal incomes of older people (pensions and income from private plots). State expenditures on older people (free public health care, large housing subsidies and state pensions) ensured a definite, albeit insufficient, coverage of their basic needs. During the 1980s, 80 per cent of elders' overall consumption came from public consumption funds, compared to 50 per cent of children's consumption and only 20 per cent of adult consumption (Slyusar 1995). The pension system did not include financial provision for many of the needs of elders, since they were already met by the public consumption funds. The size of the pension corresponded to the existing pricing system, in which production of most food products was subsidised by the state, and the retail prices were formed appropriately.

In the early 1990s a state pensioning system for all state-owned farm employees and collective farmers was introduced. At the same time, so-called 'social pensions' were implemented for those who did not have enough length of service, and the linking of pensions to the inflation rate was approved. However, the transition crisis reduced the values of all kinds of pensions, and by 1996 old age pensions were worth no more than a third of the average monthly wage.

Despite the country's socialist past, there have been some variations in the values of pension benefits. During the Soviet era, there were the following types of benefits: full old age pensions, those granted due to the loss of a breadwinner, and disability pensions. Higher-value pensions were awarded to a small number of groups such as retirees receiving state prizes or awards, honoured specialists, and former statesmen. Those retirees in receipt of a seniority or privileged pension continue to have the greatest incomes today, owing to the value of their pension and access to secondary employment.

In the period of transition, there was a breakdown in the balance of pricing, pensions and public consumption funds. Price reforms, particularly for food and housing maintenance services, did not proceed in parallel with pension reforms. The principles of housing space distribution, health care financing and social protection have changed, and this has resulted in a marked reduction of the living standards of older people.

Ukraine's public health care system was formed during the Soviet era, when disease prevention was a top priority. Despite a steadily increasing spend on various health care needs, cost-effectiveness was not a priority. During the 1970s, particular attention was given to universalising access to public health care. It is estimated that about 75 per cent of health care spending in the 1980s was derived from public funds. However, in succeeding years the demand for resources began to exceed state capacity, and the share of public spending in overall health care expenditures gradually dwindled. At the same time, an approach was taken to use the patients' and other private resources to compensate for the problems of public provision. Rather than lead to a system of equal medical services for all, this has enabled wealthy patients to pay informally to get better quality care (Chaikovskaya 2000).

In recent years the real volume of state expenditures on public health care has fallen considerably. State-owned medical institutions face many difficulties associated with an acute deficit of medicines and equipment, and non-payment of wages. As a consequence, the quality of treatment has worsened greatly. The rural health care system has been most seriously affected: the number of medical-obstetric stations has fallen by 7 per cent and 20 per cent of hospitals have been found to lack ultrasound equipment. The level of *reported* morbidity in villages is 25 per cent lower than in towns. (State Statistics Committee of Ukraine 2001a). Rather than better health, it is thought that this reflects inferior access to health facilities (and hence under-reporting of health problems).

The effectiveness of the state social welfare system in providing general care services for older people depends on how the general state budget is managed. In the case of NISs, where spending is greater than real revenues, it is optimistic to expect any extension of state social services. This is not just the experience of Ukraine. There is a global shift away from policies of full state responsibility for long-term care provision towards pluralism and drawing on elders' personal resources. In Ukraine, as elsewhere, this creates a need for new sorts of formal social support networks, aiming to keep older people in their natural environments.

The long-term care of older people is managed through a network of boarding houses, territorial centres and social welfare departments. There are now 57 boarding homes for older and disabled people, 14 nursing homes and 147 psycho-neurological boarding homes. Together, these have a capacity of 47,800 residents. The state pays for the lion's share of these services, although residents still have to contribute up to 90 per cent of their pensions (10 per cent is left as pocket money). In recent years state support for these institutions has fallen. In 1998 spending on boarding homes was only 79 per cent of the needed sum, and many of these institutions are accumulating substantial debts (Chaikovskaya 2000).

State-supported welfare for older people living beyond the reach of domiciliary services is funded from the federal and municipal budgets. Today, the care of disabled elderly people living alone is carried out through 631 territorial social service centres and 130 social welfare units: 38,000 social workers provide social domiciliary assistance for 500,000 needy persons. Scarce resources preclude the development of more services or improvements to them. The municipal and local social welfare bodies only guarantee services for some categories of older people (those who live alone, those with low incomes and those with registered disabilities). For these groups, a limited range of services (mainly 'meals on wheels' and 'home help') is provided. There is also a system of daily living services (laundry, hairdressing and dry cleaning), which is provided by local authorities on a contract basis with third party organisations. However this system is not commonly used, and it is especially underdeveloped in rural areas.

NGOs are increasingly involved in the provision of social services for elders. They include religious, veterans', and voluntary youth organisations. Efforts are being taken to develop a voluntary movement, to ensure its entry into the system of formal support, and to extend cooperative work and an exchange of experience between the volunteers and professionals.

The socio-economic position of older people under conditions of economic crisis

During the transition to a market-based economy, the gap in incomes between the working population and non-working pensioners has markedly increased. Between 1985 and 1986 the average monthly old age pension was equivalent to more than 40 per cent of an average salary, but this proportion had fallen to 28 per cent by 1998 (State Statistics Committee of Ukraine 1999b).

A survey of income formation dynamics in families with different levels of wealth permits us to observe the ways these families attain a given level of wellbeing under changing economic conditions (Table 4.3).

Table 4.3 Income structure for families with different average
***per capita* household income, Ukraine 1992–98 (%)**

Years	Salaries	Pensions and other social transfers	Earnings from personal subsidiary plots	Other sources
		Low-income families		
1992	46.2	19.4	23.4	11
1995	45.8	13	20.2	21
1998	36.2	12.7	13.4	37.7
		Medium-income families		
1992	59	9.4	20.6	11
1995	44.9	8.7	29.4	17
1998	43.7	10.3	27.1	18.9
		High-income families		
1992	66.3	7.3	17.2	9.2
1995	36.5	7.7	42.1	13.7
1998	55.6	9.3	22.1	13

Sources: Ministry for Statistics of Ukraine, 1993–1996b; State Statistics Committee of Ukraine, 1998–1999b.

At the beginning of the transition, families where the wages of working members were relatively high or in which there were many working members were in the best position. Between 1993 and 1995, the role of labour remuneration in household income gradually fell, and families receiving income from personal plots of land were the best-off. Further changes such as the restructuring and stabilisation of the labour market, the transformation of informal employment into formal sources of earnings, growing unemployment and the marginalisation of unsuccessful businessmen have strengthened the relative position of those families whose permanently working members received high wages. At the same time, economic exclusion emerged due to unemployment and low salaries. Impoverishment of old age pensioners grew due to limited opportunities for gaining income from personal plots and family dependence on social transfers. Members of pensioners' families began to earn their living through providing petty services or selling/reselling food products and goods of their own manufacture, as well as goods procured from industrial enterprises, shops and other individuals. Financial assistance from relatives and friends has become another important source of income for these families.

Considerable changes occurred in the structure of consumption of food, goods and services. From 1991 to 1999 the purchasing capacity of the population fell drastically, and this was reflected in the sales volume for consumer durables, such as TVs, audio equipment, refrigerators, laundry machines and vacuum cleaners (State Statistics Committee of Ukraine 2000). This trend was paralleled by the obsolescence of older household items, making the quality of life of older people markedly lower. With the rising cost of living, compulsory payments increasingly determine the volume of services used. In 1999, housing-communal costs (mainly rental payment) accounted for 43 per cent of all paid services, compared to only 13 per cent in 1991 (State Statistics Committee of Ukraine 2000). As a result, spending in areas such as health care and recreation fell sharply.

There have been sharp falls in the nutritional intake of low-income families, and a deterioration in the quality of poor people's diets (Ministry for Statistics of Ukraine 1993, 1996b; State Statistics Committee of Ukraine 2000). Of special concern is the nutrition of single disabled older people who are dependent on outside care and assistance. A study of the nutrition of this population group shows the inadequacy of their diet relative to the physiological norms of their needs for nutrients and energy (Figure 4.5). Even their consumption of basic products such as bread, cereals and sugar (for which pre-transition consumption exceeded the norms) is now well below recommended levels. More generally, a survey of 1500 individuals aged 60 and over between 1995 and 2000 found that falling family incomes had significantly reduced their capacity to meet their most basic needs (Table 4.4).

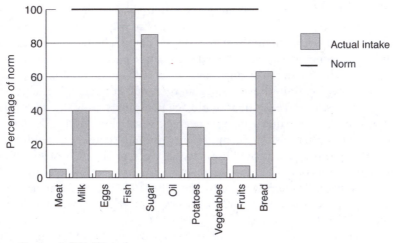

Source: Sineok et al., 2001: 196.

Figure 4.5 The deviation from recommended norms of actual daily food intake among older, non-working dependent persons, Ukraine

Table 4.4 Older people who report limitations in buying basic consumption goods and in using services as a consequence of falling incomes, Ukraine★

Limitations reported	Share reporting limitations (%)	
	Men	Women
Food intake quantity	6.7	13.2
Nutritional quality	75.0	67.4
Purchase of general goods	87.1	89.2
Use of daily living services	92.8	92.3
Obtaining information	82.0	91.7
Use of cultural services (museums, theatres, cinemas, etc.)	48.5	49.3
Use of health-improving strategies	24.9	27.8

★ Results obtained from the Social Hygienic Enquiry concerning Older Citizens in Kiev, conducted by the Laboratory for Medical Demography, Institute of Gerontology, 1995.

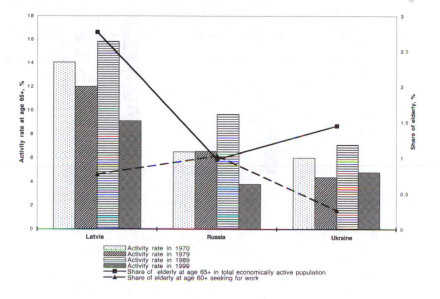

Source: ILO 2001.

**Figure 4.6 Economic activity of older people
in the European NISs, 1970–99**

Older people's contributions to national development go unrecognised

Poverty among older people has become more acute because of reduced opportunities to earn money. With increasing unemployment, older workers are seen as non-competitive. According to ILO data (2001), in some NISs the level of economic activity among persons aged 65 or more fell almost twofold from 1989 to 1999, even though the demand for paid jobs among older workers persists (Figure 4.6).

Compared to the Russian Federation, the situation in Ukraine appears to be relatively good. In 1999 older people accounted for a higher proportion of Ukraine's total economically active population. Similarly, a higher proportion of the population aged 65 or more were economically active, and fewer older people reported that there were seeking a job. The real cause of such statistical 'wellbeing' is not state policy towards employment of old age pensioners, but quite the reverse. As stated by World Bank experts (IBRD 1999), Ukraine is the most reluctant of the NIS countries to abandon a policy that aims to preserve full employment by all means. Artificial maintenance of high employment has led to underemployment and hidden unemployment

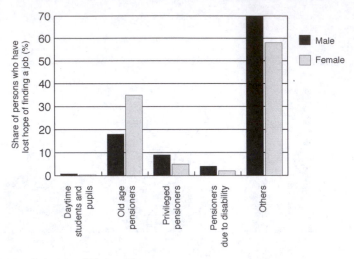

Source: Ministry for Statistics of Ukraine, 1996a.

**Figure 4.7 Social status of persons
who have lost hope of finding jobs in Ukraine, 1995**

on the largest possible scale. Some workers have been sent on long 'administrative vacations' and do not receive salaries. Many preretirement age workers are not labelled as unemployed, since they have received the status of 'retired ahead of time'. As a rule, older workers continue holding their job positions either because of contract commitments or simply because they are allowed to produce some objects for sale, using the plant or factory capacities.

Figure 4.7 shows that old age pensioners account for a large portion of people who have lost hope of finding a job. There is real cause for pessimism among older people seeking work: the discriminatory manpower policy of many Ukrainian enterprises. A 1998 survey of 911 heads of enterprises and establishments asked whether they would be prepared to employ people beyond the standard working age. It found that only 18 per cent agreed to create such work places according to their enterprise capacities; 62 per cent agreed on condition of receiving help from the state; and 20 per cent refused to employ older workers on any conditions.

Aggravation of gender problems among the older population

Experiences of later life in Ukraine are highly gendered, and there are many areas in which the wellbeing of older women is generally much worse than that of men. The years of transition have ushered in changes to traditional gender relationships, and to the relative socio-economic status of men and women. There has been an accelerating decline in female incomes and a growing gender gap in material welfare. The transition has increased psychological pressures on women in their roles as mothers, responsible for family wellbeing. Gender disparities are particularly apparent with respect to lifelong earnings and accumulated pension entitlements. However, when the occupaional history, health status and life expectancy of older men and women are also considered, the picture becomes rather more complex and confusing.

As in other countries studied in this book, there is a high incidence of widowhood among older women. In part, this reflects women's greater life expectancy. Also, Ukrainian men tend to marry younger women and few older women marry again. Widows have been found to be a particularly vulnerable group, and are more likely to live alone on a low income. Recent rises in adult male mortality have increased the incidence of widowhood, particularly in rural areas where the over-65 gender ratio (men to women) fell from 1:2.2 to 1:2.4 between 1989 and 2000. Rural out-migration of young adults has increased during the transition. This, along with increased mortality among the working population, has led to a reduction in the potential support ratio (number of persons aged 15–64 years old per person at age 65 or more) from 3.7 in 1989 to 3.3 in 2000. In rural areas, where physically hard and low-paid manual work prevails, women lose their health during the life course and are awarded a miserable pension at retirement. Being widowed and getting negligible assistance from migrant children, older women in rural areas very often become the victims of economic, juridical and even physical abuse.

An important indicator of gender inequity is the health status of older men and women. The national constitution includes the right to equal health protection for men and women. As mentioned above, in the context of economic transition, the Ukraine's state health care system is close to collapse. There is an acute lack of drugs, medical equipment and materials. Their costs are partly paid by low-income elderly consumers of medical services, among whom women comprise the greatest and least wealthy portion.

Elderly male mortality from so-called 'socially determined' causes of death, like tuberculosis, alcoholism and suicides has historically been higher than for women, but the gender gap has rapidly widened in recent years (Figure 4.8). The health status of older men and women is not only a reflection of transition, but is also a cumulative effect of the life-course and past working conditions. This includes sharp gender disparities in employment by area of activity. Here the position of women seems more advantageous. The 1989 Population Census found

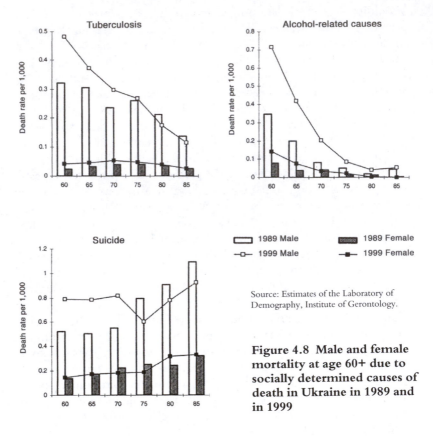

Source: Estimates of the Laboratory of Demography, Institute of Gerontology.

Figure 4.8 Male and female mortality at age 60+ due to socially determined causes of death in Ukraine in 1989 and in 1999

100 women per 136 men engaged in manual work (Ministry for Statistics of Ukraine 1992). A significant proportion of men were employed at sites where, owing to harmful conditions, women were not allowed to work. An important factor limiting access to secondary and higher education (and thus to a healthier life) for youths aged 18–21 is mandatory military service. For this reason, within the structure of personnel with higher education, men prevail only in a few branches of the economy such as forestry and construction (UNDP 1999b). Especially marked differences in favour of women are found in activities for which education is required such as information and computing services, research, health care, finance and credit management. It should be noted, however, that historically, these sorts of positions have tended to pay less than blue-collar jobs.

A tradition of early childbearing is another reason why many younger women withdraw from employment in hazardous, out-of-date production environments (Steshenko and Gkhosh 2000). This leads to

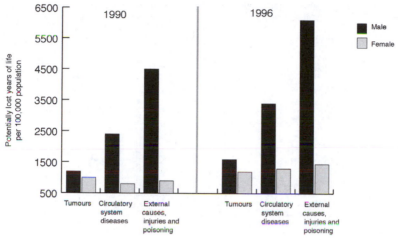

Source: UNDP 1999b.

Figure 4.9 Potentially lost years of life from birth until age 65, by major causes of death in Ukraine in 1990 and in 1996, and by gender

an excess mortality of young men and is reflected in the shortening of their life expectancy at birth and in the reduction of their working age. The increasing incapacitation of young men is echoed in the increase of their mortality at old age. Inequity in male access to education and better working conditions is seen in the dynamics of potentially lost years of life from birth to age 65 from the main causes of death (Figure 4.9).

According to the United Nations Development Programme (UNDP 1999b), about 70 per cent of old-age pensioners are women. However, men account for about 60 per cent of privileged pensioners (high-ranking civil servants in ministries, chiefs of departments, military servicemen; retirees from harmful jobs like miners where pensions are much higher than usual old age pensions). There is also a gender gap in pension benefits that has an economic and legislative basis. The value of a pension reflects workers' salaries and the period for which contributions were made. Women's salaries tend to be lower than men's, and they have a shorter period of social insurance contribution. The law specifies the pensionable age: 60 for men; 55 for women. Women's social insurance contributions are also reduced by breaks from salaried work due to childcare. Childbirth and caring for one child over three years reduces a mother's pension contributions by 7–11 per cent compared to a childless woman; the birth of two children by 14–21 per cent and of three children by 21–30 per cent (Machulskaya 1999). As a result, the average length of service at time of retirement is 36 years for

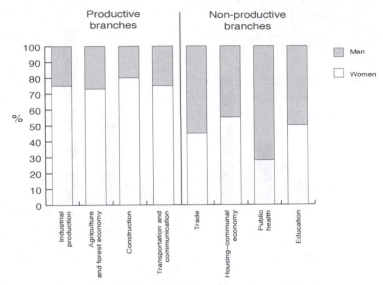

Source: The Ministry for Statistics of Ukraine, 1996a.

Figure 4.10 The structure of older (60+) workers' employment, by gender and branches of the economy, Ukraine

men and 29 for women. The difference in life expectancy for men and women means that the ratio of average periods for obtaining pension benefits and for contributing to the pension fund differs depending on sex: men pay fees for almost double the period of time that they receive pensions. Conversely, women pay fees during a shorter period (by about two years) than they receive a pension. The establishment of gender justice in the field of pensions would require an increase in the pensionable age of women. It would also require state financial support in the form of 'family bonuses', in order to bring the pension benefits of childed women into line with those of childless ones (Stashkiv 2000).

A serious gender problem exists in the labour market. All people who are able to work, irrespective of their age and sex, are now striving to get a paid job. The gender ratio for workers aged 60 and upwards was roughly even (Ministry for Statistics of Ukraine 1996a). However, data on the educational background of older workers suggest that older women are more likely to be employed in low-paid unqualified occupations. The structure of male and female employment at age 60 and over in various branches of the economy shows clear disparities between the 'productive' and 'non-productive' sectors, with women prevailing in the latter (Figure 4.10). This is important because wages are generally lower in 'non-productive activities' and there are fewer opportunities to obtain a second job. Official surveys have identified widespread discrimination in employing women at pre-retirement ages (Cabinet of Ministers of Ukraine 2000). It is likely that discrimination occurs for later ages, albeit at lower levels of intensity.

The role of the older generation in the formation of new families: does society perceive it adequately?

The modern family system in Ukraine is exposed to huge socio-economic pressures. Recent surveys shows that in up to 80 per cent of families the monthly *per capita* income is under US$19; in a third it is between US$10 and US$19, while in half it is less than US$10. Due to financial shortages, many families are forced to make some food products and perform all domestic work by themselves, regardless of their physical capacity. Hence the members of many families are overburdened with the tasks of daily living, leaving them little free time for meaningful communication with each other. Against this background of crisis, sociologists observe the appearance of mass social stress-induced derangement and feelings of hopelessness and despera-tion (Lavrinenko 1999). Older family members are especially liable to such stress.

During the Soviet era, the state occupied a paternalistic position in relation to the family, taking on material responsibilities (the provision of free education, medical care, housing, and recreation activity for all generations), and performing instructional and legal functions. In that period relationships between the family and the state entailed an active intrusion of the state into family life, excessive attention to spousal and matrimonial affairs, and an education system which propagandised societal and public ideals and 'life senses'. The state and public organisa-tions sought to supervise the family and ensure its stability. This paternalistic hierarchy of 'dominant (state)/dependent (family)' relations was transferred to the family level, forming the established psychological conditions of the 'soviet person' within a family hierarchy based on 'dominant (parents)/dependent (children)'. Such a hierarchy ensured a strong position in the family for the older generation throughout their adult lives and old age (Lavrinenko 1999).

Present relations between the family and the state are built on the principle of independence and non–interference. Under these conditions young family members, as a rule, perceive their social surroundings as hostile towards them, and therefore hold an aggressive-defensive position towards both society as a whole and the older generation in particular. The individualistic principles so enthusiastically acquired by the younger generation are contradictory to the older population's mentality and life scenarios, which had been formed under communal conditions. At the family level, this promotes an accumulation of intergenerational tension and reduces the scope for intra-familial integration.

On the other hand, because current conditions oblige most families to strive to survive, new types of family ties are being formed, in which family members of all generations are perceived and valued as the bearers of definite resources: material, physical, and emotional. In circumstances of very limited resources, the value of moral or physical support of an aging member increases immeasurably.

Family material wellbeing is often created through the work of several generations, and the cohabitation of three to four generations ensures their survival, as they all find themselves dependent on each other. According to the UNDP (1999c), only 20 per cent of young families have their own dwelling, and about 60 per cent live together with one of the spouse's parents. Certain psychological problems arise for young couples and the parents' family alike. Prior to forming their own small group within the already existing family, the young couple has not only to determine rules and roles inside their own family, but also to align them with the norms and rules of the parents' family. Parents view self-determination of the young family negatively, and try to destroy the boundaries being built by the young couple, in order to preserve the primary family foundation. As a rule, the young reject close contacts, appraisals and, sometimes, control on the part of the parents. This leads to tension and even conflicts in this multigenerational family.

In developed Western societies, the main functions of the family have become the birth and socialisation of children and 'psychological protection', love and mutual support of each other. In Ukraine, among life priorities, the economic function has taken first place in the majority of families. In the hierarchy of family values there has been a shift towards the satisfaction of prime needs and the struggle for elementary physical existence, in which the older generation is playing the key role.

Almost all young married couples are given many forms of assistance by their parents (Lavrinenko 1999). Only 10 per cent of families have been found to receive no help from their parents. Forms of parental assistance vary and cover all aspects of the economic functioning of the family (Figure 4.11). More than 30 per cent of families receive monthly monetary assistance from parents; nearly two thirds of families get regular assistance in food, clothes and things of everyday use; one third of families are helped with housing problems. The low share of young married couples receiving help in caring for children is primarily explained by the low share of childed young families. This demonstrates the key role played by the older generation in the formation and survival of new families.

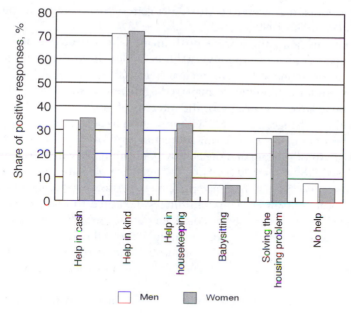

Source: Lavrinenko, 1999.

Figure 4.11 An evaluation of provision by the older generation of material and functional assistance to young families, Ukraine

The role of older people in Ukrainian society: opposite viewpoints

The attitudes of older people to the transition are based on their life values, which emphasise a communal mode of existence, and the stereotypes of collective thinking and depersonalisation induced by life under a totalitarian regime. These conflict with the new life outlooks of younger generations. The causes of serious social conflict between generations of 'parents' and 'children' include different outlooks on life, differences in life positions and attitudes to societal rearrangement. For the older generation, this conflict threatens to deepen their social isolation and turn them into social outcasts. As shown by Tanasjuk (1999), with regard to the political orientations of people of different ages, there exist certain discrepancies in their preferences for the future of the country. Thus, return to a socialist past is positively perceived by 37 per cent of elders and by only 10 per cent of the young. Preferences for future capitalism were given by 4 per cent of older respondents and by 19 per cent of the young. During the 1998/9 election, the pro–

communist parties received 60 to 70 per cent of their votes from elderly voters (Voitenko 1999).

For many years there were no human rights-oriented policies for older people. There were long-established councils for war and labour veterans, operating at local municipal, regional and national levels, but these were formal, politically managed agencies. As such, they did not function as advocacy groups for the interests of older people. However, the political changes associated with transition have seen these organisations become more involved in protection and advocacy of the rights and interests of veterans and the elderly population as a whole (Bezrukov and Verzhikovskaya 1994). These veterans' organisations now have representatives in the national parliament. Also, the parliament and many local councils contain committees dedicated to the concerns of the veterans and groups such as disabled people. Several important new organisations have emerged, including the Ukrainian Pensioners' Association. This is a public, non-profit, voluntary organisation, the major goals of which are to give financial assistance to pensioners, improve their health, maintain their social status, restore their dignity in society, and provide opportunities for their self-realisation (Dzjobak 2002).

Older peoples' attitudes to the transition are reflected in recent life satisfaction indices, which show that 43 per cent of people aged 55 and over were not satisfied with their own lives, compared to 19 per cent of people aged under 30 (Tanasyuk 1999). However, there may be an intrinsic age effect on satisfaction indices, regardless of the context in which ageing is occurring. Ukrainian elders are more likely to feel that their wellbeing depends on things beyond their personal control rather than their own agency, making them feel particularly vulnerable to the forces of transition (Tanasyuk 1999).

Given their educational and professional characteristics, as well as their value systems, older cohorts have a specific world outlook and social psychology. According to stereotypes, older people are thought to be less tolerant of negative societal changes than are youth below 30. This would seem to be contradicted by a survey which found that people aged 56 and over were able to adapt to the social tensions of the transition rather better than did younger groups (Panina and Golovakha 1999). It is likely that the life wisdom and the accumulated social experience of older generations played an important role in helping them to face social upheavals. The hard historical experience of the older Ukrainians (two world wars, pre- and postwar periods of hunger, and years of repression), means that they can be more stoical than younger generations are about present-day circumstances.

Looking to the future with hope

Ukraine and other European NISs began the transition from centrally planned to market-based economies under similar conditions. The divergence of their economic pathways by the mid-1990s indicates the importance of appropriate economic policies and development strategies for the success of transition and the maintenance of living standards. In Ukraine the period of transition has seen a sharp fall in the level of average incomes, along with the disappearance of cheap food and goods, for whose production the state had previously allocated special resources. Although old age pensions are paid by the state, they leave people just over the poverty line. In the case of the rural elderly, a long delay precedes the payment of these small pensions.

The negative impacts of transition on older people include human losses, such as depopulation and reduced life expectancy. Changes in the morbidity structure and hence in the structure of mortality (caused by growth in the diseases of later life and a shift in the pattern of vulnerability to include younger patients) reflect an acceleration of individual aging processes. An unprecedented growth of poverty among older people has led to an unbalanced and insufficient nutritional intake, even starvation, as well as the spread of 'diseases of poverty', such as tuberculosis, other infectious diseases, and food poisoning.

The position of older people has been undermined further by growing unemployment, limiting the chances of finding a paid job for people beyond retirement age. Inequality and open age discrimination against elders in the labour market have added not only to their economic deprivation but also to their social isolation, thereby leading to loss of human dignity. The hard economic position of older people has been aggravated by an exacerbation of social problems in different spheres: gender, familial and public.

The present condition of older people in Ukraine remains poor. Nevertheless, certain positive shifts should be stressed. Annually, the real size of pensions increases, albeit slowly. Health care reform has resulted in some modest improvements. Both the public and private social welfare systems are gradually developing. Older people are getting more involved in public life and politics. Worthy of special note is the voluntary movement started and run by war and labour veterans. It seems likely that at least a part of the heterogenous older population has already adapted to the new conditions.

Today, Ukraine stands at a crossroads. The country should not choose short-term actions but rather an economic strategy that will determine the development of the economy for the next decade, thus bringing it onto the road of long-awaited economic growth and success.

As stated by the World Bank (IBRD 1999), Ukraine has huge unused production capacities and big labour resources. With an efficient use of available production funds and manpower, the Ukrainian economy could see growth of output even with minimal investments. On this basis and under conditions of more urgent and resolute reform, the World Bank has predicted a take-off for stable economic growth for 2002 (an optimistic scenario) or at least by 2005 (basic scenario) (IBRD 1999). This will bring about a rise in incomes and improve living standards. Nevertheless, if the government continues to promote economic growth through an inflationary monetary policy and foreign borrowing or by a return to centralised planning, Ukraine will face economic collapse as soon as 2005, according to the same forecasts.

With unprecedented demographic ageing, Ukrainian society should understand that the 'non-active' part of population does not live at the expense of the 'active' part. Under normal socio-economic conditions, retired people neither live at the expense of others nor 'burden' anybody economically. With stable socio-economic development, pensioners are viewed not as dependants but as 'rentiers' of the capital accumulated from the surplus of wealth formed by pensioners over the capital which they had spent on their own current needs during their years of economic activity. Each generation leaves behind more than it has consumed, and this promotes societal progress. An enormous strain in the formation and division of current consumption funds has now emerged in Ukraine. This is a consequence not of the 'overloading' of the working population by pensioners, but of the disappearance of an overwhelming part of the national 'pension capital' and almost all personal savings in the course of unsuccessful experiments with economic reform. This, along with the production breakdown, has led to low pension values and a rise of poverty among older people.

Overcoming negative attitudes to ageing – when the supposed conservatism and inertia of an increasing number of older people are associated in the collective consciousness with hampering socio-economic development – is a major challenge for countries in transition. The wider community needs to recognise the role played by older people in the social life of present-day Ukraine. It also needs to recognise their aspirations and skills to realise their economic, intellectual and moral potential for the sake of building a new society. This is needed for the harmonious entry of the 'third generation' into a long-awaited future of wellbeing.

REFERENCES

Barnet, T., A. Whiteside, L. Khodakevich, J. Kruglov and V. Steshenko (1998) 'Estimation of possible demographic and social-economic consequences of HIV/AIDS spreading in Ukraine', *Studies on Demography*, 20: 81–106.

Bezrukov, V. and N. Verzhikovskaya (1994) 'USSR Former', in Jordan I. Kosberg (ed.), *International Handbook of Services for the Elderly*, Greenwood Press, Westport.

Cabinet of Ministers of Ukraine, State Statistics Committee of Ukraine and UNDP (2000) *The Gender Statistics on Monitoring the Gaining an Equity of Men and Women in Ukraine.*, Cabinet of Ministers of Ukraine, The State Statistics Committee of Ukraine and United Nations Development Programme, Kiev.

Chaikovskaya, V. (2000) 'The quality and efficacy of medical care for retirees', *The Problems of Aging and Longevity*, 9 (2): 162–70.

Dzjobak, V. (2002) 'Introductory message', *Our Generation*, 1: 2–3.

IBRD (1999) *Ukraine. Growth Recovery on the Principles of Justice: Memorandum on Economic Development of Ukraine*, International Bank for Reconstruction and Development/ World Bank, Kiev.

ILO (2001) *Yearbook of Labour Statistics, 2000*, International Labour Organisation, Geneva.

Lavrinenko, N. B. (1999) 'The specifics of family life activity during the transition', in *The Ukrainian Society: Monitoring Social Changes (1994–1999). Information-Analytic Materials*, Institute of Sociology NAS Ukraine, Kiev.

Machulskaya, K. E. (1999) 'Social welfare reforming and need of legislation coding', *Proceedings of Moscow University*, 6: 8.

Ministry for Statistics of Ukraine (1992) *Social and Professional Branch Structure of the Population of Ukraine*, Ministry for Statistics of Ukraine, Kiev.

—— (1993) *National Economy of Ukraine in 1992: Statistical Yearbook*, Technika, Kiev.

—— (1994) *National Economy of Ukraine in 1993: Statistical Yearbook*, Technika, Kiev.

—— (1995) *Statistical Yearbook of Ukraine for 1994*, Technika, Kiev.

—— (1996a) *Economic Activity of the Population of Ukraine in 1995: Statistical Yearbook*, Ministry for Statistics of Ukraine, Kiev.

—— (1996b) *Statistic Yearbook of Ukraine for 1995*, Technika, Kiev.

Ministry for Statistics of Ukrainian SSR (1991) 'Sex and Age Composition of Population in Ukrainian SSR at 12th January 1989 (data of 1989 All-Union Population Census)', Ministry for Statistics of Ukrainian SSR, Kiev, unpublished.

Panina, N. V. and E. I. Golovakha (1999) 'The social wellbeing of the Ukrainian population', in *The Ukrainian Society: Monitoring Social Changes (1994–1999). Information-Analytic Materials*, Institute of Sociology NAS Ukraine, Kiev.

Sineok, L. L., L. A. Podust, Yu. G. Grigorov, T. M. Semesko, S. G. Kozlovskaya and I. V. Sapozhnikov (2001) 'Nutrition of single non-working elderly, the takers of social welfare services, and the ways for its improvement', *Problems of Ageing and Longevity*, 10 (2): 190–9.

Slyusar, L. (1995) *Social Consumption Funds Within a Modern System of Population Reproduction Provision in Ukraine*, Kiev: Demographic–Economic Studies, Institute of Economics NAS Ukraine.

Stashkiv, B. (2000) *The ways of improving the pension legislation: gender approach,* Proceedings of the Conference 'The Equity of Men and Women in Ukraine: The Legislative Aspects', Kiev.

State Statistics Committee of Ukraine (1998) *Statistical Yearbook of Ukraine for 1997*, Technika, Kiev.

—— (1999a) 'Age and sex composition of population in Ukraine at 1st January 1999', The State Statistics Committee, Kiev, unpublished.

—— (1999b), *Statistic Yearbook of Ukraine for 1998*, Technika, Kiev.

——— (1999c) *The Social Protection of the Population of Ukraine in 1998: Statistical Bulletin*, State Statistics Committee, Kiev.

——— (2000) *Statistical Yearbook of Ukraine for 1999*, Technika, Kiev.

——— (2001a) *The Social-Economic State of Rural Residential Settlements in Ukraine: Statistical Book Collection*. State Statistics Committee of Ukraine, Kiev.

——— (2001b) *The Social-Economic State of the Rural Settlements in Ukraine: Statistical Book Collection*, State Statistics Committee of Ukraine.

Steshenko, V., O. Khomra, O. Rudnitskiy and A. Stefanovskiy (1999) *Demographic Perspectives for Ukraine until 2026*, Report preprint, Institute of Economics NAS Ukraine, Kiev.

Steshenko, V. and M. Ghosh (2000) 'The demographic and demopolitical changes in Ukraine after the International Conference of Population and Development: short review', *Studies on Demography*, 22: 7–46.

Tanasjuk, O.V. (1999) 'Age-specific differences in life values of people and their attitudes to societal transformations', in *The Ukrainian Society: Monitoring of Social Changes (1994–1999). The Information-Analytic Materials*, Institute of Sociology NAS Ukraine, Kiev.

Voitenko, V. P. (1999) *The Parties as Viewed by a Demographer. Election-98 and Election-99*, Hippocrate Publishers, Kiev.

UNDP (1999a) *Report on Human Development in the European and NIS Countries*, United Nations Development Programme, Moscow.

UNDP (1999b) *The Gender Analysis of Ukrainian Society*, State Statistics Committee of Ukraine, UN Office for Ukraine, Kiev.

UNDP (1999c) 'Part 4: The social-psychological problems of family', in *Family in Ukraine*, United Nations Development Programme.

UNDP (2000) *HIV/AIDS Epidemic in Ukraine. The Socio-Demographic Aspect*, United Nations Development Programme, Kiev.

UNDP (2001) *Human Development Report 2000*, UNDP, New York.

WHO (2001) *Health for All Data Base*, World Health Organisation, Regional Office for Europe, Updated: January, <http://www.who.dk/hfadb>

CHAPTER 5

Potential Consequences of Population Ageing for Social Development in China

DU PENG & DAVID R. PHILLIPS

Population ageing in China

China is the most populous country in the world, with some 1.28 billion people at the end of 2001. Unsurprisingly, China also has the largest population of older persons, 128 million persons aged 60 and over, representing 10 per cent of the national population, as well as more than 90 million people aged 65 and over, 7 per cent of the total population. With fertility well under replacement level and a life expectancy of greater than 71 years, China is now experiencing particularly rapid population ageing (Table 5.1).

Table 5.1 Age composition of China's population

Indices	1953	1964	1982	1990	2000
Total population (millions)	567.5	694.6	1,003.9	1,133.7	1,265.8
0–14 (%)	36.28	40.69	33.59	27.62	22.89
65+ (%)	4.41	3.56	4.91	5.57	6.96

Source: Data for 1953-90: Population Research Center, CASS (1986); *Almanac of China's Population*. Social Science Press, Beijing. 2000 Data: Key results of 2000 population census, *People's Daily*, 28 March 2001.

Especially since the late 1980s, demographic ageing in China has been accelerating. By the 2020s, when baby boom cohorts from the pre-one-child policy era will reach their sixties, China is expected to reach its peak period of population ageing. This will last for about three decades (Table 5.2). It is projected that, by the middle of this century, the percentage of people aged 65 and over in China will be around 23

Table 5.2 Projected population ageing in China (thousands)

Year	Total population	Population aged 65+	Percentage of older persons (%)
2005	1,321,364	99,473	7.5
2010	1,366,215	110,943	8.1
2015	1,410,217	131,508	9.3
2020	1,446,092	166,887	11.5
2025	1,470,787	194,793	13.2
2030	1,484,619	233,725	15.7
2035	1,490,726	283,283	19.0
2040	1,490,465	319,572	21.4
2045	1,480,932	327,533	22.1
2050	1,462,058	331,602	22.7

Source: Population Division of the Department of Economic and Social Affairs of the United Nations Secretariat, *World Population Prospects: The 2000 Revision,* United Nations, New York.

per cent, and that the absolute number of older persons in China will be more than 330 million. This will pose a major challenge in the coming decades, and policy makers in China now recognise the need to address it urgently.

As in other countries population ageing does not just signify an increase in the number of older people; it also leads to the ageing of the elderly cohorts themselves. The number of people aged 80 and above is currently estimated to be about 12 million, but will reach 27 million by 2025 and 90 million by 2050 (Du 2000). Given the expected changes in demands for health and social care that generally accompany such demographic trends, policy makers recognise the need for substantial reforms in these areas of provision.

As in all countries, the speed and pattern of population ageing have been largely shaped by rapid fertility decline and mortality decline. However, compared to most developed countries, the demographic transition started much later in China, and the process of population ageing really only started from the mid-1960s or later. With rapid socio-economic development following the founding of the People's Republic of China in 1949, the mortality rate declined sharply and life expectancy at birth increased from 40.3 years in 1953 to 71 years in 2000. China experienced baby booms in the 1950s and 1960s. However, since the mid-1960s, and especially after 1973, strict and effective national family planning policies contributed to a rapid decline in the total fertility rate (TFR) and birth rate. Indeed, from the mid-1960s to the year 2000, China's TFR declined from 7.5 to 1.7. The scale of this decline ensures rapid demographic ageing for many decades to come. Although population ageing is caused by both mortality decline and fertility declines, the more important determinant of population ageing is usually fertility decline (Jones 1993; Phillips 2000). But as China's TFR has already reached a relatively low level, further mortality decline will arguably play an increasingly important role in the future process of demographic ageing in China (Du 1994).

In the process of population ageing, China's family planning policy has played a pivotal role and, in some places, especially in the large cities, it has underpinned the emergence of families with an 'only child'. This has been part and parcel of declining family size and simpler family structures. It has been accompanied by changing living arrangements for older persons and, in combination, these features pose serious challenges to the traditional family support system, the main source of provision for older persons over many centuries.

The Chinese government believes that population size and composition will continue to be a pressing issue for China well into the 21st century. Annual net population growth will be more than 10 million at the start of this century and the population will not decline until it reaches a peak of at least 1.6 billion later in the 21st century. Therefore, the government has confirmed that China will stick to its family planning policy for the foreseeable future. For at least the next decade, China's population policy will be to stabilise the already low fertility rate and to improve the health of newborn children, which will also contribute to further population ageing.

In the State Council's *White Paper on Population in China*, published on 19 December 2000, the Chinese government announced its targets for the national population and development programme:

▸ China aims to restrict its total population to 1.33 billion by 2005 (excluding the population of the Hong Kong and Macao Special Administrative Regions and Taiwan Province). A basic social security system is to be established in urban and some rural areas.

▸ China aims to restrict its total population to 1.4 billion by 2010. China will redouble its efforts to tackle issues relating to ageing by this time, and a preliminary nationwide social security system will be established.

▸ By the mid-21st century, the total population is likely to reach its peak of 1.6 billion. An efficient and comprehensive social security system should by then be in place.

Current population policy indicates the desire and efforts of the Chinese government to balance the structure and size of the total

population and to prevent serious consequences arising from demographic ageing. The government admits that the strict family planning
regime is a special product of a special period to meet the special needs
of overpopulation. The Chinese government has realised the potential
negative impacts of this family planning policy on demographic
structures and would like to adjust it.

In part to introduce greater flexibility, the government is decentral-
ising policy relating to birth planning from the national level to the local
provincial level. All provinces have their own local population and
family planning regulations, including regulations for birth planning. A
trend toward a slight relaxation of birth planning is observable in these
local regulations. For example, 26 out of 31 provinces allow families in
rural and urban areas to have two children if both husband and wife are
only children. Because the 'one-couple, one-child' policy has been
implemented principally in the urban areas since the early 1980s, this
adjustment allows for a *de facto* two-child policy in rural areas although
not all single-child couples would necessarily wish to have two
children (Yu 2000). To some extent, the effects of this policy relaxation
will influence the speed and pattern of population ageing in the near
future.

The diversity of socio-economic development and its impacts on older persons in China

China has undergone fundamental social and economic transformations
which have progressed with unprecedented speed and touched almost
all areas and parts of society. An open-door policy and economic reform
were started in the later 1970s. The spirit of China's reform was
symbolised by the saying of the late Deng Xiao-ping: 'it does not matter
if a cat is black or white as long as it catches the mouse', indicating that
the fundamental task of the reforms was to develop China's economy
pragmatically and improve its living standards.

During the last two decades, many fundamental social and economic
reforms have been carried out. The process of reform was initiated in
rural areas where, for instance, a new rural household responsibility
system (moving away from the old collective form of agricultural
production) was first introduced in 1978 in Anhui province, and
diffused widely across the country. In 1983 the people's commune
system, dating back to 1958, was formally abandoned. At the same time,
the system of unified and fixed state purchase of agricultural products
was abolished. These measures of rural reform have drastically increased
agricultural production and helped to solve the food problems facing
China's huge population. Rural reform has also released millions of

rural labourers from agricultural work, involving a great impact on the rural economy and accelerating the process of urbanization.

The comprehensive reforms have underpinned a dramatic social and economic transformation. *Per capita* GDP has doubled over the last two decades and many obvious changes have taken place in all aspects of life. Reforms of the systems of household registration, public health, social security, education and retirement, have all achieved remarkable progress although some important challenges have inevitably been created by the process of change itself.

Generally speaking, economic reform in China has brought about great improvements in the quality of life and notable changes in the freedom and range of opportunities available to individuals. This general development can clearly be seen in the temporal trend of China's Human Development Index (HDI). This index, prepared by the United Nations Development Programme (UNDP), is based on three indicators: longevity (measured by life expectancy at birth); educational attainment (measured by a combination of adult literacy and the combined gross primary, secondary and tertiary enrolment ratios); and standard of living (real GDP per capita, $PPP). According to UNDP estimates, China's HDI was 0.51 in 1975, since when it has increased steadily and continuously, to 0.701 in 1997. Today, China is classified as having achieved medium-level human development, ranking 98th among the 174 countries or regions in the world for which the UNDP calculated the HDI (UNDP 1999).

However, as might be expected in such a geographically large and populous country, the development process does not progress evenly and there are tremendous regional variations. Table 5.3 shows the HDI and its component indicators for each of China's provincial units. There are 13 provinces where the HDI exceeds the national index, whilst it is below the national average in the remaining 17 provinces. The HDI value for three major Chinese cities, Shanghai, Beijing and Tianjin, and for Guangdong province, all located in the eastern coastal region, has already reached a level that the UNDP classifies as high. By contrast, the level in Qinghai, Tibet and some other western inland provinces is very low. The extremely low value of the HDI in Tibet is mainly caused by its low education index components.

While the percentage of persons aged 65 and over was 7 per cent nationally in 2000, there are remarkable variations among provinces. According to data from the 2000 population census, Shanghai has the highest level of ageing in China with 11.53 per cent of people being aged 65 and over. At the other end of the scale, Qinghai province had the lowest percentage of people aged 65 or more, 4.33 per cent (Table 5.4).

Table 5.3 Regional differences in China (1997) – the Human Development Index and its components

Region	Life expectancy at birth (years) 1990	Literacy (%)	School enrolment %	*Per capita* GDP (in US$) 1990	Human Development Index (HDI)	Ranking in China	Ranking in the world
Beijing	72.86	92.36	67.4	9404.72	0.867	2	27
Tianjin	72.32	90.16	62.6	7753.06	0.852	3	30
Hebei	70.35	85.7	56.3	3416.27	0.73	11	84
Shanxi	68.97	90.13	54.4	2661.53	0.679	16	106
Inner Mongolia	65.68	83.22	55.4	2636.24	0.645	21	113
Liaoning	70.22	91.79	56.8	4709.19	0.831	5	37
Jilin	67.95	91.87	57.3	3093.13	0.71	12	96
Heilongjiang	66.97	90.82	55.3	4070.42	0.766	10	56
Shanghai	74.9	89.83	67.4	14470.96	0.877	1	25
Jiangsu	71.37	80.72	59	5251.13	0.817	7	41
Zhejiang	71.78	81.62	57.2	5909.21	0.821	6	40
Anhui	69.48	79.83	54.3	2467.09	0.642	20	114
Fujian	68.57	82.55	55.9	5202.8	0.802	8	44
Jiangxi	66.11	87.53	54.2	2335.02	0.635	22	115
Shandong	70.57	77.36	55.9	4265.42	0.77	9	55
Henan	70.15	85.12	53.1	2489.57	0.661	18	111
Hubei	67.25	84.95	58.5	3315.12	0.707	14	96
Hunan	66.93	88.73	55.3	2609.27	0.662	17	111
Guangdong	72.52	90.39	55.9	5860.32	0.843	4	34
Guangxi	68.72	84.88	52.7	2447.98	0.649	19	112
Hainan	70.01	85.89	51.7	3202.16	0.709	13	96
Chongqing	66.33	83.18	51.8	2501.93	0.635	22	115
Sichuan	66.33	82	52.9	2264.21	0.617	24	120
Guizhou	64.29	74.12	49.3	1244.78	0.516	30	137
Yunnan	63.49	74.48	50	2271.52	0.583	27	126
Tibet	59.64	45.94	38.5	1794.96	0.452	31	147
Shaanxi	67.4	83.66	56.8	2083.26	0.617	25	119
Gansu	67.24	73.23	53.6	1762.93	0.57	28	129
Qinghai	60.57	56.38	50.6	2285.01	0.528	29	135
Ningxia	66.94	74.17	52.4	2261.97	0.603	26	124
Xinjiang	62.59	88.48	55	3317.93	0.685	15	104
Total	69.8	82.9	69	3130	0.701	NA	98

Note: Ranking in the world means the ranking among the 174 nations and regions.
Sources: UNDP, *China Human Development Report 1999*, UNDP, New York, 1999.

Table 5.4 Regional differences in the percentages of persons aged 65+, China, 2000

Region	Proportion (%)	Region	Proportion (%)
Total	6.96	Henan	6.96
Beijing	8.40	Hubei	6.31
Tianjin	8.33	Hunan	7.29
Hebei	6.86	Guangdong	6.05
Shanxi	6.20	Guangxi	7.12
Inner Mongolia	5.35	Hainan	6.58
Liaoning	7.83	Chongqing	7.90
Jilin	5.85	Sichuan	7.45
Heilongjiang	5.42	Guizhou	5.79
Shanghai	11.53	Yunnan	6.0
Jiangsu	8.76	Tibet	4.50
Zhejiang	8.84	Shaanxi	5.94
Anhui	7.45	Gansu	5.00
Fujian	6.54	Qinghai	4.33
Jiangxi	6.11	Ningxia	4.47
Shandong	8.03	Xinjiang	4.53

Source: Census Office of State Council and State Statistical Bureau, *Key Figures of the 5th Population Census,* China Statistical Press, Beijing, 2001.

China can be divided into three broad regions in terms of levels of human development and population ageing (Du and Guo 2000). The first, the eastern coastal region, is characterised by high HDI values, high population density and high levels of population ageing: it includes major centres such as Shanghai, Beijing, Tianjin and Guangdong. The second region is the central part of the country, with medium-level development and moderate population ageing: it includes the provinces of Henan and Hebei. The third type of region includes the north-western, west and southern provinces, home to many minority nationalities, such as Qinghai, Tibet and Xinjiang. Generally speaking, this third type of region has a less developed economy and is more sparsely populated. Moreover, fertility levels in the third region have been relatively high over the past dozen or so years, resulting in a younger age structure and a lower level of demographic ageing.

Given the heterogeneity of demographic ageing geographically across China, it is essential to note the huge differences between urban older persons and their counterparts in rural areas. In general, urban elderly residents are well covered by the social protection system and can lead mainly independent later lives with a fair quality of life. By contrast, many older rural citizens now still have to depend on their children's economic support and have a lower economic status; this is especially true for females, who are facing greater pressures and problems in their daily life. The current pension system regulations mean that urban retirees can usually obtain a pension equal to about 75 per cent of their basic salary before retirement. Therefore, whilst retirement does imply a decreased income level compared to the younger generations, urban retirees are still regarded as very lucky because almost all of their rural counterparts have no pension at all and many rural older persons may have to continue working on farms to maintain an income in later life.

The family's economic resources often remain very important for the economic status of older persons. In traditional Chinese families, older persons usually controlled the economic resources of the family and therefore they could play a dominant role in the family. However, over the past 50 years, China has experienced a dramatic shift from an agricultural to an industrialised society and increasing numbers of young people are living in the cities, separately from their old parents. At the same time, the elderly generation may have lost control over their children working outside the family and, instead of giving their salary to their old parents, the young generation usually just give their parents some money for food, clothing and daily expenses.

Although China has been improving its social security system and has expanded the pension scheme coverage, only one quarter of older persons now have a pension. As a result, the majority of Chinese older persons have to depend on the economic support of their children. This can seriously affect the economic status of older persons, and many regard themselves as an economic burden on their children. Previously, the economic resources of many Chinese older persons used to come from their work and family members. However, in the process of industrialisation and urbanisation, more and more urban older persons have their own pensions, which have become a main economic resource for them. By contrast, few rural dwellers have a pension: the differences in income between urban and rural older persons are therefore increasing.

In research and policy terms, during the 1990s, demographic ageing in China gained increasing attention. In part because of the social changes noted above, the question of who will provide for older persons in China has become a crucial issue today. To try to guarantee the economic resources of older persons, the Law of the People's Republic of China on Protection of the Rights and Interests of the Elderly came into force on 1 October 1996. Article 10 of this law stipulates that older persons shall be provided for mainly by their families who should care for and look after them. Article 11 further stipulates that supporters of older persons shall perform the duties of providing for, taking care of and comforting them and catering for their special needs. Therefore, providing economic support to older persons is recognised as a very important legal responsibility for the younger generation.

Historically, a much lower proportion of older Chinese women has worked in paid employment as compared with men. Although there was no significant sex difference in earnings when they did work, the mandatory retirement age in China gives an advantage of 5 to 10 years to male workers. Female workers retire at 50 while male workers retire aged 55 or 60. Because the amount of pension is based on salary before retirement, in a rapid developing economy like China, 5 or 10 years' earlier retirement can lead to a significant pension disparity between men and women. Therefore, for older persons of the same age, females usually have lower pensions and income levels and a higher proportion depend on the financial support of relatives. Other factors that also influence the generally poorer economic status of older women include high rates of literacy and economic participation. As a result, more than 80 per cent of female older persons depend mainly on their children's economic support. The gender gap in economic well-being is especially noticeable for older people in rural areas.

Considerable differences in regional development levels have led to large-scale internal migration, especially in the form of 'floating population' (temporary migrants). This increased dramatically from the second half of the 1980s, and the total 'floating population' was estimated at about 50 million in 1989 (Ai 1989). High rates of economic growth and continued regional disparities, have seen this population almost trebling, to reach an estimated 144 million by the end of 2000. The huge scale of official and unofficial migration and floating population has had various and far-reaching effects on social and economic development in China. Migration itself (mainly focused on the cities and eastern provinces) poses challenges to the traditional family support system that has prevailed in rural areas for thousands of years. This is because the majority of migrants are young adults from rural areas who pour into cities in the hope of a better living and who increasingly leave their parents alone in the rural areas. Older persons only comprise a very small percentage, 3.9 per cent, of the huge total of migrants. Amongst these older migrants, 23.1 per cent moved to join their children or other relatives and 15.2 per cent moved with their children or family members (Population Census Office 2002).

The vast differences in natural environments, culture and socio-economic development between China's rural and urban areas and among provinces are also reflected in health and mortality statistics.

According to 2000 population census data, there is a growing gap in life expectancy of 5.66 years between urban (city and town) and rural (county) areas.

In spite of the above differentials, generally speaking, many older Chinese people have declared themselves satisfied with their lives. For example, in a survey of older people conducted in Beijing in 2000, 75.8 per cent of respondents claimed to be satisfied with their lives; 94.4 per cent said they were living better than older persons in the past, 55 per cent said that young persons paid especial respect to older persons, and 81 per cent believed that the government is now paying more attention to ageing issues (BWCA 2002). The rapid socio-economic development of the past two decades has been perceived as benefiting older persons. The increasing coverage of pensions and the health care system and better living environments have all contributed to the satisfaction of older persons. At the same time, however, during a period of such dramatic social and economic transition, many older persons worry a great deal about social instability and the risk of unemployment for their children, and these factors have to some extent tempered their feelings of well-being.

Potential consequences of population ageing for social development in China

The ageing of the population is justifiably regarded as a major achievement in China's social development. After many years of family planning, China now has low fertility levels and the total population is projected to stabilise in about 40 years' time, a huge success for the country, even if achieved at a cost. Nevertheless, the percentage of older persons is still low compared to that in most developed countries, and China has been experiencing the lowest overall dependency ratio period in its history which will last for another two decades. Even so, population ageing has already begun to impact on development.

The lack of a basic national social protection system and the rapid increase in the number and proportion of the elderly population means that population ageing has had multifaceted impacts on China's socio-economic development, culture, politics and intergenerational relationships. As a rapidly ageing developing country, China recognises the need to establish the basic networks for social protection and community services. The country still contains a huge rural population which is not protected by social security programmes or the medical system, as well as very diverse levels of regional socio-economic development. These characteristics make it difficult to meet the challenges of population ageing. In 2000 the government announced that China was now an 'aged society', spurring concerns about ageing issues and the need to develop effective policy responses (Du and Guo 2000).

This review has identified a number of key potential consequences of population ageing for social development in China. In summary, six prominent features and challenges may be seen. These are often visible in other developing countries but, in China the weight of numbers and the rapidity and extent of socio-economic change mean they assume even greater importance.

1. Huge numbers of older people need to be covered by the newly evolving social security system

In China the social security system exists mainly in urban areas, but the urban population only represents about one third of the total. For the majority of older people, especially those in rural areas, children remain the best investment for old age security and, even in large cities today, many older people still believe that to have a son is their most reliable form of security for later life (Du and Guo 2000).

Although China has long had a retirement system for government officials, this never became universal. Traditionally, older people obtained support from their families. In 1951, shortly after the founding of the People's Republic of China, a pension system was established for all enterprises with more than 100 workers. Old age pensions covered 50 to 70 per cent of workers' wages. Seventy per cent of enterprise contributions was retained locally to pay pensions while 30 per cent was transferred to a national master fund. The All China Federation of Trade Unions managed both the local payment procedures and the master fund. Thus, the Chinese pension system started as a unified one so far as urban enterprise workers were concerned. However, during the years of the Cultural Revolution, 1966 to 1976, the pension funds that had been accumulated were used for other purposes.

After 1976, supervisory responsibilities were transferred to local labour bureaux, while the responsibility for managing payments was transferred to enterprises, who paid the pensions of their own workers out of current revenues. The cradle-to-grave welfare system called for the state-owned enterprises (SOEs) to be solely responsible for the welfare of their employees, including life-long employment, medical care and pensions. The economic reforms that started in 1978 made evident the problems of an enterprise-based pension system. Many older enterprises, often facing difficult financial conditions in their core businesses because of technical and economic changes, had placed on them the additional burden of pensions.

In rural areas, farmers were allotted plots of land in the 1950s, but no system of social insurance has been established, and it is assumed that families provide support for those who need it. The state and the collectives are held responsible to fulfil 'Five Guarantees' to childless and infirm older persons. These Guarantees cover their needs with respect to food, clothing, medical care, housing and burial expenses (Joseph and Phillips 1999). Such older people have often been institutionalised in nursing homes across the country.

Since the 1980s China has been carrying out numerous reforms in old age support and medical care. In 1992 the Ministry of Civil Affairs issued and carried out a nation-wide Basic Scheme for Rural Social Security for Old Age Support at the Country Level. This stipulates that raising funds for old age support should follow the principle of relying mainly on individual payments, with some additional support from village or township committees. This additional community support is tax-exempt, entailing an indirect state subsidy. Since 1995, each province has devised programmes to reform the pension system. The guiding principle for these reforms is that old age insurance must be in keeping with the requirements of the market economy, applicable to employees from all sectors, funded by multiple sources, and managed collectively. A notable feature of the new social insurance system is that individuals are required to pay for part of the insurance premium for old age support. The new system consists of three components: basic old age insurance paid by the government; additional insurance premiums paid by employers and the individual savings insurance paid by employees.

During the last five years, there have been efforts to set up a multi-tier old age security system in the urban areas, involving basic state old age insurance, complementary employer-supported schemes and individual insurance through savings. In rural areas, the old age security system remains largely based on personal savings, in addition to a degree of support from the state, the collectives and the family. In addition to the pension funds, there have been efforts to set up a poverty line security system in all urban areas.

China is increasing efforts to create a network of pensions and unemployment insurance to cover about 200 million people, the largest of its kind in the world, which will replace its outdated and unsupportable 'cradle-to-grave' welfare system. In 2000, China injected 87.6 billion yuan (over US$10 billion) into the programme, about one third more than in the previous year. At the fourth session of the Ninth National People's Congress (NPC) held in 2000, Premier Zhu Rongji said it remains a 'major task' for China in the coming five years to improve its social security system. Under the current Tenth Five Year Plan (2001–5), more Chinese people will be covered by the pension system, and the pension system for urban employees that integrates unified financing and individual accounts will be further improved.

At present, a basic framework of the social security system has taken initial shape, focused on schemes for pensions, medical care and unemployment insurance, as well as the minimum living standards pro-grammes for urban groups. Despite the extension of the system, there are still large gaps in social protection provision for rural and urban areas. It is argued that the social security system will be tested in urban areas. Meanwhile, in rural areas families will continue to bear the main responsibilities for providing for their older persons and the government will improve the Five Guarantees system to provide for older persons without family support. Generally speaking, the numbers of rural older people who directly benefit from the Five Guarantees are very small, and so families remain by far the most important source of support in old age.

In spite of the progress over recent decades, the overall coverage of social security in China remains relatively low and fewer than one third of older persons are covered under the current social security system. Since 1951, China has implemented pension schemes in enterprises and government agencies. Because most workers and government servants were young at that time, the number of pension beneficiaries took some time to increase. In 1978 this stood at just over 3 million. Since then, there has been a rapid increase, with the number of beneficiaries rising to 8.2 million in 1980, and 30 million in 1995. According to data from the 1 per cent Population Survey of 1995, the total number of urban older persons exceeded 37 million. In other words, the majority of older people in urban areas now receive pensions, implying they have much better income security than in the past. Most of them can live on their pensions, independent of support from their children. Therefore, to some extent, they have a higher economic status than in the past.

Currently, China's social security system is not perfect, and problems persist such as single fund-raising channels for social insurance, narrow insurance coverage and management weaknesses. In some cases pen-sioners do not receive their benefits on time due to funding bottlenecks. Although the transition is well under way, it will be a hard and long task to establish a social security system independent of enterprises and institutions. The various development priorities in China are oriented mainly towards cities and industries, yet developing the social security system in rural area is also crucial. The rationale for leaving rural older people to their families has increasingly been challenged because, with higher costs and lower returns in agriculture, the ability of rural families to provide for their older members is weakening. At the same time, the collection of routine social security system contributions from farmers is another obstacle because, unlike urban workers, farmers often do not have monthly incomes. Often, farmers only obtain an income after the harvest and, in the current agricultural context, it would be very difficult to establish a collection system across huge rural areas in the short term. The government needs to take concrete steps to support the social protection system in rural areas and to convert it from a voluntary to a mandatory and universal system.

2. Increasing dependency ratios and challenges to intergenerational solidarity

As the ratio of older persons to those of working age (the so-called elderly support or dependency ratio) increases in the coming decades, issues will arise concerning intergenerational conflicts in families and the wider society. This is crucial in China because, as noted, the majority of older persons still depend to a greater or lesser extent on their children's support and the existing social security system is essentially one of pay-as-you-go.

Population ageing will eventually increase the ratio of older persons to those of working age as well as changing the composition of the total dependency ratio in China. Whilst dependency ratios are by no means perfect measures of social and economic 'burden', they do give some indications. By the end of 2000, the total dependency ratio in China was 49 (children and older persons): 34 for children and 15 for persons aged 60 and over. Projections show that the number of elderly persons supported by every 100 people of working age is likely to increase to 30 in 2025 and 49 by 2050 (Wu 1999). This implies that the ratio of older persons to those of working age will be as large as the current total dependency ratio. The total dependency ratio will also increase from 49 in 2000 to 77 by 2050. It is expected that, by 2025, the elderly dependency ratio will exceed the child dependency ratio which itself may start a new round of debate about the potential social burden. To some extent, the increase of the dependent population can increase the burden on the 'active' labour force.

As its population ages, China has been experiencing a sharp decline in the workers-to-retirees ratio: there were 30.3 state and urban collective workers for every pensioner in 1978, and only 3.4 in 1998. Under current population policy and ageing trends, the ratio of workers to pensioners will continue to decline whilst the rate of growth of the older population will continue to outpace growth in the potential labour force (those of working age). The present baby-boomers, currently of the young working-age level, will shift close to or into the retirement age groups by 2025.

China's new social security system will face challenges posed by population ageing. The basic social pillar of social support will pay retirees a partial pension equal to 20 per cent of the average salary of current workers, a 20 per cent replacement rate. To keep this replacement rate stable, with the workers–retirees ratio at current levels (4 to 1), workers will only need to pay 5 per cent of their salary for their pension contribution. However, when population ageing decreases the ratio, workers will have to increase their contribution to as high as 20 per cent of their salary (Zuo 2001). 'Who is providing for older persons?' has been a topic of debate for a long time regarding intergenerational relationships, and this prospect alerted the Chinese government to prepare in advance to avoid intergenerational conflicts.

The other important issue is how to expand pension coverage, which is especially crucial for rural areas. Since the 1950s, China has tried its best to improve the old age security system in urban areas but the two thirds of the Chinese older persons living in rural areas are mainly outside the coverage of pension schemes. However, as family sizes shrink, households are becoming smaller and more and more young people are pouring into cities, often leaving older persons behind in the rural settings. Support and care from their children will therefore no longer be available, or less readily available in a practical sense. The expansion of coverage of the old age security system will thus be crucial to promoting greater intergenerational relationship in these circumstances.

3. More active roles for older persons

As the new and future cohorts of older persons will have undergone a more extended education than previous cohorts, followed by more intellectually demanding and professional work experience, China will need to meet not only their needs for material support but also for spiritual life in order to raise their quality of life. Effective measures have to be taken to promote the welfare, education, culture, health care and sporting inclinations of older citizens with the purpose of creating an appropriate and pleasant environment for them.

Huge numbers of older persons are also likely to exert a strong political influence in the near future. As China's elderly population is increasing, its composition is also changing and the proportion of better-educated retirees who once worked in enterprises or government agencies has been increasing rapidly. These people are changing the composition of the elderly population as they have more active attitudes to participation in social and political affairs and greater willingness to express their opinions in public.

The 1996 Law on Protection of the Rights and Interests of the Elderly defined the rights of older persons in family life, social life and participation in social activities. With strong support from older persons, other new laws are expected to be drafted in the near future, among them the Law of Elderly Care, the Law of the Social Participation of the Elderly and the Regulation of the Management of the Elderly Welfare Facilities. A survey of older persons conducted by the Beijing Ageing Studies Centre in 1999 showed 'protecting my legal rights' as one of the top three priorities that the government should address. In addition, China is increasingly democratised and widespread direct election of grassroots leaders has given a chance for older people to demonstrate their power and interests. With the increasing number of older persons and the ongoing social and political reform, older persons in China will definitely play a more active and an increasingly important role in local and national politics.

4. Challenges to the traditional support system

The challenge emerges strongly of how to share the responsibilities of support for older persons among state, society, family and individuals. Traditionally, this was the responsibility of the family, especially in rural settings, except during the collective farm era. Emotional attachment and mutual support among family members are very strong in China. However, population change is exerting an impact on the capacity of families to provide old age support. The most important factor is a considerable decline in fertility, which leads to a reduction in the number of children available to provide support for older persons. As filial piety is predicted to become more and more unreliable, it is likely that further legislation may be required to guarantee the rights and benefits of older people.

In spite of the scale of socio-economic change, families remain an essential basis for old age support in China and their basic functions will not be replaced by social protection. The Chinese government promotes the traditional family function of old age support; indeed, the relevant laws and national policies on ageing emphasise that the major responsibility for providing for older persons rests on the family. Meanwhile, the government has been doing its best to perfect the social protection system and to develop community services to complement the weakening function of families to provide for their older members as individuals.

5. Demographic ageing demands the establishment and development of community services

Increasing numbers of older persons, dramatically declining family size and changing living arrangements have resulted in an increasing number of frail older people who are obliged to live alone. Can they manage to continue to stay at home or will they need to enter institutions? Over the past 50 years, former employers have taken on some responsibility for their care in later life. However, with the extensive economic reforms, the majority of older persons have lost such support. They therefore have to seek help from their communities and, as they will spend most of their time in the community, community-based services and long-term care are increasingly crucial for senior citizens.

Since the later 1990s, China has been facing an increasing need to establish and develop community services, the system likely to benefit older persons the most. It is government policy to develop community services to satisfy the needs of community residents. Now the most popular services include nursing services for older persons with diseases, daily life assistance, accompanying services and cultural and sports activities. Efforts have also been made to develop the management of the community through the organisation of volunteer programmes and the utilisation of younger older persons to serve the older-old and people with disabilities. In the past, the government was the only sponsor responsible for the establishment of nursing homes, hostels and activity centres for older persons. Today, in addition to the government continuing to provide support, society is becoming more involved. Existing community services are provided in line with the increasing needs of older persons based on local conditions. As more and more older persons realise that they may be the beneficiaries of community services in the future as well as service deliverers while they are still capable, increasingly, elderly volunteers are joining the community services.

The ageing of China's population and associated health status changes pose a new set of challenges as the need for long-term care is steadily increasing. Government policy and intervention in this area will strongly influence the quality of life and needs of older persons and their families, as elsewhere in the region (Phillips and Chan 2002). In addition to developing community services to ease the burden on family members of providing long-term care, China faces at least two other related tasks. These are the reform of the administration of existing care institutions and the provision of more nursing homes, rehabilitation facilities and hospices. At least three major aspects will need to be dealt with to develop formal social care services: improving the primary health care system; strengthening the functioning of community services and developing services for the family; and strengthening the prevention of chronic disease to reduce the prevalence of functional disability, involving lifelong health education.

6. Population ageing has become better integrated into the national development plan

Even after 20 years of dramatic economic development, older persons still form one of the most vulnerable groups in China. They contributed during their lives to national socio-economic development and deserve a later life of good quality. Although the government, community, family and individuals are sharing the responsibilities of care for older persons, the government has to date been playing the most important role. By integrating ageing issues into national development plans, the government can take advantage of available resources and balance equity and efficiency in the process of socio-economic development. These factors and others have encouraged the Chinese government to develop and actively implement a long-term strategy. In 1999 China set up an unprecedented, highest-level committee on ageing, the China National Committee On Ageing (CNCOA), chaired by a senior vice-premier. This aims to guarantee services for older persons and to cooperate to make comprehensive policies related to older persons' different needs. The high profile of this Committee attests to the priority China is now giving to these concerns.

Since the mid-1980s, China has used the Five Guarantees as a framework for policy making for older people. These stipulate that 'older people should be supported, have medical care, contribute to society, be engaged in lifelong learning and live a happy life'. The government states that they have to meet not only the special needs of older persons for material living but also their spiritual needs in order to enhance their quality of life. Measures have to be taken, as we have seen, to promote the welfare, education, culture, health care and sporting activities of older persons. However, the government has also emphasised that responsibility for supporting older persons should be shared among the state, the society, families and the individual. From the year 2000 on, investment in ageing issues will be increased by allocating specific funds according to a certain percentage of the government budget. The funds allocated specially to ageing issues will be used for the construction of service facilities for older people, as well as personnel training and scientific research.

Conclusions

This chapter has reviewed the challenges posed in China by demographic ageing and the rapid development process, many of which are also to be seen to a greater or lesser extent in other developing countries, especially those in the Asia-Pacific region. They raise a number of important questions, including whether national policies in ageing exist and how these should be developed (Phillips and Chan 2002). The huge size of China's population, the large absolute numbers of older persons and the extraordinary scale and pace of socio-economic and environmental change in China mean that these phenomena are rarely replicated in their totality or with such intensity in other countries

(Phillips 2000). Population ageing in China has occurred in a less developed economy and one with an incomplete social security system. Many questions arise. Who will support China's huge elderly population? How much will the rapid demographic ageing influence socio-economic development and social stability in the near future? How will regional differences in socio-economic development and ageing be addressed? Given the dramatic shifts in society and weakening family support from generations with fewer children, these questions represent very serious challenges that China must take up without delay.

Finally, it is clear that China will enter its fastest ageing period 20 years from now. Fertility levels will remain low and many future issues will be linked increasingly with the ageing population, such as poverty, health care opportunities, social security coverage, women's social development, the positions of ethnic minorities, intergenerational relationships, lifelong education, social participation, HIV/AIDS and the like. The changes in China's age structure have arguably been more important than changes in the social economy and institutions, including shifts in conventions and traditions in Chinese society. As well as complex policy questions, the most crucial challenges posed by population ageing are often immediate practical ones, such as how to provide adequate health care and adequate economic and social support for older persons.

REFERENCES

Ai Xiao (1989) 'Current floating population reaches 50 million in China', *People's Daily*, 4 April.

BWCA (Beijing Working Committee on Ageing) (2002) 'Improving the quality of life of older persons', *Proceedings of the National Conference on Quality of Life of Older Persons*, China National Working Committee on Ageing, Beijing.

Census Office of State Council and State Statistical Bureau (2001) *Key Figures of the 5th Population Census*, China Statistical Press, Beijing.

Du, Peng (2000) *Ageing Issues and Policies in European Union Countries*, China Population Press, Beijing.

Du, Peng (1994) *Process of Population Ageing in China,* People's University Press, Beijing.

Du, Peng (2002) 'Implications of rapid demographic change and the impact on sustainable social structures in China', in *Sustainable Social Structures in a Society for All Ages*, Department of Economic and Social Affairs, United Nations, New York.

Du, Peng and Zhi-gang Guo (2000) 'Population ageing in China', in D. R. Phillips (ed.) *Ageing in the Asia-Pacific region*, Routledge, London.

Jones, G. (1993) 'Consequences of rapid fertility decline for old-age security', in R. Leete and I. Alam (eds.), *The Revolution in Asian Fertility*, Clarendon Press, Oxford.

Joseph, A. E. and D. R. Phillips (1999) 'Ageing in rural China: impacts of increasing diversity of family and community resources', *Journal of Cross-Cultural Gerontology*, 14: 153–68.

Liu, X., J. Liang. and S. Gu (1999) 'Flows of social support and health status among older persons in China', *Social Science and Medicine*, 41 (8): 1175–84.

People's Daily (2000) *White Paper on Population in China*, 19 December.

Phillips, D. R. (ed.) (2000) *Ageing in the Asia-Pacific region*, Routledge, London.

Phillips, D. R. (2002) 'Family support for older persons in East Asia: demise or durability?' in *Sustainable Social Structures in a Society for All Ages*, Department of Economic and Social Affairs, United Nations, New York.

Phillips, D. R. and A. C. M. Chan (eds.) (2002) *Ageing and Long-Term Care: National Policies in the Asia–Pacific,* Institute of Southeast Asian Studies, Singapore.

Population Census Office (under the State Council and Department of Population, Social, Science and Technology Statistics, National Bureau of Statistics of China) (2002) *Tabulation on the 2000 Population Census of the People's Republic of China,* China Statistics Press.

Population Division of the Department of Economic and Social Affairs of the United Nations Secretariat (2001) *World Population Prospects: The 2000 Revision,* United Nations, New York.

Population Research Centre, CASS (1986) *Almanac of China's Population,* Social Science Press, Beijing.

State Statistical Bureau (SSB) (2001) 'Key results of 2000 Population Census', *People's Daily*, 28 March.

Qiao Xiaochun (1998) 'The old social security in rural China', *Population Research*, 3: 8–13.

Shang Xiaoyuan (2001) 'Moving toward a multi-level and multi-pillar system: changes in institutional care in two Chinese cities', *Journal of Social Policy*, 30: 2.

Song Jian (2000) 'Emergence and development of "four-two-one" structure', *Population Science of China*, 2: 41–5.

UNDP (1999) *China Human Development Report 1999*, UNDP, New York.

Wu, Cangping (ed.) (1999) *Social Gerontology,* Publishing House of Renmin University of China, Beijing.

Yu, Xuejun (2000) *China's Response to Demographic Pressures: The Ageing Complex,* EF Texts and Reports Economic Policy and Poverty Reduction – Issue Notes and Background Papers, Development Policy Forum (EF), German Foundation for International Development.

Zhen, B. (1997) 'A study of Chinese community service policy', in G. White and X. Shang (eds.) *Reforms in Chinese Social Assistance and Community Services in Comparative Perspective*, Institute of Development Studies, Brighton.

Zuo, Xue-jin (2001) 'Challenge and options: elderly supporting system in the course of rapid ageing', *Chinese Journal of Population Science*, 3.

PART II

Formal Social Protection
and Older People

The evolution of formal social protection policy for older people over recent decades is typical of wider shifts in social protection philosophy. These have sought to respond to a generalised perception of a social policy 'crisis', and the need to reappraise the role of the state. They have been closely associated with an apparent paradigm shift away from state-centred welfarism, which emphasised solidarity and aspired to universality. In its place has come a neoliberal model that emphasises individual agency and institutional pluralism, while redefining the role of the public sector. This shift is reflected in international debates about social policies for older people, including pension reform and health care (Lloyd-Sherlock 1996). However, some of the basic precepts underlying this apparent paradigm change are open to question. Revisionists have cast some doubt on claims that Western welfare states are inherently inefficient and unsustainable (Stephens 1996). While social policies in developing countries suffer many shortcomings, they have often contributed to rapid improvements in basic indicators of well-being (Jolly 1997; Ghai 1997). In his discussion of pension programmes Barrientos finds that state-centred models (South Africa and Brazil) can sometimes out-perform those structured along neoliberal lines (Chile).

These debates are reflected in alternative models of financing, providing and regulating formal social protection. The first of these is the traditional state-centred model (Figure II.1), in which the public sector plays the leading role in provision, financing and regulation. The bold lines represent the boundaries of state action. The second is the idealised neoliberal model (Figure II.2), in which the public sector's main responsibilities are limited to safety nets and regulating other actors. These non-state actors may operate within a competitive framework (although there may be scope for widespread market failure), and may be subject to a combination of self-regulation and state oversight. As well as making tax payments, users are expected to meet at least part of the costs of state and non-state services. It should be stressed that these are ideal type models: even in the most developed welfare states there is an important element of non-state provision and financing.

The shift away from state involvement in social protection has been particularly noticeable in middle-income countries. Here, fiscal constraints remain acute, and the influence of multilateral organisations such as the World Bank and International Monetary Fund is much larger. The impact has been especially significant in middle-income countries where social policies were already reasonably well-developed, and where there was therefore more to be lost. In low-income countries, the situation is rather different. McIntyre's description of health in sub-Saharan Africa fits into the neoliberal approach mainly by default – states in the region simply lack the resources and infrastructure to play a larger role.

By contrast, few developed countries have profoundly reoriented their welfare policies in response to neoliberal dictates. In some cases, such as the USA, there was little scope for further reducing state involvement in social provision (barring occasional calls for the break-up of MEDICARE). In others, a strong ideological attachment to state welfarism and political barriers have precluded a radical overhaul of social policy. To some extent, the fiscal imperatives of the 1980s have relaxed somewhat since that time. A further reason is that hard evidence that privatised social policies work better than traditional models remains weak and highly contested (Colclough 1997; Uplekar 2000). While the wholesale privatisation of the social sectors may never have been a serious likelihood in developed countries, it is true that governments are becoming increasingly concerned about medium- and long-term financial pressures on existing arrangements. Efforts to promote efficiencies in the public sector and to stem the rise of public sector liabilities have encouraged a new paradigm, which locates state responsibilities within a more pluralistic model of social protection (Le Grand and Bartlett 1993; Londoño and Frenk 2000).

This third model, which might be termed the 'quasi-market alternative', is schematised in Figure II.3. Here, the public sector is still afforded a leading role in financing through social insurance, and may be allowed to compete with other actors in providing services. While originating in the North, this model is becoming increasingly influential in middle-income countries. The chapter by Ogawa examines a new initiative to establish a quasi-market in long-term care for older people in Japan. However, it is difficult to assess the effectiveness of the new system, as it has only been in operation for a short period. The chapter by Redondo examines similar systems that provide health insurance for pensioners in Argentina and the United States. The Argentine case is a cautionary one, demonstrating the pitfalls of a quasi-market approach when implemented in a context of weak regulation and governance. As Figure II.3 shows, quasi-market systems are more organisationally complex than neoliberal or state-centred ones. Advocates of quasi-market systems from other countries should not underestimate these problems.

The chapters in this section demonstrate that there is no single model of organising social protection for older people whose advantages clearly outweigh all the others wherever it is applied. It is becoming clear that no sector, be it the private sector, the state or the informal sector, can be expected to perform this role alone. Combining them in a way which both meets the needs of the most vulnerable older people and achieves intergenerational consensus represents the greatest challenge to policy makers over the coming decades.

REFERENCES

Colclough, C (ed.) (1997) *Marketizing Education and Health in Developing Countries. Miracle or Mirage?*, Clarendon Press, Oxford.

Ghai, D. (1997) 'Social development and public policy. Some lessons from successful experiences', UNRISD Discussion Paper No. 89, UNRISD, Geneva.

Jolly, R. (1997) 'Profiles in success: reasons for hope and priorities for action', in S. Mehrotra and R. Jolly (eds.), *Development with a Human Face: Experiences in Social Achievement and Economic Growth,* Clarendon Press, Oxford.

Le Grand, J. and W. Bartlett (eds.) (1993) *Quasi-Markets and Social Policy,* Macmillan, London.

Lloyd-Sherlock, P. (1996) 'The roles of the public and private sectors in providing economic support for the elderly', in P. Lloyd-Sherlock and P. Johnson (eds.), *Ageing and Social Policy: Global Comparisons,* Sticerd Publications, London.

Londoño, J. and J. Frenk (2000) 'Structured pluralism: towards an innovative model for health system reform in Latin America', in P. Lloyd-Sherlock (ed.), *Healthcare Reform and Poverty in Latin America,* Institute of Latin American Studies, London.

Stephens, J. (1996) 'The Scandinavian welfare states: achievements, crisis and prospects', in G. Esping-Andersen (ed.), *Welfare States in Transition: National Adaptations in Global Economies,* Sage, London.

Uplekar, M. (2000) 'Private health care', *Social Science and Medicine,* 51 (6): 897–904.

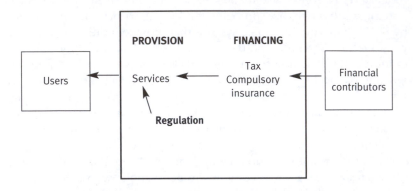

Figure II.1 The state–centred model of social protection

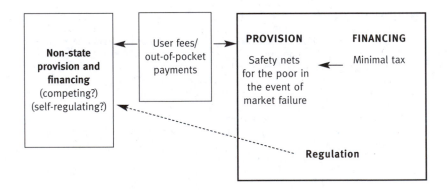

Figure II.2 The neoliberal model of social protection

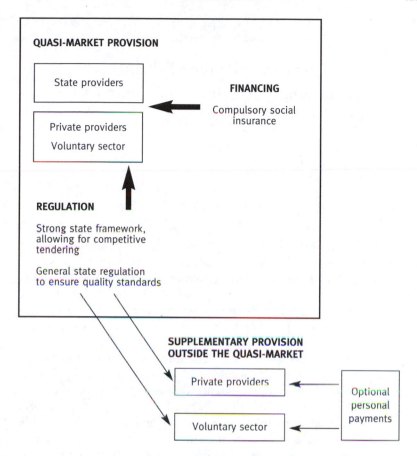

QUASI-MARKET PROVISION

State providers

Private providers

Voluntary sector

FINANCING

Compulsory social insurance

REGULATION

Strong state framework, allowing for competitive tendering

General state regulation to ensure quality standards

SUPPLEMENTARY PROVISION OUTSIDE THE QUASI-MARKET

Private providers

Voluntary sector

Optional personal payments

Figure II.3 The quasi-market model of social protection

CHAPTER 6

Comparing Pension Schemes in Chile, Singapore, Brazil and South Africa

ARMANDO BARRIENTOS

The 1990s could well qualify as the decade of global pension reform. A number of countries in Latin America and transition economies radically transformed their pension provision, and moved swiftly in the direction of privately provided individual retirement plans. The blueprint for pension reform in these countries was provided by Chile's 1981 pension reform (Barrientos 1998). The World Bank has played a key role in supporting and financing this model of pension reform elsewhere in the developing world. The spread of pension reform can be seen as a response to the accelerated demographic and epidemiological transitions in developing countries thrusting the issue of old age support to the forefront of development policy. In fact, pension reform has been embedded within structural adjustment, and has largely constituted a response to fiscal deficits and labour market liberalisation. This has narrowed the potential range of policy responses to demographic change available to developing countries. This chapter uses a comparative perspective to examine the role of pensions in old age support, and to draw attention to the variety of pension provision in the developing world.[1]

The issue of how to organise pension provision and old age support in developing countries is now increasingly coming to the fore. The World Bank's 1994 report on 'Averting the old age crisis: policies to protect the old *and* promote growth' raised the profile of ageing as an issue in the context of development policy, but within an unfortunate context of 'crisis' (World Bank, 1994). Although the report recommended developing countries adopt multi–pillar pension systems, the Bank subsequently focused almost exclusively on supporting the introduction of individual retirement saving plans. This was rationalised in terms of significant economic advantages claimed to flow from these plans, including improved work and saving incentives, the strengthening of capital markets and reduced fiscal deficits. The OECD's 1998 report 'Maintaining prosperity in an ageing society' reflected a more balanced approach to the policy responses needed to accommodate population ageing (OECD 1998). According to this report, pension reform is needed in the context of a wider 'active ageing' framework. It suggests a more gradual approach to pension reform in developed countries, focusing on raising the economic contribution of the old by extending their economic activity and supporting interventions that improve their wellbeing.

With the spread of pension reform in the 1990s, and the discussions that have attended it, insufficient attention has been paid to the variety of pension provision in the South. The selection of countries for this comparative study makes this point well. Chile's individual retirement plans have taken a paradigmatic role in pension reform among developing countries. Employees contribute a fraction of their earnings to a retirement account managed by private pension fund managers. These collect the contribution into a fund which is invested in a range of financial assets. At retirement, employees use the balance of their individual accounts to purchase an annuity. To date, pension fund returns have been satisfactory, but administrative costs are high, and the proportion of the labour force contributing on a regular basis has declined. Singapore's Central Provident Fund provides a different model of old age support. Compulsory payroll contributions are collected into a fund managed by the government, and the individual accounts are credited with a fixed rate of return. Affiliates can use their savings for a range of merit expenditures, including health, housing and education. The proportion of the labour force contributing on a regular basis is high, and the administration of the fund minimises administrative costs. Individual retirement plans and the provident fund model reflect dominant models of pension provision in Latin America and South Asia respectively.

Less conspicuous, but very important in the context of development policy, are the experiences of pension reform during the 1990s in South Africa and Brazil. In South Africa, the fall of apartheid led to the universalisation of pension benefits, by abolishing the discrimination in entitlements and access to pensions suffered by blacks. The social pension provides a regular source of income to elders and their house-holds, and is proving to be a powerful instrument of development, by supporting households' economic activity and raising investment in physical and human capital. The 'social pension' has led to a significant improvement in the status of elders within their households. In Brazil, a new constitution adopted in 1988 extended social security entitlements (*prêvidencia rural*) to elders in rural communities and in informal employment. Implemented in 1993, rural pensions have provided a significant boost to households' economic activity and have had an important impact on poverty. The experiences of Brazil and South Africa show that universalising basic pension schemes can have a measurable impact on poverty, the wellbeing of elders and economic development.

A comparison of pension schemes in Chile, Singapore, South Africa, and Brazil can yield important lessons for old age support policies in developing countries. There are, of course, technical issues of design and implementation which a comparison of this sort can illuminate, but the main concern of this chapter is to examine the significance of pension schemes for the livelihoods and security of older people in selected developing countries. The chapter begins by explaining what pension schemes do. The following section outlines the main features of pension provision in the selected countries. Separate sections discuss the significance of pension benefits within old age support, and the population and risk coverage of pension schemes. A final section summarises the main conclusions.

What can pensions do?

Pension plans perform three main functions: consumption smoothing, insurance and redistribution. Differences in pension design reflect differences in the social values and policy priorities of pension designers and have implications for the extent to which pension plans can perform these functions. In large measure, the current debate on pension design is really about the capacity of pension plans to address specific policy objectives. These issues are explored in this section and provide a foundation for the discussion that follows.

The main functions of pension plans

Income varies significantly over the life course of an individual and the household, and this is especially true for the majority who rely on labour earnings as their main source of income. The need arises to shield household consumption from some of the variation in income. In stylised descriptions of the life course during the 'golden age' (see Figure 6.1), consumption exceeds income during an initial phase including the period of family formation. Then, as earnings rise with age and household expenditures decline as children leave home, income rises above consumption up to retirement. During retirement, households use their accumulated savings to provide the necessary income. In Figure 6.1, consumption is represented as a constant over the life course.[2] A key function of pension plans is to enable individuals and

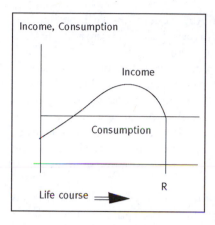

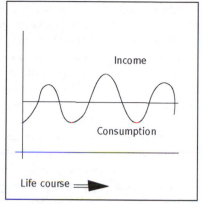

Figure 6.1 The golden age   **Figure 6.2 The 'age of insecurity'**

households to smooth consumption over the life course, by collecting saving during people's working lives and transferring this income to retirement.

Current economic conditions are very different from those in the 'golden age'. Economic crises, cuts in public programmes and labour market insecurity ensure that income variation over the life course is much greater (see Figure 6.2). This is the 'age of insecurity', perhaps, and as a consequence the capacity of households to ensure steady consumption is greatly diminished. It is to be expected that pension plans would need to cope with added pressures in order to smooth consumption in the new conditions.

A second function of pension plans is to provide insurance against a range of contingencies that otherwise may affect household consumption adversely. A key contingency covered by pension plans is longevity risk, the risk that we may outlive our accumulated resources. Uncertainty over the time of death is a primary factor in explaining the establishment of pension plans.[3] Pension plans also insure against short lives, especially through benefits to dependent survivors in the event of the death of the breadwinner. Pension plans cover risks to the length of the working life, such as sickness, disability, or unemployment. Depending on the detail of pension plan design, other contingencies may be covered. Some pension plans have indexed pension benefits, and therefore protect beneficiaries against inflation risks. Where pension plans calculate benefits with a formula based on some averaging of earnings, they effectively provide insurance against gaps in employment or variations in earnings.[4] The insurance function of pension plans is extremely important (especially in the age of insecurity), but the insurance properties of pension plans are little understood, and as a result greatly undervalued (Diamond 1996).

Pension plans can also perform a redistributive function. They collect contributions from one group and pay benefits to a different group, enabling the pursuit of social norms and policy objectives with regards to the distribution of income in society. Pension plans can redistribute income across generations, for example by transferring income from those in work to those in retirement. They can also redistribute income within generations, for example by skewing entitlements in favour of women, or poorer pensioners.

When focusing on pension outcomes, it is easy to conflate the effects of the insurance and distributive functions. *Ex post*, insurance redistributes premium income towards those groups affected by the insured contingencies. In travel insurance, for example, premium income will be allocated to the insured who experience cancellations, sickness or loss of luggage. *Ex ante* insurance results in *ex post* redistribution (Diamond 1996). This is different from discretionary redistribution, for example, where entitlements are calculated on the basis of a unisex formula purposely benefiting women who on average live longer than men. In this case, an *ex ante* redistributive pension formula results in *ex post* income redistribution. The distinction is important. We may rightly argue over the desirability and effectiveness of *ex ante* redistribution, and over the right amount of redistribution, but *ex ante* insurance is generally agreed to be welfare-enhancing.

Pension plan design and functions

Differences in pension plan design reflect different social priorities and norms, as well as judgements concerning the effectiveness of pension plans in performing the functions above. The wide variety of pension plan designs in the world demonstrates an equally wide range of views on this (Palacios and Pallarés-Millares 2000). It would be useful at this point to run through some typologies of pension plans. In *unfunded* pension plans, the contributions of active members are used to pay for the benefits of pensioners, and there is no fund accumulation. These are also known as pay-as-you-go pension plans. *Funded* pension plans accumulate the contributions of an individual or a group into a fund which is used to pay for their pension benefits. Some pension plans set the benefits according to a pre-established formula and vary contributions to cover the resulting liabilities. These are known as *defined benefit* pension plans. *Defined contribution* pension plans, in contrast, set the contribution level and allow pension benefits to vary. *Contributory* pension plans link entitlements to the contribution history of individual

members, while *non-contributory* pension plans provide entitlements independent of past contributions, but associated with old age or a specific
contingency such as disability. *Provident funds* enjoy a dual role in
providing basic social security (old age pension included) and as a source
of long-term finance for development projects (McKinnon 1996).

A less traceable distinction is the one existing between *public* and
private pension plans. It is hard to find purely private pension plans, and
it is increasingly difficult to find purely public pension plans. Governments have in most countries a substantial role in establishing private
pension plans by legislating compulsory affiliation, and discharge an
even larger role in regulating, supervising and guaranteeing seemingly private pension plans. On the other hand, public pension plans
increasingly rely on private fund managers and advisers, as well as on
private contribution collection, record keeping and benefit payment.

Pensions in Chile, Singapore, Brazil and South Africa

This section provides a brief outline of the main pension schemes in the
four selected countries. Table 6.1 presents these in summary form.

Chile

Pension provision in Chile dates back to the 1920s, when social
insurance funds (*Cajas de Previsión*) were established for specific categories of workers providing old age and retirement pensions (Arellano
1980). These were funded from payroll contributions from employees
and employers, with benefits determined by final earnings and
contributory history. After the 1950s there was rapid growth in the
number and coverage of social insurance funds. By 1976 there were
over 35 social insurance funds covering three quarters of the labour
force against a wide range of contingencies including disability, dependants, health costs and unemployment. This expansion was financed by
raising contribution levels and by fiscal transfers. The military
government, which took power in 1973, imposed fundamental reform
of social insurance in 1980 (Barrientos 1998). Individual retirement
saving plans managed by private pension fund managers were
introduced for new entrants to the labour force, while existing workers
were offered substantial inducements to switch their pension entitlements to the new pension plans. Concerns over the sustainability of the
old social insurance pension plans, and the initial high investment
returns of the new saving plans, led a majority of workers in the old
social insurance schemes to migrate to the new saving plans.

In the new individual retirement plans, workers contribute 10 per
cent of their earnings to a retirement saving account kept with one of

Table 6.1 Main features of pension schemes in Chile, Singapore, Brazil and South Africa

	Chile	Singapore	Brazil	South Africa
Main pension plan:				
Type	Individual retirement saving plans	Provident fund	Social insurance[a]	Social assistance
Pension beneficiaries	0.365 million	n/d	7.05 million	1.42 million
Pension benefit	Annuity from account balance at retirement	Lump sum withdrawal at retirement	Benefit formula based on contribution record and final salary	Difference between maximum benefit and means tested income
Financed through	Payroll contributions: employee 10% of earnings	Payroll contributions: employee 20% of earnings, employer 20% of payroll	Payroll contributions, taxes on profits, and output, general tax revenues	General tax revenues
Minimum pension benefit	4/5 minimum wage	None	1 minimum wage	Maximum benefit
Other contributory pension plans:				
Type	(i) Social insurance (payg[b] – closed to new entrants) (ii) Military and police (payg – defined benefit)	(i) High civil servants (closed to new entrants) (ii) Individual retirement saving plans (non-residents)	Private complementary plans (defined benefit and defined contribution)	Private occupational plans (defined benefit, defined contribution, and provident fund)
Number (millions) of members or accounts	0.243 members	n/d	1.65 members	9.3 accounts
Number of funds	2	2	362	16,000
Assets as % GDP	Not applicable	Civil servants fund 7.3	14.0	73
Other assistential pension programmes:				
	For over 70s, ¼ of minimum wage	n/a	For those aged 67 and over in urban areas (6.5m.); and 60/55 in rural areas (6.5m), 1 minimum wage	n/a
Public expenditure on pensions as a % of GDP	5.9 (1996)	1.4 (1996)	7.8 (1995)	2–3 (1990)

[a] Social insurance includes contributory and assistential pension plans, but the latter are described below.
[b] pay-as-you-go; n/a – not applicable; n/d – no data
Sources: Compiled from a number of data sources (Chan and Cheung 1997; Case and Deaton 1998; Central Statistics Service 1998; Camarano 1999; Mideplan 1999; Barrientos 2000; ILO 2000; UNDP 2000).

the pension fund managers (*Administradoras de Fondos de Pensiones*). These manage the retirement savings with the returns being credited to the individual retirement accounts. The pension fund managers are permitted a range of charges including a fixed monthly commission and an earnings–related commission on contributions. On paper, pension fund managers compete for affiliates on their rates of return, commission levels, and quality of service, and workers can switch pension fund managers in search of the best deal. In practice, competition is rather limited as pension fund managers have very similar results, and administrative constraints make transfers possible only twice yearly (Barrientos 1999).

The government retains a substantial role in pension provision. It mandates affiliation to a pension plan for workers in dependent employment. It licenses and regulates pension fund managers as regards their financial products, rates of return, incidence of commissions, investment portfolios and information disclosure. It guarantees retirement savings against pension fund failure, and underwrites poorly performing pension fund managers. It partially guarantees pension annuities, and guarantees a minimum pension for workers with twenty years of contributions but insufficient funds. Given the substantial role of government, it is difficult to describe pension provision in Chile as private.

Singapore

Singapore established a provident fund in 1955 as a means of encouraging saving for retirement (Asher and Karunarathne 2001). Colonial administrators had a large role to play in designing provident funds as a provisional scheme until such time as economic development created the conditions for the establishment of social insurance (McKinnon *et al.* 1997). Provident funds have a number of specific features distinguishing them from social insurance pensions. In common with all contributory pension plans, provident funds collect earnings–related contributions into a fund which is invested in interest-yielding assets, but in addition to retirement-related withdrawals, provident funds allow withdrawals for a range of merit expenditures. In Singapore, these include housing, health and tertiary education. Compared to conventional pension schemes, provident funds are broad saving instruments and extend beyond pension provision. A feature of Singapore's provident fund is that the accumulated balances are invested in government debt issued for this specific purpose and unavailable for trade in secondary markets. The investment of the savings collected by the provident fund is largely determined by government's social and economic objectives, and the rates of return paid to individualised saving accounts are the outcome, in practice, of an administrative process.

In Singapore, native and permanently resident workers in dependent employment are required to contribute to the provident fund, and their employers are also required to make an additional contribution on their behalf. Independent workers can contribute to a retirement account on a voluntary basis, but are required to contribute to a health insurance account. Smaller pension schemes are available for high-ranking civil servants and foreign workers (Asher and Karunarathne 2001).

Brazil

In common with other Latin American countries, pension provision developed in the 1920s in Brazil based on social insurance principles. In 1964, the social insurance funds were consolidated into a nationwide public social insurance system. Brazil's large share of informal employment restricted the coverage of social insurance, and only one in two dependent workers, and one in ten independent workers, contributed to the system. The coverage of contingencies was more ambitious. The social insurance system provided old age, service, disability and survivor pensions, as well as sickness and work-related injuries benefits, maternity leave, health care, and support for childbirth and funeral costs, family benefits and unemployment. Pensions were generous in terms of entitlement conditions and the value of the benefits. Among pensioned civil servants, one in two men and two in three women retired before reaching the age of 55 (Barreto de Oliveira and Iwakami Beltrao 2001). The system was financed by contributions from workers, employers and the government. Payroll contributions rose significantly over time to around 40 per cent of earnings [5] and became a matter for concern because of their impact upon employment, and labour market segmentation (Amadeo, Paes e Barros *et al.* 1995; Amadeo and Camargo 1997). The acute deterioration in labour market conditions in the 1980s reinforced a vicious circle of rising payroll contributions, triggering a rise in informality, evasion, avoidance and fraud, in turn leading to ever higher contribution rates. Social insurance deficits, at present around 1 per cent of GDP, are predicted to rise to 5 per cent of GDP in 2050.

The return to democracy after 20 years of dictatorship encouraged a new 'social contract' which crystallised in the 1988 constitution.[6] Issues of social protection and social insurance took centre stage, and the new constitution enshrined the principle of universal entitlement to social security. In terms of pension provision in rural areas, this involved a significant extension of pension entitlements. A social assistance pension introduced in rural areas in the early 1970s paid a flat rate benefit of around one half of a minimum wage to elders from age 65. As the pension was restricted to one person per household, women were in most cases excluded. The implementation of the new constitutional principle meant the elimination of this restriction, the reduction of the age of entitlement to 55 for women and 60 for men, and the increase in the level of the benefit to one minimum wage (Delgado and Cardoso 2000). At the same time, social assistance pension provision has been targeted on poor urban elders.

In parallel, complementary private pension provision experienced significant growth. Brazil is unique in Latin America in having a large private occupational pension market. There are 362 pension funds in Brazil covering 1.61 million workers and controlling assets valued at around 14 per cent of GDP (Yermo 2000; Barreto de Oliveira and Iwakami Beltrao 2001). More recently, the new Plan Gerador de Beneficios Livres, modelled on the USA's defined contribution 401k plans, has expanded rapidly.

The need to curb rising deficits in the public social insurance system, and to regulate private pension provision more effectively, led the Cardoso government to submit proposals for reform. After a long process of scrutiny by parliament, a constitutional amendment was approved in 1998, and gradually since then enabling legislation has been coming on stream. A key change is the reformulation of pension benefits in the public system. The new formula *Fator Previdenciário* introduces an adjustment to pension benefits that takes account of a person's contribution record, and her age and life expectancy at retirement. This is intended to discourage early retirement and will be phased in over a five-year period. As regards private pension provision, new regulations aim to standardise products and to clarify their tax exemptions with a view to encouraging their expansion.

South Africa

In South Africa, pension provision dates back to the 1920s with the development of occupational pension funds for whites.[7] Pension provision has been strongly segmented along racial lines, reflecting the social structure in South Africa. From 1956, occupational pension plans were established for less skilled white workers in formal employment, and over time they were extended to include other races. Van der Berg (1998) reports that by 1993 there were 9.3 million members in 16,000 pension funds controlling assets valued at 73 per cent of GDP. Around 40 per cent of the labour force are covered by occupational pension plans, but rates of coverage for blacks are significantly lower. As affiliation to an occupational pension plan is not mandatory, and private pension providers are not regulated, occupational pension plans show a variety of defined benefit, defined contribution and provident fund design (Aitken 1999).

The main source of old age support for the majority of elders is the social pension, a non-contributory pension plan paying a means-tested old age, disability and survivor pension benefit. It evolved from a safety net pension for poor whites, but was later extended to coloureds in 1928 and blacks in 1944 (van der Berg 1998). Blacks faced more stringent means tests and received much reduced pension benefits, compared to whites (Lund 1993). The fall of apartheid led to full parity in entitlements to the social pension and to a rapid rise in take-up rates among blacks. The social pension is financed through general tax revenues. Entitlements start at age 60 for women and 65 for men, and require a means test of the income of the beneficiary and spouse. This assesses private income and assets, but excludes output from subsistence agriculture and housing assets. Below a threshold level of income, the pension benefit, around US$70 per month, is paid in full. Above this threshold, the benefit is reduced at a rate of 50 per cent of extra income.

How important are pensions to older people's livelihoods?

It is important to place pension provision within the broader context of old age support. Although a detailed comparative analysis of the livelihoods of older people in the countries under investigation is beyond the scope of this chapter, brief reference will be made to labour force participation, household support and income sources of older people.[8] Table 6.2 below provides basic country information.

Participation in the labour market among elders is higher in Chile and Brazil, and markedly lower in Singapore and South Africa. Cross-country studies of the labour force participation of elders have concluded

Table 6.2 Some indicators of older people's livelihoods

	Chile	Singapore	Brazil	South Africa
Share of population over 60 (%)	10.2	10.5	7.8	5.7
Labour force participation of over-64s (%)	37.4	9.7	15.9	12.8
Mean size of households with older people	c3.3	n/a	2.98	6.0[a]
Per cent of older people living alone	9.6	3.0	17.1	n/a
Per cent of older households with children	n/a	35.4	49.1	58.3[a]

n/a not available
[a] refers to households with a pension recipient.
Sources: Chan and Cheung 1997; Case and Deaton 1998; Central Statistics Service 1998; Camarano 1999; Mideplan 1999; Barrientos 2000; ILO 2000; UNDP 2000.

it is inversely related to the coverage and generosity of pension provision, and the share of formal employment (Clark *et al.* 1997, 1999). The higher labour force participation of elders in Chile and Brazil reflects both gaps in pension entitlements and the incidence of informal employment. In South Africa, the fact that the social pension is means-tested is likely to discourage employment among elders. The low rate of labour force participation among elders in Singapore results from the strength of old age support, and relative affluence. In Brazil, Chile and Singapore, the majority of economically active elders work on their own account, as opposed to formal salaried employment (Barrientos 2000; Delgado and Cardoso 2000).

The living arrangements of older people can provide some indication of the strength of household support, although great care needs to be taken here not to assume intra-household support directly from co-residence. In Singapore, a very small fraction of elders who had at least one child live alone, around 3 per cent. The overwhelming majority of elders live with their children and grandchildren (Chan and Cheung 1997). In Chile, households with older persons are on average smaller, with fewer children and more females, than households without them (Mideplan 1999). The same is true of Brazil (Camarano 1999). In South Africa, Case and Deaton (1998) find that households with at least one pension beneficiary are larger and have more children than households without one. When disaggregated by race, an important difference emerges between white and black households. While the majority of white older people live alone, or with other older people, three-generation households are the rule among black households with pensioners. The incidence of co-residence of children with older people is high. In South Africa, Case and Deaton find that of 'the 11.9 million African children under the age of 16, 3.8 million (32 per cent) live with a social pensioner' (1998: 1340). In Brazil, nearly one half of households with older people have co-resident children. Co-residence of elders and children provides some indication of the significant role of households in providing old age support, and suggests pension provision is likely to have a wider impact on the households of beneficiaries.

How important is the contribution of pension income and labour earnings to household income? Pension income is 44 per cent of average household income among blacks in South Africa, and income from labour a further 40 per cent. Among whites, pension income is only 7.3 per cent, with labour earnings contributing another 26 per cent. For Chile, pension income for the average household with a member over 60 is 42.8 per cent of all household income, with labour income contributing a further 44.9 per cent. Among poorer households in Chile, those in the lowest quintile of per capita household income, non-contributory pensions and widows' pension benefits provide 40 per cent of household income. In Brazil, older persons contribute a significant share of household income, at 53.5 per cent. As the contribution of their labour earnings to household income is much lower at 7.1 per cent, it is likely that their pension income accounts for a large part of the difference. In Singapore the identification of separate sources of income is more difficult because of substantial intra-household transfers and the availability of withdrawals from the provident fund. In a survey of old persons in Singapore, Chan reports that 52.3 per cent of respondents were primarily self-supporting, with the remaining 47.7 per cent identifying allowances from children as their main source of financial support (Chan and Cheung 1997).

We can be much less confident in discussing the level and adequacy of older people's income. Reported figures on the income of older people need to be interpreted with great care.[9] In Chile, the incidence of poverty among older people appears to be lower than for the population as a whole. Headcount poverty is 16.6 per cent in rural areas and 9.7 per cent in urban areas for over-60s, compared to 20.7 and 27.6 per cent respectively for the population as a whole (Mideplan 1999). For South Africa, Case and Deaton report that the ratio of per capita household income for households with a pension recipient to the per capita income for all households is 0.6 for blacks and 0.9 for whites (Case and Deaton 1998). In Singapore, the mean independent income of elders is not very high, with just under 60 per cent of elders reporting income below one half of average earnings in 1995 (Chan and Cheung 1997; Asher and Karunarathne 2001). However, the vast majority of elders find their financial status is adequate (89.2 per cent of males and 89.1 per cent of females), mainly because of significant transfers from their children.

In sum, household transfers, labour earnings and pension income are the main sources of old age support in the countries under investigation. Labour force participation among elders is highest in the two Latin American countries, and probably this in part reflects the very large informal sector in the region. A majority of elders works on their own account. Only a minority of elders live alone; the majority co-reside with their extended family and children. The extent of co-residence is greatest among blacks and lowest among whites in South Africa. Household support for the elderly is extensive in Singapore, to the extent that it is difficult to identify independent income sources of the elderly. Pension income is a significant contributor to household income, and this is especially the case for poorer households in South Africa, Brazil and Chile.

What protection do pension schemes provide?

The effectiveness of pension schemes in providing an insurance component of old age support can be gauged by considering pension scheme coverage, both in terms of risks and population. Table 6.3 below presents summary indicators of coverage.

Table 6.3 Pension scheme coverage

	Chile	Singapore	Brazil	South Africa
Population coverage				
Pensioners as % of population	4.0	3.0	3.2	4.0[a]
Pensioners as % of population over 64	61.1	52.0	67.3	61.1[a]
Active contributors as % of labour force	45	65	40	n/a
Informal share of urban employment	30.3	n/a	48.2	17.4
Risk coverage				
Longevity risk	yes	no	yes	yes
Disability risk	yes	yes	yes	yes
Dependent survivor	yes	no	yes	yes
Inflation risk	yes	no	partial	partial
Political risk	low	high	medium	medium

[a] refers to social pension recipients and age-qualified recipients only.
n/a – not applicable
Sources: Chan and Cheung 1997; Case and Deaton 1998; Central Statistics Service 1998; Camarano 1999; Mideplan 1999; Barrientos 2000; ILO 2000; UNDP 2000.

Starting with population coverage, Table 6.3 provides information on two key indicators: the proportion of the old who are currently receiving pension benefits, and the proportion of the labour force who are contributing to a pension plan. The share of pensioners in the population is very similar across the countries involved, at around 3–4 per cent. For the purposes of this measure, pensioners are those receiving a pension benefit from the main pension schemes. The share of pensioners in the older population as a whole is also similar across countries at around 60 per cent. However, the factors explaining why a significant proportion of the old are not receiving pensions are different in different countries. In Chile, Singapore and Brazil, pension entitlements are dependent on contribution history. Those not entitled to a pension benefit are mainly women who did not participate in the labour market for significant periods of their working lives, and a minority of very wealthy individuals who were never in a pension scheme. In Chile and urban Brazil, where safety net pensions are available from a very late age (70 and 67 respectively) for those without any means of support, elders under the age of entitlement are an important group among the poor. In South Africa, on the other hand, the fact that social pensions are means-tested implies that those not receiving a pension benefit are on the whole those with significant income from other sources. Some in this group are probably in receipt of a private pension. In Singapore, the majority of those not entitled to a pension are women and those previously self-employed.

The proportion of the labour force contributing to a pension plan provides a good indication of future pension receipt coverage among pensioners. As can be seen from the figures in Table 6.3, a majority of current workers in Chile and Brazil are not contributing to a pension scheme, with the implication that a majority of the future elderly will not be entitled to pension benefits. The explanation for this is straight-forward: the decline in pension scheme coverage among workers in Latin America is the mirror image of the expansion of informal employ-ment in the region. In Singapore the majority of those not contributing to one of the main pension schemes are the self-employed and workers with low earnings and irregular employment.

As regards coverage of contingencies, longevity risk is not covered by the provident fund because there is no requirement that retirement withdrawals be used to purchase an annuity or equivalent. In the Chilean case, retirees have a choice of taking up an annuity or agreeing a scheduled withdrawal with a formula taking account of life expec-tancy. Longevity risks are covered by the pension schemes in Brazil and South Africa because the benefits are paid until the death of the beneficiary. All pension schemes provide insurance against the death or disability of the breadwinner. Only Chile's pension scheme provides coverage against inflation because the annuity contracts are set in inflation-adjusted units (*Unidades de Fomento*). There is partial coverage in Brazil because the pension benefit has to be at least one minimum wage, and coverage against inflation risk depends on the mechanism for adjusting the minimum wage. In South Africa, the pension benefit is adjusted for changes in prices, but this is a discretionary policy variable.

Because all pension schemes have a significant government input, pension income is subject to political risk, sometimes referred to as 'policy risk' – the risk being that government decisions have a large impact upon pension income. Because of its multi-dimensional nature, political risk is more difficult to evaluate. In the Chilean case, government is limited in its ability to alter the parameters of the pension scheme, which is why a low score was awarded to political risk (Diamond 1994). Having said this, projections of future pension benefits suggest that as many as one half of current workers will only receive the government-guaranteed minimum pension, and the level for this is a policy variable. In Singapore, the government determines the rate of return applied to provident fund accounts, and because of this a 'high' score was awarded. In Brazil and South Africa, the nature of the pension scheme means that governments have a direct input into contribution rates or the benefit formula, or both. On the other hand, strong political support for the pension schemes sets definite limits to the scope for government interventions.

Conclusions

The chapter has provided a comparative analysis of pension schemes in Chile, Singapore, Brazil and South Africa, in the context of their role in old age support in the developing world. The recent spread of pension reform in the developing world has drawn attention to the importance of pensions in contributing to the livelihoods and security of older people in developing countries. There is a wide range of pension provision in developing countries, justifying a comparative analysis. Chile relies on individual retirement plans, managed by private providers. Singapore's main pension scheme is the Central Provident Fund, which collects payroll contributions and manages individual accounts for its members. In contrast to the Chilean pension scheme, it allows withdrawals for merit expenditures on tertiary education, housing and health. Brazil and South Africa have attempted to universalise basic pension provision. In South Africa the social pension provides a basic benefit targeted on the poor. In Brazil, the expansion of social insurance to workers in informal and rural employment has resulted in a large increase in coverage of the rural older population. These pension schemes demonstrate the range of pension provision models in the developing world.

Pension income is an important component of the income of older households, although labour earnings and intra-household transfers are also important. In the countries studied, there is strong evidence of co-residence of elders with their children and grandchildren, and labour force participation rates are higher for the two Latin American countries, where older people are predominantly self-employed. Pensions make a significant contribution to the livelihoods of older people and their households.

Pensions also make a key contribution to the security of older people and their households, although the population coverage of pension schemes varies significantly across countries. The proportion of the labour force contributing to a pension scheme is below 50 per cent in Chile and Brazil, but around 65 per cent in Singapore. This is in large part explained by the incidence of informal employment in the first two countries. The proportion of the population over 65 receiving a pension is similar across countries, ranging from 52 per cent in Singapore to 67 per cent in Brazil. There are also important differences in the coverage of contingencies across countries.

There are important lessons from this comparative analysis for the future of pensions in the developing world. Pensions are important to older people's livelihoods and security, but they are also an important instrument of social protection and poverty reduction, and can make an important contribution to economic development. The variety of pension provision in the developing world helps identify the relative effectiveness of different elements of pension design, but warns us against fixing on a single, unique pension design suitable for all developing countries. The broad objectives of pension reform are as important. The examples of Brazil and South Africa show that attempts at universalising pension provision focused on the poor can be effective and can attract popular support. In the context of the accelerated demographic and epidemiological transitions currently under way in the developing world, the main challenge will be to develop pension schemes into integrated old age support programmes covering health and long-term care.

NOTES

1 I am grateful to Francie Lund, Peter Lloyd-Sherlock and Ana Maria Camarano for helpful comments and information. The errors that remain are all mine.
2 This is grounded on economic theory. Given the assumptions first that individuals derive the same utility from a dollar of consumption throughout their life course, and second that utility declines at the margin when consumption rises, it follows that total lifetime utility is maximised when consumption is the same through the life course.
3 As a general rule, people's expectations of length of life are based on observation of previous cohorts. As there are large improvements in life expectancy from one cohort to another, length of life expectations are very likely to be wrong by an order of magnitude.
4 In the UK, for example, the calculation of the state basic pension benefit takes account of up to ten years of home responsibility (indicated by receipt of child or disability care benefits).
5 Barreto de Oliveira and Beltrao (2001) note that employee contributions are on average 10 per cent of earnings, while employer contributions are on average 22 per cent, and in addition the unemployment insurance contribution is 8 per cent. There are also employer contributions calculated on profits and revenues.
6 Brumer (2002) traces the influence of political mobilisation on the extension of social insurance.
7 On the background to the social pension in South Africa see Devereux (2001). There

are a number of papers providing a overview of pension provision in southern Africa (Barbone and Sanchez 1999; Fultz and Pieris 1999).

8 The section draws from papers examining the livelihoods of older people using household survey data collected in the 1990s (1993 for South Africa, 1995 for Singapore, 1996 for Brazil, and 1994 and 1998 for Chile) (Chan and Cheung 1997; Case and Deaton 1998; Central Statistics Service 1998; Camarano 1999; Mideplan 1999; Barrientos 2000).

9 There are few comparative studies on the adequacy of older people's income. Whitehouse (2000) looks at a sample of countries, mainly advanced economies, and finds that older people are under-represented in lower-income groups and over-represented in higher-income groups. The income measures normally used are biased against finding poverty among the old (Barrientos 2002). The conventional methodology is to add all sources of household income and divide by the number of household members, generating a measure of *per capita* household income. As noted above, older people live predominantly in smaller households with fewer children, except for South African blacks. Because the relative cost of children is lower than older people, and because of the presence of economies of scale in household consumption, this measure biases poverty incidence among the old downwards (Deaton and Paxson 1997, 1998).

REFERENCES

Aitken, I. M. (1999) 'South Africa: the occupational pension scheme', *Journal of Pensions Management*, 5 (1): 69–75.

Amadeo, E., R. Paes e Barros, J. M. Camargo and R. Mendonca (1995) 'Brazil', in G. Márquez (ed.), *Reforming the Labor Market in a Liberalized Economy*, Inter-American Development Bank, Washington DC.

Amadeo, E. J. and J. M. Camargo (1997) 'Brazil: regulation and flexibility in the labor market', in S. Edwards and N. C. Lustig (eds.), *Labor Markets in Latin America: Combining Social Protection with Market Flexibility*, Brookings Institution Press, Washington DC.

Arellano, J. P. (1980) 'Sistemas alternativos de seguridad social: un análisis de la experiencia Chilena', *Colección de Estudios CIEPLAN*, 4 (November): 119–57.

Asher, M. G. and W. Karunarathne (2001) 'Social security arrangements in Singapore: an assessment', mimeo, University of Singapore.

Barbone, L. and L. A. Sanchez B. (1999) 'Pensions and social security in sub-Saharan Africa: issues and options', Africa Region Working Paper Series 4, World Bank, Washington DC.

Barreto de Oliveira, F. E. and K. Iwakami Beltrao (2001) 'The Brazilian social security system', *International Social Security Review*, 54 (1): 101–12.

Barrientos, A. (1998) *Pension Reform in Latin America*, Ashgate, Aldershot.

—— (1999) 'The emerging pension fund management market in Latin America', *Journal of Pensions Management*, 5 (1): 60–8.

—— (2000) 'Work, retirement, and vulnerability of older workers in Latin America. What are the lessons for pension design?', *Journal of International Development*, 12: 495–506.

—— (2002) 'Old age, poverty, and social investment', *Journal of International Development*, 14 (8): 1133–42.

Brumer, A. (2002) 'Gender relations and rural social security in Southern Brazil', in C. Abel and C. Lewis (eds.), *Exclusion and Engagement: Social Policy in Latin America*, Institute of Latin American Studies, London.

Camarano, A. A. (1999) 'Como vai o idoso Brasileiro?', *Discussion Paper 681*, IPEA, Rio de Janeiro.

Case, A. and A. Deaton (1998) 'Large scale transfers to the elderly in South Africa',

Economic Journal, 108 (450): 1330–61.

Central Statistics Service (1998) *Living in South Africa: Selected Findings of the 1995 October Household Survey*, CSS, Pretoria.

Chan, A. and P. Cheung (1997) 'The interrelationship between public and private support for the elderly: what can we learn from the Singaporean case?', *Elderly in Asia Research Report Series 97–41*, Population Studies Center, University of Michigan, Ann Arbor.

Clark, R. L., E. A. York and R. Anker (1997) 'Retirement and economic development: an international analysis', in P. R. de Jong and T. R. Marmor (eds.), *Social Policy and the Labour Market*, Ashgate, Aldershot, pp. 117–45.

Clark, R. L., E. A. York and R. Anker (1999) 'Economic development and labour force participation of older persons', *Population Research and Policy Review*, 18: 411–32.

Deaton, A. and C. Paxson (1997) 'Poverty among children and the elderly in developing countries', mimeo, Research Program in Development Studies, Princeton University, Princeton.

Deaton, A. and C. Paxson (1998) 'Economies of scale, household size, and the demand for food', *Journal of Political Economy*, 106 (5): 897–930.

Delgado, G. and J. C. Cardoso (eds.) (2000) *A Universalizacao de Direitos Sociais no Brasil: a Previdencia Rural nos anos 90*, IPEA, Brasilia.

Devereux, S. (2001) 'Social pensions in Namibia and South Africa', IDS Discussion Paper 379, IDS, Falmer.

Diamond, P. (1994) 'Insulation of pensions from political risk', Working Paper 4895, National Bureau for Economic Research, Cambridge MA.

Diamond, P. (1996) 'Government provision and regulation of economic support in old age', in M. Bruno and B. Pleskovic (eds.), *Annual World Bank Conference on Development Economics 1995*, World Bank, Washington DC.

Fultz, E. and B. Pieris (1999) 'Social security schemes in Southern Africa', Discussion Paper 11, ILO/SAMAT, Geneva.

ILO (2000) *World Labour Report 2000: Income Security and Social Protection in a Changing World*, International Labour Organisation, Geneva.

Lund, F. (1993) 'State social benefits in South Africa', *International Social Security Review*, 46 (1): 5–25.

McKinnon, R. (1996) 'The public management of national provident funds for state-led development: the case of Malaysia's Employees Provident Fund', *Public Sector Management*, 9 (1): 44–60.

McKinnon, R., R. Charlton and H. T. Munro (1997) 'The national provident fund model: an analytical and evaluative reassessment', *International Social Security Review*, 50 (3).

Mideplan (1999) *Situación de los adultos mayores en Chile. 1998*, Documento 10, Ministerio de Planificación y Cooperación, Santiago.

OECD (1998) *Maintaining Prosperity in an Ageing Society*, Organisation for Economic Co-operation and Development, Paris.

Palacios, R. and M. Pallarés-Millares (2000) *International Patterns of Pension Provision*, Pension Primer Paper, World Bank, Washington DC.

UNDP (2000) *Human Development Report 2000*, United Nations Development Programme, New York.

van der Berg, S. (1998) 'Ageing, public finance and social security in South Africa', *Southern African Journal of Gerontology*, 7 (1): 3–9.

Whitehouse, E. (2000) 'How poor are the old? A survey of evidence from 44 countries', Pension Primer Paper 1, World Bank, Washington DC.

Yermo, J. (2000) 'Institutional investors in Latin America: recent trends and regulatory challenges', in OECD (ed.) *Institutional Investors in Latin America*, Organisation for Economic Cooperation and Development, Paris, pp. 23–120.

CHAPTER 7

Ageing in Japan: An Issue of Social Contract in Welfare Transfer or Generational Conflict?

TETSUO OGAWA

Population ageing is a major consequence of Japanese social and economic developments in the post-war era. Japan, with the second largest GDP[1] in the world, has a pattern of welfare very different from that of Western industrial countries (Esping-Andersen 1990; Esping-Andersen and Gallie 2002). It also differs from Anglo-Saxon countries in other ways relevant to national development, in particular financial and capital markets, corporate culture and industrial relations (Mishra 1999). In Japan, the scope of state welfare programmes and the level of social expenditure remain low compared with the OECD average (OECD 1997).[2] Even though Japanese social development is often described as unique, the current issues with which the country is faced are relevant to those of OECD member states with regard to ageing. These member states have identified many challenges for governments due to the long-term effects of ageing, and have set out a challenging mix of policies.[3] However, responding to the challenges of shifting demographic forces is a complex and difficult task for Japan as well as other OECD states because the implications are both diverse and profound (OECD 1997). Strategic frameworks need to be in place at the national level in order to harmonise and sustain ageing reforms, as well as to build up public understanding and support (ISSA 2002).

A set of policy principles has been developed to guide reforms in Japan. Since the early 1990s, the government has prioritised reforms in pensions, health and social care in order to respond to ageing issues. At the same time, sociologists, legal experts, economists and political scientists are giving much attention to these policy proposals. It is important to point out that long-term policies on ageing require a broad view of the Japanese economy in order to understand the government's capacity to generate resources, and a long-term view of demographics in order to understand the demands that will be placed on the economy (OECD 1997). Under Japan's social protection system, the national burden as a percentage of national income was 36.5 per cent (13.9 per cent of social security contributions and 22.6 per cent of taxes) in the fiscal year 2000. This rate is extremely low compared to other developed countries: 35.8 per cent in the USA (9.7 per cent of social security contributions and 26.1 per cent of taxes), 48.3 per cent for the United Kingdom, 55.9 per cent for Germany, 65.3 per cent for France and 70.3 per cent for Sweden (MHLW and MOF 2001).

The Japanese government has sought to coordinate ageing policy with economic policy in order to sustain the low level of social protection expenditures and to avoid excessive financial pressures (OECD 1997; Ogawa 2000). However, the current economic situation is stagnant and the government has been tackling ageing issues in a new way. As the proportion of those aged 65 and over is now 17.2 per cent of the total population, the number of older people who are bed-bound, suffering from senile dementia and in need of long-term care is rapidly increasing. Under the current socio-economic system, the roles of family and community are changing and those changes have made it difficult for the family alone to look after older people. While family care as informal care was in the past emphasised as part of welfare policy, it also reflected the preferences of most older people.

In Japanese society, there are many channels of informal and formal welfare. These may involve exchanges between generations, and take place within four sectors: the informal sector, the statutory sector, and the voluntary and private ones (Knapp 1996). In Japan the public pension and health care systems are universal and comprehensive, but other areas of social provision are less advanced, particularly in the area of personal social services for older people (MOF 2001). Thanks to informal social protection, the costs of personal social services have been lower than those of European countries (MHLW 2001). Because of an historical absence of a comprehensive government social care policy, the extent of institutional care for older people has been less than in other industrialised societies (Martin 1989). However, since the early 1990s the government has implemented a series of new initiatives for older people, including new social care policies. These social care policies are known as the Gold Plans (Gold Plan, 1990; New Gold Plan, 1994; Gold Plan 21, 1999) and they have been combined with the recently established Long-Term Care Insurance System (LTCIS, 2000). The LTCIS[4] has been implemented as a compulsory state care insurance scheme to cover all older people since April 2000. The scheme, based on the fundamental principles of wide care coverage, represents a major new social policy in response to population ageing (MHW 1996; Satomi et al. 1997).

This chapter tries to analyse how family care provision can be replaced by state care provision with the implementation of the Long-Term Care Insurance System (LTCIS 2000). Several consequences of the policy change will be discussed. I give a brief account of old age in Japan and also examine the shifts in welfare transfer modes away from traditional family-based support to other mechanisms, which reflect wider changes in Japanese society and social policy. There are several concepts that are convenient to this analysis: intergenerational welfare transfers through pension funds, health care and long-term care, and the search for a new social contract to avoid generational conflicts relating to socio-economic, demographic, cultural forces and policy imperatives.

Old age in Japan

The crisis of intergenerational relationships

Welfare production involves four sectors and their combinations. These sectors are the informal sector, such as family, relatives and neighbours; the statutory sector, such as local authorities; the private sector, such as private corporations (for profit and private); and the voluntary sector, such as charity organisations and NGOs (non-profit and private). In Japan, most older people have relied heavily upon the informal sector, for cultural and historical reasons. However, welfare production is now being transformed from traditional means to a new mixed pluralistic welfare system, combining all the above four sectors (Ogawa 1999).

Traditionally, families have provided a substantial amount of care for older people in Japan, and in most cases their main caregivers have tended to be women rather than men. These caregivers were usually daughters-in-law rather than daughters or sons (Ogawa 1999). For older people needing care, co-residence with children remains virtually the only source of support. A large-scale survey conducted by the Tokyo Metropolitan Government (TMG) in 1995 found that 88 per cent of older people with disabilities were cared for by co-resident family members, and a further 5 per cent by children or relatives living apart. The survey found that 32 per cent of principal caregivers were wives, many of whom are themselves older people, 23 per cent were daughters, and 22 per cent were daughters-in-law (Koyano 1999).

However, recent family trends have seemingly weakened such inter-generational relationships between children and their parents (Okazaki 1994). This can be seen in decreasing levels of co-residency. By 2000, 13 per cent of Japanese older people were living alone and a further 32 per cent were living as a couple (MHLW 2000). The intention to rely on children in old age has diminished, and the proportion of people choosing hospitals or social welfare institutions for care in cases of senile dementia or the patient being bed-bound has risen (Okazaki 1994). These changes have been influenced by several factors, relating to socio-economic, demographic and cultural forces in Japan. They include a decline in fertility, rural to urban migration linked to industrialisation, the increasing longevity of older people, increased participation of women in the work force, and changing cultural attitudes (Kumagai 1984; Maeda 1986). These factors also seem to have led to wider changes in family care and the dynamics of other care services supported by statutory, voluntary and private bodies.

The policy challenge to replace traditional generational contracts with a new social contract

Several issues have arisen in parallel with social policy debates in Japan. Since there was a tendency for family care to be regarded as essential, most older people relied heavily upon it. They also disliked institutional care because of its stigma, despite the fact that older people without alternative sources of care could not help but resort to institutional care as a last option. As there were far fewer alternatives for care in Japan than Western European countries, choices of steps in support from family care to institutional care were less varied. This was mainly because the development of social care services was delayed due to the government's emphasis on economic policy rather than social policy (Walker 1986). In addition, the family itself felt obliged to look after their older parents in line with Japanese tradition. It is often pointed out that family care costs the state less than institutional care. However, a comparison of costs between institutional care and informal care is controversial, as methods of cost calculation depend upon to what extent and by which criteria we take into consideration the costs of informal care.

In addition, the taxation system in Japan is often described as an influential factor in decisions towards intergenerational relationships. High levels of inheritance tax may serve as a disincentive for younger generations to care for older people, since the size of future bequests will be diminished. They may also encourage high levels of consumption in later life, since the incentive to accumulate assets for inheritance is weakened. In Japan inheritance tax was substantially increased during the 1990s. The current Liberal Democratic government proposed a new policy to reduce the basic allowance by up to 20 per cent, and to revise and reduce the highest inheritance tax rate from 70 per cent to 50 per cent. The new policy is intended to ease the overall fiscal burden, but may have also been adopted with half an eye to older people's care needs.

It has been necessary for the government and several generations of the public to find a consensus and a new contract to cope with the expanding demands for elder care. Past policy involvement was not enough to cover the costs of informal care or to provide it. The new Long-Term Care Insurance (LTCIS 2000) aims to actively intervene in families in order to reduce the burdens on them. Another aim of the new care policy is that women and care givers in private household settings should be discharged from traditional caring roles for older parents. Many such women quit their jobs after getting married and entering their husbands' homes. However, the new care policy has significantly changed people's attitudes towards care, as it has been found that many Japanese women wish to continue to work outside the family unit (Ogawa 1999). If they do so and are employed in the labour market, they can support their older parents financially via social security and pension transfers rather than actual care giving. However, the scope for this type of familial support is presently limited by Japan's economic situation, as many young and middle-aged people are unemployed.

Because of these complex structural constraints on elder care, the state has had to seek alternative means to satisfy social responsibilities for the care of older people over the next few decades. The traditional Japanese family obligation based upon kinship, which also stressed the importance of community collaboration, has been weakened by urbanisation and the migration of younger people into urban areas. The practice of elder care is clearly different between urban and rural areas because of different local cultures. Older people in rural areas are more supported by their families than those in urban areas. If the notion of community collaboration is used effectively, it could contribute to elder care in spite of the decline of family care. In reality, in some areas local community members have already begun to perform 'informal' community care without policy involvement. This demonstrates the potential for local community members to organise home help and home nursing spontaneously by themselves.

Policy solutions towards long-term care

In 1994 a government council on Health and Welfare for the Aged recommended the establishment of a public insurance system for the social care of older people. The report called for elder care services to be provided, in principle, to those aged 65 and over, and the financial costs to be borne by contributions from those aged 40 and over. In December 1997, the bill was passed through the Houses of Representatives and Councillors. Since April 1999 those aged 40 and over have started to contribute, and the scheme was implemented in April 2000. Japan's Long-Term Care Insurance System (LTCIS) is a compulsory state programme which covers all older people who are in need of care.

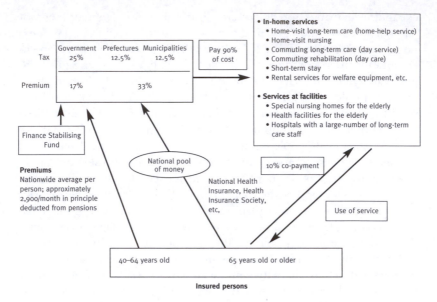

Source: MHLW (2002)

Figure 7.1 Outline of the Long–Term Care Insurance System in Japan

Figure 7.1 shows the structure of the LTCIS. Municipalities act as the insurer, and are responsible for long-term care provision for older people in every local authority. People aged 65 years and over are fully insured by the scheme, and people aged between 40 and 65 contribute through different mechanisms that vary between local authorities. The LTCIS is funded 50 per cent by contributions and 50 per cent by general taxation. Since April 1999 care insurance contributions have been collected by several means, one of which is the local authority's responsibility to levy JPY 2,500 per month from those aged 40–64, and JPY 1,250–3,750 from those aged 65 and over, according to each local authority's decision on the levying rates. These rates are currently under revision (MHLW 2002).

The rationale for implementing the LTCIS

In the face of accelerating demand for elder care, the state was not able to meet these needs and remained heavily dependent upon the involvement of the informal sector, especially families. In 1993, about two million older persons required care (MHW 1996). It was estimated that their spouses or children in private households cared for most of them, while only 3 per cent were in residential accommodation. At the same time, the question of accessibility to residential accommodation has arisen among older people who could not be cared for in their private households.

The Gold Plan 21 contains an ambitious range of measures, including attempts to manage the capacity of such residential accommodation for older people (Figure 7.2). However, the lists of older people who are waiting for admission to residential accommodation increased despite attempts by the government to expand the amount of social care accommodation. According to data from the Tokyo Metropolitan Government for 1992, 8,800 older persons were waiting for admission to residential homes, while the capacity of social care institutions was only 15,200. The government neglected to expand home-based care services for older people in private households for long periods, even when seriously ill older persons were not able to enter residential accommodation. Since the 1963 Law of Social Welfare had not been able to anticipate the subsequent increase in the numbers of older people in need, the provision of accommodation and home helpers was insufficient in quantity and quality, even though the increase in the number of older people remained moderate over several decades. In some cases, where the provider of care was not a family member or another informal carer, local authorities failed to support older people. At the same time, Japanese society stigmatised older people who could not receive informal care from either their families or other kin. As a result, both older persons and informal carers were overburdened by the state's lack of care support.

In order to resolve these complex issues, the central government has sought to increase the capacity of social care institutions and the number of qualified professional carers according to the Gold Plan 21 (1999). It has made efforts to establish a care needs assessment system for older people at the community level. This reflects a wider shift in central government policy away from prioritising residential-based care and towards home-based care. This has mainly occurred in response to the rapid increase of the older population. Policy guidelines have attempted to expand home-based care services for older people rather than increase the number of residential homes. These changes have made a difference in the degree of local government involvement in policy planning for older age care. After assessing local care needs in 1989, each local authority had to produce a community care plan. However, local authorities suffered from a lack of finance for care since there had been no funds available for implementing their plans. One response was to seek to expand the care capacity of local communities. Despite this, financial pressures on local authority care programmes remained acute, as did pressures on human resources. While discussions about these issues continued, the Long-Term Care Insurance System (LTCIS) was introduced at the national level in April 2000.

Figure 7.2 Overview of measures for the Gold Plan 21, Japan   *Source:* MHLW (2002)

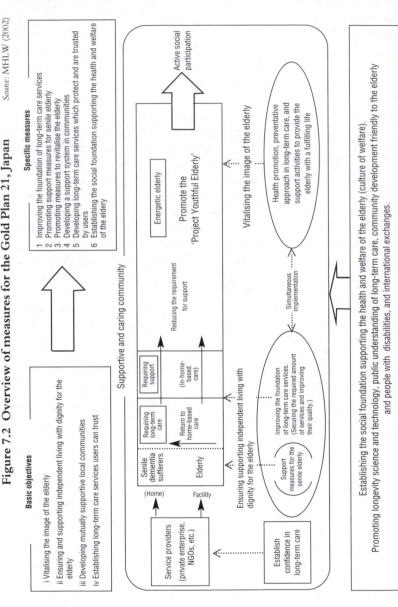

Shaping policy

Policy developments are the results of interaction between many interests, including the political parties, pressure groups and public opinion. Ideological positions and the strengths of various interests may shape and influence elder care policy, but it is often said that there were limited prospects for further major reform of the Japanese social care system except for the LTCIS. Under Japan's ministerial budget ceiling system, which is pre-set by the previous year's public social expenditure, it was not possible for the Ministry of Health, Labour and Welfare (MHLW) to increase the budget of social services exclusively for older people. Also, tax increases were not favoured by the coalition government of that time. This limited scope prevented policy makers from choosing funding methods other than social insurance for the new care system.

Table 7.1 State expenditure on pensions, health care for older people and elder care in Japan, compared with total social security expenditure

Fiscal year	Pension benefits	Medical care benefits	Welfare service benefits	Subsidies for elderly employees	Total	Annual rate of increase	% of total (A)	(A) Total Social security expenditure	Annual rate of increase
	Hundreds of millions of yen	Hundreds of millions of yen	Hundreds of millions of yen	Hundreds of millions of yen	Hundreds of millions of yen	%	%	Hundreds of millions of yen	%
1973	10,756	4,289	596	–	15,641	–	25.0	62,587	–
1974	19,204	6,652	877	–	26,733	70.9	29.6	90,270	44.2
1975	28,924	8,666	1,164	–	38,754	45.0	32.9	117,693	30.4
1976	40,697	10,780	1,489	–	52,966	36.7	36.5	145,165	23.3
1977	50,942	12,872	1,798	–	65,612	23.9	38.9	168,868	16.3
1978	61,329	15,948	2,060	–	79,337	20.9	40.1	197,763	17.1
1979	70,896	18,503	2,306	–	91,705	15.6	41.7	219,832	11.2
1980	83,675	21,269	2,570	–	107,514	17.2	43.4	247,736	12.7
1981	97,903	24,280	2,822	–	125,005	16.3	45.4	275,638	11.3
1982	109,552	27,450	3,129	–	140,131	12.1	46.6	300,973	9.2
1983	120,122	32,660	3,306	–	156,088	11.4	48.8	319,733	6.2
1984	130,497	35,534	3,467	–	169,498	8.6	50.4	336,396	5.2
1985	144,549	40,070	3,668	–	188,287	11.1	52.8	356,798	6.1
1986	163,140	43,584	4,316	–	211,040	12.1	54.7	385,918	8.2
1987	175,081	46,638	4,278	–	225,997	7.1	55.5	407,337	5.6
1988	185,889	49,824	4,569	–	240,282	6.3	56.6	424,582	4.2
1989	201,126	53,730	5,106	–	259,962	8.2	57.9	448,822	5.7
1990	216,182	57,331	5,749	–	279,262	7.4	59.1	472,203	5.2
1991	231,909	61,976	6,552	–	300,437	7.6	59.9	501,346	6.2
1992	249,728	66,685	7,456	–	323,869	7.8	60.2	538,280	7.4
1993	266,199	71,394	8,171	–	345,764	6.8	60.9	567,975	5.5
1994	286,248	77,804	9,066	–	373,118	7.9	61.7	604,727	6.5
1995	311,565	84,525	10,902	117	407,109	9.1	62.9	647,314	7.0
1996	326,713	92,166	11,537	369	430,785	5.8	63.8	675,475	4.4
1997	341,699	96,392	12,743	567	451,401	4.8	65.0	694,187	2.8
1998	362,379	101,092	13,797	773	478,041	5.9	66.3	721,411	3.9
1999	378,061	109,443	15,101	954	503,559	5.3	67.1	750,417	4.0

Unit: JPY 100,000,000 in medical care benefits denotes the 'general medical care cost'.
Source: National Institute of Population and Social Security Research (2002).

The lives of older people are also affected by general fiscal policy. Table 7.1 shows that increases in pension, national health expenditures (for those aged 65 and over) and elder care expenditures are substantial compared with the increases of general health care expenditures. In addition, these increases exceed those of national income. Even with this rapid increase in spending on care, the pace of population ageing means that further sources of funds are needed. The LTCIS seeks to meet this need.

The Japanese government states that the aims of the LTCIS are:

1 to facilitate a system in which society as a whole supports those who are facing the need for long-term care;
2 to establish a system in which the relationship between benefits and burdens is made clear, by introducing a social insurance approach that can easily command public understanding;
3 to reform the present system, vertically divided between health, medical and welfare services, and to establish a system offering users comprehensive services from a variety of institutions of their choice;
4 to separate long-term care from coverage of health care insurance, and to establish a system which aims to decrease cases of 'social hospitalisation' as the first step toward restructuring the social security system as a whole.

The performance of the LTCIS

Table 7.2 shows the recent situation of older people covered by the LTCIS. From April 1999 to March 2001 the number of older people insured by the LTCIS increased from 21,562,000 to 22,422,000. By

Table 7.2 The development of the LTCIS
and the situation of older people in Japan (1999–2001)
Comparison of service usage before
and after the implementation of the long-term care insurance (LTCIS)

	Monthly average in 1999	November 2000	May 2001
Home–visit long-term care	3,550,000	5,390,000	6,450,000
Commuting long-term care	2,500,000	3,400,000	3,840,000
Short stay	918,000 days	849,000 days	1,092,000 days
Group homes for older people with dementia	266 places (number of operating cost subsidies in 1999)	870 places (March 2001)	1,312 places (September 2000)

Source: MHLW (2002)

March 2001 the number of older people receiving care through the LTCIS was 13,602,000. The number of older people who were in care institutions was 6,642,000. Of these, 3,156,000 were in social care facilities and 2,409,000 were in health care facilities.

Relationships between the public and private sector

Before the LTCIS, the difference between the public (including the voluntary sector) and private sectors was very clear. The 1963 Law of Social Welfare for the aged offered care services free at the point of use or at a minimum cost (according to local authorities' charging policy). Private providers offered a range of services which they sold to users directly without government intervention. The principal differences which defined the public–private boundary were the prices and the quality of service (MHLW 2000). Surveys (MHLW 2000) have shown consistently that a significant proportion of the population was dissatisfied with public services (including the voluntary service totally financed by public funding) (MHLW 2000). However, there was no other alternative than those services for those who could not afford to pay. The main goals of the Gold Plan and New Gold Plans (1990; 1994) have been to make the statutory service sufficient to meet needs, and to offer greater care services mainly in community care, in particular in the area of home-based care services, such as home help services, day care services and short stay services (respite care services). In addition, the new Gold Plan 21 (1999) has encouraged private companies to enter into the area of social care.

Prior to the LTCIS, the availability of care services under the statutory services was in a critical state. The choice of care service was extremely limited, and most care users had complaints about the quality and availability of public services (MHW 1994). A particular example is residential care, where currently about 98 per cent of the services are provided by the statutory and voluntary sectors, and which are financed totally by local authority and central government. Figure 7.3 shows the proportion of service providers in the informal, statutory, commercial and voluntary sectors. The introduction of the private sector has been relatively recent, while the voluntary sector has a longer tradition of co-operation with local authorities (Ogawa 1999). The informal sector, such as volunteer groups, has become more influential as a provider of community care services. It is true that the areas they have entered are extremely limited, since their skills in care and methods of service provision determine the tasks they can perform. Overall, it is possible to observe a diversification of community care service providers in each area and the monopoly of local authorities as the single service provider has been reduced.

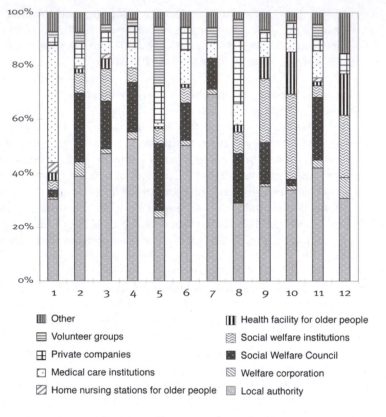

**Figure 7.3 Diversification of service providers
in elder care services in Japan**

Service Types: (1) Home nursing and rehabilitation service; (2) Home help service; (3) Visiting bathing service; (4) Futon exchange service; (5) Meals on wheels; (6) Visiting medical care service; (7) Call alarm service (8) Day care service; (9) Short stay service; (10) Information service; (12) Information service for accommodation.
Source: Statistics and Information Division, Ministry of Health and Welfare, Survey of Demands for Health and Welfare Related Services, 1997.

The most important aspect of the relationship between public, voluntary and private sectors is that the state, in its regulatory role, can permit the voluntary and private sectors to operate as service providers, or it can prevent them. In Japan both voluntary and private sector providers may only operate under a strict regime of admission and registration. A would-be private provider is regulated strictly according to the legal regime of local government and must be recommended for registration. Until recently, they registered with the Association of Elder Service Providers, but now must do so with the local authority, a shift that emphasises local government control. Because of these regulations and laws, many private care service providers hesitate to enter the LTCIS. In the worst case, private corporations are fined or shut down. In contrast, the voluntary sector has a long tradition of co-operating with local authorities, and they are also substantially financed by the local authorities. An important way in which local government determines the coverage of care services is in the regulation of service providers and the coverage of services. Usually, it only allows new service providers to enter the area of home-based care services, such as nursing care, home help, short stay services and day care. These services have been emphasised in the various Gold Plans (MHW 1994).

The state does not allow service users to select providers of their own choice. Care service provision is decided by a welfare office of the local authority by means of needs assessment and care package plans. While the most common providers of care services for older people are local authorities themselves, the Gold Plan (1990) and New Gold Plan (1994) have had a significant influence on private sector providers by encouraging structural links between public and private services. The New Gold Plan 21 (1999) has also encouraged private companies to enter the area of social care. Statutory services have not been able to keep up with the expanding needs of older people, and have not been able to satisfy users' needs and demands. In many cases private care users enjoy access to a wider set of care services than those who cannot afford to go private. This situation is expected to increase demands for private provision.

Efficiency and equity considerations in the LTICS

The LTICS and welfare pluralism

The most economically efficient system of social care is one that combines the compulsory LTCIS administered by the local authorities, along with greater use of the voluntary and private services, financed by top-up payments from the LTCIS (Ogawa 1999). However, the introduction of the LTCIS has become a threat to the voluntary sector, which had previously been financed wholly by local authorities. It has been pointed out that the cost effectiveness of the current care system does not always make the voluntary sector a good alternative to the private one, and in fact makes it less attractive than previously thought. The implementation of the LTCIS has presented wider opportunities for private companies. By providing a clearer basis for allocating resources and available services, the LTCIS has opened the way for private companies to provide new services that may do much to satisfy previously unmet needs for public care.

Care sharing and cost sharing by generating a new generational contract

Each local authority has been taking measures to control the cost of social care for older people, but conditions vary between them owing to the distinct financial position of each local authority. In addition, there seems to have developed a considerable divergence of service provision in local authorities in Japan since the implementation of the LTCIS. The methods employed by local authorities vary according to the ways in which their social care service systems and provision are organised and implemented. Variations in the implementation of the LTCIS depend on whether or not local authorities have to charge co-payments. They also reflect the extent to which users receive services from the local authorities, as opposed to other sectors (Koyano 1999; Ogawa 2001).

The goal of the LTCIS is a system that promotes care sharing and cost sharing in order to socialise care (Tochimoto 1997; Koyano 1999). Government regulation can influence the supply of services by the different sectors. The most influential factor affecting service provision in systems such as this is control through direct regulation (Le Grand, 1993). Patterns of provision are also affected by differential subsidies for providers. Taking the social care system as a whole, a key factor is that since the advent of the LTCIS care financing is no longer constrained by tight ministerial budget ceilings (Ogawa 1999). Nevertheless, regulations and subsidies influencing the supply side of care may need to include the introduction of social care expenditure ceilings in prospective budgets, reinforced by controls on manpower costs. The introduction of a less costly manpower policy is also based on ideas of authorising, regulating and subsidising service providers and carer groups, regardless of whether these are newly established private providers or long-established voluntary sector organisations. This aims to limit social care budgets by choosing less costly services, while at the same time providing high-quality care by offering providers and formal carers incentives to be more cost-effective. This is also likely to include co-payments for services, although the level of these should reflect the situation of local authorities. Any co-payments would need to be accompanied by an effective system of exemptions for older people with low incomes.

Professional carers have an important role in shaping care policy, although their role and importance are often ignored (Satomi *et al.* 1997). According to Table 7.3, the number of home-helpers needs to be increased greatly for the implementation of the Gold Plan 21 (1999). A particular issue is the supply of labour to the informal care system and the scope to employ overseas workers. This links to wider concerns about the need for replacement migration in response to Japan's shifting demographic structure. To date, the use of foreign labour has been very limited, owing to the extremely restrictive labour and immigration policies of the Japanese government.

Table 7.3 Estimates of the needs of older people and service users under the new LTCIS social care system in Japan

Users (estimated)	1999	2000	2005	2010
Older people in need	708,000	708,000	940,000	1,200,000
Frail older people	1,300,000	1,300,000	1,600,000	1,900,000
Home-based care				
Home helpers	170,000	220,000	340,000	560,000
Day care service	17,000	21,000	32,000	53,000
Short stay	73,000	91,000	140,000	230,000
Home nursing	6,000	8,000	12,000	20,000
Residential care				
Special nursing homes	287,000	290,000	316,000	332,000
Health facility	249,000	280,000	274,000	288,000
Residential medical care	156,000	190,000	171,000	180,000

Source: Ministry of Health, Labour and Welfare, *Needs Estimations under the New Social Care System*, 2000.

Conclusion: two policy challenges for rebuilding a generational care contract

The first dimension – intergenerational equity for social solidarity
In Japan, some form of welfare state restructuring has taken place in policy areas. As a result of policy changes in parallel with sociodemographic changes, the Japanese have entered into debates about the merits of pluralistic welfare systems, and about the balance of intergenerational equity and social solidarity (Walker 1996). These sought to avoid intergenerational conflicts and provide a long-term solution to the issue of old age care. There is still argument about how many resources for older people should be equitably allocated, and how every generation should reach a consensus for resource allocation. Under the combined

influence of Japan's population ageing and economic stagnation, it has been argued that the government should pursue a more pluralistic social welfare system in determining the level of resource allocation than it has in the past. Considering the nature of elder care in Japan, some also argue that the LTCIS should be moved beyond being a form of insurance for those aged 65 and over and towards being a form of lifetime saving to cover lifetime care needs for every generation, including people with disabilities (Satomi *et al.* 1997).

At present, discussions regarding social care expenditure are balanced between the needs of older people and the quantity of care provision. It is true that the bulk of social care costs can be met by the LTCIS, to which contributions are collected from those aged 40 and over. Previously, local authorities had not adopted the ideas of care sharing and cost sharing to cover the total social care costs. The LTCIS has had great influence on the mechanisms of care provision and care planning, and has facilitated a new generational consensus. However, its implementation has varied considerably between local authorities (Koyano 1999). In other words, the concepts of care sharing and cost sharing introduced by the LTCIS have diverged owing to the limitations of local authorities which must insure people, collect contributions from them and provide sufficient services to those in need. In the past, the most economically efficient method of limiting social care provision was a budget ceiling for the whole of social care expenditure or for specific aspects of it, such as manpower costs. Since the adoption of the LTCIS some resources are free from budget ceilings that had considerably restrained social care expenditures in the past. Local authorities now have separate budgets from central government. In addition, supplementary budgets for other emergent uses are available, since social care is not ring-fenced under the new scheme, even for those who never contributed to it (Niki 1997). These issues are still being actively debated in order to generate consensus around intergenerational equity and social solidarity. The aim is that the current social care system, in conjunction with new reforms of state pension schemes, should be seen as equitable and socially just.

The second dimension – the deterioration of intergenerational relations as a by-product of formal policy involvement
Having analysed policy imperatives behind the development of a new social care system (Gold Plan 21 1999; LTCIS 2000), the discussion moves to the second dimension of generational relations: relationships between kin. The main focus is upon the caring relationship within the family and the question of whether the new social care policy would accelerate the deterioration of traditional intergenerational and kinship relations. The newly established social care structure, which has a strong

ideological basis, is central to the social reproduction of the caring relationship. However, as a result of the formal policy involvement, it may
lead to the decline of kinship obligations and a shift in the quality of
intergenerational relations. One of the objectives of the LTCIS has been
achieved through the introduction of the idea of rationing in social care
by recreating a new social contract for future generations. The concept
of the LTCIS embodies a principle of collective provision and finance of
elder care, but on the other hand, it results in greater user preference for
individual choice of private care (Tochimoto 1997). The principle of
the LTCIS is to develop comprehensive social care rather than individualistic choice (Satomi *et al.* 1997). In this sphere, the state and people
should be more cautious about some consequences. It appears that the
lack of a formal care policy encouraged the primacy of the family in
welfare transfers. In reality, by accepting the leading role of the family in
caring, the state could minimise its financial commitment. Nonetheless,
the continued absence of such a comprehensive care policy means that
tensions are placed on the caring relationships between kin, as they need
to respond to the fundamental changes in intergenerational welfare transfer patterns and responsibilities as well as socio-demographic changes in
Japanese society. In addition, an objective of the LTCIS is to make care
insurance more compatible with the universal use of elder care services.
The LTCIS aims at the introduction of resource allocation through
rationing by means of a needs assessment system for care planning in
each local authority. The mode of the LTCIS is regarded by the state
more as a transfer model of administration and finance than as a market
model as used by private insurance companies (OECD 1997). Some
have argued that the marketisation of elder care should be avoided after
the introduction of the LTCIS, since such privatisation of elder care
tends to jeopardise the realisation of 'intergenerational' solidarity and
altruistic behaviour. It is appropriate to observe whether the LTCIS
functions in a way that would achieve the ideal of 'social' or 'civil' care.

As far as these two dimensions of intergenerational relationship are
considered, the chapter concludes that they are interactively linked
through family functioning and social care policy. As Walker (1996)
emphasised, 'while there are distinct macro and micro social features of
generational relations, one effect of this dichotomous scientific construction of the social world is to underplay the degree of interaction
between them'. This is widely observed in dramatic shifts in social
norms for the provision of care and in the balance of affect and
reciprocity that governs receipt of care within families (Stark 1995;
Ogawa 1999). In terms of intergenerational welfare transfers, these
phenomena are comparable with those of many other countries that are
currently establishing social care policy for older people.

NOTES

1 Japan's GDP in 2000 was US$4.8 trillion (as compared with US$9.87 trillion for the United States) and GDP *per capita* was US$37,676 (US$35,032 for the United States) (Economist Intelligence Unit 2001).
2 Japan's social protection expenditure was 11.57 per cent of GDP in 1990 compared with an average of 21.61 per cent for OECD countries, and tax revenue was only 29.1 per cent of GDP in 1993 compared with the OECD average of 38.7 per cent (OECD 1997).
3 The OECD emphasises comprehensive approaches to the issues, including the need to consider ageing as a lifetime issue; the importance of coordinating fiscal policy, private sector activity and government service delivery at national, regional and local levels; and the need for comprehensive strategies of information and consultation (OECD 1997).
4 Based on a recommendation by the Council for Health and Welfare for Older People in 1994, a bill to establish long-term care insurance was discussed by the Coalition government of the Liberal Democratic Party (LDP), the Social Democratic Party (SDP) and the Sakigake Party, and finally passed by parliament in December 1997.

REFERENCES

Economist Intelligence Unit (EIU) (2001) *National Facts,* The Economist, London.
Esping-Andersen, G. (1990) *The Three Worlds of Welfare Capitalism,* Polity Press, Cambridge.
—— and D. Gallie (2002) *Why We Need a New Welfare State,* Oxford University Press, Oxford.
ISSA (2002) *International Social Security Review,* 55 (1).
Knapp, M. (1996) 'Private and Voluntary Welfare', in M. Sullivan (ed.), *The New Policies of Welfare,* Macmillan, London.
Koyano, W. (1999) 'Populations ageing, changing in living arrangements, and the new long term care system in Japan', *Journal of Sociology and Social Welfare,* 26 (1): 155–67.
Kumagai, F. (1984) 'Modernisation and the family in Japan', *Journal of Family History,* xi: 371–82.
Le Grand, J. (1993) *The Theory of Quasi-Markets,* Macmillan, London.
Maeda, D. (1986) 'Health services for the elder in Japan', Information for the Workshop on Health and Ageing, Groningen.
Martin, L. (1989) 'The Graying of Japan', *Population Bulletin,* 44 (2): 1–41.
Ministry of Finance (1997; 2001) *White Paper,* Government Paper, Tokyo.
Ministry of Foreign Affairs (2001) *White Paper,* Government Paper, Tokyo.
MHW (Ministry of Health and Welfare) (1994) 'The Implementation of a New Gold(en) Plan', The Latest Information for Retirement Life, *Series 12,* Akebi Syuppan, Tokyo.
—— (1995) *Annual Report on Health and Welfare 1993–1994,* Japan International Corporation of Welfare Services (JICWELS), Tokyo.
—— (1994–8) *Kousei Hakusho* (White Paper), The Ministry of Health and Welfare, Tokyo.
MHLW (Ministry of Health, Labour and Welfare) (2000; 2001; 2002) White Paper, Government Paper, Tokyo.
Mishra, R. (1999) *Globalization and the Welfare State,* Edward Elgar, Cheltenham.
National Institute of Population and Social Security Research (NIPSSR) (2002) *Social Security Expenditures,* NIPSSR, Tokyo.
Niki, R. (1997) *Objections to the Public Care Insurance Scheme,* Minerva, Kyoto.
OECD (1997) *Ageing in OECD Countries – a Critical Policy Challenge,* Organisation for

Ecoonomic Cooperation and Development, Paris.

Okazaki (1994) *The Basic Knowledge about the Ageing Society*, Chuo Houki Shyuppan, Tokyo.

Ogawa, T. (1999) 'Decentralisation and diversity in the delivery of social care services for older people in Japan – the development of community care policy and social care markets', doctoral thesis submitted to the University of Sheffield.

Ogawa, T. (2000) 'Japanese women and elder care – changing roles?', *Asian Women*, 13: 135–67.

—— (2001) 'Long-term care for older people in Japan, the Social Care Insurance Scheme (SCIS) and marketisation of elder care', Working Paper No.14, Oxford Institute of Ageing, Oxford.

Satomi, K., R. Niki and T. Ito (1997) *Keouteki Kaigo Hokenn ni Igi Ari – Mouhitostu no Teiann.* (Objection to the public care insurance – another proposal), Minerva, Kyoto.

Stark, O. (1995) *Altruism and Beyond – an Economic Analysis of Transfers and Exchanges within Families and Groups,* Cambridge University Press, Cambridge.

Tochimoto, I. (1997) *Kaigo Hoken – Fukushi no Syakai Ka –* (The care insurance – the socialisation of welfare), Ieno Hikari Kyokai, Tokyo.

Tokyo Metropolitan Government (TMG) (1991) *Annual Report of Social Welfare and Statistics of the Tokyo Metropolitan Area,* TMG, Tokyo.

Walker, A. (1986) 'The political economy of privatisation', in J. Le Grand and R. Robinson (eds.), *Privatisation and the Welfare States,* Hyman and Unwin, London.

Walker, A. (ed.) (1996) *The Generational Contract: Intergenerational Relations, Old Age and Welfare,* University College London Press, London.

CHAPTER 8

Health Policy and Older People in Africa

DI McINTYRE[1]

The aim of this chapter is to consider health policy issues, with a particular focus on health sector reforms, in relation to the likely impact of these policies on older people in Africa. It is particularly difficult to discuss issues relating to older people in chronological terms in the African context, given that average life expectancy in sub-Saharan Africa is a relatively low 48.8 years and that only two countries, Cape Verde and Mauritius, have an average life expectancy at birth of 60 or greater (United Nations Development Programme 2001). Thus, if one uses chronological categorisations in the absence of a viable alternative, it is more appropriate to consider issues relating to those who are 50 years or older. Another constraining factor is that there has been virtually no consideration of the impact of health sector reforms from the perspective of older people. No empirical literature could be found documenting these impacts.

In order to address these constraints, this chapter begins by providing a brief contextual analysis of the characteristics and experience of older people in African countries. This analysis focuses on demographic, socio-economic and health-related issues of relevance to older people in Africa. It draws extensively on routinely published statistics that unfortunately focus largely on the population who are 65 years or older. In order to explore the issues using a more appropriate chronological definition in the African context, namely the population who are 50 years or older, the Living Standards Measurement Survey (LSMS) databases for three countries are also analysed. In an effort to highlight the diversity of experience of the elderly in Africa, LSMS data were reviewed for one country in each of the following regions: West Africa (Côte D'Ivoire), East Africa (Tanzania) and Southern Africa (South Africa). This context then allows me to draw on the existing health sector reform literature in exploring the likely impact on older people.

It is important at the outset to indicate the perspective of the analysis presented in this chapter. An equity perspective is adopted for this analysis and in particular, the question is posed as to whether older people in Africa are being treated equitably in relation to health policy and through health sector reforms. There is considerable debate about the definition of health equity, but there is consensus that equity refers to fairness and justice. Whitehead (1992) argues that inequities relate to differences in health that are not only considered unfair and unjust, but that are *unnecessary* and *avoidable*. Whitehead's perspective highlights the importance of focusing not on differences between groups, in this case age groups, that are due to unavoidable factors (such as biological factors) but rather on those health differences that are unnecessary in the sense that cost-effective health service and other health-promoting interventions exist which could avoid these differences.

The analysis presented here also draws on the notion of vertical equity. Mooney (1996) argues that 'if, as is normally the case, ill health is not randomly distributed across different groups in society, might that society not want to give preference, *on vertical equity grounds*, for health gains to those groups in that society who are on average in poor health?' (Mooney 1996: 102). This implies that there should be preferential health policy action, or expressed differently 'positive discrimination', in favour of those who are particularly disadvantaged or vulnerable. Vertical equity also has implications for the way in which health services are financed. In particular, vertical equity requires that persons (or families) with different abilities to pay should make appropriately dissimilar payments for health care (Wagstaff and van Doorslaer 1993).

Using these concepts, the focus of analysis in this chapter will be on assessing the equity implications for the elderly of recent health policy developments in Africa, especially certain health sector reforms. In particular, the extent to which the elderly, or subgroups within the category of older people, can be viewed as vulnerable or disadvantaged will be considered. In addition, information will be reviewed on whether health sector reforms have resulted in unfair, unnecessary and avoidable inequalities or whether positive discrimination towards those older people who are considered vulnerable occurs through health policy action in Africa.

Overview: key issues affecting older people in Africa

Demographic issues
Demographic ageing, which refers to increases in the percentage of the population who are 65 years or older as a result of declines in fertility rates and increases in life expectancy, is occurring in all regions of the world. Sub-Saharan Africa is the region that has seen the least dramatic

demographic ageing, with only 3 per cent of the population aged 65 and above in 1999 compared with the world average of 6.9 per cent, an average of 5 per cent for all developing countries and 12.9 per cent for OECD countries (United Nations Development Programme 2001).

The process of demographic ageing in sub-Saharan Africa is confounded by the HIV/AIDS epidemic. As the epidemic grows, the percentage share of the population who are 65 years or older increases even more dramatically than one might expect in the African context given that HIV/AIDS deaths primarily affect working-age adults and babies born to HIV-positive mothers. As the epidemic approaches its peak within a country, life expectancy falls, which will ultimately result in a falling share of the population who are 65 years or older.

Although the percentage share of the population of older persons will fluctuate in countries affected by the AIDS epidemic, the absolute numbers of older people will continue to increase in African countries. The number of people aged 65 and above is projected to increase by about 10 million in sub-Saharan Africa between 1999 and 2015. While the overall population size in this region will increase by 47 per cent during this period, the growth in the number of people of 65 years or older will increase by 57 per cent (United Nations Development Programme 2001). Social sector policies in Africa, thus, do have to take account of the growth in the number of older people over time, but should address the particular needs of the elderly as a matter of urgency in countries in the midst of an AIDS epidemic, given the greater vulnerability of older persons during this time (see next section).

Socio-economic issues

Papers by Apt (2002) and McIntyre (2002) present considerable evidence that many older people in Africa are vulnerable from a socio-economic perspective. This is supported by the analysis of LSMS data, which shows that older people (in this case defined as 50 years of age or more) live in households which generally fare worse in socio-economic terms than households without older members. For example, households in Côte d'Ivoire without an older member have average household income levels that are 1.5 times that of households with a member who is 50 years or older. In South Africa, the percentage of households with access to piped water is 64 per cent and 48 per cent respectively. The elderly are frequently concentrated in rural areas in African countries (Zohoori 2001) where the highest levels of poverty and lowest levels of human development are found (United Nations Development Programme 2001).

In most cases, the elderly have a limited ability to generate income. Nevertheless, they often contribute to the households in which they live in very important ways (caring for grandchildren, for example, which allows other adults to engage in income-generating work activities). They are also able to make important financial contributions when entitled to non-contributory pensions provided by the state. However, such pension systems are only available in a few sub-Saharan African countries, namely Botswana, Mauritius, Namibia and South Africa (Charlton and Rose 2001).

While older people in Africa make significant contributions to households, often of a non-monetary nature, they tend to be heavily reliant on informal family and community support systems for access to financial, food and other essential resources. There is evidence that these informal support systems, particularly family networks, are breaking down in many African countries. Of particular concern within the African context is the decline in the population share of working-age adults who are able to provide financial support in extended families. While this is partly attributable to the impact of lengthy civil and other wars in a large number of African countries, an increasingly important factor is the impact of HIV/AIDS. Older people, particularly older women, are shouldering a greater share of responsibility for family needs at a time when they themselves are less able to meet these needs. 'The AIDS epidemic in sub-Saharan African countries has been called the "grandmother's curse", because it is the grandmothers who must care for adult children with AIDS, as well as for grandchildren who have AIDS or who have been orphaned' (Charlton and Rose 2001: 2427S). The extent to which the elderly do or do not have direct access to financial resources, or indirect access through functioning support networks, has significant implications for their ability to engage in health-promoting activities (such as healthy eating) and to access health services when in need.

Although data on the socio-economic status of older people relative to other age groups in Africa are limited, evidence supports the assertion that many elderly people in Africa are vulnerable, particularly within the context of the HIV/AIDS epidemic. In a vertical equity approach, policy actions should be designed to impact preferentially on those older people who live in impoverished households, as well as other vulnerable groups. What is of concern is that most policies of relevance to socio-economic issues, including poverty-reduction strategies, over-whelmingly focus on children (health and education) and reproductive health issues, with limited or no reference to the particular situation of those older people who are impoverished or vulnerable in other ways (HelpAge International 2000).

Health and health service issues

As has been shown internationally, there are relatively higher levels of reported illness among the very young (less than 5 years), and even more so among older adults, in African countries. Table 8.1 indicates that reported illness tends to be above average from the age of 40 years onwards, but particularly high from the age of 55 years in the three African countries for which LSMS data were analysed.

Table 8.1 Reported illness by age group (% reporting illness in preceding two weeks in South Africa and in preceding four weeks in Côte d'Ivoire and Tanzania)

Age category	Côte d'Ivoire	South Africa	Tanzania
0–4 years	24.3	9.1	25.1
5–19 years	11.0	4.4	11.4
20–39 years	18.2	6.8	17.5
40–49 years	23.5	10.2	21.7
50–54 years	25.3	13.1	22.7
55–59 years	28.0	18.1	27.3
60–64 years	36.4	17.7	21.7
65 years and above	36.4	19.5	27.7
Average	18.3	7.8	17.3

A review including the majority of African countries indicated that the major causes of death for older people were:

▸ Diseases of the circulatory system (accounting for 34 per cent of deaths in those aged 45–64 years and 41 per cent of deaths for those aged 65 or older);

▸ Infectious and parasitic diseases (which accounted for 28 per cent of deaths in those aged 45–64 years and 19 per cent of deaths for those aged 65 or older); and

▸ Cancers (accounting for 14 per cent of deaths in those aged 45–64 years and 9 per cent of deaths for those aged 65 or older) (World Bank 1994).

As detailed in McIntyre (2002), three other important causes of ill-health and premature mortality for older people in Africa are malnutrition, mental health problems and blindness.

The higher incidence of ill-health among older persons is to some extent related to biological factors, but some of the ill-health and premature mortality in the elderly may be regarded as inequitable. It is well established that a wide range of socio-economic factors influence health status. Morbidity and premature mortality that result from the inter-relationship between poverty and health may be described as inequitable, as they stem from inequity in socio-economic status between groups and are thus potentially avoidable and unnecessary, as well as being unfair and unjust.

A greater level of ill-health may also be considered inequitable, in that it is potentially avoidable and unnecessary where it is related to health service deficiencies (such as problems in accessing health services or poor-quality health services). While particular policy consideration is often given to the health service needs of children and younger women, 'there is scant recognition of the specific health needs of older people' (Heslop 1999: 27). It is of concern that 'older people say health care is for them the most important yet often least accessible service – with barriers caused by attitudes as much as service design' (HelpAge International 2000: 7).

The LSMS data sets provide some evidence that being able to use health services at a time of need is particularly problematic for older persons. For example, while an average of 32.6 per cent of all respondents who were reportedly ill in the preceding four weeks in Tanzania did not seek treatment, 38.7 per cent of respondents who were 50 years and older did not seek treatment despite reporting illness. The differential in Côte d'Ivoire was even more striking with the overall average for those not seeking treatment when ill being 53.8 per cent compared with 68.1 per cent of those aged 50 or older.

A wide range of factors contributes to whether or not someone will use a health service when ill. Geographic access is of particular concern to older persons in Africa, given that a high proportion of those aged 50 or older live in rural areas where health service provision is generally less extensive (Heslop 1999). Financial access is also of importance, not only in terms of the cost of services but also the cost of transport to the health facility. The LSMS data sets suggest that greater financial costs are incurred by older people than by younger age groups in African countries. Payments for health services used in a specified recall period (two weeks in South Africa and four weeks in Côte d'Ivoire and Tanzania) indicate that the average *per capita* expenditure on health services was 1.3 times greater for respondents aged 50 years or more than for those below the age of 50 years in Tanzania, 1.6 times greater in Côte d'Ivoire and a staggering 4.5 times greater in South Africa. While the higher expenditure levels reflect the relatively greater health care needs of older people (see Table 8.1), much of this expenditure is out-of-pocket. Thus, the major concern is that older people have to bear a higher health care financing burden at a time when they can ill afford these costs. Other factors such as staff attitudes and perceived quality of care are equally important in influencing utilisation. If one is concerned to promote equitable use of health services through health policy actions, including health sector reforms, all of these obstacles need to be addressed.

Health sector reforms in Africa

African health systems, like those in a wide range of other countries, have undergone substantial reforms or restructuring for the past two or more decades. Health sector reform has been defined as 'sustained, purposeful change to improve the efficiency, equity and effectiveness of the health sector' (Berman 1995:15). Within the sub-Saharan African context, the focus was initially on the introduction of user fees, community financing initiatives (especially pre-payment schemes) and decentralisation of health services. Since the early to mid-1990s, there has been considerable pressure to create an enabling environment for the private health sector to grow, both in terms of health care financing and provision, alongside initiatives to restrict government financing and provision of health services to an essential package. More recently, a number of African countries have begun to consider seriously the introduction of social health insurance. Although many of these reforms have been under discussion and implementation to varying degrees for almost one and a half decades now, they are still very much among the key health policy concerns in African countries at present.

Each of these health sector reforms is critically evaluated below in relation to their likely impact on older people in Africa. The emphasis in these reforms has been on improving health sector efficiency, with unexpected adverse equity impacts often ignored during and after the implementation of reforms (Gilson 1998). It is for this reason that the emphasis in this chapter is on the equity impact of health sector reforms. In addition, the most recent initiative to impact on health policies in Africa, Poverty Reduction Strategies, will be considered briefly.

User fees
User fees refer to patient charges at the point of service in public health sector facilities. The major motivation for introducing user fees cited by national level policy makers and international organisations such as the World Bank, who were particularly vociferous advocates of this form of cost recovery, is that of revenue generation (de Ferranti 1985; Akin *et al*. 1987; Griffin 1988). Economic difficulties in many countries stemming from low or negative economic growth and increasing indebtedness, particularly since the 1980s, limited the resources available to

government for financing and providing health services (Gilson 1995; Gilson and Mills 1995). Fees were seen as an important mechanism for addressing the resource gap in financing public sector health services.

Substantial evidence existed from an early stage that user fees adversely affect health service utilisation, particularly for the poorest groups which, as argued previously, include a large share of the elderly population (Chernichovsky and Meesok 1986; Gertler *et al.* 1987; Stanton and Clemens 1989; Yoder 1989). For example, when user fees were first introduced in Kenya in December 1989, utilisation of services at facilities charging fees fell by a massive 52 per cent (Mwanzia and Mwabu 1993). However, studies in Cameroon and Niger suggest that where fee revenue is retained at facility level and used to improve service quality, overall utilisation may be increased in the longer term, especially for the poorest (Litvack and Bodart 1993; Diop *et al.* 1995). It should be noted, however, that these were studies of small-scale pilot interventions, and that there is no large-scale experience of fees having been used to improve the quality of health services in developing countries.

Studies of user fee impacts on health service utilisation indicated that ability to pay such fees is critically dependent on the disposable income of patients and their families as well as on family and community support networks (Waddington and Enyimayew 1989; McPake *et al.* 1993; Russell 1996). As indicated earlier, support networks for the elderly are becoming more tenuous, particularly in countries most affected by the HIV/AIDS epidemic. There are growing concerns that fees could lead to long term impoverishment if debts are accumulated or assets are sold to cover health care expenses (Corbett 1989).

There are no published studies that explicitly consider the impact of fees on older people. However, information presented earlier indicates that households with members who are 50 years or older tend to have lower *per capita* income levels. In addition, the elderly have higher levels of reported illness, and health care expenditure is considerably higher per person for older people than for those under 50 years of age. This suggests that older people are likely to face considerable financial constraints on health service utilisation. Unsurprisingly, the LSMS data indicate that use of health services when ill is greater among younger than older household members.

Analysis of a panel household data set (KwaZulu–Natal Income Dynamics Study – KIDS) in South Africa indicates that the use of public sector primary care services increased substantially after user fees were removed from these services in 1996. Utilisation increases were particularly dramatic for older people (see Figure 8.1). These data indicate that, of those who reported being ill or injured in the preceding

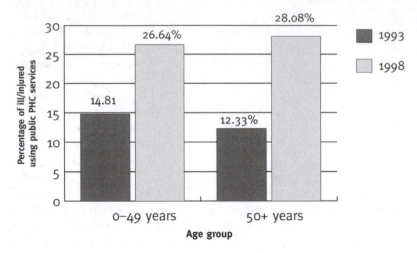

Figure 8.1 Change in utilisation of public sector primary care services in KwaZulu–Natal, after user fees were removed

two weeks, a much higher percentage of older people were able to use public sector primary care services after the free primary care policy was introduced. Although these data only relate to one province (KwaZulu–Natal), the data set does contain information on health service utilisation by the same households before (1993) and after (1998) user fees were removed. Thus, although the data set is somewhat limited, this analysis represents the first empirical evidence that user fees have a particularly deleterious effect on older people and, conversely, that older people derive relatively more benefit from their removal.

In order to minimise the adverse health service utilisation effects of fees, there need to be effective mechanisms for exempting those who are unable to pay fees for health care. A number of studies have indicated that exemption mechanisms are relatively ineffective in practice (La Forgia 1992; McPake et al. 1993; Gilson et al. 1995; Willis and Leighton 1995). While many African countries have some form of income-related exemption, there are also a wide range of fee exemptions for different health services (immunisations, for example) and demographic groups. However, the elderly (usually defined by policy makers as those over the age of 60 or 65 years of age) are infrequently exempted (Russell and Gilson 1995). Even where the elderly are officially eligible for fee exemptions, many are unaware of this fact and may thus not receive the full benefit of this policy (Ahenkora 1999).

In summary, user fees can have a substantial adverse impact on access to and use of health services. There is extremely limited evidence of successful exemption mechanisms, or of targeting the additional resources generated from fee systems to benefit the most vulnerable. It is of interest that two African countries have recently removed fees from some or all health services (fees were removed from primary care services in South Africa in 1996 while all fees were abolished in Uganda in 2001). Unless effective strategies for protecting vulnerable groups are devised, it may be more appropriate to pursue other mechanisms of cost sharing (some of which are discussed in other sections) and to follow the bold example set by Uganda.

Community-based pre-payment schemes

As indicated in the preceding section, there are considerable potential adverse effects of user fees, largely related to the fact that fees can place a heavy burden on patients at the time of using health services. An alternative approach is for community members to contribute to a pre-paid scheme and receive care free or at a reduced cost (Eklund and Stavem 1996). Pre-paid schemes are decentralised (being community-based), small-scale initiatives with considerable community involvement. They usually cover rural communities, although there are a few which cover informal sector workers in urban areas (in the Democratic Republic of Congo, for example) (Shepard *et al.* 1996).

Most rural pre-paid community schemes receive contributions either once or twice a year (Arhin 1995; Eklund and Stavem 1996; Shepard *et al.* 1996). As these payments are timed to coincide with harvests, there is greater ability to pay scheme contributions. There is thus the *potential* to generate more revenue than user fees, which rely on the full fee being paid at the time of service use. Arhin (1995) found that a significant proportion of rural dwellers express a preference for pre-payment schemes as opposed to user fees.

Pre-paid community schemes usually have a flat-rate contribution per member or per household. As the poor tend to have a greater incidence of morbidity (Abel-Smith and Dua 1988), a flat pre-payment may be less regressive than levying fees for every service used. This would be particularly relevant to the elderly, especially if they are suffering from a chronic illness requiring regular visits for monitoring and dispensing of medication.

Family, as opposed to individual, membership not only reinforces social cohesion but it also reduces adverse selection (where high-risk individuals are more likely than others to take insurance cover) (Lambo 1998; Shepard *et al.* 1996). Family membership of pre-payment schemes is likely to be particularly important in protecting the elderly against high health care costs.

A criticism of pre-paid and other community financing schemes is that they place the burden for health care financing on those least able to afford it (poorer rural communities) (Stinson 1984; Hoare and Mills 1986). Such financing mechanisms will be particularly inequitable if free (entirely tax-funded) health services are provided in urban areas (Abel-Smith and Dua 1988). However, if the quality of care at rural public sector facilities is very low, individuals may already be incurring significant costs by purchasing care in the private sector or by travelling long distances to use better-resourced public facilities in urban areas. Pre-payment schemes which generate resources to improve the quality of public sector health services, particularly the supply of drugs, may in fact reduce the amount that individuals have to pay for health care. Service quality improvements have been reported in all schemes evaluated in the literature, with the exception of the CAM card scheme in Burundi (Arhin 1994; Arhin 1995; Shaw and Griffin 1995).

In summary, community-based pre-payment schemes are seen as being a more sustainable alternative to user fees. However, equity can be undermined if these schemes only exist in rural areas with limited cost-recovery efforts in urban areas. It is particularly important that such community financing initiatives are supported by adequate and equitable allocations of government health funds to rural facilities to ensure accessible and quality health services.

Decentralisation

While there are varied objectives for health service decentralisation in different countries, some of the most frequently cited objectives (Brijlal et al. 1998) include:

▶ bringing about community participation;

▶ promoting local self-reliance;

▶ promoting political representation, 'good governance' and the accountability of the government to the population; and

▶ improving management, including more effectively meeting local needs.

From the perspective of older people, decentralisation may be a positive development if it promotes improved recognition and meeting of their specific health care needs. The nature of community participation in decentralised health service management, and the extent to which the 'voice' of older people, especially those who are impoverished, is heard, is of particular importance in this regard.

There is often an interrelationship between decentralisation (which is a reform of health sector organisation) and health care financing reforms. For example, the promotion of local revenue generation through user fees and/or community pre-payment schemes is often implemented along with greater decision-making responsibility and authority at the local level. However, user fees, community pre-payment schemes and other forms of cost sharing will not generate sufficient revenue to fund decentralised health services in their entirety. If decentralisation is to be successfully implemented, it is incumbent upon central government to ensure that lower levels of government have adequate resources to provide services for which they have been given responsibility. As the bulk of general tax revenue is usually collected at the central level, there is a need for increased inter-governmental transfers with decentralisation (unless taxation authority is also decentralised).

Decentralisation can result in greater inequity in resource availability as historically disadvantaged (especially rural) areas are unable to generate substantial local revenue. It is thus critical that decentralisation of service provision responsibility is accompanied by a mechanism for equitably allocating centrally collected revenue. This may take the form of a needs-based resource allocation formula, one of the critical elements of which is the demographic profile of geographic areas (DHSS 1976; McIntyre et al. 1990; Doherty and van den Heever 1997). This allows the relatively greater levels of ill health and need for health services among the elderly (as well as very young children and women of child-bearing age) to be taken into account. Given that the elderly predominantly live in rural areas, if such a resource allocation approach is not adopted, older people are likely to be particularly disadvantaged in access to appropriately resourced health services.

One of the more recent forms of decentralisation, namely that of developing autonomous institutions, may also pose problems in health service access for the elderly. A number of central, and other, hospitals in African countries now enjoy greater management autonomy, and are expected to increasingly fund their services through cost-recovery efforts (McPake 1996). The search for increased financial self-sufficiency leads these hospitals to focus more on serving patients who are covered by some form of health insurance and/or individuals, usually employed, who have a sufficiently high income to pay fees that approximate (or exceed) the cost of service provision. Such hospitals, therefore, are less likely to be willing to serve patients, such as the elderly, with relatively high levels of ill-health and more frequent need for use of health services, but with limited ability to pay for these services.

172 FORMAL SOCIAL PROTECTION AND OLDER PEOPLE

Creating an enabling environment for the private sector

Most countries' health systems have both public and private sector involvement in health care financing and provision. Changing the public/private sector mix has been one of the central issues in health sector reform initiatives in a wide range of low- and middle-income countries as well as in some high-income countries. More specifically, these reforms have focused on mechanisms for increasing the role of the private sector (Bennett 1992; Gilson and Mills 1995).

The World Bank has played a particularly important role in promoting the growth of the private health sector. The 1993 *World Development Report* (World Bank 1993) strongly argued for government to restrict itself to financing health services with significant externalities and an 'essential package' of care (see next section). This should be complemented by the creation of an enabling environment for the private health sector to grow and to finance and provide all services outside of this essential package.

There is a wide range of private health care providers in African countries, including:

▶ traditional healers;

▶ non-governmental organisations (NGOs), including mission hospitals and health centres as well as a range of community-based service organisations;

▶ private-for-profit providers, including independent practitioners, dispensaries/pharmacies, health centres and hospitals; and

▶ a growing number of 'informal' or unqualified providers such as street drug vendors.

In many African countries, NGOs, particularly mission facilities, are a very important source of health services in rural areas. Given the concentration of older people in rural areas and their frequently lower access to financial resources, NGOs are likely to be one of the more important private providers for the elderly in Africa.

Formal voluntary private insurance schemes, usually employment-based, are less extensive than other forms of private health care finance (such as user fees and pre-payment schemes) in Africa at present. Private voluntary insurance is unlikely to be of major benefit to the elderly in the African context. The international trend in private health insurance organisations is not to include parents as dependants – that is, to restrict cover to the principal member and his/her spouse and children. The elderly may benefit if they are able to continue their membership of the private insurance scheme on retirement. However, many private insurance schemes have risk-rated contributions, which would make membership prohibitively expensive for the elderly, given that they are usually regarded as high-risk and are thus charged the highest premiums. Recent South African experience highlights some very concerning trends in relation to the impact of private insurance on the elderly. In particular, many South Africans contributed to medical schemes throughout their working lives, while claiming limited benefits, in the mistaken belief that in later life they would be entitled to draw more benefits than their contribution levels given the inherent cross-subsidisation in the initial design of these schemes. However, as medical scheme expenditure began to spiral out of control from the mid-1980s, the goalposts shifted, and pensioners found themselves forced either to pay massive contributions with ever-declining benefit packages or to leave the schemes and rely on public sector health services (Cornell *et al.* 2001; Söderlund *et al.* 1998).

It is clear that the private health sector has a potentially important role to play in African countries, both in terms of financing and provision, given that macro-economic conditions make it difficult for governments to fund and provide all the health services required by their populations. The goals of NGOs are generally more closely aligned with those of national health policy and it will be particularly important to seek ways to support these private providers. The growth in for-profit providers cannot be ignored and it is important to instal appropriate regulation and incentive mechanisms to promote the private sector contribution to national health policy goals and to protect vulnerable groups, including the elderly. Similarly, an adequate regulatory framework is required for private voluntary insurance schemes.

Essential package policies

As indicated in the preceding section, the 1993 *World Development Report* argued that governments should only finance those public health services that have *substantial* externalities, listed as 'infectious disease control, prevention of AIDS, environmental pollution, and behaviours (such as drunk driving) that put others at risk' (World Bank 1993: 6). In addition, it was argued that governments should finance a defined package of essential clinical services. It was recommended that the essential package should include cost-effective health services which address the major health problems within that country (determined in terms of the 'burden of disease').

The World Bank team developed a specific methodology for measuring the burden of disease within a country, namely the DALY (Disability-Adjusted Life Year) (World Bank 1993; Murray 1994; Murray and Lopez 1994). The DALY combines losses from premature death (the difference between the actual age at death and life expectancy at that age) and loss of healthy life resulting from disability. The cost-effectiveness of particular clinical interventions can be determined in terms of their cost per DALY. It was argued that the essential package of services within a particular country should include those with the lowest cost per DALY, taking into consideration budgetary constraints (World Bank 1993).

There has been considerable debate about the methodology for calculating DALYs and about the use of cost per DALY estimates for determining an essential package (Ugalde and Jackson 1995; Barker and Green 1996; Anand and Hanson 1998; Paalman *et al*. 1998). One of the most controversial aspects of the DALY calculation is the differential age weighting applied to life years lost (Barendregt *et al*. 1996). Murray (1994: 438), a key designer of DALYs, argues that it is valid to weight life years lost for working-age adults higher than for young children and the elderly, given that 'because of social roles the social value of that time may be greater' and that it is purely 'an attempt to capture different social roles at different ages'. Anand and Hanson (1997: 691) highlight the extent of age discrimination by noting that 'in the construction of a DALY, a year lived at age 2 counts for only 20 per cent of a year lived at age 25 where the age-weighting function is at a maximum, while that lived at age 70 counts for 46 per cent of the maximum'. The effect of this age weighting is that if two people have the same illness and can be treated effectively for the same cost, a young adult will be treated rather than an older person. A number of authors have argued that the age weights should be considered 'inequitable in principle' (Paalman *et al*. 1998: 17; Anand and Hanson 1997).

Given the considerable age weighting included in the DALYs, and hence in the cost-effectiveness analyses, older people and very young children living in poor households, particularly in rural areas where there is more limited access to health services, are likely to be most adversely affected by the burden of disease and essential package approach. Despite growing concerns about the serious methodological and data limitations in existing 'cost per DALY' studies, a large number of African countries have been persuaded to adopt this approach and have defined an essential package of services to be provided through public funding. In many instances, donor funding is also earmarked for providing this essential package of services.

From the perspective of older people in Africa, it is extremely concerning that the essential package of care is heavily biased in favour of reproductive, maternal and child health. For example, as indicated previously, malnutrition is increasingly recognised as being a serious health problem among the elderly in Africa. However, the basic package focuses on nutrition for young children and pregnant and lactating mothers only, with the exception of information, education and communication (IEC) on nutrition which would presumably have some benefits for a wider group. Curative care at health centre level, which would have been one category that could benefit the elderly, is explicitly prioritised for young children. In addition, chronic care is restricted to tuberculosis treatment, which the epidemiological profile presented earlier suggests is not one of the most critical health problems for the elderly in Africa. The costs of services outside of this very limited package are expected to be borne by the patient. Given that the 'essential package' approach dominates much of health policy in Africa, it would appear important to continue to challenge the assumptions underlying the DALY approach, and to advocate a more equitable method of priority setting to benefit Africans of all ages according to their needs.

Social health insurance

While there are many variants of social health insurance (SHI) internationally, the major characteristic of this form of health care financing is that of *compulsory* (that is, required by legislation) contributions by formal sector employees and their employers, in the first instance, into a health fund (Hoare and Mills 1986). In some countries this has been extended gradually until universal population coverage is achieved. Social solidarity, which implies cross–subsidisation of lower income earners by the wealthy and of the ill by the healthy, is a fundamental concept of SHI (Ron *et al.* 1990).

There has been a particular focus on the potential application of SHI in African countries since the 1990s (Abel-Smith and Rawal 1994; Shaw and Griffin 1995; Shaw and Ainsworth 1996) but to date relatively few have moved to implementation. Most advocates of SHI argue that it removes the burden of financing health care for employed persons, and frequently their dependants, from the state. In this way, scarce tax-funded resources can be released to improve the delivery of cost-effective services for the non-insured population, particularly the poor (Griffin and Shaw 1996). However, costs to the government (such as employer contributions to SHI for civil servants) may exceed the public resources released through SHI cover (Kutzin 1995). It is thus important to evaluate prior to implementation whether or not SHI will improve the distribution of government subsidies (Kutzin 1998).

The major disadvantage of SHI, from an equity perspective, is that it creates a two–tier health system with differentiation in access to health services on the basis of contribution status (Ensor 1995; Kutzin 1995). The quantity and quality of health services are usually greater for those who are covered by SHI (Hoare and Mills 1986; Bachmann 1994).

There are considerable concerns about the potential impact on the elderly of introducing SHI in African countries. The majority of older people are not in formal employment and will thus be excluded from SHI cover, unless they qualify as dependants. This may serve to marginalise the elderly, along with other vulnerable groups such as the unemployed. In general, the elderly, particularly those in rural areas, will only benefit from the introduction of a SHI if the government resources released by the SHI exceed the amount that the government contributes to SHI. In addition, the net gain in resources would have to be explicitly targeted to services which would benefit the most vulnerable. The limited experience of SHI in Africa is not encouraging in this regard: either the introduction of SHI has resulted in a net loss in resources for spending on general public sector health services or there has been little attempt actively to redistribute government resources to benefit the non-insured. It is thus critical to undertake a detailed review of who will benefit from an SHI, and to what extent, before pursuing SHI and, if it is implemented, to establish mechanisms for promoting equitable distribution of limited government health care resources.

Poverty reduction strategies

In September 1999, the World Bank and International Monetary Fund (IMF) decided that each country being considered for concessional lending by the World Bank's International Development Association or for debt relief under the Heavily Indebted Poor Countries (HIPC) Initiative had to prepare a Poverty Reduction Strategy Paper (PRSP). While the PRSPs were to be developed by the country concerned, the World Bank has produced a very detailed manual, called the *PRSP Sourcebook*, on how to draft a PRSP (www.worldbank.org/poverty/ strategies).

Importantly, there are repeated cautionary statements about the adverse effects of user fees in the health chapter of this sourcebook. For example, the introduction states that 'Out-of-pocket payments for health services – especially hospital care – can make the difference between a household being poor or not' (Claeson *et al.* 2001: 1). The authors also argue that governments 'can mitigate the effects of low income on health outcomes by reducing the price poor people pay for health and other key goods and services, through, for example, health insurance, fee-waivers, and targeted food subsidies' (Claeson *et al.* 2001: 2). This implies a policy change within the World Bank, given the previous heavy emphasis on user fees as a key health care financing mechanism, with insufficient attention to minimising adverse equity effects. The PRSP health chapter goes further than considering alternative financing mechanisms; it also addresses the improvement of other aspects of health service access and quality to promote their use by the poor in times of need.

Despite the numerous positive features of the PRSP health chapter and associated technical annexes, as with many other recent international health policy initiatives there is an almost exclusive focus on children and women of reproductive age in this document. For example, although nutrition and mental health problems are key causes of ill-health for older people, the nutrition interventions recommended focus exclusively on children, adolescents and women of childbearing age, while the mental health section also makes no mention of the particular challenges for the elderly. Indeed, the only reference to older people in the technical annex was a brief statement that chronic illnesses increase with demographic ageing.

The PRSPs developed by each country included in the PRS initiative, most of which are in Africa, will have a dramatic impact on their health policies. The *PRSP Sourcebook*, thus, provides valuable insights into the likely future direction of health sector reforms in Africa. While it is extremely encouraging that there has been some recognition of the adverse consequences of certain of the previous reforms, it is also of concern that this important initiative for addressing poverty and its consequences pays virtually no attention to the plight of older poor people.

Key issues and future research

Although there are extremely limited empirical data on the issue, it is likely that most of the health sector reforms that have been introduced in African countries over the past decade or more have had adverse consequences for many older people. It has been shown that many older people in Africa live in rural areas and in households falling into very low-income categories. The elderly, although making considerable contributions (often of a non-monetary nature) to the households they live in, are frequently heavily dependent on family and other social support networks for access to financial resources. Older people in African countries with a high incidence of AIDS are particularly vulnerable when they have to assume responsibility for caring for their HIV-infected adult children and/or orphaned grandchildren.

Health sector reforms in Africa have focused particularly on increasing private sources of finance for health services and increasing the relative role of the private health sector. The introduction of, or increases in, user fees has potentially the most serious adverse impact on access to health care for the elderly. This relates to the fact that one needs ready access to money at the time of seeking health care, which is a particular constraint for the elderly living in poor households. Given that older people do report ill-health more frequently than other age groups, the requirement of ready access to funds would impact more heavily on the elderly and their families.

It is precisely because of the risk of incurring substantial health care costs that health insurance vehicles were created. A range of insurance or pre-payment mechanisms has been promoted through reforms of African health systems. However, very few older people are likely to be covered through voluntary private or social health insurance schemes, unless they are included as adult dependants of a formal sector employee. In the limited number of African countries where older people are principal members of private insurance schemes, through continuation membership on retirement, there has been a trend of rapid increases in contribution rates and declining benefit packages for this high-risk group. The results have been declining membership of these schemes among the elderly and heightened reliance on publicly funded services. The major concern in relation to SHI is that the elderly will become an increasingly marginalised group, and that gradually public resources will come to be concentrated on funding SHI contributions for civil servants and subsidising those for other SHI members, with correspondingly lower resources being devoted to those who are dependent on publicly funded services.

Community-based pre-payment schemes are likely to have the least adverse consequences for older people, if some form of private contribution to health care funding is required. The reason for this is that membership is usually on a family or household basis, and is thus more likely to include the elderly than voluntary private or social health insurance. In addition, as the contribution is usually an annual flat rate contribution with no additional charge per visit, the elderly will be able to access (at least outpatient) health services at the time of need. However, as these schemes usually operate in rural areas, it is essential that urban dwellers who have the ability to pay for health services are also required to contribute to the costs of their health care. In addition, these mechanisms for generating private health care contributions must be supplemented by equitable allocation of central government health care resources between geographical areas and individual facilities.

It is of considerable concern that there is still substantial pressure from some international organisations for governments in African countries to restrict their financing of health services to an essential care package. The recommended package has a heavy bias towards maternal and child health, which translates into very limited availability of the type of publicly funded health services most needed by the elderly.

The almost exclusive focus on children and women of childbearing age is seen in a wide range of international initiatives relating to health services, including the recent Poverty Reduction Strategy initiative.

While many children and young women in Africa are vulnerable, the elderly should also be recognised as a vulnerable group, particularly those in households of low socio-economic status, with limited access to support networks and those affected by the HIV/AIDS epidemic.

Although the percentage of the population who can be described as elderly is still relatively small in Africa at present, the number of older people is increasing and will continue to do so in future. It is essential that governments and international organisations pay closer attention to older people, particularly those who are poor, and their health needs in order to develop policies that minimise adverse impacts on this section of the population and instead preferentially advantage this group. This will only occur through advocacy for such an approach, which needs to be supported by sound research.

At present, there is a dearth of research around health policies and the elderly in Africa. There are household survey data available which, as has been demonstrated through the albeit limited analyses presented in this chapter, can be used to:

▶ better understand the characteristics and experience of older people, and which subgroups are particularly vulnerable;

▶ investigate their specific health needs;

▶ analyse health service utilisation by the elderly and what determines utilisation patterns; and

▶ review the impact of specific health policy actions.

In addition to household survey data analyses, monitoring and evaluation of new health policies should include consideration of their impact on the elderly, as well as other population groups.

It is only through improved understanding of these issues that health policies and strategies can be developed which will be of benefit to all Africans.

NOTE

1   I am greatly indebted to two colleagues in the Health Economics Unit, University of Cape Town, who contributed to this chapter by undertaking analyses of various household survey data sets. Okore Okorafor analysed the LSMS data sets for Côte D'Ivoire, Tanzania and South Africa to provide contextual socio-economic and health care utilisation and expenditure information. Michael Thiede analysed the KIDS data set to determine the effect of the removal of user fees for primary health care services in South Africa. I am also grateful to Peter Lloyd-Sherlock and Michael Thiede for extremely helpful comments on earlier drafts of this chapter.

REFERENCES

Abel-Smith, B. and A. Dua (1988) 'Community-financing in developing countries: the potential for the health sector', *Health Policy and Planning*, 3: 95–108.

Abel-Smith, B. and P. Rawal (1994) 'Employer's willingness to pay: The case for compulsory health insurance in Tanzania', *Health Policy and Planning*, 9: 409–18.

Ahenkora, K. (1999) *The Contribution of Older People to Development: The Ghana Study*, HelpAge International and HelpAge Ghana, London.

Akin, J., N. Birdsall and D. de Ferranti (1987) *Financing Health Services in Developing Countries: An Agenda for Reform*, A World Bank Policy Study, The World Bank, Washington, DC.

Anand S. and K. Hanson (1997) 'Disability-adjusted life years: a critical review', *Journal of Health Economics*, 16: 685–702.

—— (1998) 'DALYs: Efficiency versus equity', *World Development*, 26: 307–10.

Apt, N.A. (2002) *Informal Care for Older People: The African Crisis*, mimeo, United Nations Research Institute for Social Development, Geneva.

Arhin, D.C. (1994) 'The health card insurance scheme in Burundi: A social asset or a non-viable venture?', *Social Science and Medicine*, 39: 861–70.

—— (1995) *Rural Health Insurance: A Viable Alternative to User Fees?*, PHP Departmental Publication No. 19, Department of Public Health Policy, London School of Hygiene and Tropical Medicine, London.

Bachmann, M.O. (1994) 'Would national health insurance improve equity and efficiency of health care in South Africa? Lessons from Asia and Latin America', *South African Medical Journal*, 84: 153–7.

Barendregt, J. J., L. Bonneux, and P. J.Van der Maas (1996) 'DALYs: the age-weights on balance', *Bulletin of the WHO*, 74: 439–46.

Barker, C. and A. Green (1996) 'Opening the debate on DALYs', *Health Policy and Planning*, 11: 179–83.

Bennett, S. (1992) 'Promoting the private sector: A review of developing country trends', *Health Policy and Planning*, 7: 97–110.

Berman, P.A. (1995) 'Health sector reform: Making health development sustainable', in P. Berman (ed.), *Health Sector Reform in Developing Countries: Making Health Development Sustainable*. Harvard University Press, Boston.

Brijlal, V., L. Gilson, J. Mahon, D. McIntyre, and S. Thomas (1998) *Key Issues in Decentralisation: Background Paper for Module 9 of the Flagship Course in Health Sector Reform and Sustainable Financing*, University of Cape Town, University of the Witwatersrand and World Bank, Washington, DC.

Charlton, K. E. and D. Rose (2001) 'Nutrition among older adults in Africa: the situation at the beginning of the millennium', *The Journal of Nutrition*, 131: 2424S–2428S.

Chernichovsky, D. and O.A. Meesok (1986) 'Utilisation of health services in Indonesia', *Social Science and Medicine*, 23: 611–20.

Claeson, M., C. Griffin, T. Johnston, M. McLachlan, A. Soucat, A. Wagstaff and A. Yazbeck (2001) 'Health, nutrition and population', in *World Bank Poverty Reduction Strategy Papers' Sourcebook*, World Bank, Washington, DC, available at <www.worldbank.org/poverty/strategies>.

Corbett, J. (1989) 'Poverty and sickness: the high costs of ill-health', *IDS Bulletin*, 20: 58–62.

Cornell, J., J. Goudge, D. McIntyre, and S. Mbatsha (2001) *National Health Accounts: The private sector report*, Department of Health, Pretoria.

de Ferranti, D. (1985) *Paying for Health Services in Developing Countries: An Overview*, World Bank Staff Working Papers No. 721, The World Bank, Washington, DC.

DHSS (Department of Health and Social Security) (1976) *Report of the Resource Allocation Working Party: Sharing Resources for Health in England*, HMSO, London.

Diop, F., A. Yazbeck and R. Bitrán (1995) 'The impact of alternative cost recovery schemes on access and equity in Niger', *Health Policy and Planning*, 10: 223–40.

Doherty, J. and A. van den Heever (1997) *A Resource Allocation Formula in Support of Equity and Primary Health Care*, Centre for Health Policy, University of the Witwatersrand, Johannesburg.

Eklund, P. and K. Stavem (1996) 'Community health insurance through prepayment schemes in Guinea-Bissau', in R. P. Shaw and M. Ainsworth (eds.), *Financing Health Services Through User Fees and Insurance: Case Studies from Sub-Saharan Africa*, The World Bank, Washington, DC.

Ensor, T. (1995) 'Introducing health insurance in Vietnam', *Health Policy and Planning*, 10: 154–63.

Gertler, P., L. Locay and W. Sanderson (1987) 'Are user fees regressive? The welfare implications of health care financing proposals in Peru', *Journal of Econometrics*, 36: 67–88.

Gilson, L. (1995) 'Management and health care reform in sub-Saharan Africa', *Social Science and Medicine*, 40: 695–710.

—— (1998) 'In defence and pursuit of equity', *Social Science and Medicine*, 47: 1891– 1896.

—— and A. Mills (1995) 'Health sector reforms in sub-Saharan Africa: Lessons of the last 10 years', in P. Berman (ed.), *Health Sector Reform in Developing Cuntries: Making Health Development Sustainable*, Harvard University Press, Boston.

——, S. Russell and K. Buse (1995) 'The political economy of user fees with targeting: Developing equitable health financing policy', *Journal of International Development*, 7: 369–401.

Griffin, C.C. (1988) 'User charges for health care in principle and practice', Seminar Paper No. 37, Economic Development Institute of the World Bank, The World Bank, Washington, DC.

—— and R.P. Shaw (1996) 'Health insurance in Sub-Saharan Africa: Aims, findings, policy implications', in R. P. Shaw and M. Ainsworth (eds.), *Financing Health Services Through User Fees and Insurance: Case Studies from Sub-Saharan Africa*, The World Bank, Washington, DC.

HelpAge International (2000) *The Mark of a Noble Society: Human Rights and Older People*, HelpAge International, London.

Heslop, A. (1999) *Ageing and Development*, HelpAge International, London.

Hoare, G. and A. Mills (1986) 'Paying for the health sector: A review and annotated bibliography of the literature on developing countries', EPC Publication No 12, Evaluation and Planning Centre for Health Care, London School of Hygiene and Tropical Medicine, London.

Kutzin, J. (1995) 'Experience with organizational and financing reform of the health sector', SHS Current Concerns Paper Number 8. Division of Strengthening of Health Services, World Health Organization, Geneva.

—— (1998) 'Health insurance for the formal sector in Africa: "Yes, but…"', in A. Beattie, J. Doherty, L. Gilson, E. Lambo and P. Shaw (eds.), *Sustainable Health Care Financing in Southern Africa*, World Bank, Washington, DC.

La Forgia, G. (1992) *Means Testing in Health Ministry Facilities in the Dominican Republic. From Platitudes to Practice: Targeting Social Programs in Latin America*, World Bank Latin America and the Caribbean Technical Department Regional Studies Program, Washington, DC.

Lambo, E. (1998) 'Aims and performance of prepayment schemes', in A. Beattie, J. Doherty, L. Gilson, E. Lambo and P. Shaw (eds.), *Sustainable Health Care Financing in Southern Africa*, World Bank, Washington, DC.

Litvack, J. and C. Bodart (1993) 'User fees plus quality equals improved access to health care: Results of a field experiment in Cameroon', *Social Science and Medicine*, 37: 369–83.

McIntyre, D. E., S. P. Taylor, W. M. Pick, D. E. Bourne and J. M. L. Klopper (1990) 'A methodology for resource allocation in health care for South Africa; Part II: The British experience and its relevance to South Africa', *South African Medical Journal*, 77: 453–55.

McIntyre, D. (2002) 'Health policy and older people in Africa', paper presented at the UNRISD Conference on 'Ageing, Development and Social Protection', 7–9 April, Madrid.

McPake, B. (1996) 'Public autonomous hospitals in sub-Saharan Africa: trends and issues', *Health Policy*, 35: 155–77.

McPake, B., K. Hanson, A. Mills (1993) 'Community financing of health care in Africa: An evaluation of the Bamako initiative', *Social Science and Medicine*, 36: 1383–1395.

Mooney, G. (1996) 'And now for vertical equity? Some concerns arising from Aboriginal health in Australia', *Health Economics*, 5: 99–103.

Murray, C. J. L. (1994) 'Quantifying the burden of disease: the technical basis for disability-adjusted life years', *Bulletin of the World Health Organization*, 72: 429–45.

Murray, C. J. L. and A. D. Lopez (1994) *Global comparative assessments in the health sector: Disease burden, expenditure and intervention packages*, World Health Organisation, Geneva.

Mwanzia, J. and G. Mwabu (1993) *User Charges in Government Health Facilities in Kenya: Effect on Revenue and Attendance Without Improvement in Medical Care Quality. Report on Study Undertaken by the Kenyan Ministry of Health in Conjunction with the World Health Organisation*, World Health Organisation, Geneva.

Paalman, M., H. Bekedam, L. Hawken and D. Nyheim (1998) 'A critical review of priority setting in the health sector: the methodology of the 1993 World Development Report', *Health Policy and Planning*, 13: 13–31.

Ron, A., B. Abel-Smith and G. Tamburi (1990) *Health Insurance in Developing Countries: The Social Security Approach*, International Labour Office, Geneva.

Russell, S. (1996) 'Ability to pay for health care: concepts and evidence', *Health Policy and Planning*, 11: 219–37.

——, and L. Gilson (1995) *User Fees at Government Health Services: Is equity being considered?* Health Policy Unit, London School of Hygiene and Tropical Medicine, London.

Shaw, R. P. and M. Ainsworth (eds.) (1996) *Financing Health Services Through User Fees and Insurance: Case Studies from Sub-Saharan Africa*, The World Bank, Washington, DC.

Shaw, R. P. and C. C. Griffin (1995) *Financing Health Care in Sub-Saharan Africa Through User Fees and Insurance*, World Bank, Washington, DC.

Shepard, D. S., T. Vian, E. F. Kleinau (1996) 'Performance and impact of four health insurance programs in rural and urban areas of Zaire', in R. P. Shaw and M. Ainsworth (eds.), *Financing Health Services Through User fees and Insurance: Case Studies from Sub-Saharan Africa*, The World Bank, Washington, DC.

Söderlund, N., G. Schierhout and A. van den Heever (1998) *Private Health Care in South Africa*, Health Systems Trust, Durban.

Stanton, B. and J. Clemens (1989) 'User fees for health care in developing countries: A case study of Bangladesh', *Social Science and Medicine*, 29: 1199–1205.

Stinson, W. (1984) 'Potential and limitations of community financing', *World Health Forum*, 5: 123–5.

Ugalde, A. and J. T. Jackson (1995) 'The World Bank and international health policy: a critical review', *Journal of International Development*, 7: 525–41.

United Nations Development Programme (2001) *Human Development Report 2001: Making New Technologies Work for Human Development*, Oxford University Press, New York.

Waddington, C. J. and N. Enyimayew (1989) 'A price to pay: The impact of user charges in Ashanti-Akim District, Ghana', *International Journal of Health Planning and Management*, 4: 17–47.

Wagstaff, A. and E. Van Doorslaer (1993) 'Equity in the finance and delivery of health care: Concepts and definitions', in E. Van Doorslaer, A. Wagstaff, and F. Rutten (eds.), *Equity in the Finance and Delivery of Health Care: An International Perspective*, Oxford University Press, New York.

Whitehead, M. (1992) 'The concepts and principles of equity and health', *International Journal of Health Services*, 22: 429–45.

Willis, C. Y. and C. Leighton (1995) 'Protecting the poor: The role of means testing', *Health Policy and Planning;* 10: 241–56.

World Bank (1993) *World Development Report 1993: Investing in Health*, Oxford University Press for The World Bank, New York.

World Bank (1994) *Better Health in Africa: Experience and Lessons Learned,* World Bank, Washington, DC.

Yoder R. A. (1989) 'Are people willing and able to pay for health services?' *Social Science and Medicine*, 29: 35–42.

Zohoori, N. (2001) 'Nutrition and healthy functioning in the developing world', *The Journal of Nutrition*, 131: 2429S–2431S.

CHAPTER 9

Social Health Insurance for Older People: A Comparison of Argentina and the United States

NÉLIDA RODONDO[1]

Both Argentina and the United States have relatively aged population structures. Despite significant economic, social and cultural differences, these two societies employ similar institutional structures to provide health care for retired persons. The United States MEDICARE system and Argentina's National Institute of Social Services for Retirees and Pensioners (INSSJP) are, in fact, the only social security agencies in the world specifically designed to provide health care for retirees and pensioners. As explained below, INSSJP was modelled on the United States MEDICARE system.

This chapter provides a comparative analysis of the two schemes. It examines key elements in their performance, including their current problems and anticipated reforms, and identifies lessons of potential relevance to other countries. The first section provides a brief history of health policy in the two countries. It focuses on the political and institutional structures out of which the two health care systems grew, highlighting the major events in their evolution. The second section examines the general characteristics of the populations served by INSSJP and MEDICARE. It goes on to analyse recent budget data for each scheme and the structure of the benefits they provide. This leads on to a consideration of ongoing discussions about reforming each scheme and a general appraisal of their respective strengths and weaknesses. This includes recommendations about the severe crisis which is currently affecting the INSSJP.

State welfare institutions in the United States and Argentina

Both Argentina and the United States have relatively aged population structures (Table 9.1). This process of ageing dates back to the early

Table 9.1 Persons over 65 years of age as a percentage of total population – Argentina and the United States, 1960–2000

Population censuses Year	Argentina % over 65	USA % over 65
1960	5.7	9.31
1970	7	9.87
1980	8.2	11.34
1991/0	8.9	12.55
2000	9.7	12.44

Sources: Argentina: National Population Censuses of 1960, 1970, 1980 and 1991, and INDEC 1996 estimates and projections for the year 2000; United States: Population 1790 to 1990 United States Summary, and USA Statistics in Brief, U.S. Census Bureau (1990–2000).

twentieth century, giving rise to long-standing debates about the role of the state in providing economic and medical protection to older people. These debates intensified after the Second World War, and saw a shift of responsibility towards the public sphere. Intergenerational transfers and obligations which had previously been in the domain of families were partly taken over by more formalised structures of social security. The emergence of MEDICARE and the INSSJP was an important part of this process.

The United States health care system

The early decades of the twentieth century in the United States saw the first discussions regarding the provision of broad-based health care. The majority of the population wanted protection against unpredictable, and potentially catastrophic, medical expenses. Debate focused principally on relative merits of public and private financing of health insurance. Given the liberal economic views that predominated in the country, opinion favoured a private-sector system, to be financed primarily in the workplace. Though private coverage grew during and following the Second World War, legislative proposals for national health insurance appeared in Congress throughout the 1940s. Political fragmentation in Congress, however, as well as determined opposition on the part of the insurance industry, physicians' groups and hospital associations, weakened consensus for such legislation (Giaimo 2001).

    The early 1960s saw the beginning of a crusade for government-funded health care for older people, driven in part by then Senator (and later President) Kennedy. In 1965, after extensive national debate (intensified by the effects of the assassination of the president) Congress passed legislation establishing MEDICARE and MEDICAID. MEDICARE was initially created to meet the medical needs of elderly individuals. Coverage for some disabled people and victims of chronic kidney disease was added in 1972. MEDICAID was designed to provide the needy with health care not adequately covered by existing public services (HCFA 2002a). Established after 50 years of intense public debate, MEDICARE was the first social security agency in the world specifically designed to provide health care for a growing elderly population.

Implementation of MEDICARE

MEDICARE was initially intended to provide beneficiaries with levels of health care comparable to those provided to individuals during their working lives by employer-funded private insurance plans. Prior to the advent of MEDICARE, the average cost of private health insurance represented between 13 per cent and 20 per cent of median income for older married couples. As a result, only half of the over-65 population and one third of those over 75 had such insurance (MEDPAC 2002).

Initially, MEDICARE designed benefits packages based on the traditional health insurance model: coverage against the risk of impoverishment due to serious illness or accident; and reduced costs for the use of particular services. MEDICARE covered almost all hospitalisation costs for acute illness, as well as home care during convalescence (*Part A*), while outpatient care (*Part B*) was an option that most MEDICARE beneficiaries could obtain by paying an additional monthly fee. The manner in which benefits were structured reflected a desire to balance health care access and financial protection for beneficiaries against the burden on taxpayers and beneficiaries.

Although the basic benefits package initially provided through the MEDICARE system remained virtually unchanged, coverage for particular services was repeatedly revised through legislation, reinterpretation of regulatory provisions and judicial rulings. The revisions significantly broadened the types of services that were covered, adding new technologies and procedures, greater convalescent care, selected preventive services, and other services for the terminally ill. However, services such as outpatient medications, and optical and dental services remained uncovered.

A series of laws passed by the United States Congress extended the range of benefits and people entitled to MEDICARE. These included: people aged under 65 who suffered from chronic kidney disease (1972); preventive services (1980); mental health services, including partial inpatient care and community-based care (in the 1980s); end-of-life care (1982) and oral cancer drugs (1993) (MEDPAC 2002). Certain advances in medical technology, such as kidney transplants and coronary and cardiac therapies, generated new demand for rehabilitation services and home convalescent care. The broadening of services and the practice of providing them through different providers (Giaimo 2001) led to inflation in MEDICARE costs, and created a need to modify the method of paying for services.

From its creation to the early 1980s, MEDICARE underwent persistent cost inflation, (from US$3 billion in 1967 to over US$33 billion in 1982). This was less a reflection of population ageing than a consequence of the fee-for-service system, which encouraged uncontrolled hospital costs and the use of complex medical technology. In view of this trend, MEDICARE commissioned a Yale University study to develop a prospective payment system. This sought to increase control over the cost and quality of hospital care for patients with different combinations of pathologies, degrees of severity and general physical conditions (OTA 1983).

In 1983, after more than a decade of studies and testing, the first version of what are called diagnosis related groups (DRGs) was adopted. The purpose of the new system of payment and quality control was to ensure the efficiency of health care, keeping rates in balance for all diagnoses and promoting the appropriate use of new technologies. The prospective payment system included care guidelines and standard payments for 467 combinations of illnesses and hospital admittances, and dealt with financial risk related to potential increases in the need for services.

Health care in Argentina

Argentina's current health care system has its origins in the first and second Peronist governments (between 1945 and 1955). In this period public health became a high priority for government policy. The result was a national health care system, which aspired to universal coverage for the population. The number of hospital beds in the country doubled, a national network of outpatient health care facilities was set up, and many doctors became state employees (Katz 1993). The Peronist health project led to improved population health, reflected in large reductions in morbidity and mortality rates, both nationally and in poorer regions.

At the same time as these important advances in the national health system, a separate health insurance model emerged. This consisted of occupation-specific health funds (known as 'obras sociales'), which were mainly managed by labour unions and overseen by the Ministry of Social Security. By the 1950s, the health system was organised on the basis of two competing models: universal public health services (promoted by the federal Ministry of Health), and selective insurance (supervised by the Ministry of Social Security).

During the 1950s and 1960s efforts were made to decentralise and deconcentrate state health care services. A lack of technical and financial support contributed to a rapid deterioration of the public health care infrastructure. By contrast, the social insurance system became increasingly widespread, and emerged as the dominant model for health care financing and provision (Isuani and Mercer 1988; Katz 1993). Most of these insurance funds contracted out to third party providers, which gave rise to a complex set of interests in the health insurance industry, including the state, labour unions and a range of provider group lobbies (Katz 1993).

At the time of establishing the INSSJP in 1970, the country's health care financing consisted of three subsectors: a downgraded public sector; social insurance funds; and a small but growing private prepaid sector. In recent years, particularly the 1990s, there have been efforts to radically overhaul the health care system. These have involved further decentralisation of the public sector (including hospital self-management), and efforts to introduce competition between the social insurance funds. While these reforms largely failed to meet their objectives, they have contributed to the rapid expansion of private financing and provision. Argentina's economic crisis of 2000/2001 was reflected in serious funding problems across the health sector as a whole. In February 2002 the federal government declared a 'state of health emergency' covering the entire nation.

The creation of the INSSJP

The INSSJP, created in 1971, is a self-sufficient social insurance fund. It was established towards the end of a period of military rule beleaguered by popular resistance. In creating INSSJP, the old military regime hoped to gain popular support and be a contender in the future democratic process. On one hand, this further strengthened its relationship with the unions by transferring the costs of providing for retirees away from the union-run social insurance funds. On the other hand, the country was ageing: many retirees had been independent workers and therefore were not part of any social insurance plan. The military hoped that by offering these benefits it would gain a future electoral base.

It is likely that the military's thinking was heavily influenced by the implementation of MEDICARE five years earlier. Nevertheless, the design of MEDICARE and the process by which it was implemented were quite different from the Argentine case. Time frames, major motivations, the range of players and the political/institutional scenarios involved were notably different. MEDICARE was the result of a broad process of democratic debate in which powerful conflicting sectoral interests were balanced, and in which organisations representing the eventual beneficiaries played a decisive role. The result was a social security health care model, in a country where there had been strong popular support for private risk coverage. By contrast, INSSJP was based on agreements with powerful sectoral groups, without active citizen participation. The differing origins of the two institutions led to different organisational models, the features of which are described below.

Implementation of the Comprehensive Health Care Programme[2] (PAMI)

According to the legislation that created it, the mission of INSSJP is to provide social and health care services to all retirees and pensioners, now numbering nearly four million. INSSJP obtains funds derived from contributions of 1 per cent of wages, 2 per cent of the pension benefits, and 3 per cent of all annual bonus salaries. INSSJP is governed by private law, and therefore its accounts are not reviewed by any public auditing agency. The decisions of its officers alone determine its budget. The organisation's management structure includes a board of directors with representatives of labour unions, retirees' and pensioners' organisations, and the State. It is headed by a president appointed by the President of Argentina.

The INSSJP model for providing services is embodied in el Programa de Atención Médica Integral (PAMI), which was the result of the first and only open bidding process in its history. In design, the system was similar to Great Britain's national health care system. It was structured with three main levels of care: a primary level based on family physicians operating at the local level; a secondary level, comprising specialists and hospitalisation for acute care; and a third level, also based on inpatient services, for geriatric and psychiatric care.

The family physician was charged with overseeing the health and medical problems of clients, and was responsible for channelling patients to other levels of the system. Since the functioning of the system depended on the primary care level, which was entirely community-based, the new organisation operated through delegations and districts. Each district had a medical-social team that included doctors, nurses, social workers, psychologists, and household assistants. The model also introduced a new system for paying family physicians based on prospective payment per patient. Physicians were paid in advance every month according to the patient load (a maximum of 1,000 patients was permitted, regardless of the medical care required). Secondary care providers, on the other hand (including private clinics, community hospitals, and union-run polyclinics) functioned on a fee-for-service basis.

Among physicians' organisations, there was strong resistance to the creation of PAMI. Nevertheless, PAMI succeeded in implementing its model in the federal capital and in a few other cities. It was unable, however, to resist the pressure from the powerful Medical Federation of the Province of Buenos Aires (FEMEBA), and its defeat in the country's most important province exposed weaknesses in its model, which have since been exploited by physicians' groups elsewhere. Thus, while the INSSJP was nation-wide, the PAMI model was restricted to a few large cities. Elsewhere, physicians' organisations and associations of private medical facilities were free to negotiate contracts between INSSJP and service providers in ways which they preferred.

Between 1977 and 1981, the domestic currency was overvalued in relation to the dollar. In this context, the fee-for-service method of payment stimulated a surge in imported diagnostic and treatment technology. A medical care model, based on treating specific illnesses and on highly complex medical services, took root at PAMI, to the detriment of its original focus on comprehensive community-based care. Since INSSJP was the principal health care funder for the nation, the demand created by this health care approach weakened the position of public hospitals, which lacked funds for sophisticated technological equipment. The most important feature of this period was the transfer of financial and organisational resources for services from INSSJP to intermediary entities. These consisted of provider groups, which were able to set fees and schedule services largely at will. As a result, the INSSJP quickly developed substantial deficits, and it has continued to accumulate them through to the present day.

This same period saw a rapid expansion of INSSJP personnel: from 1,600 to 12,000 between 1976 and 1983. Since then, levels of employment have remained constant, despite two costly drives for voluntary retirement (1986 and 1995), each of which initially reduced the number of employees by about half. Never in the history of the institution has there been a competitive process for open selection of professional, technical or management personnel.

By the mid-1980s, when inflation was high, the Institute was facing a deepening crisis. By the end of the decade, it was clear that it could not continue funding an extensive and unusual collection of services that went well beyond basic medical and social care, to include housing mortgages, and generous psychiatric provision. In the early 1990s, in response to its worsening crisis the INSSJP implemented a new fixed capitation payment system which covered the total package of medical services provided to its members. It invited bids from third parties for supplying 'comprehensive packages'. In this way, INSSJP avoided hundreds of dispersed contracts with different intermediaries, transferring responsibility for services to a few private sector organisations that assumed the risk of increased demand for care in exchange for fixed revenue.

Stocker *et al.* (1999) correctly point out that the transplantation of the American health care model to Latin American countries was essentially limited to the application of techniques for controlling expenses in medical care. Thus, quality control and studies on the health care needs of the target population received little attention. In the case of INSSJP, the overall capitation values were not established on the basis of actuarial risk nor on valid, reliable statistics relating to the rate at which services were used. As at other times in the Institution's history, the capitation rate emerged from rudimentary negotiations between INSSJP officials and provider associations. These negotiations succeeded in bringing costs into line with available budgetary resources. However, there is also evidence of widespread corruption in contracting with providers. A significant proportion of the payment for services was being 'returned' to political officials (not to the INSSJP). These so-called 'returns' contributed to maintaining the political *status quo*. Since the providers were generally the same ones that had been operating since 1978, it is probable that the payment of 'commissions' to obtain contracts was a practice that had already been in effect for some years.

The new form of contracting based on capitation rates creates an incentive for underserving, since revenue is determined independent of whether clients make use of the services. As in any change, there were winners and losers. In the 1990s, the big winners were the pharmaceutical industry, which increased its share of the budget, and the health care administrators, which received major amounts for intermediation of contracts. The losers were providers of highly complex therapies, those responsible for delivering services, including clinical physicians, and, in general, human resources in the health care system, who lost power, prestige and remuneration.

Affiliation and benefit structures for the INSSJP and MEDICARE

There are significant differences between Argentina and the United States that must be taken into account when comparing their respective health care systems. In 2000, Argentina's *per capita* GDP was estimated at US$7,988.70. INSSJP's budget for 2000 was US$2.3 billion, representing 0.8 per cent of the country's GDP. Its expenditures, on the other hand, were US$2.6 billion, or 0.9 per cent of GDP for the year, representing around US$750 per client per year. In 2000, the United States had a *per capita* GDP of US$33,900. In 2000, the MEDICARE budget was US$224.4 billion, or 2.3 per cent of GDP, representing US$5,754 per client per year. Given these large variations, it is not surprising that there are important differences in the operation of each health scheme.

There is general agreement that INSSJP and MEDICARE specialise in providing health care for the elderly population. Nevertheless, here is where the first point of divergence between the two systems can be seen. While the over-65 population served by INSSJP represents 64 per cent of that age group in Argentina, MEDICARE serves 97 per cent of the over-65 population in the United States (Figure 9.1).

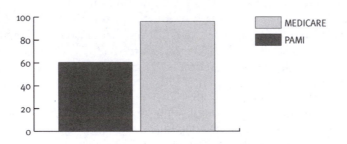

Figure 9.1 Population covered by INSSJP in Argentina and MEDICARE in the US as a percentage of the total over-65 population in those countries in 2000

Sources: Author's figures, based on data from the INSSJP Information Technology Office (2002a), INDEC (1995), Health Care Financing Administration (HCFA, 2002b) and US Census Bureau (2000).

The differences can be explained by the different conditions for admission to the two programmes. INSSJP includes retirees and pensioners from the old National Pension System, as well as dependent family members (spouses, children who are under 21 or disabled, parents and parents-in-law). In the 1990s, INSSJP also extended its services to veterans of the Falklands/Malvinas War. MEDICARE covers retirees who receive social security benefits; in terms of dependants, only their spouses are eligible. To be eligible for services, one must have made contributions to MEDICARE over a period of more than 10 years of work, but the contribution becomes effective only upon reaching 65 years of age. People who wish to do so may pay privately for coverage once they reach that age. Exemption from the age limit is granted only in the case of the disabled, renal patients and, more recently, individuals suffering from multiple sclerosis.

Thus, while MEDICARE is specifically designed to provide coverage for older and disabled persons, INSSJP does not define its target by age,

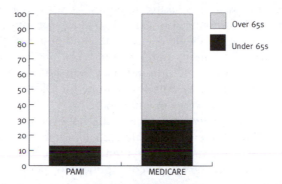

Figure 9.2 Proportion of persons under 65 as a percentage of all INSSJP clients in 2001 and all MEDICARE users in 1999

Source: Author's figures based on data from the INSSJP Information Technology Office (2002a) and from the Health Care Financing Administration (HCFA, 2002b).

but rather, in terms of the retired population, their dependants, and the health risks to which these individuals are subject. Hence, of the 3,211,000 clients covered by INSSJP as of December 2000, 30 per cent were under 65 years of age, while only 13 per cent of MEDICARE users were in that age bracket (Figure 9.2). Moreover, while roughly 30 per cent of INSSJP users are either adults, young people or children, the basic capitation rate that INSSJP pays to providers is the same for all ages. In other words, INSSJP pays for everyone as if all were geriatric cases. With the exception of the design for specific pediatric services, INSSJP does not differentiate between outpatient and inpatient care, and the available services are defined identically for all age groups.

In Argentina, there is a disparity between retirement and old age, due, in part, to political and institutional factors. Early retirement has been a common feature of the Argentine system, and it was used in the 1990s to make adjustments in the labour market and to grant political favours. Early retirement, indeed, is one of the reasons for the financial burden now being borne by INSSJP and is responsible for the fact that younger wives and dependent children figure significantly in social welfare programmes. Moreover, INSSJP provides less coverage of the over-65 population, owing to the high number of informal workers who do not pay social security and thus are not entitled to participate in the system. This proportion is set to grow for future cohorts of older people.

From the beginning, INSSJP made an effort to broaden its range of benefits to provide full coverage for the needs of its users. Since it was primarily designed to serve older people, it initially offered long-term geriatric care, as well as leisure activities. Starting in 1978, cash grants were gradually introduced to extend coverage for long-term care, and to cover housing needs and debts. By the end of the 1970s, INSSJP was offering loans for housing purchases; in the 1980s it created real-estate developments to provide housing on a loan-for-use basis, and in the 1990s it organised the Welfare Programme for Older People to provide supplemental food aid for those in need.

A comparison between 2000 and 2001 shows a 10 per cent annual decline in INSSJP's revenue (Table 9.2). This is a direct consequence of unemployment and underemployment, which reduce active contributions, while also reducing the contributions of pensioners. This trend will increase in the coming years, reflecting cuts in retirement benefits, as well as continuing falls in pension coverage.

Table 9.2 INSSJP accrued revenue, by source, in 2000 and 2001 ($Arg millions)

	2001	%	2000	%
Revenue	2,142.3	100	2,335	100
Contributions, active workers	1470.9	68.7	1624.2	69.6
Retirement contributions, public system	581.1	27.1	601.4	25.8
Retirement contributions, private funds	17.6	0.8	11.8	0.5
Miscellaneous revenue	72.8	3.4	97.7	4.2

Source: Author's figures, based on data from the INSSJP Economic and Financial Office (2002b).

With falling revenues, INSSJP services ought to have been adjusted. Expenditures in different categories are shown in Table 9.3. This shows that, despite falling revenues, expenditures for servicing external and internal financial debt increased (category IV, Financial Expenditures). There was also an increase in the relative weight of administrative expenses.

Comparison with MEDICARE reveals the extent to which INSSJP funds have been diverted from its original mission (Table 9.4). MEDICARE, which, like INSSJP, contracts with third parties for medical services, spends only 3.25 per cent of its budget on administrative expenses, while PAMI spends 15 per cent, to which must be added nearly 3 per cent for debt service.

Between 1999 and 2000 MEDICARE's budget increased by 4 per cent, and similar increases were projected for subsequent years (CMS 2002). Since 1997 there have been increased payments to managed care

**Table 9.3 Accrued expenditures on services and inputs,
by type of service, INSSJP, 2000 and 2001 ($Arg millions)**

Type of service	2001 ($Arg million)	%	2000 ($Arg million)	%
Total categories I, II, III, IV	*2477.8*	*100*	*2618.8*	*100*
I. Medical benefits	*1506.5*	*60.8*	*1586.3*	*60.6*
Capitated comprehensive medical care agreements	781.7	31.5	798.4	30.5
Dental services	37.6	1.5	37.9	1.4
Medical services not included in agreements	268.7	10.2	268.8	10.8
Prescription medications	315.8	12.7	345.9	13.2
Special benefits (optical, prosthetic, oxygen, etc.)	98.8	4.0	132.5	5.1
Other medical benefits	3.8	0.1	2.6	0.1
II. Social benefits	*363.2*	*14.7*	*390*	*14.9*
'Probienestar' programme	89.2	3.60	118	4.51
Burial	50.7	2.05	55	2.10
Geriatric care	109.3	4.41	112.1	4.28
Services for the handicapped	75.1	3.03	62.6	2.39
Cash grants	25.5	1.03	25.1	0.96
Subsidies related to retirees and pensioners	13.4	0.54	17.2	2.60
III. Administration	*371.7*	*15.0*	*387.7*	*14.8*
Personnel	302.4	12.2	318	12.1
Other administrative expenses	69.2	2.79	69.7	2.66
IV. Financial expenses	*73.1*	*2.9*	*61*	*2.3*
V. Withholding	*163.3*	*6.6*	*193.8*	*7.4*

Sources: Author's figures, based on data from the INSSJP Economic and Financial Office (2002b).

organisations, both under *Part A* and *Part B* of the membership options (see p. 186 above), with a corresponding reduction of payment in fee-for-service arrangements. This indicates a switching of expenditure toward managed health care, both in hospital spending and general medicine. Despite this, MEDICARE cost inflation has been sustained, with its budget rising from US$7.5 billion in 1970 to US$111.0 billion in 1990, and stabilising at more than US$200.0 billion in 1996.

MEDICARE spent US$370 per beneficiary in 1970, US$3,240 in 1990, and currently spends approximately US$5,700 per beneficiary. The increase arises from greater coverage for services and benefits, primarily due to high-complexity and high-technology services. On the other hand, administrative costs dropped from 14.2 per cent of the total

Table 9.4 Expenditure on health services and inputs, by type of service, MEDICARE, USA, 2000

Type of service	US$ billion	%
Total	224.4	100
Personal health care	217	96.70
Hospital care	126.7	56.46
Clinical and medical services	59.6	26.56
Dental services	0.1	0.04
Other professional services	4.7	2.09
In-home health care	9.2	4.10
Prescription medications	2.3	1.02
Non-prescription medications	1.3	0.58
Durable medical equipment	4.6	2.05
Care in geriatric care facilities	9.5	4.23
Administration	7.3	3.25

Source: Center for MEDICARE, Office of the Actuary, National Health Statistics Group, 2001.

budget in 1970 to the current level of 3.3 per cent (CMS/OACT, 2002). Despite this inflation in health care costs, MEDICARE beneficiaries increasingly pay out of pocket for essential services.

While MEDICARE has an office specifically devoted to actuarial studies and to collecting and publishing statistics and projections, INSSJP only has a statistical office for processing the data submitted on an occasional basis by providers. It has no actuaries on staff, and has no information system of its own that allows it to monitor providers. Finally, INSSJP does not publish information on its budget or spending.

Medical benefits
Providing health care is the organisational *raison d'être* for both INSSJP and MEDICARE. However, there are significant differences between them in terms of how much of the budget is allocated to particular types of benefits; the range of benefits offered; assessment of the quality of services provided; and the information provided to users and, hence, users' ability to access services.

The first and most significant difference lies in the percentage of budget used to pay for medical benefits. INSSJP allocates slightly over 60 per cent for this purpose, while MEDICARE uses almost all of its funds (97 per cent). This striking difference is due, in part, to the 18 per cent of the INSSJP budget that is consumed by administrative costs and debt servicing, and to the fact that INSSJP provides social services that represent close to 15 per cent of its total budget. However, the percentage allocated for medical benefits is, in fact, even less than these figures would seem to indicate, since the health care administrators also earmark a certain percentage of contracts for their own administrative costs. Data about the scale of these costs do not exist, but they are thought to be substantial.

Somewhat surprisingly, the INSSJP offers a greater diversity of services and more-nearly universal coverage (at least on paper) than MEDICARE does. The basic *(Part A)* MEDICARE plan provides complete hospital coverage, with virtually no out-of-pocket outlays by beneficiaries, for almost all beneficiaries. Outpatient care for all specialties – diagnosis and treatment – does involve supplementary payment of approximately US$45 for a great proportion of beneficiaries *(Part B)*. There are optional plans to cover these services, but they, too, require additional payment, except in the case of the elderly poor, where MEDICAID subsidises such services. Services offered are precisely defined and published online (*www.cms.gov*), as well as in pamphlets or other print formats. Service provider databases are available on a state-by-state basis, and different evaluations of quality of service by service providers are available, including the results of user surveys.

INSSJP offers a vast array of services, which, as evidenced in the current guidelines, have practically no limits to coverage. Only medicines and long-term geriatric care require some type of co-payment by users. The crucial problem in terms of coverage is the system's complete lack of transparency. PAMI does not publish a list of the services it offers, let alone the way in which (or the procedures by which) the services may be accessed. The service strategy of INSSJP is to offer all types of services, while preventing beneficiaries from knowing about them and, hence, from requesting them. In addition to this general strategy, outsourced services are organised in such a way as to force users to go to different establishments, often separated by large distances, in the course of obtaining primary care. Nor do providers generally know with any precision the points of referral, forcing the client again to contact the family physician or INSSJP headquarters for referral purposes. In the specific case of coverage for the elderly population, INSSJP's strategy is highly inequitable, since accessibility problems are particularly onerous for the very old. This group has more difficulty in moving around, and has more health care needs but less money to pay for transport. The barriers are especially severe for older people without children able to help them. Also, it should also be noted that INSSJP has no mechanisms for monitoring and evaluating the quality of services provided by contractors.

Social benefits

So-called 'social benefits' represent around 15 per cent of INSSJP's budget. From the beginning, INSSJP emphasised that these were part of its plan for *comprehensive* health care, going beyond the traditional medical paradigm. Long-term geriatric care in third-party institutions or, in a few cases, in INSSJP institutions, is the longest-standing social benefit offered by INSSJP. Some social benefits have been discontinued, but surviving ones include food parcels, cash grants for housing needs, home help, special care for disabled people, and geriatric inpatient care.

In 2001 0.5 per cent of affiliates were receiving geriatric inpatient care. This level of coverage bears little relation to the real demand for these services. Eligibility criteria are not known, and there is no publication of lists of applicants or of those admitted to the system. By contrast around 14 per cent of affiliates were receiving food parcels and emergency relief from the Welfare Programme for Older People. The programme is carried out through retiree centres, whose directors are responsible for purchasing the food and distributing it among financially disadvantaged users living in their areas. Despite its community-based operation, INSSJP publishes neither the list of retiree centres in the programme nor the funds dedicated to the project. Coverage of the many other social benefit programmes is not known. There are concerns that many cash grants are awarded on a highly discretionary basis, as there are no transparent criteria for the selection of beneficiaries.

In summary, INSSJP social benefits do not seem to contribute to a truly comprehensive system of health care and social services. Rather, they give the impression of unfairly distributing resources to small privileged groups. Information regarding such resources and the means of accessing them is not publicised. Thus, they remain unknown to nearly all users of the system, while services are offered on a discretionary basis, sometimes in response to emergencies, and often in the context of clientalist relationships. Many benefits are channelled through retiree centres, which are often steeped in political clientalism, and where resources and favours are distributed in exchange for votes (Auyero 2001). MEDICARE offers no services comparable to 'social benefits' of this type. This is because services to poor or needy older people are provided with supplementary funds from MEDICAID.

Comparative analysis of reform proposals for MEDICARE and INSSJP

Throughout their histories both the INSSJP and MEDICARE have been the subjects of an almost continuous stream of reform proposals. Reform debates have become particularly intense over the past few years. However, the nature and the severity of the problems they address are very different.

MEDICARE reform proposals are concerned with the problem of inadequate service provision. One key issue is a lack of coverage for out-patient medication (especially for treatment of common ailments such as diabetes, coronary disease, cholesterol and mental illness) and for services closely associated with personal independence, such as eye-glasses, hearing aids and dental health. There is also widespread belief that the traditional system does not promote coordination between providers and care facilities. The provision of services is fragmented by care centre locations and by specialties, with few mechanisms or financial incentives to make providers oversee patients with multiple problems through the entire service circuit (White House, 2002).

MEDICARE's affiliate base is expected to grow in the coming years. In part, this is because the older population is expected to increase as the post-war 'baby boomer' generation reaches later life. As in other countries, there has been a rapid expansion of very old age groups, which are more likely to require MEDICARE services. Also, there has been an increase in the number of people under 65 with disabilities that make them eligible for MEDICARE. However, the effects of these changes on health care spending by beneficiaries cannot be accurately anticipated, since this will depend on a complex of interacting trends. An increased need for assistance in daily activity, as well as more long-term medical care, is expected. Yet there was a decline in the percentage of persons requiring help for daily activities between 1984 and 1999 (from 24 per cent to 19 per cent) (Cutler 2001, cited in MEDPAC 2002).

Another situation generating demand for reform is the uneven impact of MEDICARE services. Although MEDICARE is acknow-ledged to be effective for most of its users, it has limitations in terms of care for patients with long-term problems, low incomes, or those who lack optional coverage. These cases may obtain additional cover from MEDICAID, but this will not happen until out-of-pocket payments have left them sufficiently poor to be eligible for such protection. Despite this concern, increased attention is now being given to extending co-funding arrangements (whereby the beneficiary is expected to cover a fixed share of the treatment). These would seek to minimise obstacles to essential care and services, while maintaining incentives to prevent the inappropriate use of services, including incen-tives to promote the use of recommended services over those consid-ered of doubtful efficacy or efficiency (MEDPAC 2002).

The Bush administration argues that MEDICARE no longer meets the most up-to-date health care standards, even though coverage for preventive care increased significantly in the last five years. According to White House estimates, MEDICARE currently covers only 53 per cent of the annual medical costs of the average elderly American. In addition to challenging what is seen as excessive administrative regulation, it points to a deficit of US$51 billion for the year 2000 (White House 2002). The goal is to correct these administrative problems by integrating management structures more effectively and bringing coverage into line with new demands. Meanwhile, the American 'grey lobby' is closely following the evolution and content of the reform agenda.

INSSJP has faced concerted reform proposals since the mid-1980s. The main objectives of successive programmes were to control inflation of medical costs, to reduce administrative spending in general and to cut staffing levels. During this period, the World Bank gave INSSJP various loans to modernise and streamline its administrative structure. In 1996, INSSJP received US$200 million for reforming its personnel structure and benefits policy. The organisation provided counterpart funds of its own, some of which were loans from the national central bank. The 3 per cent of the budget earmarked for debt service (Table 9.3) is largely a result of the obligations incurred from these loans.

The process of rationalisation, administrative reform and institutional strengthening at INSSJP included assessments by consultants, payment for voluntary retirements and compensation, nation-wide staff training, and computerisation. Despite the enormous expenditure, the current staffing level is higher than ever before. Benefit reform was strongly resisted by an array of vested interests including providers and pharmaceutical firms. The training and consultancy programmes were largely ineffective: INSSJP still does not have a proper computer network to monitor benefits, permit users to ask questions, or to carry out administrative procedures. Sustained decline in revenues and a lack of financial and administrative adjustments led to a marked increase in INSSJP debt, which had reached 75 per cent of its annual operating budget by 2002.

In 2001, two radical reform proposals come onto the agenda. One proposal, based on neoliberal thinking, was that health care for older people be deregulated, so that they could freely choose between affiliating to INSSJP or a range of other private or social insurance funds. A key problem with this is that most older people cannot afford to pay monthly health insurance premiums. Another proposal was for INSSJP to be decentralised to the provinces. However, there were concerns that INSSJP funds might be diverted to rescue bankrupt provincial public health systems. Both of these reform proposals were formally rejected in 2002. Since then there has been a plethora of new proposals, but few signs that these will be implemented effectively, or that they would have a major effect on improving the Institute's fortunes. In the meantime, the level of provision for INSSJP affiliates continues to deteriorate, and in some regions services have been completely suspended.

MEDICARE and PAMI: agencies with similar functions but different histories

Though similar in concept, these two social security agencies have followed divergent paths in regard to performance. Because they operate through multiple contractors, they have both suffered from cost inflation and lack of integration in patient care. Since geriatric patients generally present with more than one pathology, the fragmentation of services has a negative impact on their care.

Despite these common problems and design features, the two organisations developed different performance patterns. In MEDI-CARE, inflation is caused by constant increases in the services it provides, and by the incorporation of high-tech medical services. Nevertheless, significant reductions in administrative costs have been continually achieved since the system was created. In order to control medical costs, the agency studied and applied prospective payment methods, with quality control exercised according to the specific pathologies involved. Achievements in transparency and accessibility of information have been significant, demonstrating that the agency is concerned with meeting the needs and demands of its users.

By contrast, INSSJP has not succeeded in containing inflation of medical costs and has totally failed to set up a rational system for monitoring the cost and quality of benefits. Administrative spending has increased from the creation of the agency to the present, despite reduced revenues and a shrinking user population. Family physicians, responsible for integrating affiliates' medical care packages, gradually lost control over services provided by other agencies. Sectoral and corporate interests pose serious obstacles to reform in this area.

An explanation of these two different situations must take into account political and institutional factors. In MEDICARE, the users are seen as 'members' of the programme and they are a socially powerful sector composed of senior citizens. Services are designed and evaluated with the needs of this group in mind. At the INSSJP, users are the 'objects' of benefits and services, while the true 'subjects' in the system are a dense network of providers, professionals, unions, consultants and employees. Representatives of retiree and pensioner organisations on the INSSJP board have been unable to ensure transparency in management or exert effective control over the quality of services. These problems are part and parcel of the country's governance problems. As in many countries in the region, 'Argentina continues to lack a set of tools that would allow all of its citizens to express their demands and enforce accountability for failure to meet them' (Gargarella 2002: 1). Powerful lobbies have had more weight in INSSJP decision making than citizen advocacy. The scale of the funds managed by the Institute leaves it vulnerable to corruption and clientelism.

As a consequence of these differences, if an increase in the scope and quality of services is to be achieved while keeping a check on spending, the respective processes of reform must take different paths. In Argentina, cost effectiveness studies and actuarial analysis will only be useful if they are part of a broad approach that takes into account complex and multi-dimensional institutional and cultural problems.

Conclusions

INSSJP and MEDICARE are the only two health insurance institutions in the world exclusively dedicated to serving the health needs of the over-65 population and younger populations suffering from specified disabilities. Both have, from their beginnings, faced cost inflation problems due to two factors: demographic pressures that result from increased life expectancy, and the increased cost of medical services resulting largely from increased use of sophisticated technology. It is generally accepted that cost inflation is more pronounced when health care services are provided by multiple contractors, which happens at both INSSJP and MEDICARE.

Given the nature of their missions, these agencies cannot reduce the probability of high or catastrophic health care costs, associated with advancing age, by extending their risk pool to include the entire individual or family life cycle of their beneficiaries. These problems, common to the two organisations, should be taken into account if the model is to be replicated in other countries. It is clear, after three decades of operation, that although their original design was similar, the paths they have taken differ considerably, as a consequence of the institutional dynamics and the role of citizen control in the respective countries.

Both INSSJP and MEDICARE must adapt to new scenarios and improve their performance in order to meet the needs of their beneficiaries in a framework of fiscal austerity. Given the ageing of their populations, both agencies should develop social and health care programmes and services designed to maximise affiliates' ability to function and make autonomous decisions, even when disabilities appear. Given expectations of an increase in the numbers of very old, emphasis should be placed on actuarial and epidemiological analysis, in order to determine the most efficient and effective means of prevention, care and rehabilitation, while holding down costs.

In order to achieve efficient, effective and transparent management susceptible to public evaluation, INSSJP needs to free itself from the interests of providers, employees, unions, politicians and financial groups, and turn its attention instead to meeting the needs of the older population. While this is easier said than done, the example of the USA may give some cause for hope. The so-called 'gerontocracy' in the United States has much more political influence than is the case in Argentina. Differences in the pressure exerted by the 'grey lobby,' as well as differences in the rules of operation and the transparency of management in the two systems, translate into diametrically opposed behaviours of the two organisations. This is seen in regard to their concern for meeting the demands and needs of their beneficiaries, as well as the extent to which they are accountable to their societies for management of the funds entrusted to them.

This comparison of the performance of MEDICARE and INSSJP makes it clear that exporting or importing ideal models of agencies or systems that provide services is not always a good recipe. A country's historical, political, cultural and social realities play a key role – one to be taken into account before formulating cross-national recommendations.

NOTES

1   The author is particularly grateful for the comments and suggestions of Peter Lloyd-Sherlock, Roberto Kaplan, Roberto Souto and José Luis Tesoro. Any error or omission is, of course, the responsibility of the author. The research was carried out with a grant from the United Nations Research Institute for Social Development (UNRISD).
2   Plan de Atención Médica Integral in Spanish.

REFERENCES

Auyero, Javier (2001) *La política de los pobres. Las prácticas clientelares del peronismo*, Ed. Manantial, Buenos Aires.

CMS (Centers for MEDICARE & MEDICAID Services) (2002) *Budget Overview,* available at <www.cms.gov>.

CMS/OACT (Centers for MEDICARE & MEDICAID Services, Office of the Actuary) (2002) *Medicare Administrative Expenses. Selected Fiscal Years*, available at <*www.cms.gov*>.

Gargarella, Roberto (2002) 'Piedras de papel' y silencio: la crisis política argentina leída desde su sistema institucional', working document, CIEPP, Buenos Aires.

Giaimo, Susan (2001) 'Who Pays for Health Care Reform', in Paul Pierson (ed.), *The New Politics of the Welfare State*, Oxford University Press, New York.

HCFA (Health Care Financing Administration) (2002a) *Medicare: a Brief Summary*, available at <www.cms.gov>.

—— (2002b) *National Health Care Expenditures Projections: 2000-2010*, available at <www.cms.gov>.

INDEC (Instituto Nacional de Estadística y Censos) (1995) *Proyecciones de la Población por*

Provincia Según sexo y Grupos de Edad 1990–2010, Serie 2 Análisis demográfico, INDEC, Buenos Aires.

INSSJP (Instituto Nacional de Servicios Sociales para Jubilados y Pensionados) (2002a) *Población Afiliada al INSSJP – Total del País – Estructura por sexo, grupo etáreo y condición de afiliación-Diciembre de 2001*, Subgerencia de Informática, Buenos Aires.

—— (2002b) *Esquema AIF base devengado. Años 2000 y 2001*, Gerencia Económico-Financiera, Buenos Aires, January.

Isuani, Ernesto A. and H. Mercer (1988) *La fragmentación institucional del sector salud: ¿Pluralismo o irracionalidad?*, Centro Editor de América Latina, Buenos Aires.

Katz, Jorge M. y colaboradores (1993) *El sector salud en la República Argentina: su estructura y comportamiento*, Fondo de Cultura Económica, Buenos Aires.

MEDPAC (MEDICARE Payment Advisory Commission) (2002) *Report to the Congress: Assessing Medicare Benefits*, available at <http://www.medpac.gov/ publications/congressional_reports/ Jun02_Titlepg_Insidecov_Acknow.pdf>.

Myles, John and Paul Pierson (2001) 'The Comparative Political Economy of Pension Reform', in Paul Pierson (ed.), *The New Politics of the Welfare State*, Oxford University Press, New York.

OTA (Office of Technology Assessment) (1983) *Diagnosis Related Groups (DRGs) and the Medicare Program: Implications for Medical Technology*, US Congress, Washington, DC.

Redondo, N., M. Bruzzese and A. Rivkin (2001) *Digesto de Normas y Procedimientos Para el Aceso a Prestaciones y Servicios del INSSJP*, INAP-INSSJP, Buenos Aires.

Stocker, Karen, Howard Waitzkin and Cecilia Iriart (1999) 'The exportation of Managed Care to Latin America', *New England Journal of Medicine*, 340 (14): 1131–6.

U.S. Census Bureau (2000) 'Table DP-1: Profile of General Demographic Characteristics for the Unites States: 2000', *Census 2000*, <www.census.gov>.

White House (2002), *Modernizing and Reforming MEDICARE*, President George W. Bush Administration, <www.whitehouse.gov>.

PART III

Older People
and the Care Economy

Many issues related to the care economy have been raised in previous chapters. Chapter 1 challenges complacent assumptions that 'the care economy can care for itself'. It draws attention to the scale and complexity of the care economy, along with its impacts on both care givers and care receivers. Chapter 7 on Japan by Ogawa explores new initiatives for financing long-term care within a framework of formal social protection. Similarly, all the chapters in Part I make substantial reference to informal protection and caring. This begs the question why it is necessary to devote a dedicated selection of chapters to these issues. In part, it is useful to counterbalance a tendency to overlook care issues in research and policy, particularly in the South. The following chapters speak for themselves in demonstrating the centrality of care to debates on ageing and development.

The four chapters in this section explore different aspects of the care economy in very different settings. In Chapter 10, Isabella Aboderin examines care and family relationships in a context of extreme poverty and minimal formal social protection. Her research makes a vital contribution to moving beyond generalisations about the impact of 'development' on intergenerational support systems. These debates fall into two opposed camps. Optimists argue that cultural norms of family responsibility are stronger in many developing countries than in the North and, therefore, informal care can largely be taken for granted. Pessimists suggest that rapid changes associated with development put families under strain and heighten the social isolation of older people.

The limited available data and research suggest a more complex and variable picture. Data on the living arrangements of older people would appear to provide some support for the optimists. Unlike their counterparts in richer countries, only a very small minority of older people in the South live alone or with an elderly spouse (Palloni 2001). Moreover, some studies have found that even where families are no longer co-resident, older people may still receive substantial care and support (Ofstedal *et al.* 1999; Ramos 1992). It is sometimes claimed that income remittances from migrant children may significantly raise their parents' material wellbeing, although this remains largely unevidenced and deeply contested.

However, the arguments of the pessimists should not be dismissed. First, it is dangerous to assume that co-residence with younger people is an effective guarantee of care for those older people who need it. Research from South Africa has exposed the vulnerability of older people to neglect and serious abuse from other household members (Burman 1996). Aboderin's chapter on Ghana falls into this pessimistic camp. She observes that a combination of deepening poverty and abrupt socio-economic change has significantly undermined support for many older people, particularly men. Her findings are in line with those of a separate anthropological study of the same country which concludes that: 'Minimal care based on minimal respect will remain available to all old people, but a comfortable and pleasant old age will probably be reserved for a minority' (van der Geest 2002: 29).

It is probably not coincidental that optimistic findings are largely taken from countries that have experienced a general rise in prosperity (Thailand, Taiwan, Singapore and the Philippines) or where social protection has bolstered the economic position of pensioners (Brazil). Where economic conditions have been less fortunate, there may be grounds for inclining towards pessimistic assumptions. In this regard, Gomes da Conceição and Montes de Oca Zavala's study of Mexico in Chapter 11 is of particular interest, as the national experience falls somewhere between these two scenarios. They find considerable diversity of experience, and that poverty is associated with lower levels of co-residence and support. In agreement with Aboderin, this study notes that poor older men are particularly vulnerable to abandonment by family members. Taken together, these different studies show the significance of wider economic conditions. They also reveal the essentially reciprocal nature of care relationships: where older people have less to offer family members, they are less likely to receive support.

Discussion of reciprocity should not overlook the importance of older people as care givers, as well as care receivers. Research from around the world has highlighted this role, and particular attention has recently been paid to older people as carers in communities affected by HIV/AIDS. In recent years, the impact of the pandemic on older people and, more so, their potential role in mitigating the effects of the pandemic have started to feature in international policy debate. This should be welcomed as a mainstreaming of older people into a key international development agenda. However, the high profile afforded these issues has not been matched by a high volume of rigorous empirical research. The work by Knodel, Saengthienchai and others in Thailand is a notable exception to this shortfall.

Knodel and Saengthienchai observe in Chapter 12 that international debate has focused on the role of older people as carers for AIDS orphans, but has overlooked other issues, including the complex indirect impacts of the epidemic on older peoples' wellbeing. Although older people may be less likely to suffer contagion than other age groups, they remain exposed to the indirect impacts of the disease. These include losses of household income, increased care requirements, psychological trauma, and meeting care and funeral expenses. In parts of sub-Saharan Africa the scale of the epidemic threatens a general social and economic crisis that is likely to have catastrophic consequences for everyone living in affected communities. One recent survey from Uganda reported that grandparents were the main group of prime carers for AIDS orphans, accounting for 34 per cent of cases (Ntozi and Nakayiwa 1999a and 1999b). Older women bear a particularly large part of the care burden for sick children and for orphaned grandchildren (Mupedziswa 1997). Such households will be highly vulnerable in the event of the death of the older carers, or if they are no longer able to continue in this role.

These accounts have played a major role in promoting the recognition of older people's contributions to development in low-income countries. However, there is a danger that they may generate over-simplified claims of symbiotic relationships between heroic grand-mothers and grateful orphans. The limited available research suggests that it is dangerous to generalise about the impact of AIDS on older people. Knodel and Saengthienchai show in Chapter 12 that in Thailand the role of elders as carers of orphans has been less significant than caring for dying children. In the Ukraine, high demographic dependency ratios mean that a key issue will be the declining supply of younger adults to care for frail elders (Barnett et al. 2000).

The final chapter in this section focuses on gender dimensions of the care economy. In Chapter 13, Martha Nussbaum observes that, although cultural attitudes to supporting the aged vary, women are almost always the main providers of functional support to those who require it. She argues that the most ubiquitous and long-lasting conception of the woman, in virtually all countries and traditions of the world, is as a giver of care: homemaker, mother, wife, tender of the needs of older people. Nussbaum claims that this care-giving function has often removed women from candidacy for full citizenship, and from many aspects of employment. She advocates a perspective based on ideas of human capability and functioning, which, she claims, can more adequately deal with issues of social justice raised by the need to provide care for older people in a state of extreme and asymmetrical dependency.

While such concerns about gender justice are ubiquitously relevant, there are important variations in the ways in which women have been incorporated into the care economy. In the North, much reference is made to the so-called 'sandwich generation' of women, who find themselves caring for older people and young children at the same time (Velkoff and Lawson 1998). This phenomenon is less prominent in most developing countries, but is likely to emerge there in future decades. Also, the potential role of men as carers should not be dismissed. Comparative research from Asia shows that men may also make important contributions, particularly in terms of economic support (Ofstedal et al. 1999). Unfortunately, policy debate about the care economy does not address this complexity and variation. All too often discussions are still framed in terms of an all-or-nothing choice: care may be provided either by families or by the state. Little has been done to develop policies which might bridge the two, particularly in the South. Very little attention has been paid to intermediary policies which recognise the scope to support older people without institutionalising them (Phillips and Chan 2002; Lubben 2002). In the absence of significant initiatives, growing strains on the care economy will be felt primarily by older people and women.

REFERENCES

Barnett, A., A. Whiteside, L. Khodakevich, Y. Kruglov and V. Steshenko (2000) 'The HIV/AIDS epidemic in Ukraine: its potential social and economic impact', *Social Science and Medicine*, 51:1387–1403.

Burman, S. (1996) 'Intergenerational family care: legacy of the past, implications for the future' *Journal of Southern African Studies*, 22 (4): 585–98.

Lubben, J. (2002) 'The future of community health for older persons – a key to successful health and welfare integration' in WHO, *Development of health and welfare systems – adjusting to ageing*, WHO, Kobe.

Mupedziswa, R. (1997) 'AIDS and older Zimbabweans: who will care for the carers?' *South African Journal of Gerontology*, 6 (2): 9–12.

Ntozi, J. and S. Nakayiwa (1999a) 'AIDS in Uganda: how has the household coped with the epidemic?' in I. Orubuloye, J. Caldwell and J. Ntozi (eds.), *The Continuing HIV/AIDS Epidemic in Africa: Response and Coping Strategies*, Health Transition Centre, Australian National University, Canberra.

——— (1999b) 'Changes in household composition and family structure during the AIDS epidemic in Uganda', in I. Orubuloye, J. Caldwell and J. Ntozi (eds.), *The Continuing HIV/AIDS Epidemic in Africa: Response and Coping Strategies*, Health Transition Centre, Australian National University, Canberra.

Ofstedal, M., J. Knodel and N. Chayovan (1999) 'Intergenerational support and gender: A comparison of four Asian countries', *Population Studies Center Report 99–54*, University of Michigan.

Palloni, A. (2001) 'Living arrangements of older persons', *Population Bulletin of the United Nations,* Special Issue No. 42 and 43, pp. 54–110.

Phillips, D. and A. Chan (2002) 'National policies on ageing and long-term care in the Asia-Pacific: Issues and challenges', in D. Phillips and A. Chan (eds.), *Ageing and long-term care*, National policies in the Asia–Pacific, IDRC/Institute of Southeast Asian Studies, Ottawa/Singapore.

Ramos, L. (1992) 'Family support for elderly people in São Paulo, Brazil', in H. Kendig, H. Hashimoto and L. Coppard (eds.), *Family Support for the Elderly*, Oxford University Press, Oxford.

Van der Geest, S. (2002) 'Respect and reciprocity: care of elderly people in rural Ghana', *Journal of Cross-Cultural Gerontology*, 17: 3–31.

Velkoff, V. and V. Lawson (1998) 'Gender and Aging. Caregiving', US Bureau of the Census International Brief IB/98-3, Washington DC.

CHAPTER 10

Intergenerational Family Support
and Old Age Economic Security in Ghana

ISABELLA ABODERIN

Material family support for older people in African countries is declining,
exposing increasing numbers to destitution and poverty. Whilst the need
for policy responses to ensure old age economic security is increasingly
recognised, different emphases exist on the kinds of policy approaches
(public, family or individual) that are required. A crucial prerequisite for
identifying which approaches are likely to be most appropriate is a solid
understanding of the nature, causes and consequences of the declines in
family support. Such an understanding, however, is so far lacking given
the conceptual and epistemological limitations in the two explanations
put forward to date – on the one hand, 'modernisation' and ageing
notions, and on the other arguments emphasising the role of growing
material constraints. Building on the findings of an in-depth
exploratory study in Ghana, this chapter develops a fuller understanding of the factors and processes that have underpinned the decline in
family support, and of the changing normative expectations that are
emerging in its wake. It reflects on the potentially crucial policy
implications of these processes and, in this context, highlights the
urgent need for further research in order to build the necessary basis for
appropriate old age economic security policy development in sub-
Saharan Africa.

Background: declining family support and old age
economic security policy in sub-Saharan Africa

In sub-Saharan Africa, the debate on old age poverty and economic
security in old age is inextricably linked with trends and emerging
patterns of family support for older people. In countries such as Ghana,
where no adequate formal old age income security provision exists for

210

the vast majority of older people, and where gainful employment opportunities for those who are able are extremely scarce, the extent of (and the trends in) material old age family support are crucial in shaping their economic well-being. Whilst caution must surely be exercised regarding claims of a wholesale 'breakdown' of family support, just as there must be caution regarding the often overly ideal portrayals of 'traditional' support in the 'golden past', there are strong indications that the *adequacy* of material support to older people – in terms meeting their basic requirements has declined, exposing increasing numbers to vulnerability and material deprivation (Aboderin 2000).

In Ghana, material protection of older people has traditionally been the responsibility of the family, with older people's dependence on family support, and especially adult children's obligation to provide it, enshrined in the customary moral code (Apt 1996; Gyekye 1996; Nukunya 1992) and encapsulated in a proverb: 'If your elders take care of you while you are cutting your teeth, you must in turn take care of them when they are losing theirs' (Apt 1996: 22). Now, however, all indications are that for many older people this family support no longer provides the necessary protection and is insufficient to meet even their basic needs (Aboderin 2000, 2001).

Moreover, though a formal old age provident fund system has existed since the 1960s and was recently superseded by a new (and theoretically universal) contributory social insurance pension scheme (Dei 1997), the reach of this security has remained elusive for the vast majority of the old. Whereas the old system applied only to public sector employees (who constitute only a tiny fraction of the labour force), the new scheme in practice covers only the formal sector, leaving the vast majority of those in the informal sector (constituting more than 85 per cent of the total workforce) without protection. Furthermore, the scheme appears unable to afford sufficient security even for those who are covered. Among the major reasons are the erosion of annuities by inflation, as well as unaffordability and low benefit levels (due to low salaries and thus low contributions) (Ahenkora 1999; ISSA 2000; Ghana Statistical Service 2000; Kaseke 2000).

In this context, the symptoms of the declining adequacy of material family support in Ghana have been increasing destitution and privation among older people. This is particularly visible in cities where many are reduced to begging, and where there is a growing concern about the increasingly frequent 'abandonment' of older people by their families in hospitals. In response to these problems, there has been an emergence of community-based initiatives, led by NGOs such as HelpAge Ghana, which try, on small scale, to improve the situation of older people today (Aboderin 2000; Apt 1996).

For tomorrow's generation of older people the situation is likely to be equally grave, if not worse, given the trends in family support and a continued inadequacy of formal old age income security provision. The scale of old age poverty on a national level, moreover, will be heightened by the rapid demographic ageing of the population projected over coming decades. In Ghana the proportion of those aged over 60 will triple, while their numbers will increase by as much as five times by 2050. The numbers of those aged over 80 will rise by a factor of more than eight (Table 10.1).

Table 10.1 Demographic trends: projected population ageing in Ghana

	2000		2050	
	Total numbers (in 1000s)	% of total population	Total numbers (in 1000s)	% of total population
Population 60+	984	5.1	5,887	14.7
Population 80+	78.2	0.4	647.4	1.6

Source: UN (2000).

In the light of these trends, and their potential impact on the development of societies as a whole, there is growing recognition, in Ghana and other African countries, of the vital need for policy responses to ensure economic security for the growing numbers of older people now and in future (HelpAge International 2002; OAU 2001a, 2001b; Kaseke 2000; UN 2002). The increasingly intense international policy discussion and debate in recent years have focused on the kinds of policy approaches needed to effectively ensure material security for older people, whilst doing justice also to the needs of the young. An additional consideration, crucial for the sub-Saharan African context, has been the need for any programmes to be compatible with broader national economic development and poverty reduction aims and strategies (Aboderin 2002; HelpAge International 2002).

    The discussions have centred on the question of what combination of family, public or individually based approaches to old age economic security is required, and what form individual strategies or schemes should take. In this context, two particular perspectives have come to dominate the African discussions in recent years. First, there have been increasingly strong arguments for the need to extend non-contributory public pension schemes, such as those in South Africa, Botswana, Namibia, and parts of India. These arguments critique the performance and impact of the existing private contributory schemes which, under advocacy of the World Bank (see World Bank 1994), were introduced in Ghana as in other African countries over the last decade. They expose, above all, the fundamental inadequacy of individually based saving schemes in which the level of old age security is based on earlier earning ability, in a context of pervasive poverty, and underemployment. At the same time, the arguments refute the orthodox view that universal, non-contributory pension systems are fiscally unaffordable for poor developing countries. They question the simplistic assumptions and analyses upon which this view has been based and note the evident feasibility of pension schemes in Botswana or Namibia, for example (Charlton and McKinnon 2001; Neysmith and Edwardh 1984; Schultz 2002; Barrientos in this volume). Research has highlighted the significant beneficial effects of such pension systems not only on the older people, but also on younger generations in their families or communities (Barrientos in this volume). There is some evidence, moreover, that rather than 'crowd out', such pension schemes can, in fact, 'crowd in' other dimensions of intergenerational support such as, for example, physical care and assistance (HelpAge International 2002; Lund 2001).

The second dominant perspective in African policy discussions on old age economic security has been an emphasis on the need to build, as much as possible, on traditional African values and systems of family obligation and support. Such a centrality of the family is stressed particularly in African contributions to the debate such as the Policy Framework On Ageing developed by the Organisation of African Unity, OAU (OAU 2001a, 2001b). Rather than simply embrace what are seen as 'Western' models of care, policies, it is argued, must 'learn from' traditional norms and practices, and thus 'promote and strengthen the role of the family' in the support and welfare of older people (Apt 2000; Apt and Grieco 1994; OAU 2001a, 2001b). Specific measures proposed include the introduction of tax concessions for those supporting older relatives, and the legal institution of a binding duty on children to provide support for older parents. Thus the OAU recommends that member states 'enact legislation requiring adult children to provide support for their parents ... the principle being that, in the same way parents have a duty of care towards their children, children should have a duty of care towards their parents' (OAU 2001a: 3)

The African emphasis on the need to build on the family is not, as one may suspect, an extension of macro-economic arguments seeking to limit public spending. Rather, it is born out of a wider concern with the kind of value model that is needed to achieve sustained social and economic wellbeing in Africa (Apt 2001). Critiquing the obvious failure of Western (imposed or all too readily adopted) models of development, it is argued that progress in Africa cannot be achieved by transferring models, institutions and techniques from other societies, but must be based on Africa's own indigenous cultures, values and institutions. Traditional African values, thus, must be 'preserved, revitalized, further developed and adjusted' to the 'present time of rapid change' (Apt 2001).

Towards formulating policy: the need for an understanding of the shifts in family support

How to reconcile, and translate into practice the common ground between the different perspectives on achieving old age economic security in Africa? How to identify what combination of public and family approaches or strategies will be most effective? One crucial pre-requisite is a solid understanding of the nature and the causes of the declining adequacy of material family support for older people, and of any shifts in expectations or attitudes that may be emerging as a result of it. In other words, we need to clarify how and to what extent family support has actually declined, and to understand how traditional norms, values and practices of old age family support have evolved and operate today, in the context of widespread societal change, 'development' and globalisation (Aboderin 2002; Apt 2000; IAG 2002).

Such an understanding, however, does not so far exist. Not only is there a lack of evidence on the past and present experiences and perspectives of older people but also, crucially, on the attitudes, expectations and values of the young – those who will themselves be old in the coming decades and who, until then, are expected to support the older generation.

Existing accounts in the literature, operating on the assumption of a real decline in family support for older people, so far put forward two main explanations for it (Apt 1996, 1997; HelpAge International 2002). On the one hand, there are 'modernisation' and ageing theory notions (Burgess 1960; Cowgill 1972, 1974). These focus on the weakening of traditional norms of family and filial obligation as a result of the influence of Western individualistic values and urban lifestyles, and a consequent growing focus on the nuclear family. The implication is that support, no longer compelled by the force of custom, has become increasingly dependent on younger people's discretion: their sympathy or affection for, and thus their *wish* to support older parents or relatives. Ultimately, these interpretations imply an increasing *unwillingness* on part of the young to provide for their older parents or relatives.

On the other hand, and in contrast, interpretations drawing on local observations and in line with materialist or political economy perspectives place emphasis on the crucial role of growing material constraints and hardship among the young. In the context of persistent (or worsening) un- and underemployment and poverty they thus point to an increasing *incapacity* (rather than unwillingness) of the young to adequately provide for their aged kin.

A further contributory factor to declines in family support considered in international discussions is a reduction in the pool of children or younger relatives available to support older individuals, as a result of falling fertility levels and out-migration (Sen 1994). Whilst this factor may be significant for other developing world regions and for specific types of family support such as physical caregiving or domestic help, it would seem to be of less relevance to the declining adequacy in material old age family support in Ghana or other African countries.

Fertility rates, though they have gradually begun to fall in recent years, have remained high in such countries (the current figure for Ghana is 4.6). Out-migration of the young, moreover, does not preclude the provision of material support. The important role of financial remittances to older people from migrated children has been noted (Blanc and Gray 2000; Ghana Statistical Service, 2000; UN 2002).

Both modernisation and 'material constraints' interpretations undoubtedly capture some of the factors underpinning declines in support, and most discussions mention them as parallel explanations. However, there has been little, if any, theoretical or empirical reflection on the relative role and merit of each in providing a real appreciation of why and how such declines have come about. In purely common sense or practical terms, if one questions whether these explanations enable an understanding of the declines, the answer is surely 'no'.

Reflection on a theoretical level, moreover, indicates that neither of the two explanatory models, nor the two in conjunction are able to provide such an understanding, as both harbour important conceptual and epistemological limitations. These are, most importantly, (1) their failure to illuminate the interrelationships between normative and material factors in causing declines in support: their failure, that is, to clarify the crucial question of the role played by changes in values or attitudes or by changing material circumstances on part of the young; and (2) their lack of grounding in or consideration of interpretive evidence on individuals' motives, experiences and interests in receiving and providing old age support either 'traditionally' in the past, or in the present (see Aboderin 2000, 2003 for a more detailed critique).

Developing a fuller understanding of declines in family support – an example from Ghana

In view of the above, the author conducted an in-depth, qualitative investigation to generate a fuller understanding of the factors, processes and shifts that have underpinned and may be emerging in the wake of the decline in material family support for older people. The investigation, conducted over nine months in Accra, the national capital, employed an entirely qualitative methodology to explore the perspectives of a purposely selected, stratified sample of adults (18+) (N = 51) of three linked generations – the oldest (G1), the middle (G2) and the youngest (G3). In-depth interviews were used to elicit each generation's past or present experiences of and attitudes to providing and receiving old age support, as well as their interpretations of the diminished level of support today. Supplementary information was obtained through investigations of cases of abandoned older people, and through consultations with social welfare and nursing staff, HelpAge officials and academics at Ghana University.

Based on the themes, patterns, and categories generated from the respondents' accounts, rather than on *a priori* theories or constructs, the investigation developed an analytical account of the nature, causes and consequences of the declines in support, using a framework of three main components. The first is an appreciation of the patterns, motivational basis, context and adequacy of old age material family support in the past. This examines why, how and to what extent material family support to older parents or relatives was provided more adequately in the past. This picture of the past was generated from the combined recollections of the older generation respondents, spanning the period from the late 1920s to early 1960s. Second, there was an appreciation of the basis, patterns and context of family support in the present, based on the older generation's current experiences of receiving, and the younger generations' perspectives in or views on providing such support. Third, and based on a systematic comparison between 'past' and 'present', as well as older people's own interpretations of the changes that have occurred, there was an appreciation of how and why support in the past differed from the motives, attitudes and wider context that underpin the increasingly inadequate support today.

The findings of this research, given its interpretive approach and small scale, can make no claims to a greater generality or universal truth. However, they may be seen as solid starting points for further discussion and research and are discussed below. Particularly relevant points are illustrated with typical quotes from study respondents (see Aboderin 2000, 2003 for a full discussion of methodology, approach, and findings).

Nature, causes and consequences
of the decline in support

The strikingly homogeneous picture revealed by the oldest generation's recollections of the past patterns of material family support confirms, above all, that such support was, on the whole, adequate. Although rare cases of non-support by children did exist, material assistance was given to older people mainly by children but also by more extended relatives. By the same token, the older respondents confirmed that, though support has not wholly 'broken down', it has clearly declined.

> In the olden days even older people who didn't have children would be alright, they would receive help from their relatives, but these days, even those who have children find it difficult. (G1)

> I am not saying that the whole system has broken down completely, but what I am saying is that when you compare what used to take place, things have definitely gone worse. (G1)

The older and younger respondents' descriptions of the changes and patterns of support today, indicate, as implied in the literature (Apt 1996, 1997), that the decline has occurred on two levels. First, there has been erosion in the support older people receive from extended family members such as nieces, nephews or siblings, shifting the responsibility of support increasingly onto spouses and children.

> In the olden days older people were cared for not just by the children but also the relatives … but now they don't do it anymore, only the children look after the old person. (G1)

The decline in extended family support, importantly, has also affected younger generations, leaving them increasingly alone in meeting responsibility for their own welfare and that of their children.

> The family? Nobody! In this Ghana here, excuse me to say, nobody looks out for their relatives, they won't help you. They only look out for their own children, but not their brother's or sister's children. So you yourself must do it, you must fight on your own. (G2)

At the same time, there has been a reduction in the support that older people receive from children. The adequacy of such support has broadly declined, and there has been an increasing incidence of children who do not support their parents (usually fathers) at all.

> These days the children, the little they give you, it cannot satisfy you. (G1)

> Formerly, when I was young children used to look after their parents but in these days … there are so many old people for example here in Accra I have seen, the children don't look after the parents at all. (G1)

The picture of the causes of these declines that emerges from the respondents' accounts shows a complex and mutually reinforcing inter-action between some of the effects of the economic strain in Ghana, and certain influences that may be related to modernisation or globalisation. This interaction, which has not so far been discussed in the literature, has led to two major processes or shifts in support.

A decreasing resource capacity to support the old
The first of these processes, as the materialist interpretations assert, has been a progressive decline in the economic capacity of younger people to provide adequately for their older parents or relatives. In the past, providing support was generally affordable and conflicted little with younger generations' own material needs and aspirations (thanks to low costs and needs of daily living and a shared responsibility within the extended family),

> Q: Was it difficult financially to support your parents?
> A: Oh formerly it was easy to look after your parents, it was not difficult at all. (G1)
>
> In those days you could feed a whole house with 2 or 4 shillings, 10 shillings went a long way...so what people received was enough for them. (G1)

Now, however, the 'opportunity costs' of supporting elders have risen. Many, given the limited resources at their disposal, have become increasingly unable to cater for the needs of their older parents or rela-tives, as well as to satisfy their own and their children's requirements. In this situation, faced with decisions on how to allocate their meagre incomes, they have begun to give priority to the needs of their conjugal family (themselves, their spouse and children), before those of older kin.

What underlies these decisions of resource allocation, it seems, is a fundamental hierarchy of priorities such that in situations of scarcity, the needs of the young (self, spouse, children) come before those of older parents, and these in turn before the needs of other (older) relatives. This hierarchy was seen as something 'natural' and inevitable by both older and younger respondents.

> Q: What should young people do if they don't have enough money for all?
> A: They and their children must come first. They are facing life … I am not saying they should ignore their parents, but they have to fend for themselves and their children first before they can think of others. That is the natural thing…. (G1)
>
> You have to feed the immediate family first, that means your wife and children, and then next your parents. Anybody else nowadays … is a secondary matter. (G1)

The essential principle embodied in this hierarchy is that the old have no 'right' to absorb the resources that younger generations need for their future. Interestingly, this is not just a Ghanaian or even African principle, but is present also in other cultures. In the West for example it is expressed in the notion of the 'processional nature' or 'transitive order' of justice between generations (Laslett 1992; Moody 1993) which has been central in the contemporary debate on the future of old age care and security provision (see Bengtson and Achenbaum 1993).

The primary causes of the declining capacity among the young, not surprisingly, have been growing un-and underemployment, the rising costs of daily living, and the rising fees of health care and education (introduced as part of cost recovery strategies under the IMF/World Bank economic recovery programme) (Government of Ghana, Technical Committee on Poverty 1996; UNDP 1997). These have reduced the income available to cover needs and requirements.

> [T]he costs of everyday living are so high that it eats deep into whatever you have. Even the basics are so costly – rents, food, rates, school fees, medicine, all the everyday things are getting more expensive and your salary can't cover it. And if you have no proper job it is hopeless. (G1)

> [M]any younger people today can't look after their parents properly because … they have no means. And when their means are small like that they will put their children first…. Formerly … there was enough to cater for everyone, but now you have to make decisions…. (G1)

In addition, however, the declining capacity has been caused by an *escalation* in the needs or requirements of the young today compared to the past. On the one hand, there has been an emergence of new inescapable needs such as rent, bills, transport or schooling, which are now deemed essential. On the other hand, there has also been an emergence of 'modern' consumer 'needs' such as TV, hi-fi, fashion items or leisure activities among the young. As a result of a shift in status criteria that has placed increasing importance on wealth and material possessions (rather than on conduct or family honour), younger people now acquire and view these things as vital for attaining a necessary basic standing in society – meaning they have even less to give to the old.

> [T]hese days people have less to give to their old parents because the needs of the modern youth are getting more and more. You see … now they think they need TVs, mobile phones, and all these things, or they think they have to go to bars and drink beer. So naturally, the money they have left to give to their parents is nothing. But the question is, where are they putting their priorities?' (G1)

> Q: What are the basic things you feel you need these days?

A: I think with civilisation you are entitled to certain things. For example ...
to a television set, a radio or hi-fi, and video cassettes for your children. That
is important because if you don't have these things the children will go to
someone else's house and that would be an insult to me.... (G2)

The crux, as perceived by many of the older generation, is that
modern consumer 'needs' should be viewed as 'wants' which the young
could – if they were willing – forgo, so as to free resources to give to the
old. Thus, within the context of a declined capacity, there remains an
element of choice on the part of the younger generation as to the extent
to which they want to do all they theoretically could to support (and
satisfy) their older parents or relatives.

That many younger people evidently do not chose to do 'all they
could' for extended older relatives (or extended relatives *per se*) is seen as
an inevitable outcome of growing economic insecurity for individuals,
and of an underlying interest in self-preservation that has always
motivated people, now as in the past. That it is accepted by the older
generation with less bitterness than the absence of support from their
own children also reflects the fact that the traditional obligation to assist
older relatives was less binding than the strict duty that commanded
support to older parents.

It is, then, a shift in the basis of this duty that has been the second
major process underpinning the decline in support from children.

A shift in the basis of filial support
In the past adult children supported their parents in fulfilment of a strict
filial duty to honour parents and support them in return for care
received from them in childhood. All older respondents, when asked
about their motives for supporting parents, expressed these *exclusively* in
terms of their duty to do so.

Q: Why did you look after your mother?
A: My mother looked after me so I should also look after her.... We have a
proverb here in Ghana that if your parents look after you when you are
growing your teeth you must also look after them when they are losing their
teeth.
Q: Why did you feel it was your duty to look after your father – you said he
didn't look after you when you were young?
A: Your father brought you into this world, so it is still your duty. (G1)

Importantly, and as not so far discussed, this filial duty had two distinct moral roots. First, it was based on a customary obligation, encapsulated in the above-mentioned proverb and flanked by strong family and
community sanctions that asked children to support their parents in
return for the care they had received from them in childhood. In other

words, it asked children to repay their parents for having fulfilled their duty to them in the past.

An important feature of this reciprocal obligation was that it contained a principle of 'conditionality'. This held that if parents had *willingly* (rather than out of a lack of capacity) neglected their parental duties (to provide food and clothing and enable the child to become self-sufficient and 'be someone'), the child, in turn and in theory had no obligation to support them.

> If the parents' didn't have the means to look after their children properly, then the children still have to care for them, but if the parents have the means and they don't do it, then it is no obligation on the children. (G1)

In practice, this conditionality was overruled by a second, and absolutely binding, God-given duty on children to honour their parents – regardless of their past conduct. This duty, and the threat of the harshest divine punishment that enforced it, was of course embodied in the biblical Fifth Commandment:

> Honour thy father and thy mother that thy days may be long upon the land which the Lord thy God giveth thee. (Exodus 20: 12).

In this context, as the older respondents described, children supported parents out of a fear of the consequences – the family sanctions and especially God's punishment that they believed would otherwise befall them.

> Q: What was your mind when you were looking after your mother?
> A: You see, I feared because of what I had been taught in the bible. In the Ten Commandments there is a line saying that if you respect your parents you will be rewarded, you will have a long life, but if not you will not have a long life.
> Q: What would have happened if you hadn't looked after your father?
> A: My family would blame me. They will call me and ask "Why are you not looking after him?' And if you don't mind them they will finish with you. So when something happens to you and you go to them … they won't help you.

Knowing thus, that supporting and satisfying parents' requirements was, in a sense, vital for their own future welfare, children on the whole did so regardless of their judgement of or feelings for them.

Now, however, filial support has become increasingly dependent on such judgements. That is, it has become dependent on the extent to which children feel a sense of obligation, or wish to help their parents out of gratitude, appreciation or affection. And this, in turn, as the middle generation clearly expressed, depends on their perception of the degree to which their parents supported them in the past and tried their best to further their prospects. Where parents are perceived not to have done so, children now increasingly do *not* do all they could to satisfy their needs.

> It all depends on the way the parents have brought up the children. Sometimes we get so attached to a parent because of something, maybe you saw how much she sacrificed for you when you were in need of something. In that way you will do it back. But if you didn't see anything like that, you don't care much and if your money too is little, you won't be trying much. (G2)

> You see today it all depends on the love. If I love my daddy I would want to do something for him but if I don't love him, I mean I don't think of doing much for him. So if you don't love your children and treat them in a way that will make them also love you, they won't even think of trying hard to take care of you. (G2)

In extreme cases, where parents (usually fathers) are seen to have wholly neglected their basic parental duties, in particular to provide education, children retaliate, withholding all support and arguing that they in turn have no duty towards their parent. In effect then, the shift in the basis of filial support has led to a situation in which parents increasingly receive support not according to fixed status rights but, in a sense, according to their 'merits', as judged by their children.

> Q: Why are you not giving anything to your father?
> A: My father didn't try for me at all.... He didn't even send us to school. So because of him I am struggling now.... If I had education I would be somewhere better. So these days I don't have and my brother, too, he won't give him anything.... I know that my father isn't satisfied but what can he say? He didn't try at all. (G2)

What has caused this development? Although the shift resembles that implied by the modernisation and ageing theory interpretations, it has clearly *not* been caused, as these interpretations suggest, by a wholesale weakening of traditional norms of filial obligation. The customary, reciprocal obligation on children to support parents in return for parents having fulfilled their duties towards them clearly persists and has come to the fore (a similar conclusion is reached in recent ethnographic investigations in rural Ghana (Van der Geest 1997, 2002).

What has weakened, however, is the absolute status of duty that in the past required children to honour and support parents regardless of whether they had [wholly] fulfilled their duty to them. At the same time the expectations have increased of what parental duty entails. On a material level, parents' duty now vitally involves the provision of decent education and training for their child – something that was not considered absolutely essential in the past. On a more principled level there seems to be a growing expectation that it is parents' duty to 'love' and thus do all they can to further the life of their child. Finally, children have become more ready to judge and critically evaluate the degree to which their parents fulfilled their duty.

> You see, nowadays the children give you marks. If you don't educate them…when you are old they won't come and take care of you…. In my days we didn't think of giving our parents marks like that. Whatever they did, we just took it like that. (G1)

These developments have emerged as the result of a mutually reinforcing interaction between a number of factors and processes. Whilst some of these may largely be seen as consequences of worsening socioeconomic pressures in Ghana, others are reflections of the growing influence of globally asserted rights values.

First, there have been the dwindling prospects that younger people without solid education or professional qualification have of finding decent, gainful employment in the current economy and thus of 'becoming someone'. In this situation, good education and/or professional training have become absolutely vital for younger people's life chances, and the onus on parents to do all they can to further their children's prospects has become greater. Accordingly, children whose parents seemingly did not try to provide such education or training have become increasingly bitter. They have begun to question a duty that requires them to part with their meagre resources so as to honour and support parents who themselves neglected their duties. Their judgement, in effect, is that these parents have no right to expect support.

> Some fathers … neglect their children…. So when the child grows up, the father shouldn't expect anything from him or her. And if the child doesn't do it, there is nothing you can say or do because you failed in your duties. (G2)

In making this judgement, children have, in a sense, been supported by the growth in Ghana (as in other nations) in awareness of and emphasis on the rights of children, in particular *vis-à-vis* their parents. These rights, embodied in the UN Convention on the Rights of the Child ratified in 1989 (UN 2002), are now legally enforceable and have been increasingly publicised in the media. They have contributed, above all, to a greater sense of empowerment of children, and to an atmosphere in which the notion of an accountability of parents (and by extension their evaluation by children) has received more currency. In addition, they have contributed to the fostering of the notion of parental love as a 'right' and, by extension, pointed to the existence of a parental duty to do all one can to further one's child's life chances.

Finally, there has been a weakening of the threat of the familial and metaphysical sanctions that formerly forced children to obey their duty to honour and support parents. The diminished fear of family sanctions, in contrast to what modernisation notions imply, is not primarily due to an increased geographical mobility, education or economic self-sufficiency of the young. Rather, the dominant cause in the current urban context has been the general decline in extended family support and protection. In a situation where individuals increasingly bear a solitary responsibility for their material welfare, threats of withdrawal of family support have, to a large extent, become hollow.

The weakened threat of punishment from God finally is not the result of an increasing secularisation. If anything, Christian faith and worship – the need for, and trust in God – have become more marked with the continued economic strain: this is reflected, among other things, in the phenomenal growth in charismatic and spiritual churches (Dovlo 1992). What has underpinned this shift is a change in the popular conception of God. Whereas in the past God was seen as a harsh punishing authority, he is now increasingly preached, perceived and experienced as a supportive and loving God whose help in achieving one's goals (economic or otherwise) is assured.

> You see, people now see God as merciful, kind and forgiving, that is how they are preaching it now... But formerly they were teaching us how to fear God. (G1)

> You see the thing is … in the bible it says God created good things for his … children. God wants us to enjoy the riches of this earth, so once I am a child of God I should enjoy everything good. (G2)

Changing normative expectations as a consequence of the decline

Although the decline in family support has not been *caused* by a replacement of traditional norms with 'Western' values of individual independence, such values may be beginning to emerge as a *consequence* of the decline, shaping the views and expectations especially of younger generations. With regard to obligations towards extended family members in general, there seems to be an increasing emphasis on the value of and need for self-reliance. While many people still hope for extended family support, those who are asked to provide it but do not increasingly justify this by asserting this 'value' of self-reliance, as expressed in the following interview response:

> Look, there are still so many people who expect their family to help them out, but this is Accra, this is 1998. It is no longer appropriate to expect that because everyone is trying to get along, to make ends meet, so you shouldn't think that you can rely on your relations. You should try and get on yourself. (G2)

Similar emphasis on self-reliance emerged in the attitudes and expectations of most younger generation respondents, and was shared by many older people. In the past the expectation of material support from children in one's old age was standard and legitimate, fostering a view of children as 'investments', a point also made in the demographic literature on Africa (Caldwell 1982; Cain 1985). Today, the legitimacy of such a view is being questioned. There is an emerging sense that, for the future, it is no longer appropriate or morally right to expect to rely on material support from children in one's old age because the financial burden on them, given the economic situation, would be too great.

> Our economy is getting more rotten each day. So if you should relax and rely on your children it is bad. It is not good because you know what they will be going through. Now it is up to the individual, you know. Some people just live by the day, they don't have the foresight ... but you have to start planning your life, planning your future. (G2)

In addition, there is increasing recognition, perhaps not surprisingly, that it is no longer *wise* to rely on one's children, because the level of their support, if provided at all, is unlikely to be sufficient.

> You just can't rely on your children. Some people still have that idea but it is wrong because you can't be sure of them. Even if you invest in them, they may not get to a position where they can look after you. So if you rely on them you are going to suffer. (G3)

As this statement already suggests, many younger people today, especially the poorest, with little education or prospects, continue to bank on their children's support in old age. In the investigation, this wish was expressed by those respondents with the least education, income or prospects who, in the current context, have little option to find or even envisage an alternative.

> My son will look after me. That is why I am trying my best to put that boy on a good foundation. He knows I am trying my best. (G2)

Tragically, it is people in this very group that are likely to be most dependent on material support in old age, at the same time as their children are likely to be the least able to support them adequately. Most other younger-generation respondents, however, espoused the value of self-reliance, and had translated this into personal expectations or intentions for their future. They stressed above all their desire and aim to be financially independent of their children:

> I am not going to depend on my children when I am old. I want to be independent because they can fail me. (G3)

> I don't want to depend on my children because if you start impinging on them they have to divide whatever they get.... They should have their life

and I will take care of myself. This is what I want to do.... The planning is very very important. (G2).

Policy implications?
Reflections and the need for further exploration

These emerging views and expectations, as well as the shifts that have underpinned the decline in material family support for older people, have important policy implications. They raise issues or questions that need to be considered in identifying what kinds of policy approaches will be most appropriate and effective in ensuring economic security for older people now and in the future.

Most immediately, the emerging emphasis on, and wish for self-reliance and independence in old age expressed by many of the younger generations, points – at least in the urban context – to a demand (and thus perhaps need) for policies or strategies that enable individuals, as much as possible, to enjoy a reasonable level of economic security *independently* of their families. This raises the question of the appropriateness of an approach, as is strongly advocated for Africa, that focuses on the centrality of family or filial support as the basis of old age security. On a normative level, the appropriateness of such an approach may be limited: it would in effect represent an attempt to lay down a particular 'moral order' of family responsibilities that no longer fully accords with the values and expectations for the future prevalent in the population today.

Questions may also be raised about the potential effectiveness of such a family-based approach. The shift in the basis of filial support towards an increasing dependence of such support on children's judgement of their parents' past conduct suggests that even a legally binding filial duty may not be readily adhered to in cases where this judgement is negative. In view of recent trends showing a rising incidence of parental neglect by fathers, this raises doubts about the ability of such a policy measure to ensure adequate economic security, especially for older men (Aboderin 2000; Robertson 1981). It would seem that the central and effective role of filial support may only be maintained if accompanied by broad change in parenting approaches. This would require, in theory, a greater emphasis on the need for parents to do all they can to further their children and, more importantly, to *communicate* these feelings and intentions to them. Such communication, if achieved in practice, would clarify for children the reasons why parents' support may be limited in practice, and would thus inform their judgement of this support.

Finally, even if filial support were generally given, it may be expected (given the continued scarcity of resources, and the fundamental hierarchy of priorities that seemingly underlies their allocation in families) that this support would not be adequate to meet older people's needs. Even if extra funds were afforded to children (for example through tax exemptions), these would be likely to remain subject to the same priorities in decisions on their allocation: the needs of the young coming before those of the old.

In contrast to the doubts raised about the suitability of family–centred policies, the trends in family support and normative expectations identi- fied in this exploratory research would point (at least for the urban context) to the appropriateness and effectiveness of non-contributory pension schemes. Such schemes would signify an acceptance of older people's right to be financially independent of their families and make claims on the state (Finch 1989; Messkoub 2001), and this would raise the crucial question of whether such pensions are sufficiently compatible with African values and ideals of filial obligation and reciprocity. While this is a subject for a different debate, one consideration may be offered here: a public pension scheme could be seen as an application of the essence of these very values at a societal level: through the state which draws on, and redistributes the resources generated by them, the young honour their obligation to support and repay the old for their earlier contributions to society.

Summary and concluding remarks

The complex interaction of factors and processes identified here as underpinning the decline in material family support for older people in urban Ghana is not recognised in the general literature. This study underscores the limited usefulness of the two existing explanatory models (modernisation and ageing theory notions on the one hand, and materialist interpretations on the other) in providing a meaningful and practicable understanding of how and why shifts in family support have occurred in countries such as Ghana. These new insights have poten- tially crucial policy implications. There is an obvious need for further and larger-scale research in Ghana and other African countries into the dynamics and motivational basis of material family support and resource allocation to older people. It is only with such an understanding that appropriate and effective old age economic security policies can be developed for the region.

REFERENCES

Aboderin, I. (2000) 'Social change and the decline in family support for older people in Ghana: an investigation of the nature and causes of shifts in support', PhD dissertation, School for Policy Studies, University of Bristol.

—— (2001) 'Decline and normative shifts in family support for older people in Ghana – implications for policy', paper presented at the Annual Development Studies Association, Manchester, UK, 10–12 September.

—— (2002) 'Building on family support and "traditional" values – an appropriate basis for developing old age economic security in Africa today?' paper presented at the Valencia Forum, Valencia, Spain, 1–4 April.

—— (forthcoming) 'Modernization and economic strain: the impact of social change on material family support for older people in Ghana', in Vern L. Bengtson and Ariela Lowenstein (eds.), *Families, Aging and Social Supports: International Perspectives*, Aldine de Gruyter, Hawthorne, New York.

Ahenkora, K. (1999) *The Contribution of Older People to Development. The Ghana Study*, HelpAge International and HelpAge Ghana, Accra.

Apt, N. A. (1996) *Coping With Old Age in a Changing Africa*, Avebury, Aldershot.

—— (1997) *Ageing in Africa*, World Health Organisation, Geneva.

—— (2000) 'The Rights and Protection of Older Persons in Africa', paper presented at the OAU/HAI Experts Meeting, Kampala, Uganda, 27 Nov.–1 Dec.

—— (2001) 'Gender, culture and social factors determining active ageing', paper presented at an Expert meeting on Ageing and Development, The Hague, Netherlands, 26 October.

—— and M. Grieco (1994) 'Urbanisation, caring for the elderly and the changing African family: the challenge to social welfare and social policy', *International Social Security Review*, 48: 111–22.

Bengtson, V.L. and W. A. Achenbaum (eds.) (1993), *The Changing Contract Across Generations*, Aldine de Gruyter, New York.

Blanc, A. K. and S. Gray (2000) *Greater than Expected Fertility Decline in Ghana. An Examination of the Evidence*, Macro International Inc, Calverton, Maryland.

Burgess, E.W. (ed.) (1960) *Ageing in Western Societies*, University of Chicago Press, Chicago.

Cain, M. (1985) 'Fertility as an adjustment to risk', in A. S. Rossi (ed.), *Gender and the Life Course*, Aldine, New York, pp. 145–9.

Caldwell, J. C. (1982) *The Theory of Fertility Decline*, Academic Press, New York.

Charlton, R. and R. McKinnon (2001) *Pensions in Development*, Ashgate, Aldershot.

Cowgill, D. O. (1972) 'A theory of aging in cross-cultural perspective', in D. O. Cowgill and L. D. Holmes (eds.), *Ageing and Modernization*, Appleton-Century-Crofts, New York, pp. 1–14.

—— (1974) 'Aging and modernization: a revision of the theory', in Jaber F. Gubrium (ed.), *Late Life*, Thomas, Springfield, IL, pp. 123–45.

Dei, H. (1997) 'Meeting the challenges of conversion: Ghana's Provident Fund becomes a pension scheme', *International Social Security Review*, 50: 63–71.

Dovlo, E. (1992) 'Comparative overview of African independent churches and charismatic ministries in Ghana', *Trinity Journal of Church and Theology*, 2: 55–73.

Finch, J. (1989) *Family Obligations and Social Change*, Polity Press, Cambridge.

Ghana Statistical Service (2000) *Ghana Living Standards Survey (GLSS) 4*, Ghana Statistical Service, Accra.

Gouldner, A. W. (1960) 'The norm of reciprocity: a preliminary statement', *American Sociological Review*, 25: 161–78.

Government of Ghana Technical Committee on Poverty (1996) *Policy Focus for Poverty Reduction*, Government of Ghana, Accra.

Gyekye, K. (1996) *African Cultural Values. An Introduction*, Sankofa Publishing Company, Accra.

HelpAge International (2002) *State of the World's Older People 2002*, HelpAge International, London.

Heslop, A. (2002) 'Livelihood and coping strategies of older people: the role of non-contributory pensions', paper presented at the Valencia Forum, Valencia, Spain, 1–4 April.

IAG (2002) *The Valencia Report 2002. A Report on the Outcomes of a Meeting of Gerontological Researchers, Educators and Providers. Providing an Evidence Base in Support of the International Plan of Action on Ageing 2002*, International Association of Gerontology, available at <http://www.valenciaforum.com/vfr.html>.

ISSA (2000) 'Social security in Africa. new realities', *African Series No. 21*, Social Security Documentation, International Social Security Association (ISSA), Abidjan.

Kaseke, E. (2000) 'Extending social security to older persons in Africa: the challenge of the new millennium', paper presented at the OAU/HAI Experts Meeting, Kampala, Uganda, 27 Nov.–1 Dec.

Laslett, P. (1992) 'Is there a generational contract?' in P. Laslett and J. S. Fishkin (eds.), *Justice Between Age Groups and Generations*, Yale University Press, New Haven.

Lund, F. (2001) ' "Crowding in" care, security, and micro-enterprise formation: revisiting the role of the state in poverty reduction, and in development', paper presented at the DSA Conference, Manchester, UK, 10–12 September.

Messkoub, M. (2001) 'Population ageing and care of the elderly: what are the lessons of Asia for Sub-Saharan Africa?', in P. Lawrence and C. Thurtle (eds.), *Africa and Asia in Comparative Perspective*, Macmillan, London.

Moody, H.R. (1993) *Ethics in an Aging Society*, Johns Hopkins University Press, Baltimore.

Neysmith, S. and J. Edwardh (1984) 'Economic dependency in the 1980s: its impact on Third World elderly', *Ageing and Society*, 4 (1): 21–44.

Nukunya, G.K. (1992) *Tradition and Change. The Case of the Family*, Ghana University Press, Accra.

OAU (2001a) *The African Common Position on Ageing: Input to the 2nd UN World Assembly on Ageing*, Conf./Trip/Draft/ Rapt-Rpt/1 Annex IV, Organisation of African Unity, Addis Ababa.

—— (2001b) *Draft Policy Framework and Plan of Action on Ageing*, Conf./Trip/Draft/ Rapt-Rpt/1 Annex III (Rev.1) Organisation of African Unity, Addis Ababa.

Robertson, C. C. (1981) *Sharing the Same Bowl: a Socio-Economic History of Women and Class in Accra, Ghana*, Indiana University Press, Bloomington.

Schultz, J. (2002) 'Are both growth and adequate pensions possible in an ageing world?', paper presented at the Valencia Forum, Valencia, Spain, 1–4 April.

Sen, K. (1994) *Aging: Debates on Democratic Transition and Social Policy*, Zed Books, London.

United Nations (2000) *World Population Prospects: The 2000 Revision*, United Nations, New York, <www.un.org/popin/data.html>.

—— (2002) *International Plan of Action on Ageing 2002*, advanced unedited copy, United Nations, 12 April.

United Nations Development Programme (UNDP) (1997) *Ghana Development Report 1997*, UNDP, Accra.

—— (2002) *Human Development Report 2002*, UNDP, New York.

Van der Geest, S. (1997) 'Between respect and reciprocity: managing old age in rural Ghana', *Southern African Journal of Gerontology*, 6: 20–25.

—— (2002) 'Respect and reciprocity: care of elderly people in rural Ghana', *Journal of Cross-Cultural Gerontology*, 17: 3–31.

Walker, A. (2002) 'Global Challenges in Securing Material Well-Being in Ageing Societies', paper presented at the Valencia Forum, Valencia, Spain, 1–4 April.

World Bank (1994) *Averting the Old Age Crisis*, World Bank, Washington, DC.

CHAPTER 11

Ageing in Mexico:
Families, Informal Care and Reciprocity

CRISTINA GOMES DA CONCEIÇÃO AND
VERONICA MONTES DE OCA ZAVALA

Over the next two decades demographic ageing will become firmly established in Mexico. According to projections, Mexico will have one of the ten largest elderly populations in the world. This chapter deals with socio-economic, cultural and family trends associated with ageing, taking into account gender differences, as well as formal and informal exchange systems. The gender perspective takes account of the fact that men and women of different generations assume different societal, familial and community roles. This reflects a complex process, whereby networks, representations, status and stereotypes related to ageing are constructed anew. Intergenerational commitments and obligations are negotiated and renegotiated by working-age adults and by older people – a process that takes place in a context of social security, family and social networks. Widowhood among women (due to their greater life expectancy) is a key issue for older people, influencing home life and income as well as social constructions and exchanges. As will be seen, working-age and older generations are currently reinforcing female roles based on caring for the home and on the routinisation of domestic activities. At the same time, the male's role as provider during adult years can lead to weak social and family networks by the end of his life. Thus, while the male is valued in his functional role as provider, he is devalued in old age.

In developing countries such as Mexico a lack of formal support systems and economic resources places older people at a disadvantage in interactions and exchange negotiations with family and community. In the supply and demand structure for support services, older individuals find themselves in a weakened position, particularly when they are ill, disabled or living in extreme poverty. Rapid population ageing is putting formal social protection mechanisms to the test, highlighting both the potential and the limitations of informal support systems.

This chapter locates the ageing process within a socio-economic context in which institutional or other formal support systems for older people are lacking, giving rise to a complex informal support system based on the family and on social networks. The central issues revolve around the support received by older adults and the types of exchanges in which they engage. Particular attention is paid to the direction of support, conflicts that arise in regard to inheritance, and expectations of reciprocity in cross-gender and intergenerational relations.

Socio-economic and demographic context

Demographic transition in Mexico has been relatively recent. As a result of continued high fertility rates, the proportion of Mexicans aged over 60 in 2000 was lower than that in 1950 (Table 11.1). Despite this, rapid growth in the population as a whole meant that the absolute number of people aged 60 or more increased from two to seven million. The pattern of demographic transition means that there is currently a good potential supply of support for older people from younger age groups (assuming that older people require such support). However, the potential support ratio will fall sharply over the next 20 years.

Table 11.1 Demographic trends in Mexico, 1950–2025

	1950	1975	2000	2025
Population aged 60+ (% of total)	7.1	5.7	6.9	13.5
Potential support ratio*	12.1	12.4	13.2	7.3

* Number of persons aged 15 to 64 for every person aged 65 or over.
Source: UN Population Division, 2002

Mexico is considered a middle-income country, and in 1999 was the world's twelfth largest economy (World Bank 2000). As in Brazil, the economy's performance during the 1980s and 1990s failed to match that of preceding decades. Mexico also mirrors Brazil in terms of high levels of inequality between income groups, regions and rural/urban settings, and high rates of poverty. In 1995 a severe economic crisis produced a sharp drop in real household incomes and a contraction of formal labour market opportunities. In 2000 24.2 per cent of the population lived in extreme poverty: a higher proportion than in 1992 (22.5 per cent) (Cortés *et al.* 2002).

The initial evolution of formal social protection in relation to the labour market in Mexico was also similar to that of Brazil. Since the

1930s, a corporatist political economy conferred varying levels of entitlement on different occupational groups (Mesa-Lago 1978). However, unlike the Brazilian case, there has been no substantial extension of social protection since the 1980s. As a result, pension coverage of older people remains relatively low: in 1996 27 per cent of women and 31 per cent of men received a pension (Wong and Parker 1999). In contrast to Brazil, households with older people were more likely to experience poverty than those without (*ibid.*). Coverage of health insurance is rather higher than pension coverage: in 1999 50 per cent of those aged 60 or more were protected. It is thought that in many cases older people are included in health plans taken out by adult children (*ibid.*).

Currently, 62 per cent of the total population are classified as economically active, but only 33 per cent of adult women engage in paid work. Women are epecially concentrated in the informal labour market. The majority of the economically active people do not work under a formal contract, do not enjoy labour protection and do not contribute to a pension plan (Gomes 2001). A key feature of Mexico is large-scale labour migration to the USA. It is estimated that this involved around 300,000 people a year during the 1990s. As will be seen, migration has important effects on household composition and on patterns of informal support. There is also an increasingly substantial wave of elderly return migrants, who have higher incomes and more valuable asset bases, but who lack formal social protection entitlements (Wong 2001).

Families, households and ageing

Analyses of the family's role in rapidly ageing societies make the assumption that everyday interaction involves support systems and socially shared resources (De Vos 1988; Chappell 1992). Given the narrowness of formal social protection, the Mexican family is seen as a key source of support and protection against economic shocks (Tuirán 1995). This is accomplished through specific survival strategies and support relationships provided through social networks (Lomnitz 2001).[1]

According to Salles and Tuirán (1996), one of the most firmly established myths in the collective mind is that the family provides a roof under which all of its members (perhaps including three or more generations) are gathered and sheltered. Such myths obscure many inequalities within families that are a function of age, gender and kinship. Also, these myths overlook the emotional dynamics of family relationships, the play of feelings, conflicts, as well as hostilities and negotiations. Other authors (Leñero 1998; Varley and Blasco 2000; Contreras de Lehr 1992) discuss the links between families and macro-social conditions, and stress the role of the family as a source of social, economic and psychological support.

This chapter identifies inherent contradictions in the role and concept of the Mexican family. On one side is the reaffirmation of a positive ideology, according to which the family serves as a protective shelter for its members; on the other are the family's internal inequalities, power relationships and differences based on gender, generation and kinship. On top of this, demographic, socio-economic and cultural shifts associated with urbanisation have changed the structure of the family, the behaviour of its members, and the perceptions and values that influence the way family is regarded.

Households containing older people
Over the last decade, family structures and dynamics have been transformed and restructured. With increased life expectancy, numerous generations are alive at the same time, creating changes in the kinship structure (Tuirán 1993 and Gomes 2001). Historically, the nuclear family has been the most common type of household in Mexico (Tuirán 1993; Rabell 1996; Del Rey 2001). The prevalence of nuclear structures reflects a near-universal preference for marriage, along with a reluctance to live with parents. At the end of the twentieth century, 68 per cent of all households were defined as nuclear, and 25 per cent were defined as extended. In recent years, population ageing has led to an increase in the number of new household forms, including extended families with female heads and adult children; one-person households; and households made up of elderly couples living alone (Gomes 2001).

These changes are related to women's greater life expectancy and to high rates of marriage across all adult generations. Men and women aged between 70 and 74 now enjoy a life expectancy ten years higher than the generation born thirty years before them. More than 90 per cent of these individuals married and were able to live with their spouses a decade longer than their predecessors. Marriages are ending increasingly late in life, since high life expectancy postpones widowhood. Moreover, separations and divorces are extremely rare in Mexico, and have been throughout the twentieth century (Tuirán 1998; Quilodrán 2001; Gomes 2001). At the same time, increased life expectancy has meant that older adults are surviving long enough to see their children and grandchildren grow to adulthood.

The increase in numbers of older people has led to the emergence of new phases in the latter parts of the life course. First, adult children marry and leave home, leaving the older couple alone in the 'empty nest'. Second, one of the couple dies (most commonly the man), and the widow may continue living alone in the now one-person household. Alternatively, she may take in an adult child, or move in with one of her children, creating an extended multi-generational household (Gomes 2002a).

Table 11.2 shows important variations in patterns of co-residence between older men and older women. In 1995 married men aged over 60 lived mostly in nuclear or extended families, with or without children. Women without spouses (mostly widows) mainly lived in one-person households and in extended families with or without their children, while another large segment of women lived in nuclear households with their children. Half of men over 60 without spouses lived in one-person households, while the rest lived in nuclear or extended families with their children.

Table 11.2 Percentages of household types, by age, gender and marital status of the head of household, Mexico 1994

Type of household		Married heads of household	Unmarried female heads of household	Unmarried male heads of household
Nuclear	• Couple, children	39		
	• Couple	23		
	• Head of household, children		23	23
Extended	• Couple, children, others	28		
	• Head of household, children, others		28	18
	• Couple, others	8		
	• Head of household, others		18	6
One-person			28	49
Other		2	3	4
Total		100%	100%	100%

Source: Gomes, 2001, based on National Household Income and Expenditures Survey (ENIGH) 1994.

Thus, in the final stage of the life course, in addition to the emergence of the extended family as a household, we see – as a function of advancing age, gender, and the end of marriage (generally due to death)

– a growing complexity of household types. Multi-generational households, which could guarantee the wellbeing of the older population, are
not a norm in Mexico. Although the country is still at the beginning of
the demographic ageing process, an increase in one-person households
is already evident (from 4.9 per cent of all households in 1990 to 6.4 per
cent in 2000). This trend is due in large part to the increase in
households headed by widows (Gomes 2002a).

Interpreting relationships bewteen household structures and the
wellbeing of older people is not an easy task. For example, studies have
found that some older widows with economic resources prefer to live
alone: a situation that does not necessarily mean isolation from family
networks and support. Living alone can mean greater autonomy, and
that female roles associated with home care will not be reproduced in
succeeding generations.

In other cases, living alone may be the result of abandonment, most
often related to lack of resources. In particular, older men without
resources may not be attractive live-in candidates for their children or
for other adult relatives (Varley and Blasco 2001). In cases of extreme
poverty, social and family networks built in earlier phases of life may be
broken, especially at times of economic crisis and when the older adult
in question is ill. Enríquez (2000) analyses the increase in cases of social
isolation among older adults in poor outlying areas of the city of
Guadalajara, where one-person households of older people are typical,
not by choice but in the wake of broken social ties, isolation and
abandonment. Enríquez views this as a result of a process of social
disintegration associated with ageing.

While it is dangerous to generalise about the living arrangements of
older people in Mexico, there are indications that families do not
provide an adequate safety net of social protection to compensate for
the limitations of the social security system. The country contains a
complex network of household types conditioned by the presence or
absence of resources, income, possession of real estate, or home ownership. Other determining elements include past experience of urban life,
migration to the city, whether the older people have children, and their
health status, especially chronic illness or physical disability. Older adults
who live in one-person households under conditions of extreme
poverty may have opted to live alone in order to ensure their own
welfare, or they may be living in extreme poverty and social isolation
without any source of formal or family support. Those who live in
extended families may be providing the living quarters in which they
and their children live, and they may be contributing with their
pensions or inheritance. In other cases they may move to the house of
one of their children, in particular when physical limitations are an

issue. We will now explore these issues in greater depth with reference to multi-generational households.

Multi-generational households

Historically, multi-generational households have been a much less frequent phenomenon than the nuclear family. Extended family living situations were much less common than nuclear families in the past, since mortality was high and parents tended not to survive long enough to see their children become adults (Rabell 1996). Today's greater life expectancy could allow for more multi-generational households. However, while multiple generations are now living contemporaneously, this does not necessarily mean that they live together in the same households.

Patterns of residence in multi-generational households are strongly influenced by the sex of the older person. Mexican women increasingly live in multi-generational households as they age, with sharp rises after the ages of 70 and 80. Conversely, men are less likely to live with their children or other adult relatives at age 80 than when they are 60 or 70 years old. This may have important implications for informal care for men and women. The socio-economic characteristics of older people, especially men, are closely related to whether they share housing with their children or other adult relatives. Older men in work or those with pensions are more likely to live with other family members (Gomes 2001).

There are several explanations for these gender effects. Because of their longer life expectancy, women are more likely to experience the death of a spouse. They are also more likely to experience chronic illness and physical and mental disability, which increase their need to live with other people and receive support. At the same time, women are considered more appealing candidates for living with other adults, because their socialisation is oriented to housework, cooking and caring for children (Chant 1996; Varley and Blasco 2001). As a result, older women are in an advantageous position to offer their own services in exchange for economic assistance and family support from their children.

Gender-related factors, such as the role of 'provider', do not allow men to establish relationships with their children that are as close as those enjoyed by mothers. Thus, when relationships end in divorce or death, an emotional break tends to occur as well, reproducing the stereotype of the male as 'unreliable' or 'picky'. This reinforces the disadvantageous position of men, who are not seen as desirable co-residents by their children and other relatives. While they may have contributed as economic providers, men who lack resources are unlikely to realise their hopes of future reciprocity vis-à-vis their children. This situation is particularly severe for older men who lack income, property or other economic assets (Varley 2001).

Older men are less likely to experience poverty than older women (Wong and Parker 1999). It might therefore be expected that they would have more to offer family members in return for their support. Older men's labour earnings are concentrated in the early stages of old age, when some adult children have not yet established homes of their own, increasing the desirability of co-residence. When men retire, it is likely that their children will have already established an independent household. Furthermore, retirement in Mexico invariably means a drastic reduction in income level, and this makes the home of the retiree less economically attractive as part of an exchange (Gomes 2001).

Similar gender effects may influence patterns of access to health insurance. Wong and Parker (1999) note that older women were rather more likely than older men to be included in health plans, even though they were less likely to have been employed in the formal sector. One likely reason for this discrepancy is that adult children are better disposed towards older women and are therefore more likely to include them in family health plans.

A small proportion of older people have clear needs to live with and receive support from other adult relatives. However, most inter-generational living is more a reflection of the economic needs of the working generation. Older people with economic resources are more likely to be part of multi-generational households, particularly if they are home owners. At the same time, there is a small number of men and women (roughly 7 per cent) who never had children and who, in the absence of economic resources, will be faced in old age with no support from children or grandchildren.[2]

In short, economic factors play an important role in multigenera-tional households. Even when individuals would prefer to live in their own home, apart from parents, the ability to do so is limited by economic constraints. Living independently requires an ability to pay for and maintain a separate household. Another factor in determining whether or not multi-generational households are the arrangement of choice is, of course, the preference of the parents. Some older parents prefer, or at least accept, living with other adults, especially when it involves their own children.

Family support networks and patterns of informal support

Informal support systems involve flows of resources within the family, and may include help from other households. Recent information provides a general view of informal support patterns in Mexico, and sheds light on the role of social and family support networks. The

National Survey on the Sociodemography of Ageing[3] (ENSE 1994) was the first survey in Mexico to focus on the social and family support networks of people aged 60 and over.

According to the National Survey, the household is the primary source for various forms of instrumental support (personal care, housework, food and money) provided to older people. At least one form of support was reported by 57 per cent of respondents. This support is more widespread than transfers from the state (52 per cent of older adults received either health services or some type of pension.) A third, more restricted but potentially significant, type of support is from other households, either in Mexico or abroad (benefiting 38 per cent of those surveyed). The primary providers of such aid are children living at a distance from the older adults (Montes de Oca 2001). The National Survey reported that 30 per cent of respondents received support primarily in the form of housework, 29 per cent as food, 26 per cent as money and 16 per cent as personal care. The main providers of such support are children (57 per cent), spouses (18 per cent), children-in-law (6 per cent), grandchildren (5 per cent) and other relatives (14 per cent).

Support within the household, from other households and from institutions varies significantly between rural and urban areas. According to the National Survey, older people living in urban areas report more support within the home than in rural areas (61 versus 55 per cent). At first sight, this trend is surprising, as it contradicts the general view that informal support is stronger in rural areas than in urban ones. It is possible that home support in rural areas is under-reported, as it is seen more as an obligation than a courtesy in this setting. Higher levels of poverty and disruption caused by migration may be other factors at play. Urban elders are also more likely to report receipt of institutional support than are their rural counterparts (68 versus 41 per cent). This difference reflects rural/urban disparities in the coverage of the social security medical system.

Although household exchange plays an important role in support, a significant percentage of persons reported no help from any relatives with whom they live.[4] This is at odds with the fact that, as described above, the majority of older adults live with someone. The National Survey indicates that support within the home increases when the older adult has problems functioning. In such scenarios, 63 per cent received support within the household unit. The pattern of support is different for these people, however. Personal care is reported much more frequently (22 per cent), and there is a slight drop in reports of housework (27 per cent), provision of food (28 per cent) and monetary contributions (26 per cent) compared to support received by people in good health.

Table 11.3 Distribution of support from older people to relatives, Mexico City, 1999

Men	Child	Parent	Brother/ Sister	Son- or daughter- in-law	Grand- child	Other relative	Other non- relative	Domestic worker	Total
Money	8.33	5.29	5.10	6.69	0.00	0.00	0.00	0.00	25.42
Services	35.32	13.00	0.00	0.00	0.00	0.00	0.00	0.00	48.32
Gifts	6.81	5.29	0.00	5.38	0.00	0.00	0.00	0.00	17.48
Child care	3.76	0.00	0.00	0.00	0.00	5.02	0.00	0.00	8.78
Other	0.00	0.00	0.00	0.00	0.00	0.00	0.00	0.00	0.00
Total	54.23	23.58	5.10	12.07	0.00	5.02	0.00	0.00	100.00

Women	Child	Parent	Brother/ Sister	Son- or daughter- in-law	Grand- child	Other relative	Other non- relative	Domestic worker	Total
Money	4.60	0.56	1.23	1.14	0.00	0.00	0.00	0.57	8.10
Services	29.75	0.54	5.64	8.50	1.76	3.31	2.42	0.00	51.93
Gifts	16.48	0.56	2.38	3.01	1.01	1.74	0.00	0.00	25.19
Child care	5.23	0.54	0.73	2.44	0.00	1.95	0.47	0.00	11.37
Other	2.16	0.00	0.00	0.68	0.00	0.57	0.00	0.00	3.41
Total	58.23	2.20	9.98	15.78	2.77	7.57	2.89	0.57	100.00

Source: United Nations SABE survey for Mexico City, 1999.

A separate survey of older people in Mexico City[5] investigated the support they provide to other household members. It found that 60 per cent of men and 40 per cent of women provided some type of support. This is most frequently provided to spouses (60 per cent of total support received), although the survey found that a substantial amount of support went to children (accounting for 20 per cent). Table 11.3 shows that older people also provided significant support to a variety of other relatives, with older women slightly more likely to offer support.

The most common type of support provided by older people consists of services. These are mainly provided by women, and directed to all family members, including household employees. Not surprisingly, monetary contributions are typically made by men and are largely directed at their children. Women are more likely to engage in child care than men are, not only for their own grandchildren, but also for the children of others. When men do provide care, it is only to their own grandchildren. A very significant exchange of services also occurs between spouses of an advanced age, and this includes services provided by men.

It is likely that the contributions of older people to their family networks are influenced by significant gaps in institutional support systems and a lack of economic resources. They reflect marked gender-dependent differences and disadvantages for women, especially in terms of participation in the labour market and retirement systems. However, women have an important cross-generational role in providing services. Patterns of gender and social inequality are extremely varied for older adults in Mexico. The family has been an important locus for the exchange of support of various types, and older people have filled important gaps in the lives of working-age adults; more by providing services, care and gifts than through financial contributions.

Inheritance practices are central to any understanding of intergenerational exchange, and often have a large bearing on informal support for older people and on the position of widows. In urban areas, few older people make wills, even among better-educated, high-income groups. This often gives rise to protracted legal disputes within families. In some cases, older people are pressured to transfer assets to children before their death. This may then be reciprocated in the form of improved support. However, the Mexican Association of Notaries has documented numerous cases where such asset transfers were followed by abandonment or abuse. In rural areas, inheritance primarily involves the transfer of land rights. Patterns of rural landholding in Mexico display a number of unusual features. Historically, a high proportion of land (especially in the centre and south of the country) has been owned communally in *ejidos*. In this system, land would be granted to individual farmers through the *ejidal* assembly. In the event of the farmer's death, the assembly would reallocate the land, usually to the farmer's oldest son. This practice has tended to exclude surviving widows from their husband's assets. Indeed, before the 1970s, women's potential inheritance rights were completely ignored by the assemblies (Espinosa 2001).

Patterns of reciprocity in Mexico City

The principle of reciprocity is implicit in relationships of support and exchange, from the simple family or parental context to the complex fabric of society and generations. Reciprocity is part of a complex of attitudes and behaviours involved in protecting and supporting, and one can expect to find it even in the simplest, family-based contexts. Analysis of reciprocity has centred on the family, with special emphasis on certain essential links (between spouses, among siblings, between parents and children, grandparents and grandchildren, parents-in-law and children-in-law, among neighbours and friends). This analysis has focused on the nature of the relationships as well as on the temporal aspect (immediate or deferred) that is involved in the exchange process (Harraven and Adams 1999; Izquieta 1996).

The theory of social exchange is based on the idea that one person provides benefits to another, and that although there is a general expectation of response, the timing and particular nature of the response is left undefined. Indeed, it must be left undefined, since any attempt to make it explicit beforehand would destroy the social significance of the exchange, making the expectation of future support into an economic transaction. Thus, reciprocity must be seen as part of a social exchange in which the provision of benefits creates a diffuse future obligation. The value parents attribute to their children and their expectations of reciprocity are fundamental in understanding the impact of ageing on the structure, relationships, commitments and obligations that link the different members of the Mexican family.

According to Donati (1999: 42): 'There is a risk of not understanding what is to be given, to whom, and how much. Nor is it clear what it is fair to take, from whom and how much'. This raises a wider issue about how to determine whether or not a form of behaviour is in some way reciprocal, and how it can be evaluated. As discussed by Nussbaum in this volume (Chapter 13), relationships of exchange often occur under conditions of real inequality, because the things being exchanged have very different meanings to the people involved. This may be a function of experience, as well as of the effort involved in obtaining them. In other cases, the normative and ethical values of society may emphasise material and financial resources above other kinds of support, such as companionship or simple personal contact. This uncertainty about what is fair lends an element of inconsistency and uncertainty to perceptions of reciprocity.

Research has been conducted on the experience and perception of old age in Mexico City, asking respondents what kind of support they receive, and from whom. This approach made it possible to take into account the network process, as well as the flow and meaning of support (Montes de Oca 1996). Some illustrative cases may help to distinguish three types of support and exchange relationships, and reveal the direction of support, the manner in which the time factor is managed, and the expectations of reciprocity. These different relationships can be illustrated with reference to specific case studies of older people. The following cases are taken from a wider study of 30 older men and women who were selected for interviewing according to a predefined guide. The respondents resided in central districts of Mexico City, and had varied living arrangements and socio-economic backgrounds (Montes de Oca 1996).

Gudelia lives with her son in a middle-class neighbourhood. She values the role played by her younger son, now that she is ill, and understands that her other children cannot be with her as much as she would like. 'My children come to visit me, and when they can help me they do, and when they can't they don't.' Despite the care she receives from her youngest son, she feels lonely and feels she 'cannot count on them'. She signed a power of attorney so that her youngest son could collect her pension now that she is ill. This concession on her part allows the son to manage an income in addition to the one he earns himself. Since she can no longer leave the house because of the illness, she has slowly lost contact with neighbours and friends. On the subject of other relatives and the significance of this, she answered, 'No! I'm telling you, they're here to be helped by me, not for them to help me. For example, my cousin lives in Tampico and never speaks to me. Juan, who is my cousin, lives in Coatzacoalcos. He speaks to me, but doesn't come to see me. But he does speak with me.' (Gudelia, an only daughter, is 68 years old and lives in Mexico City, but is originally from Tamaulipas. She receives a pension, has five children, is a widow, owns her home, and suffers from chronic illness.)

In this case, family reciprocity is based on immediate return, with specific arrangements for exchange between the older adults and their families. The number of children is very important in the flow of support, but whether it actually leads to more support depends on how it combines with other factors. When the parents are better off, there are ways of supporting the children – and, in such cases, without an expectation of return, either immediately or in the long term. Gudelia's pension alone makes her financially independent, but she also owns her own home. Hence, she is able to meet her own financial needs. Despite her illness, she continues supporting one of her children with money, shelter and food. In this case, illness was a factor in reducing contact with other children and relatives. Geographical distance from relatives also diminishes the flow of support from them, at least on the emotional level. The lack of reciprocity of the other children is excused on the basis of their work and family obligations. When necessary, support is given without expectation of receiving anything in return.

Brígida lives with her father, who is in his eighties. She currently considers herself married, though it is some time since she lived with her husband, and indeed she has lost contact with him. She has a place to live thanks to her work as a caretaker in a building, and is the head of her household, but she does not own a home. Since childhood she has done domestic work. She married at the age of 29 and had three sons, two of whom survived. She worked doing washing and ironing, enabling her to contribute substantially to the welfare of the family. At 50, she stopped working, and her children began supporting her. Now, she works as a caretaker in a building, where she cleans, thus earning her living space. She sees her children almost every day, and the oldest is her primary source of funds. Despite their humble origin and the conditions in which they were brought up, Brígida sees her children as fulfilled, with good jobs and financial security. She depends financially on her oldest son, and she visits all the families weekly. It is important to her at this stage to live with her children, especially the eldest son. She will soon be without housing, and will most likely go to live with her oldest son. She has difficulty speaking of this. She does not seem to have a history of problems in her family relationships. (Brígida is 68, lives in Mexico City, originally comes from San Luis Potosí, works, has one sister, two children, is separated, and does not own her own home.)

Brígida does not have many children, but she feels a sense of support from her oldest son. She sees her son as returning the effort she made for him, but she no longer has anything to give to her children, despite the fact that she needs help from them. It is worth noting that she continues to work in exchange for her living space. This strategy reflects a hidden area of concern: she lives with and takes care of her father, and the two of them cannot live in the house of one of her children. Her work puts her in touch with people, who constitute the social support network that keeps her in contact with people and support mechanisms. This is a case where support goes from children to older people, and where the arrangement is perceived as a deferred exchange in return for the older person's past efforts.

Antonio lives with his wife and children in a working-class neighbourhood. They work in retailing. He owns the house in which they live, but family relations are very tense. There is no support relationship. Antonio is financially independent, and his children are grown up. He feels that his children do not show him respect, that he has to demand his place in family affairs. His frustration is rooted in the fact that the large amount of time he has had to spend working has made it impossible for him to pay enough attention to his children and, now that they are grown up, their attitude toward him has changed. 'When they were children they were a joy when I got home at night, but I almost didn't exist in the house. I left at five in the morning to work, and sometimes got back at four or five in the afternoon, or as late as eight in the evening. The point is that I had to earn money. There were seven children and they were all in school.' Antonio has not only been mistreated but has been hit by his sons and daughters-in-law. He definitely expects no support, but does feel he can demand respect at this stage of his life. (Antonio had 13 siblings, has no pension, owns his own home, has eight children, and suffers from diabetes).

This case illustrates a situation where older adults do not receive support from their close relatives. Although Antonio supported them in the past and once had great expectations of reciprocity, this has evaporated as family conflicts have proved intractable. There is also evidence of abuse by his children, which is borne out by records of complaints showing that Antonio's own sons are his principal aggressors. Antonio fulfilled his role as provider, and in his old age he hoped for respect from his children. But the family alliances, in which the children side with the mother, have excluded him from the basic solidarity that family ties ordinarily provide. He lives with them, but not in a relationship of mutual support. In this case, the family reciprocity tie has been broken, and he is left with only the social networks created in the context of work.

These three cases cannot be taken as in any way representative of the wide variety of experiences of older people in Mexico. However, they can be taken as a good reflection of the wider findings of the qualitative survey from which they were taken (Montes de Oca 1996). They illustrate the complexity of relationships between informal exchanges and reciprocity and the wellbeing of older people. They also reveal different expectations of reciprocity depending on the differing relationships of support and on the financial circumstances of older persons and their relatives. In some cases, reciprocity is limited by a scarcity of children, and by their difficult financial and family circum-stances, as well as by geographical distance. In other cases, disabling illness limits contact and the ability to maintain relationships with relatives and friends. This deactivates family and social support networks. On occasion, reciprocal exchange takes place immediately, but in other cases it takes place over time, once children are grown and have resolved their own problems.

Final comments

Along with demographic change, Mexico's economic situation reduces opportunities for the population as a whole and has far-reaching effects on families. More people in the family must work in order to generate household income. At the same time, fertility and mortality rates are declining, leading to a reorganisation of families and households. These units create complex systems of informal self-protection, which seek to meet the needs of the various generations. However, informal support systems operate within the limits of households, according to gender, social, cultural and economic dynamics.

Most households containing people over 60 are either nuclear, extended or mono-person. There are also multiple-family and other complex arrangements, some of which are contained within households, while others extend beyond household boundaries. Complex household arrangements hamper accurate assessment of support strategies and the direction of support. In addition, economic factors affect whether parents and adult children live together. Households with higher levels of income and education are more likely to contain two generations. With advancing age, women in Mexico more often live with their children than do men. This is partially due to illness, but also to the fact that women are in a position to exchange services for support. At a less advanced age, men also live with their children, but they cease to do so with advancing age, as a result of their financial situation and gender-based issues.

Households provide significant support to older people in a number of areas. These include housework and food preparation, as well as providing money and personal care. These activities tend to increase when the older person suffers disability or illness. However, support from the family is not universal or uniform, and thus it does not compensate for the poorly developed formal social protection system. It is apparent that households assist and care for their older members differently, depending on the advantages or disadvantages represented by the older person. In some cases, caring for an ill older person is made easier by the presence of financial resources, home ownership and property that can be drawn on in an emergency.

Older people provide an extensive and varied range of support to other family members. While older men mainly help their families with money, women provide a wide range of services, gifts and care to their dependent relatives. The principal recipients of support are spouses, followed by children, and then by other relatives. Older people often act as primary care givers when adult children are ill, and they take full responsibility for grandchildren in cases where the grandchildren's parents die. Overall levels and patterns of support provided by older people are strongly shaped by economic factors. When financial resources are particularly limited, this is reflected in the types of support which predominate.

Reciprocity between generations is a key, albeit implicit, principle in support and exchange relationships. However, it tends to vary according to the socio-economic situation both of the older adults and their children. Pensions and other monetary resources make old people more attractive or less of an inconvenience for the working-age generation, as well as giving the older generation autonomy and the ability to decide whether or not to share their living space with children and grand-children. Both options may or may not involve solidarity networks, negotiation or conflict. The number of children also affects the perception of reciprocity and the exchange relationship. A large number of children who lack a solid economic position may not be a source of any support whatsoever, while a smaller number of children who are better off can mean an expectation of support and reciprocity. Reciprocity may be immediate or deferred, although non-familial support networks usually require immediate reciprocity. While intergenerational exchange remains central to Mexican society, there are grounds for questioning the long-term survival of norms of reciprocity in family care giving and support. These include concrete sociological changes such as decreasing family size, the dissolution of kinship ties, an increase in one-person households, migration and increasing distance between family members. They also include less tangible effects, relating to shifts in attitudes and emotional ties between the generations.

NOTES

1 This thinking may also be applied to other strongly Catholic countries, such as Spain and the Philippines (Izquieta, 1996).
2 According to the National Survey the current generation over 60 years old have had an average of 6.6 children born alive, and 6.3 of their children still alive. Only 6.9 per cent of people over 60 years old have never had children (Gomes 2003).
3 The survey is representative at the national level, drawing on a sample of slightly over 5,000 men and women 60 years of age or over (46.9 per cent and 53.1 per cent respectively). The survey employed a non-self-weighted probabilistic sample.
4 The population not receiving support within the household may still receive support from outside the home or from state transfers. Only 10 per cent of the population aged 60 or over reported receiving no support from any of these sources.
5 In 1999 the United Nations sponsored household surveys in seven Latin American

cities, including Mexico City. These examined family support networks, health and ageing. The Mexico City sample represents the city's entire elderly population, consisting of 1,881 cases, of which 73 per cent were women over 50 and 27 per cent were men over 60. In order to make the data comparable for men and women, this analysis only takes into account the surveyed individuals over 60, 44 per cent of whom were men and 56 per cent were women.

REFERENCES

Chappell, Neena (1992) *Social Support and Aging*, Butterworths, Toronto.
Cortés, Fernando, Daniel Hernández, Enrique Hernández, Miguel Székely and Hadid Vera (2002) *Evolución y características de la pobreza en México en la última década del siglo XX*, SEDESOL, México.
De Vos, Susan (1988) 'Extended family living among older people in six Latin American countries', *Journal of Gerontology*, 45 (3): pp. 87–94.
Donati, Pier Paolo (1999) 'Familias y generaciones', *Desacatos. Revista de Antropología Social*, 2: 27–49.
Enríquez, Rocío (2000) 'Redes Sociales y Envejecimiento en Contextos de Pobreza Urbana', paper presented at the Sixth National Meeting on Demographic Research, Mexican Demographic Society and Colegio de México, Mexico, 31 July.
Espinosa, Rosaurora (2002) *Informe Final del Segundo Monitoreo al Programa de Educación, Salud y Alimentación* (PROGRESA), report presented at the 29th meeting of the Red Nacional de promotoras y Asesoras Rurales, Puebla, Mexico.
Gomes, Cristina (2003) 'Intergenerational exchanges in Mexico: types and intensity of supports', paper presented at the International Conference on Intergenerational Relations in Families' Life Course, Committee on Family Research, International Sociological Association, Institute of Sociology, Academia Sinica, Taipei, Taiwan, 12 March.
—— (2002a) 'Life course, households and institutions: Brazil and Mexico', *Journal of Comparative Family Studies*, 33 (3): 317–44.
—— (2002b) 'México, un país de jóvenes, en rápido proceso de envejecimiento. Participación laboral, pensiones y salud', in Verónica Montes de Oca and Cristina Gomes (eds.), *Envejecimiento demográfico y políticas públicas para adultos mayores. México en Iberoamérica ante el nuevo siglo*, Instituto de Investigaciones Sociales-UNAM, Mexico.
—— (2001) *Dinámica Demográfica, Familia e Instituciones, Envejecimiento Poblacional en Brasil y México*, PhD Dissertation, Colegio de México, Mexico.
Hareven, Tamara and Kathleen Addams (1999) 'La generación de en medio. Comparación de cohortes de ayuda a padres de edad avanzada dentro de una comunidad estadounidense', *Desacatos. Revista de Antropología Social*, 2 (Autumn): 50–71.
INEGI (1997 and 2000) *Encuesta Nacional de Ingresos y Gastos del Hogar – México; Censos Generales de Población y Vivienda; Encuesta Nacional de la Dinámica Demográfica – ENADID; Los Hogares en México; Información Estadística del Sector Salud y Seguridad Social*, Mexico: INEGI.
Izquieta, José Luis (1996) 'La protección y ayuda mutua en las redes familiares. Tendencias y retos actuales', *Revista Española de Investigaciones Sociológicas*, 74 (April–June): 189–208.
Leñero, Luis (1998) 'Tercera edad en sus implicaciones familiares y sociales', *El Cotidiano. Revista de la realidad mexicana actual*, 88 (March–April): 42–8.
Lomnitz, Larissa (2001) *Redes sociales, cultura y poder. Ensayos de Antropología Latinoamericana*, FLACSO, Mexico.

248   OLDER PEOPLE AND THE CARE ECONOMY

López, Barajas, Ma. De la Paz and Haydea Izazola (1994) *El perfil censal de los hogares y las familias en México*, INEGI, IIS-UNAM, Mexico.
Mesa-Lago, Carmelo (1978) *Social security in Latin America. Pressure groups, stratification and inequality*, University of Pittsburgh Press, Pittsburgh.
Montes de Oca, Verónica (1996) 'Como viven los ancianos en la ciudad de México. Sociodemografía, experiencias institucionales y percepciones sobre la vejez', Instituto de Investigaciones Sociales, mimeo.
—— (1998) 'Política social y sociodemografía de la vejez', *El Cotidiano. Revista de la realidad mexicana actual*, 88 (March-April): 49–56.
—— (2000) 'Experiencia institucional y situación social de los ancianos en la ciudad de México', in Rolando Cordera and Alicia Ziccardi (eds.), *Las políticas sociales en México al fin del milenio. Descentralización, diseño y gestión*, Coordinación de Humanidades/ Facultad de Economía/ IIS-UNAM /Miguel Angel Porrúa, Mexico.
—— (2001) 'Envejecimiento en México: un análisis sociodemográfico de los apoyos sociales y el bienestar de los adultos mayors', PhD. Dissertation, El Colegio de México, Mexico.
Quilodrán, J. (2001) *Un siglo de matrimonio en México*, El Colegio de México, Mexico.
Rabell, Cecilia (1996) 'Trayectoria de vida familiar, raza y género en Oaxaca colonial,' in Cecilia Rabell and Pilar Gonzalbo A. (eds.), *Familia y Vida Privada en la Historia de Iberoamérica*, El Colegio de México and UNAM, Mexico.
Salles, Vania and Rodolfo Tuirán (1996) 'Vida familiar y democratización de los espacios privados', in Mario Luis Fuentes *et al.*, *La familia: investigación y política pública*, UNICEF/DIF/El Colegio de México, Mexico.
Tuirán, Rodolfo (1993) 'Vivir en familia: hogares y estructura familiar en México, 1976–1987', *Revista de Comercio Exterior*, 43 (7): 662–76.
—— (1995) 'Cambios y arraigos tradicionales', *DEMOS*, 8: 30–31.
—— (1996) *Las trayectorias de vida familiar en México: una perspectiva histórica*. SOMEDE, Mexico.
—— (1998) *Family-related life-course patterns in México: A long-term perspective*. PhD Dissertation, University of Texas at Austin.
UN Population Division (2002) *World Population Ageing: 1950–2050*, UN Population Division, New York.
Varley, Ann and Maribel Blasco (2000) 'Intact or in tatters? Family Care of older women and men in urban Mexico', *Gender and Development*, 8 (2): 47–55.
—— (2001) 'Cosechan lo que siembran. Mujeres ancianas, vivienda y relaciones familiares en el México urbano', in Cristina Gomes (ed.), *Procesos sociales, población y familia. Alternativas teóricas y empíricas en las investigaciones sobre vida doméstica*, FLACSO, Mexico.
Wong, R., Soldo, Beth J. and C. Capoferro (2000) 'Generational Social Capital: the Effects on Remittance Streams in Mexico', paper presented at the Annual Meeting of the Population Association of America, 23–25 March, Los Angeles.
Wong, Rebecca (1999) 'Transferencias intrafamiliares e intergeneracionales en México,' *Envejecimiento Demográfico de México: Retos y Perspectivas*, CONAPO, Mexico.
—— (2001) 'La migración y la población mayor', *DEMOS*, 14: 16–17.
—— and Susan Parker (1999) 'Welfare of the elderly in Mexico: A comparative perspective', mimeo, September.

CHAPTER 12

AIDS and Older Persons: The View from Thailand

JOHN KNODEL & CHANPEN SAENGTIENCHAI[1]

The global AIDS epidemic is typically associated with adults under 50, and with the young children they leave behind as AIDS orphans. However, older adults are also impacted by the epidemic. Not only do older adults contract HIV themselves but, far more commonly, they experience multiple consequences as parents and relatives of younger adults who become ill and die from AIDS. Older persons often serve as care givers to their infected sons and daughters and as foster parents for their orphaned grandchildren. They have considerable untapped potential for contributing to efforts by the government and other formal channels to expand and improve the treatment of persons with AIDS. Yet little research has been conducted on how AIDS has affected and has been affected by the older adult population, especially in developing world settings. Here we report on our analysis of the impact of the AIDS epidemic on older adults in Thailand. Our primary focus is on the consequences for and the contributions by older persons in their role as AIDS parents (the term we use to refer to parents of persons with AIDS).

Older persons as infected and affected individuals

Although major risk behaviours and thus infections are less common among persons of 50 and over, AIDS has no age limit. In Thailand, 5.4 per cent of reported AIDS cases through 1998 were among persons aged 50 and older, a level typical of the developing world as a whole (UNAIDS and WHO 2000; Knodel *et al.* forthcoming). In populations with significant epidemics, the absolute numbers of infected older persons can be quite substantial.

Far greater numbers of older people, however, are affected by AIDS through the infection and death of others, particularly their adult children. Since most people who die of AIDS are in their twenties and thirties, one or both of their parents generally survive them, and are most often in their fifties, sixties or seventies. In Thailand, where recent reports estimate that 225,000 adults had died of AIDS by the start of 2000 (TWG 2001), well over 300,000 older persons have lost an adult child to AIDS. Although this number is at least four times greater than the cumulative number of AIDS orphans in Thailand (Rhucharoen-pornpanich and Chamratrithirong 2001; UNAIDS 2000),[2] AIDS parents receive far less attention than AIDS orphans (UNAIDS 1999; UNICEF 2000). Recent micro-simulation studies indicate that 8–13 per cent of Thais over age 50 are likely to experience the loss of at least one adult child to AIDS during their remaining lifetime (Wachter et al. 2002; Wachter et al. forthcoming). While AIDS is not the only cause of death among young adults, the micro-simulations suggest it increases the chances by up to 70 per cent.

In addition to the individual-level consequences of the AIDS epidemic, it has potential macro-level economic and societal impacts that affect persons of all ages (Barnett and Whiteside 2000; Bloom and Lyons 1993; Godwin 1997; World Bank 1997). Although a discussion of these macro-level impacts is beyond the scope of this chapter, it is important to recognise that they may have specific negative impacts on older-aged persons. For example, if AIDS removes significant numbers of working-age persons from the labour force, the old-age dependency burden rises. Formal programmes designed to benefit older persons that depend on taxation and other forms of mandatory contributions from the current workforce could consequently suffer. Also, large numbers of persons with AIDS could compete with older persons for limited health services. Finally, to the degree that the AIDS epidemic lowers national productivity and increases national health care costs, it may weaken the economy, affecting older people along with the general population. In spite of the significance of these potential consequences, however, the loss of an adult child to AIDS often affects older persons more directly and far more immediately than macro-level changes.

Pathways and consequences of family-level impacts
Table 12.1 presents a framework describing the multiple pathways through which the illness and death of an adult child with AIDS can affect parents, and the specific consequences for four dimensions of well-being: emotional, economic, physical and social. Systematic research on these potential family-level impacts on older persons is rare, except in the case of grandparental fostering of AIDS orphans. Although we frame our discussion in terms of AIDS parents, we note that other older-generation relatives could experience many of the same consequences.

Table 12.1 Potential pathways through which the AIDS epidemic may adversely impact the wellbeing of AIDS parents, and their possible specific consequences

Potential pathway	Dimension of wellbeing and possible specific consequence (see codes for possible specific consequence below)			
	Emotional/ psychological	Economic/ financial	Physical health	Social
Care giving	ABC	A	AB	ABC
Co-residence	AC	–	B	B
Providing financial/ material support during illness	D	B C	C	–
Sponsoring the funeral	CD	B C	C	D
Fostering grandchildren	CD	B C	C	ABC
Loss of child	DE	D E	–	–
Negative community reaction	C	F	–	BD

Possible specific consequences
(note PDA = person who dies of AIDS)

I Emotional/psychological consequences
A Psychological pain of seeing suffering and decline of PDA's health
B Feeling overwhelmed by caregiving demands
C Psychological pain from anticipated or enacted negative community reaction
D Anxiety concerning consequences for economic security
E Grief from loss of PDA

II Economic/financial consequences
A Opportunity costs of time taken from economic activities
B Indebtedness from borrowing money to cover expenses
C Depletion of savings or sale of assets to cover expenses
D Disruption of PDA's contributions to parents' household
E Loss of future support when parents are in old age
F Loss of business from former customers out of fear of contagion

III Physical health consequences
A Physical efforts required by care giving
B Risk of exposure to HIV (very low) or opportunistic diseases (especially TB)
C Strain of additional economic activity needed to cover expenses

IV Social consequences
A Time taken away from social activities
B Avoidance of social contact by others
C Strained intra-familial relations
D Strained social relations

Care giving. Providing care to an ill adult child can affect all four dimensions of wellbeing of the older-aged parent. Parents may experience psychological pain witnessing the suffering of their child. They may also feel upset over anticipated or actual negative reactions from community members who associate care giving with contamination by HIV. Care giving demands enormous time and effort, especially at the terminal stage of AIDS. This may lead to adverse financial consequences when care giving takes time from earning a livelihood, or to social isolation when care giving leaves little time for social activities or when it prompts others, who fear contamination, to avoid social contact. Perceived inequities in the care-giving contribution of other family members can strain intra-familial relations. Finally, physical tasks associated with care giving, such as lifting an ill adult child, may lead to physical strains and risks of exposure to the opportunistic diseases associated with AIDS (especially TB).

Co-residence. Adult children may reside with their parents during illness either because they were living with parents prior to the onset of symptoms or because illness prompted them to return to their parental home. Such co-residence, even when parental care giving is not involved, can have some of the same consequences as care giving, including the psychological pain of witnessing the child's decline, concern over negative community reaction, exposure to opportunistic infections, and a restricted social life if community members avoid contact.

Providing material support. Parents may pay for the medical and living expenses of their ill child or for the upkeep of his or her dependants. Parents may go into debt, deplete their savings, or sell assets to cover these extra expenses and thereby threaten their own economic security. Parents may take on extra work to cover the costs, which, if physically taxing, could adversely affect their health.

Arranging the funeral. Funerals can involve significant costs for surviving parents and affect their economic wellbeing in the same ways as the expenses prior to the death. If community members avoid the funeral or act offensively at the funeral (refusing food, say, or avoiding the corpse), parents suffer socially and emotionally.

Fostering grandchildren. Parents of deceased AIDS victims may inherit responsibility for orphaned grandchildren, with obvious financial consequences. Again, the additional costs may lead to physical strain if parents take on supplemental work required to cover them. Also, negative community reaction toward AIDS orphans or worries about child care costs may be stressful. Foster care may diminish social activities, lead friends and neighbours to avoid contact for fear that the grandchildren are infected, or create intra-familial conflicts over custody of the grandchildren.

Child loss. An adult child's death can lead to lasting grief (Sanders 1980). In addition, economic wellbeing may decline if the child who died contributed financially to parental support or household economic activities. Parents also lose potential support that the deceased child might have provided in their old age. These situations could create anxiety and psychological stress.

Community reaction. Negative reactions from community members toward the parents, either during the time of the illness or following the death, could cause psychological, economic, and social distress. For example, a shopkeeper whose child dies of AIDS could lose business because customers fear contagion. If other family members have a similar fear, strained intra-familial relations may result.

Of these seven pathways of impact, the first five result from largely volitional actions on the part of the parents, who thus maintain some degree of control over them. Parents have little ability, however, to avoid losing their children or to manage negative community reaction, the last two pathways. The extent to which any of these potential impacts actually occur remains largely for systematic empirical research to determine. They are likely to be context-sensitive and thus to vary across different settings.

The Thai setting

Thailand's AIDS epidemic began in the 1980s and by the mid-1990s large numbers were becoming ill with and dying of AIDS (Rhuch-aroenpornpanich and Chamratrithirong 2001). By the end of 2001 cumulative numbers of HIV/AIDS approached 1 million and over 300,000 had died (TWG 2001). Despite falling incidence in response to an aggressive campaign to combat the epidemic, annual AIDS deaths are projected to hover around 50,000 for the next decade (Phoolcharoen *et al.* 1998; UNAIDS 1998). Adult prevalence of almost 2 per cent in 2001 places Thailand second only to Cambodia in Asia (UNAIDS 2002). Moreover, in some upper northern provinces over 15 per cent of military recruits tested seropositive in the early 1990s, and the overall death rate more than doubled between 1990 and 1996, swollen by tens of thousands of deaths attributable to AIDS (Im-em 1999; Nelson 1998; van Griensven *et al.* 1998).

As in many developing countries, heterosexual intercourse is the dominant route of HIV transmission in Thailand (UNAIDS and WHO 2000). Much of the epidemic has been driven by commercial sex patronage, a relatively unstigmatised behaviour in Thailand, at least until the AIDS epidemic (Knodel et al. 1996). More recently, infected men are spreading HIV to their wives and non-commercial partners, resulting in women accounting for almost half of all new infections (Chitwarakorn et al. 1998; TWG 2001).

During much of the AIDS epidemic, Thailand experienced rapid economic growth that had begun a decade or more earlier. However, Thailand's economy was hard hit during the Asian economic crisis that erupted in mid-1997 (Gragnolati 2001; UNDP 1999). In assessing the economic consequences of the AIDS epidemic on a societal, familial, or individual level, other influences, including the turbulent economic situation, should be kept in mind.

Between the late 1960s and the early 1990s, the total fertility rate in Thailand fell from approximately 6 to 2 children per woman and has remained low ever since. This has an important bearing both on the number of adult children that an older-aged parent has and on the number of orphans left behind when an adult son or daughter dies.

Intergenerational exchanges of support and services are pervasive in Thailand as in much of the developing world, a situation that conditions the consequences of losing an adult child (Knodel, Chayovan et al. 2000; World Bank 1994). Widespread norms supporting filial obligations to parents, including old-age support and co-residence, underlie existing behavioural patterns (Knodel et al. 1995). Parents also continue to feel an obligation to their children. One result of these intergenerational exchange norms is that approximately half of the adult children of Thais aged 50 and over live in the same locality as their parents, and half of these co-reside with parents. Moreover, the vast majority of adult children who live elsewhere maintain close contact with their parents (Knodel et al. 2001).

For a developing country, Thailand has a relatively well-established public health system. Local health stations and district hospitals are widely accessible. Government provides affordable health insurance through various programmes including a voluntary pre-paid health card system entitling household members to health services and a welfare programme covering medical costs for the indigent. Private enterprise employees have health cover through a mandatory social security programme, government employees have their own health insurance scheme, and a programme to provide universal inexpensive coverage is being implemented. Prior to late 2001, however, none of the various health insurance schemes covered antiretroviral therapy (ART) for HIV.

Data sources and methods

Our findings draw primarily on two components of our research project that permit quantitative analysis: interviews with key informants and direct survey interviews with AIDS and non-AIDS parents.[3]

Key informant study. In 1999 we interviewed informants in 85 rural and urban sites in eight provinces throughout Thailand who were know-ledgeable about community members who were infected with or had died of AIDS. Most informants were staff of local health centres. They provided basic information on living arrangements and care giving for more than 1,000 individual cases, and more detailed data, including information on economic and social impacts, for almost 300 cases they knew best.

Direct interview survey. In 2000 we conducted face-to-face interviews, using a structured questionnaire, with parents of 394 persons who had died of AIDS, usually within the prior three years, and a control group of 376 parents of similar ages and backgrounds who had not experienced the recent death of an adult child. Interview sites were selected from three provinces in three subregions to reflect a broad range of circumstances. In cases where both parents were living together, some items referred separately to each parent, generating information for 649 AIDS parents and 621 non-AIDS parents. Local health personnel served as intermediaries in identifying respondents.

Comparison of sources. Because neither the key informant study nor the direct interview survey is based on a probability sample, the results cannot be statistically generalised in any rigorous fashion. However, they have complementary strengths and weaknesses and together should reasonably represent the situation. While in the key informant study all information was provided by a proxy, in the direct interview survey the respondents provided information about themselves and their own deceased son or daughter. Thus the direct interview survey provides more detailed and surely more accurate information for individual cases. However, as discussed below, the key informant study is probably more broadly representative of AIDS parents generally.

In the key informant study, local informants provided information for adults in the local area who were currently symptomatic or who had died of AIDS, regardless of whether the parents lived locally or elsewhere or were deceased. In the direct interview survey, inter-mediaries identified local parents who had lost an adult child to AIDS. They could generally identify parents whose child died locally, since such deaths are typically known, especially to health personnel, but they had difficulty identifying parents whose child died elsewhere. Since such parents are less likely to provide care giving and probably less vulnerable to some of the economic and social impacts under investigation, their under-representation biases the overall sample. However, the large subset of parents within the sample who provided care to their ill adult child should not be particularly biased. The key informant study may also be broader-based because, unlike the direct interview survey, inclusion of a case did not depend on the willingness of a parent to be interviewed. Despite these differences, the age distributions of AIDS parents in both sources are very similar, with approximately half aged 60 or older and most of the rest aged at least 50.

Living and care-giving arrangements for persons with AIDS often change during the course of the illness. Some who live elsewhere at the onset of symptoms may return to their place of origin as the illness advances and they can no longer earn a living or they need care assistance. Thus the extent of parental care giving and other forms of support provided during illness are fully evident only for cases in which the adult child had already died. Moreover, the full extent of some economic, social, emotional and physical impacts of this care giving are manifest only after the death of the child. We thus limit our analysis mainly to parents whose children had already died, although we still cannot capture truly long-range impacts given that the deaths were relatively recent.

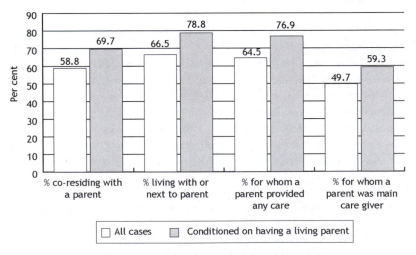

Figure 12.1 Living and care-giving arrangements at terminal stage of illness for adults who died of AIDS in Thailand

Source: Key informant study.

Care-giving and living arrangements

Overview. Older Thais are extensively involved with their AIDS-infected adult children through both living and care-giving arrangements. Figure 12.1 presents results from the key informant study that, as explained, is representative of a broad range of AIDS parents. Of adults who died of AIDS, 59 per cent co-resided with a parent at the terminal stage of illness and fully two thirds either co-resided with or lived next to a parent. Moreover, parents assisted in personal care giving for almost two thirds of adults who died of AIDS and were main care givers for half. Among adults who had at least one living parent, almost 70 per cent co-resided and almost 60 per cent had a parent as a main care giver.[4]

Gender differences. Results in Table 12.2 illustrate the gender dimension to personal care giving. In general, mothers are more likely than fathers to provide personal care and are particularly more likely to be a main care giver. This reflects in part the greater likelihood that an adult person with AIDS has a surviving mother than a surviving father. Nevertheless, as the direct interview survey results show, even for cases in which both parents were alive, the mother was 2.8 times more likely than the father to be a main care giver. Instrumental help outside the household (such as help with transportation, shopping, or arranging for welfare benefits) shows far less pronounced gender differentials. When both parents are alive, fathers and mothers are about equally likely to provide some instrumental help, although mothers are still more likely than fathers to be the main instrumental help provider.

Routes to parental care-giving. In understanding the high prevalence of parental terminal-stage AIDS care-giving in Thailand, it is useful to recognise that about half of *all* adult children of older-aged parents live with or nearby their parents, which facilitates parental involvement when a son or daughter falls ill. In addition, return migration of seriously ill adult children, especially in cases of a fatal and incurable disease such as AIDS, is common in the Thai context (Williams *et al.* 1996). Thai hospitals shy away from long-term care of AIDS cases, and hospices for persons with AIDS have very limited capacities. Unless adult children who leave their home communities have a spouse who can provide care and financial support, they often have little choice but to return to their parents. Even in the case of married children, a need for assistance in care giving or material support may prompt the couple to move in with or near to parents. Moreover, some have strong emotional reasons for wanting to die at home.

258   OLDER PEOPLE AND THE CARE ECONOMY

Table 12.2 Parental care givers and instrumental helpers, by gender, Thailand

	Per cent distribution (cases in which at least one parent provided the type of assistance specified)			Ratio of mothers to fathers[a]
	Mother only	Father only	Both parents	
All cases of assistance (including widows and widowers)				
Key informant study				
Any personal care	48.5	8.6	42.9	1.8
Main personal care giver	70.0	9.8	20. 2	3.0
Direct interview survey				
Any personal care	37.6	8.1	54.3	1.5
Main personal care giver	72.6	15.3	12.1	3.1
Any instrumental help	39.1	24.6	36.3	1.2
Main instrumental helper	58.9	34.1	7.0	1.6
Cases of assistance in which both parents were alive				
Direct interview survey				
Any personal care	22.3	4.7	73.0	1.2
Main personal care giver	70.0	15.0	15.0	2.8
Any instrumental help	25.5	27.4	47.1	1.0
Main instrumental helper	51.6	40.4	8.1	1.2

Note: [a] Mother only + both parents/Father only + both parents.

Table 12.3 Parental care-giving duration, by return migration status of adult child who died of AIDS, Thailand

		Return migration status	
Care-giving duration	All cases (%)	In parental locality before onset of symptoms (%)	Returned to parental locality following onset of symptoms (%)
Less than 1 month	33.3	32.4	35.4
1–2 months	35.0	34.0	37.2
3–5 months	17.2	16.6	18.6
6–11 months	7.3	9.5	2.7
1 year or longer	7.1	7.5	6.2
Mean	2.9	3.1	2.5
Median	1.0	2.0	1.0
Number of cases	354	241	113

Source: Direct interview survey.

Both the key informant study and the direct interview survey indicate that a substantial share (between a third and two fifths) of adult children with AIDS who were cared for by parents at the terminal stage had returned home from elsewhere (Knodel and VanLandingham forthcoming). That they return at a late stage of illness is evidenced by findings of the direct interview survey indicating that almost a fifth of the adult children died within a month and almost half died within three months of returning home (results not shown).

Care-giving duration. As Table 12.3 shows, the duration of care giving is somewhat shorter for adult children who returned from elsewhere than for those who lived in the parental locality at the onset of symptoms. Under both circumstances care giving usually lasted for only a few months and, in about a third of cases, lasted less than a month. Even among those who lived near their parents from the start of their illness, less than a fifth received care for 6 months or more. The moderate duration of parental care giving reflects short survival times after the onset of AIDS in Thailand combined with attempts by many adult children to care for themselves for as long possible. Despite the short duration, however, care giving occurs during the most disabling stage of the illness and is thus likely to be intensive and emotionally and physically draining for both parent and child.

Care-giving tasks. AIDS care giving by parents involves a wide variety of tasks ranging from those that likely would be done even for a healthy co-resident child to others associated with extreme debilitation. Table 12.4 provides findings from the direct interview survey about specific tasks that were performed by at least one parent. If both parents were involved in any care giving, the question referred to their combined efforts without distinguishing who did which task. Thus gender differences in parental assistance can be distinguished only when just one parent provided care (if, for example, the other parent was deceased).

Watching over the ill adult child and preparing food were the two most common tasks of AIDS parents. In a majority of cases, parents helped with very basic needs such as feeding, using the toilet, bathing, and dressing. Parents were also commonly involved in the interactions between their ill adult children and the health system, including transporting them to health facilities, helping administer medicines, and consulting with health care personnel.

The frequency with which most tasks were mentioned differs clearly according to which parent provided assistance. For most tasks, parental help was more frequent when both parents rather than just one provided assistance. For many tasks, however, parental assistance was

Table 12.4 Percentage of parents performing specific tasks of care giving and instrumental help among parents who gave either type of assistance to their adult child with AIDS in Thailand

	Total	Which parent provided any assistance		
		Mother only	Father only	Both parents
Type of activity				
Watching over	91.3	91.1	83.9	92.4
Preparing food	85.5	86.3	58.1	89.1
Shopping for food	78.3	80.5	58.1	80.0
Providing transportation, e.g. to clinic or hospital	74.7	67.2	58.1	81.5
Lifting and moving	72.4	68.5	54.8	77.3
Preparing and giving medicine	72.1	72.6	61.3	73.5
Feeding	67.8	66.1	51.6	71.1
Helping with toilet; changing soiled linen	66.9	63.7	41.9	72.5
Cleaning, laundry, doing dishes	66.8	71.0	32.3	69.5
Consulting with health care providers	65.1	65.9	38.7	68.6
Bathing	62.3	61.3	35.5	66.8
Dressing	60.7	62.9	38.7	62.6
Helping apply for welfare benefits	22.9	20.3	12.9	25.8
Arranging legal and financial affairs	16.9	14.8	22.6	17.3
Cleaning wounds	16.5	14.8	16.1	17.6
No. of cases	366	124	31	211

Note: Excludes cases in which a parent provided neither personal care nor instrumental help.
Source: Direct interview survey.

only modestly less frequent when just the mother, rather than both parents, provided help, but was substantially less frequent when just the father provided help.

Although not asked about in direct survey interviews, providing emotional support was frequently mentioned in open-ended interviews conducted as part of our research (Saengtienchai and Knodel 2001). These interviews made it clear that trying to relieve despair and boost the morale of a person facing a fatal and severely debilitating disease is particularly challenging and stressful. The task is all the more difficult when the person being cared for is one's own adult child.

Health impacts on parents

The relatively advanced age of many AIDS parents makes them particularly vulnerable to physical strains associated with care giving. As direct interview survey results in Table 12.5 show, substantial proportions of parental care givers experienced health problems. Almost three quarters reported experiencing nervousness or anxiety and over two thirds reported insomnia, suggesting that care giving is accompanied by considerable emotional stress. Over half also reported fatigue, and sizeable minorities experienced strained muscles, headaches, and stomach aches. For both mothers and fathers, being a main personal care giver increased the chance of experiencing each health problem, usually to a substantial extent. Gender differences in health problems among main personal care givers are modest. However, since mothers are much more likely than fathers to take on a care-giving role, and particularly to be a main personal care giver, they are also more likely to experience the health problems associated with care giving.

Table 12.5 Health problems experienced during care giving by parents who gave care to an adult child with AIDS in Thailand

	All parents who assisted with personal or instrumental care			Parents who assisted but were not main personal care giver*		Parents who were main personal care giver	
	Total	M	F	M	F	M	F
Health problem							
Strained muscles	41.4	49.1	30.7	45.6	25.3	50.4	41.9
Headaches/ stomach aches	31.0	34.6	25.9	29.2	20.8	36.7	36.5
Fatigue	55.5	60.6	48.2	50.0	39.0	64.8	67.6
Insomnia	68.7	74.9	59.9	70.8	52.9	76.5	74.3
Nervousness/anxiety	73.4	80.3	63.9	75.3	60.1	82.2	71.6

Notes: * Includes parents who were main instrumental helpers but not a main personal care giver.
M = mother F = father
Source: Direct interview survey

Results in Table 12.6 show that compared to control parents, AIDS parents were less likely to report that their current health was much better or somewhat better than three years ago, and more likely to report that their health was worse or much worse. This differential

Table 12.6 Percentage distribution of self-reported change in health over the previous three years in Thailand: a comparison between parents who lost a child to AIDS and parents who did not

Self-reported change in health over last 3 years	Both sexes		Fathers		Mothers	
	AIDS parents	Control parents	AIDS parents	Control parents	AIDS parents	Control parents
Much better	2.2	3.7	1.8	4.0	2.5	3.5
Somewhat better	8.2	10.0	7.0	6.9	9.1	12.5
About the same	31.0	34.2	37.5	39.3	25.9	30.1
Somewhat worse	50.2	46.0	46.0	43.6	53.4	47.8
Much worse	8.5	6.1	7.7	6.2	9.1	6.1
Total per cent	100	100	100	100	100	100

Source: Direct interview survey.

holds for both mothers and fathers. Apparently losing a child had a lasting, if modest, detrimental impact on parental health.

Psychological and emotional strain commonly accompany parental care giving, with the terminal stage being particularly stressful as parents witness their ill child suffer and realise that death is inevitable. The loss of an adult son or daughter to AIDS can result in lasting grief and sorrow (Saengtienchai and Knodel 2001). Responses to questions about happiness in the direct interview survey appear to reflect this. Compared to the control group, AIDS parents were more likely both to say they were currently unhappy and to report a decline in happiness over the previous three years (results not shown).

Fostering grandchildren

Caring for grandchildren who become orphaned because of AIDS can have substantial long-term implications for the grandparents. As Table 12.7 shows, however, less than half of all parents whose adult children died of AIDS had grandchildren who were orphaned as a result.[5] This proportion is relatively low primarily because, according to both the key informant study and the direct interview survey, about 30 per cent of the adult children who died of AIDS had never married and a substantial minority of those who married were childless. Moreover, according to the direct interview survey, 71 per cent of the deceased adult children who were themselves parents had only one child, reflecting the recent low fertility in Thailand. Moreover, orphaned children typically have both maternal and paternal grandparents, only

Table 12.7 Percentage of AIDS parents in Thailand involved in the care and living arrangements of AIDS orphans

	Key informant study	Direct interview survey
% of AIDS parents whose deceased son or daughter had a surviving child	44.4[a]	43.8
% of AIDS parents who ever cared for an AIDS orphan		
Among all AIDS parents	18.3[b]	31.3
Among AIDS parents whose deceased son or daughter had a child	34.4[b]	68.4
% of AIDS parents who ever lived with an AIDS orphan		
Among all AIDS parents	n.a.	25.7
Among AIDS parents whose deceased son or daughter had a child	n.a.	58.8
% of AIDS parents who currently live with an AIDS orphan		
Among all AIDS parents	n.a.	20.8
Among AIDS parents whose deceased son or daughter had a child	n.a.	47.5

Note: The unit of analysis for this table is an AIDS parent. In cases where both parents are surviving each counts as a case.
n.a. Not applicable
[a] Based on all cases for whom it was known that there was a surviving parent.
[b] Based on parents of the subset of persons who died of AIDS for which the key informant provided supplemental information.

one set of which will adopt them. Thus when *all* AIDS parents are considered, only a minority report ever caring for an AIDS orphan.

If results are conditioned on having at least one surviving AIDS-orphaned grandchild, however, the proportion is much higher, with a third of the parents in the key informant study and two thirds in the direct interview survey reporting the provision of some form of care for these grandchildren. The higher levels of grandparental fostering indicated by the direct interview survey are likely to be biased upwards because, as noted above, the selection of cases is almost certainly skewed towards AIDS parents who lived with or near their deceased son or daughter, or provided care for them. Open-ended interviews with AIDS parents suggest that such persons are particularly prone to inheriting responsibility for orphaned grandchildren (Saengtienchai and Knodel 2001). The key informant study, however, may underestimate grandparental involvement in caring for AIDS orphans, because the informants may have neglected to mention (or been unaware of) situations in which grandparents provided care that was short of primary responsibility. In contrast, direct interview survey respondents knew about such care, even if they did not take primary responsibility for their grandchildren.

Results from the direct interview survey indicate that, among all AIDS parents, only a fourth ever lived with an AIDS orphan and only a fifth currently were doing so. However, when results are conditioned on having an orphaned grandchild, involvement more than doubles in both instances. Although these findings suggest that only about half of the grandparents of AIDS orphans have been involved in fostering them, several caveats are called for. First, neither of our data sources takes into account the likelihood that some AIDS parents who are not currently fostering their grandchildren will do so in the future. According to the key informant study, approximately half of the children of persons who died of AIDS were being cared for by a surviving spouse. Some significant proportion of these spouses are themselves infected by HIV and likely to die before the dependent child grows up (Knodel, Saengtienchai et al. 2001). In such cases, grandparents are likely to take over responsibility for the orphans. Second, the results in Table 12.7 refer to the loss of one adult child per parent, which underestimates the likelihood of fostering grandchildren in another way. Some parents have lost or will lose more than one adult child to AIDS and thus are at additional risk of having orphaned grandchildren. Third, the impact on those who foster grandchildren orphaned to AIDS is likely to be substantial and lasting. These older Thais are at a point in life when they may expect to receive some material and instrumental support from their adult children. Instead, they may be losing that possibility while incurring the added responsibility of raising another young child.

Economic impacts

The illness and death of an adult child from AIDS can have significant economic repercussions for older-age parents, the most immediate of which are likely to stem from expenses associated with treatment and care giving. If parents sell property or possessions or go into debt to cover expenses, or if the deceased child had been contributing to the parents' household income, the effect may be a sustained reduction in economic wellbeing.

Table 12.8 summarises several key measures of economic impact based on the direct interview survey. Because the survey is skewed towards parents who were involved in care giving and who lived with or near the deceased child during the terminal stage of AIDS, the proportion that acted as main care givers is quite high (over 70 per cent compared to 50 per cent from the key informant study). Thus the results are likely to overstate the economic impact on AIDS parents generally, although the results for those who were main care givers should be representative of this large segment of AIDS parents.

Table 12.8 Potential influences on economic impact on AIDS parents in Thailand, by care-giving and economic status

% of cases of adult children who died of AIDS in which:	All cases	Was a parent a main care giver?		Economic status		
		No	Yes	Better-off	Average	Poorer
A parent was a main care giver	71.3	0.0	100.0	69.3	70.2	72.7
A parent was a main contributor to expenses during adult child's illness	61.9	38.9	71.2	70.7	67.2	54.5
A parent had to curtail economic activities	47.0	23.9	56.2	41.3	46.6	49.2
Parents helped pay for funeral:						
Any net cost	74.3	63.6	78.5	76.0	83.1	67.2
Substantial net cost (B5,000+)	62.0	49.1	67.0	70.7	71.5	51.4
Parents went into debt to pay expenses	38.6	26.5	43.4	30.7	37.4	42.8
Parents sold property or possessions to pay expenses	20.1	15.0	22.1	16.0	20.6	21.4
The deceased adult child contributed to parental household income during year prior to becoming seriously ill:						
Any contribution	71.3	66.4	73.3	64.0	65.6	78.6
Main contributor	32.2	28.3	33.8	17.3	26.0	42.8
Parents provided support to dependants of deceased adult child	31.6	29.2	32.6	36.5	30.5	30.6

Source: Direct interview survey.

Parents were main contributors to treatment expenses for their ill adult child in slightly over 60 per cent of the cases (compared to 52 per cent from the key informant study (Knodel, Saengtienchai, *et al.* 2001).[6] Being a main care giver is associated with both a far greater likelihood of being a main contributor to expenses during illness and a better economic status.

Among all respondents to the direct interview survey, about half reported having to curtail their economic activities, but this necessity was over twice as likely among parents who were main care givers than among parents who were not and, in general, was more likely among parents with lower economic status. The key informant study indicates that about a fifth of all AIDS parents, and 29 per cent of parents who were main care givers, had to reduce their economic activities during their adult child's illness (results not shown).

Funerals are major social events in Thailand and can be expensive. Thais commonly join local funeral societies as a form or insurance (Bryant and Prohmmo 2002), and those attending funerals customarily contribute toward expenses. Nevertheless, as Table 12.8 shows, AIDS parents incurred net funeral costs in almost three quarters of the cases and in over 60 per cent had substantial net costs. Poorer parents were somewhat less likely than better-off parents to have a net cost, particularly a substantial one, which probably reflects their inability to afford an expensive funeral. Parents had to borrow money in almost 40 per cent of cases and sell property or possessions in about a fifth of all cases to pay for expenses associated with the illness and death of the deceased adult child. Both occurred more frequently when a parent was a main care giver. In addition, poorer parents were more likely than better-off ones to borrow or to sell something for this purpose.

In over 70 per cent of cases, the deceased child provided some material assistance to the parents during the year prior to becoming ill, and in almost a third was the main income provider. It is particularly noteworthy that deceased children of poorer parents were more than twice as likely to have been the main income earner than those of better-off parents, probably reflecting differences in their parents' dependence on them for support.

As discussed, supporting orphaned grandchildren can be a significant expense that lasts for years. In almost a third of the cases from the direct interview survey, the parents reported providing support to the dependants of their deceased adult child – a result that varies little by care-giving or economic status.

Given that most AIDS parents had their children when fertility levels were high, in only 2 per cent of the cases did the death of their adult child leave the parents childless. Thus most of these AIDS parents have

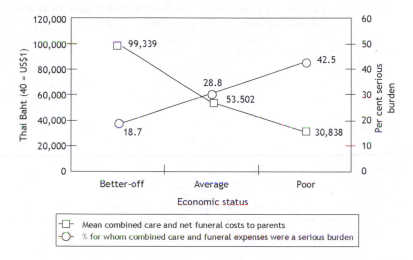

Figure 12.2 Mean combined care and net funeral costs to AIDS parents, and percentage for whom costs were a serious burden

Source: AIDS parents survey.

other adult children who could compensate for lost support from the deceased child, although this is less likely when the deceased child was the main earner for the parents. Thus when asked if the amount of support received from children had changed over the past three years, considerably more AIDS parents than those in the control group said that support had declined (42 versus 26 per cent, results not shown).

Only a third of the overall sample of AIDS parents in the direct interview survey said the expenses they incurred in connection with care giving and the funeral were a serious burden to them (results not shown). One reason this was not higher is that in 60 per cent of the cases the deceased adult child was covered by basic health insurance, mainly through some government plan. Although the insurance did not cover expensive antiretroviral treatments, at the time of the survey such drugs were not widely available or commonly known about (Im-em *et al.* 2001). In about half of the cases in which the adult child had insurance, or about a third of all cases, the parent said that the insurance was a major factor in covering the medical expenses.

Parents can moderate the economic impact of losing an adult child to AIDS by adjusting their spending to their financial circumstances. Indeed, parents of little means have few resources they can mobilise once they exhaust their own funds. Results in Table 12.8 indicate that poorer AIDS parents were less likely pay for expenses associated with

Table 12.9 Community reaction in Thailand to AIDS parents during
the illness and after the death of their adult child,
by care-giving status (%)

	During the illness			After the death		
	All cases	Was a parent a main care giver?		All cases	Was a parent a main care giver?	
Type of reaction		Yes	No		Yes	No
Only positive	67.6	67.4	68.2	74.7	73.9	76.6
Some negative but mostly positive	14.2	14.9	12.7	11.5	13.2	7.2
Mostly/only negative	7.3	8.3	4.5	4.2	5.1	1.8
Neutral/other	10.9	9.4	14.5	9.7	7.7	14.4
Total per cent	100	100	100	100	100	100

Source: Direct interview survey.

their child's illness and death. Yet poorer parents appear to be particularly vulnerable to adverse economic consequences from the loss of
an adult child to AIDS. For example, compared to other AIDS parents,
those of poorer economic status were more likely to curtail economic
activities, to go into debt, to sell property or possessions, and to lose a
child who was contributing to the household income, and may well
have been a main income earner.

Figure 12.2 clearly illustrates that spending and adverse impact are
related to economic status in opposite directions: the lower their
economic status, the less AIDS parents spent on care and funeral
expenses, but the more they reported being seriously burdened by the
costs. Thus, even if expenses were not large in absolute amounts for
poor parents, they were more likely to be severely taxing relative to
their resources.

Social impact

AIDS is a stigmatised disease throughout much of the world, although
the nature, degree and consequences of stigma are likely to vary across
settings and over time (Leary and Schreindorfer 1998). Stigma may
extend to those closely associated with the infected person, especially to
those providing personal care (Brabant 1994), and may prevent the
infected person and their family care givers from asking for assistance or
seeking health or social services (Ory et al. 1998). Our research suggests,
however, that by the late 1990s most community reaction experienced
by AIDS parents in Thailand was relatively sympathetic, although
negative experiences continue to affect some.

According to respondents in the key informant study, community reaction had improved over the course of the epidemic in almost every site and current reaction was not generally negative. For 71 per cent of the sites, key informants reported that members of the community generally did not act unusually toward families with a member infected with AIDS, and for only 12 per cent of the sites did they report a predominant reaction of avoidance and/or criticism. Case-specific information for the subset of families the informant knew best indicates that only 28 per cent experienced negative community reaction during the time of illness and that less than 10 per cent experienced negative community reaction following the death of the person with AIDS (results not shown).

Quite possibly key informants would not know about the more intimate social relations and personal experiences of the families of AIDS-afflicted persons. Direct interview survey results, however, present a very similar picture of community reaction. As Table 12.9 shows, fully two thirds of respondents reported that they experienced only positive reactions such as expressions of sympathy or offers of help, during the time their adult child was ill and three quarters said that reactions following the child's death were all positive. Whether or not a parent served as a main care giver makes little difference. Most who reported experiences with negative reaction indicated that their experience was mixed and only a small minority indicated their reaction was solely or mainly negative.

Over 90 per cent of respondents said that other community members visited during the adult child's illness; almost two thirds said some brought food; more than a third reported that friends and neighbours helped in looking after their ill adult child or in providing transportation; only a quarter reported that others gossiped about them; only a fifth said some in the community avoided visiting during the illness; and only one in seven said that some avoided talking with them (results not shown). Following their child's death, 95 per cent of these AIDS parents said community members helped with the funeral; just over 90 per cent said that funeral attendance was large or normal; and 90 per cent reported social visits following the death. At the same time, only one in six reported gossip about their situation following their child's death, and less than 10 per cent reported that some community members refused to attend the funeral, refused to eat at the funeral, or avoided social contact. Thus most parents of persons with AIDS find sympathy and support from community members and only a minority suffer negative social consequences as a result of losing a child to AIDS. The fact that most Thais have reasonably accurate knowledge of AIDS and know that HIV is not transmitted through casual contact may help explain the lack of widespread stigmatisation of AIDS parents (Im-em *et al*. 2001).

Conclusions

Several major findings from our analysis deserve emphasis. The most important is that substantial numbers of older-aged persons are adversely affected by the AIDS epidemic through the infection of their adult children. The number of AIDS parents far exceeds that of older persons who are HIV-infected themselves and, at least in Thailand, the number of AIDS orphans. While the plight of orphans has received extensive publicity, older-aged AIDS parents have been largely overlooked by national governments, international organisations, and private organisations concerned with the epidemic.

Although AIDS parents can suffer a wide variety of adverse consequences as a result of their adult child's illness and death, only their role in fostering orphaned grandchildren has been widely recognised, giving the misleading impression that this is both the most common and the most significant way that older people are affected. Even in high-fertility African countries hit by the epidemic, fostering AIDS orphans probably involves only a minority of older persons who lose an adult son or daughter to the disease. At the same time, increasing evidence indicates that, as in Thailand, parental care giving to infected sons and daughters is very widespread in Africa (Knodel and VanLandingham forthcoming). By providing home care, AIDS parents, particularly those who act as main care givers, take a tremendous burden off the health care system even while they incur a range of hardships for themselves. Our Thai research also reveals that parents act as critical links between their ill adult children and the health care system – accompanying them to health service outlets, staying with them in hospitals, consulting with their health care providers about appropriate treatment, and administering their prescribed medications. Yet there is little recognition in Thailand or elsewhere of this contribution, nor are there programmes to provide guidance to AIDS parents as they carry out this arduous and painful role.

In Thailand, the loss of an adult child to AIDS appears to have serious economic impacts for only a minority of parents. Those who spent substantial amounts on treatment tend to be better-off economically and hence better able to afford to do so without lasting financial hardship. Although the poor spend less on treatment, care giving, and funerals, they are the most adversely affected economically because these expenses have the potential to drain their modest resources. Interventions to help older-aged parents deal with the financial strains associated with losing an adult child to AIDS should take into account the considerable variation in vulnerability that exists, and target those who are particularly susceptible to economic hardship.

Some impacts of losing an adult child to AIDS, such as the loss of a potential provider of care or material support in old age, may not become apparent until long after the child's death. Our research cannot assess these potential long-term effects because at the time of the studies insufficient time had passed for them to manifest themselves. Most current AIDS parents in Thailand, however, have other surviving children on whom they can depend. Yet if the epidemic continues on a significant scale, subsequent generations of AIDS parents will have fewer children, and losing one adult child might seriously threaten their old-age security. Moreover, in countries where HIV prevalence is far higher than in Thailand and parents are at greater risk of losing multiple adult children, they have greater vulnerability to erosion of filial old-age support.

While negative community reactions are not absent in Thailand, sympathetic and supportive reactions are far more common. Anecdotal evidence of extreme negative reaction, especially during early stages of the epidemic, was not supported by findings from this study. This pre-dominance of positive community reaction suggests that programmes designed to build on community support to assist families affected by AIDS would meet little resistance. It also may lower barriers to home care by increasing the willingness of an ill adult child to return home and the willingness of parents to accept care giving responsibility.

A society's culture, politics and levels of socio-economic develop-ment, as well as the dimensions and characteristics of the epidemic, influence the manner and the scale of the AIDS impact on older persons. Thailand shares some important relevant characteristics with many countries experiencing serious HIV/AIDS epidemics. These include the predominance of heterosexual transmission and dependence on adult children for old-age support. Thailand is also distinguished from other developing countries – particularly Africa, where the severity of the epidemic is far worse – in features likely to moderate the impact of AIDS on older-aged parents. These features include a well-developed public health system, widespread government health insurance, open-ness to confronting the epidemic and educating the public about it, and low fertility among adults in the prime AIDS ages. Thailand is also strongly influenced by Theravada Buddhism, which contributes to a distinctive cultural setting within which the causes and consequences of the epidemic play out and is probably related to the relative tolerance of persons with AIDS within the community (Keyes 1987). Thus, while the findings of the present study are likely to have considerable relevance for other developing countries with AIDS epidemics, they also need to be understood in terms specific to the Thai context.

NOTES

1   We acknowledge financial support for this study from the National Institutes of Ageing as part of the project 'Socio-demographic Impact of AIDS on Older Persons' (grant AG15983). Guidance and assistance were provided throughout the research process by our co-investigators, Wassana Im-em, Jiraporn Kespichayawattana and Mark VanLandingham.

2   According to a 1994 nationally representative household survey, adults aged 20–44, the age range of most AIDS deaths, have on average 1.5 living parents. Even if we allow for the fact that some modest proportion of persons who die of AIDS are siblings (and thus have the same parents), the number of AIDS parents generated by an AIDS death in this age range would be modestly less than 1.5.

3   For details of the methodologies see Knodel, Saengtienchai et al. (2000) and Knodel et al. (2002).

4   See Knodel, Van Landingham et al. (2001) for details of how these estimates were adjusted for the 8 per cent of cases in which the key informant did not know if the parents were alive.

5   For the purpose of this discussion, we refer to any child who loses a parent as an AIDS orphan, regardless of whether or not the other parent is still alive.

6   In this section, comparisons with the key informant study refer to the subset of cases for which supplemental information was collected and in which at least one parent was alive at the time of death.

REFERENCES

Barnett, Tony and Alan Whiteside (2000) *Guidelines for Studies of the Social and Economic Impact of HIV/AIDS*, Best Practice Collection, UNAIDS, Geneva.

Bloom, David and Joyce Lyons (1993) *Economic Implications of AIDS in Asia*, UNDP Regional Project on HIV and Development, New Delhi.

Brabant, S. (1994) 'An overlooked AIDS affected population – the elderly parent as caregiver', *Journal of Gerontological Social Work*, 22: 131–45.

Bryant, John and Aree Prohmmo (2002) 'Equal contribution and unequal risk in a North-east Thai Village funeral society', *Journal of Development Studies*, 38 (3): 63–75.

Chitwarakorn, Anupong, Werasit Sittitrai, Tim Brown and Doris Mugrditchian (1998) 'Thailand', in Tim Brown (ed.), *Sexually Transmitted Diseases in Asia and the Pacific*, Venereology Publishing Inc., Armidale.

Godwin, Peter (1997) 'Socio-economic implications of the epidemic', in Peter Godwin (ed.), *Socio-economic Implications of the Epidemic*, UNDP Regional Project on HIV and Development, New Delhi.

Gragnolati, Michele (2001) 'The social impact of financial crises in East Asia – evidence from the Philippines, Indonesia and Thailand', discussion paper series, East Asia Environment and Social Development Group (EASES), World Bank.

Im-em, Wassana (1999) *Mortality Trends and Levels to Verify the AIDS Epidemic in Thailand: Analysis from Death Registration Statistics, 1984–1997*, Institute for Population and Social Research, Mahidol University, Bangkok.

Im-em, Wassana, Mark VanLandingham John Knodel and Chanpen Saengtienchai (2001) *Knowledge and Attitudes of Older People about HIV/AIDS in Thailand: a Comparison with Young Adults*, University of Michigan, Ann Arbor.

Keyes, C. (1987) *Thailand, Buddhist Kingdom as a Modern State*, Westview, Boulder.

Knodel, John, Mark VanLandingham, Chanpen Saengtienchai and Anthony Pramual-ratana (1996) 'Thai views of sexuality and sexual behavior', *Health Transition Review*, 6: 179–201.

Knodel, John, Napaporn Chayovan, Siriwan Graiurapong and Chutima Suraratdecha. (2000) 'Ageing in Thailand: an overview of formal and informal support', in D. Phillips (ed.), *Ageing in the Asia–Pacific Regions: Issues and Policies*, Routledge, London.

Knodel, John, Chanpen Saengtienchai, Wassana Im-em and Mark VanLandingham. (2000) *The Impact of Thailand's AIDS Epidemic on Older Persons: Quantitative Evidence from a Survey of Key Informants*, Institute for Population and Social Research, Mahidol University, Bangkok.

Knodel, John, Chanpen Saengtienchai, Wassana Im-em and Mark VanLandingham (2001) 'The impact of AIDS on parents and families in Thailand: a key informant approach', *Research on Aging*, 23: 633–70.

Knodel, John, Chanpen Saengtienchai and Werasit Sittitrai (1995) 'The living arrange-ments of elderly in Thailand: views of the populace', *Journal of Cross-Cultural Geron-tology*, 10: 79–111.

Knodel, John, Mark VanLandingham, Chanpen Saengtienchai and Wassana Im-Em (2001) 'Older people and AIDS: quantitative evidence of the impact in Thailand', *Social Science and Medicine*, 52: 1313–27.

Knodel, John, Mark VanLandingham, and Susan Watkins (forthcoming) 'AIDS and older persons: an international perspective', *Journal of Acquired Immunodeficiency*.

Knodel, John, Wassana Im-em, Chanpen Saengtienchai, Mark VanLandingham and Jiraporn Kespichayawattana (2002) *The Impact of an Adult Child's Death Due to AIDS on Older-Aged Parents: Results From a Direct Interview Survey*, Institute for Population and Social Research, Mahidol University, Bangkok.

Knodel, J. and M. VanLandingham (forthcoming) 'Return migration in the context of parental assistance in the AIDS epidemic: the Thai experience', *Social Science and Medicine*.

Leary, Mark and Lisa Schreindorfer (1998) 'The stigmatisation of AIDS: rubbing salt in the wound', in V. Derlega and A. Barbee (eds.), *HIV and Social Interaction*, Sage, Thousand Oaks.

Nelson, K. E. (1998) 'The demographic impact of the HIV epidemic in Thailand', *AIDS*, 12: 813–4.

Ory, M. G., D. L. Zablotsky and S. Crystal (1998) 'HIV/AIDS and aging: identifying a prevention research and care agenda', *Research on Aging*, 20: 637–52.

Phoolcharoen, W., K. Ungchusak, W. Sittitrai and T. Brown (1998) 'Thailand: Lessons from a strong national response to HIV/AIDS', *AIDS*, 12 (supplement B): 123–135.

Rhucharoenpornpanich, Orratai and Aphichat Chamratrithirong (2001) 'Demographic Impact of AIDS on the Thai population', *Asia–Pacific Population Journal*, 16 71–88.

Saengtienchai, Chanpen and John Knodel (2001) *Parents providing care to adult sons and daughters with HIV/AIDS in Thailand*, UNAIDS, Geneva.

Sanders, C. M. (1980) 'A comparison of adult bereavement in the death of a spouse, child, and parent', *Omega-Journal of Death and Dying*, 10: 303–22.

TWG (Thai Working Group on HIV/AIDS Projection) (2001) *Projections for HIV/AIDS in Thailand: 2000–2020*, Thai Ministry of Public Health, Bangkok.

UNAIDS (1998) *Connecting Lower HIV Infection Rates with Changes in Sexual Behaviour in Thailand: Data Collection and Comparison*, UNAIDS Best Practice Collection, Geneva.

UNAIDS (1999) *Children Orphaned by AIDS: Front-line Responses from Eastern and Southern Africa*, UNAIDS, Geneva.

UNAIDS (2000) *Report on the Global HIV/AIDS Epidemic*, UNAIDS, Geneva.

UNAIDS (2002) *Report on the Global HIV/AIDS Epidemic*, UNAIDS, Geneva.

UNAIDS and WHO (2000) *Thailand, Epidemiological Fact Sheet on HIV/AIDS and*

Sexually Transmitted Infections: 2000 Update, UNAIDS/WHO, Geneva.

UNICEF (United Nations Children's Fund) (2000) *The State of the World's Children*, United Nations, New York.

UNDP (United Nations Development Programme) (1999) *Human Development Report of Thailand 1999*, UNDP, Bangkok.

van Griensven, F., S. Surasiengsunk and Panza A. (1998) *The Use of Mortality Statistics as a Proxy Indicator for the Impact of the AIDS Epidemic on the Thai Population*, Institute of Population Studies, Chulalongkorn University, Bangkok.

Wachter, Kenneth, John Knodel and Mark VanLandingham (2002) 'AIDS and the Elderly of Thailand: Projecting Familial Impacts', *Demography*, 39: 25–41.

Wachter, Kenneth, John Knodel and Mark VanLandingham (forthcoming) 'Parental Bereavement: Heterogeneous Impacts of AIDS in Thailand', *Journal of Econometrics*.

Williams, A., E. Bennet, V. Himmavanh and F. Salazar (1996) '"They just go home and die": Health care and terminal illness in rural northeast Thailand', *Asian Studies Review*, 20: 98–108.

World Bank (1994) *Averting the Old Age Crisis: Policies to Protect the Old and Promote Growth*, Oxford University Press, Oxford.

World Bank (1997), *Confronting AIDS: Public Priorities in a Global Epidemic*, Oxford University Press, New York.

CHAPTER 13

Care, Dependency and Social Justice:
A Challenge to Conventional Ideas
of the Social Contract

MARTHA C. NUSSBAUM

It will be seen how in place of the *wealth* and *poverty* of political economy come the *rich human being* and *rich human need*. The rich human being is ... the human being *in need of* a totality of human life activities.

Marx, *Economic and Philosophical Manuscripts of 1844*

An acute problem of justice

All societies contain people in need of care. Indeed, all people in all societies are in need of care. Even so-called 'normal' and 'able-bodied' adults rely constantly on care provided by others in the fabric of their lives: people who cook meals and tend the home, providers of regular health care, people who prepare the external environment so that it is safe and conducive to ordinary functioning. At times during their lives the 'normal' have more acute needs for care: during an illness, for example, or after an accident. But of course 'normal' adulthood is itself a temporary phase of a human life. It is preceded by a very long period of childhood, much longer than in most animal species, during which basic needs for food, comfort, shelter, cognitive development and social interaction must be met by the constant involvement of adult givers of care. This period can last for over twenty years in many cases, though of course the nature of the needs in question shifts over time.

The phase of 'self-sufficient' adulthood is usually followed, in turn, by a period of increasing dependency, as ageing gives rise to new physical and mental needs. The increasing life expectancy in many nations of the world is giving rise to a new, or newly numerous, set of dependencies, as children who have just raised their own children, or are still doing so, must care for their own parents in their physical and/or mental decline.

There are many citizens in every society, moreover, who are asymmetrically dependent upon others throughout their lives. In some cases these dependencies result from unusual physical disabilities. All human beings are disabled beings, with many imperfections in judgement, understanding, perception and bodily functioning. But society is typically arranged to cater for the most typical disabilities. Thus we do not find staircases so high that only the giants of Brobdingnag can climb them, nor do our symphony orchestras play at frequencies inaudible to the human ear and audible only to canine ears. When a person is blind, or deaf, or has to go around in a wheelchair, societies are not so well adjusted to making such persons fully mobile, fully able to occupy public space on a basis of equality. What blind law professor Jacobus Ten Broek calls 'the right to be in the world' is unevenly extended to its citizens, and people who could perfectly well get around if the streets were maintained in a particular way, for example, are put by social contingency in a position of dependency – on a dog, other humans, a network of support.[1]

Other citizens have disabilities that make dependency on others a virtually inevitable fact of their daily lives. People with severe mental disabilities, for example, may never be able to live on their own, and some rely on care givers for their most basic bodily needs.

Who does all the work that care requires? In a vast majority of the cases, women.[2] Indeed, the most ubiquitous and long-lasting conception of the woman, in virtually all countries and traditions of the world, is as a giver of care: homemaker, mother, wife, tenderer to the needs of the elderly – in general a supporter of the needs and ends of others. Often this conception of the woman sees her as a *mere* means to the ends of others, rather than as a source of entitlements in her own right, a being who ought to be treated as an end in herself. Thus, women's care-giving function has often been understood to remove them from candidacy for full citizenship, and for many aspects of employment.[3] Even when women are legally entitled to work and participate in citizenship, their heavy responsibilities in the home often make it difficult for them to do so.

Nancy Folbre uses a vivid image for this situation:[4] it is as if society, in trying to get ahead, allows some people to run in the race without any handicap. Others have to run carrying other people (children, the sick, the elderly). Obviously enough, those in the second group will lag behind from the point of view of their personal goals and their contribution to society outside the home, even though the work they are doing is obviously essential to the survival and wellbeing of society.

The problem of care has at least three distinct aspects on the side of the care giver: the allocation of care-giving responsibilities within the household, the support (or lack of support) for care giving on the part of the public sector, and the structure of careers. Women are disabled by care-giving responsibilities, to the extent that they are, in part because men do not do anywhere near half of the housework, child care, and elder care, even in two-career households. Public sectors in different countries vary greatly in the extent to which they subsidise parental leave, public child care and elder care. And careers differ greatly as to whether they provide the flexibility that many caregiving adults need if they are to fulfil both work responsibilities and care-giving responsibilities. Young lawyers in the US have no chance of advancement to partner if they choose the flexible part-time 'mommy track.' Academics have a slightly better time, because a lot of their work can be performed in the home and when they choose.

The problem of care has, of course, another face: that of the recipient of care. Children, the elderly, the disabled, and the so-called normal adult who simply needs to have food and shelter, all these need care appropriate to their capacities and stage of life, including development of their faculties, social interaction and the conditions of self-respecting life. Meeting these needs for care in a way that is compatible with social and political functioning, cognitive development, emotional health and self-respect is a major part of the work that needs to be done in any society.

So: care must be supplied to those who need it, without exploiting the givers of care. At present, in all nations of the world, this difficult social problem has not been solved. Women do a vast majority of care-giving work, receiving either no pay or inadequate pay. Often this work is not even recognised as work. The need to provide care hinders women in many areas of their lives.

These problems need to be approached from many angles. We need better data about their extent, and more comprehensive accounts of how different nations and local governments are addressing them. We need more comprehensive studies of different career structures, in order to be able to imagine models that promise good solutions for caregiving adults.[5] But we also need to ask whether there are deeply entrenched ways of thinking in many societies that militate against the full and fair solution of these problems. The present chapter will pose that question, and offer an affirmative answer.

This chapter, then, will be a conceptual and theoretical essay, intended to complement the more empirical treatments of the problem of care by other chapters in this book. The chapter criticises dominant models of society as a social contract and recommends a new theoretical perspective based on the idea of fostering human capabilities. I shall argue that the general way of thinking about society, its citizens and its goals fostered by the social contract tradition and now widely disseminated around the world is one large part of our problem. It has created a blinkered way of thinking about need, dependency and dignity that make it hard to place care in a sufficiently prominent place on the agenda of society, and to give it the support it deserves. By contrast, I shall argue that a perspective based on ideas of human capability and functioning can more adequately deal with issues of social justice raised by the need to provide care for the elderly, the lifelong disabled and others in a state of extreme and asymmetrical dependency.

Abstract images of human interaction may seem far away from the daily stuff of political problem solving. And yet we all think of ourselves in ways influenced by abstract pictures of what a human being is, and these ways shift over time. The importance of such abstract concepts is well known in the history of feminist thinking about law and social justice. For example, it used to be thought that a woman who had an active sex life, especially outside marriage, could not be raped: thus defence attorneys would get their clients acquitted by offering evidence of the woman's prior sexual conduct. The underlying image governing this exceedingly strange way of thinking was that of the woman as either chaste or a whore, and of the whore, it must be added, as a being so low that her consent to intercourse could be taken as given in advance of the question. This image deeply influenced the lives of real women. Now we use different images of a woman's sexual autonomy: we think, or at least are coming to think, that active consent to the particular sex act in question is a necessary condition of its legality. This shift in our legal thinking is a sign that we no longer hold onto the underlying image of the woman as either chaste or whorelike: instead, we now see women as free agents who may say yes in one instance and no in another. The type of conceptual criticism carried out by the feminist movement and its methods of 'consciousness raising' have turned out to be profoundly practical.

This is just one example of the way in which pervasive images of the person shape social and political thought, and the reflective critique of such images can reshape thought. I shall argue that the social contract tradition has shaped widespread ways of thinking about care, in ways that have deformed our conceptualisation of the problem and its solution. I shall offer a critique of the image of the citizen proposed in that tradition and argue for a way of reshaping it that retains many of its best insights concerning the importance of dignity, agency, and reciprocity, but lacks its most troubling defects.

The social contract perspective

Western philosophy's dominant approach to formulating an account of basic social justice has been to imagine society's institutions as resulting from a 'social contract', in which parties come together to achieve the benefits of cooperation.[6] Typically the parties are imagined as roughly equal in ability, and the partnership is imagined as one that is profitable to them all: by cooperating they each get more than they could get by not cooperating. This very structure itself requires a situation of rough parity among the parties, for the arrangement will only prove profitable to all if no one is so placed as to dominate the others, as David Hume and John Rawls point out. For this reason, theorists in the social contract tradition omit situations of asymmetrical or lifelong dependency from their accounts of how society's basic institutions are designed. In this section I examine the problems this creates for John Rawls's account of justice, and the challenge posed to that theory by Eva Kittay and other feminist philosophers. I argue that the difficulties are deep and cannot be remedied by a mere modification of the contractarian perspective.

The general idea of the social contract tradition is that we can generate a morally satisfactory account of the principles underlying political cooperation if we imagine a hypothetical situation in which people come together to choose the principles in accordance with which they will henceforth live. This situation does not represent any real historical situation; instead, it is a model embodying some of our deepest moral convictions, and it is supposed to help us think about the moral core of political principles. Similarly, the contractarian thought experiment is not claiming that the people it represents are realistic models of actual people: they may be simplified in many ways, and in some cases the relevant attributes of persons may be represented as features of the model situation, rather than of the psychology of the hypothetical people.

It is important to keep these facts in mind. John Rawls's contracting parties in the famous 'original position' have frequently been criticised by feminists for lacking compassion and altruism, and the inference has been made that Rawls thinks these attributes of persons unimportant. This is a misreading of Rawls.[7] The imaginary people represent just one part of what Rawls thinks moral rationality involves: the aspect of prudential rationality. Altruism and moral impartiality are represented by the Veil of Ignorance, which denies them knowledge of their particular place in the resulting society. Rawls repeatedly states that the combination of prudential rationality with ignorance is meant to capture the real-life moral agent, who takes up the standpoint of impartiality in order to be just.[8] Thus, we cannot quickly infer from the absence of a particular feature of human life in the representation of the parties in a contract situation the further fact that this feature of human life is missing in the situation taken as a whole. We must look at the entire situation as it is modelled.

We should also note that contractarian theories adopt an implicit idea of the whole point of social cooperation. People will not cooperate unless there is some point to doing so, the idea goes. As David Hume puts it, there are certain circumstances, the 'circumstances of justice', in which choosing principles of justice has a point, and other circumstances where it would not have a point.[9] Rawls follows Hume here. The circumstances are, to put it very crudely, that people are so placed that there are both shared interests (such as an interest in cooperation, which makes life better for all) and also conflicts of interest that need to be resolved by principles of justice. These conditions, in turn, will only be met if people are in certain objective circumstances: occupying a definite territory that they must somehow share; vulnerable to attack; roughly similar in physical and mental powers, in the sense that no one of them can dominate all the others; and living under conditions of moderate scarcity. Rawls also draws attention to certain subjective circumstances: people must have roughly similar but at the same time complementary needs and interests, so that cooperation achieves something; they also have their own plans of life, and view their different conceptions of the good as deserving of recognition and respect. They also have various shortcomings of judgement and knowledge (Rawls 1971: 126–7). These features all play a role later on in determining the shape of the principles to which the parties will agree.

Let us now focus on just one feature of this account of the 'circumstances of justice', shared by not only Hume and Rawls, but the entire social contract tradition. This feature is not directly implied by the assumption of rough similarity and non-domination, but it is a particular and controversial way of interpreting and further expanding that assumption. This is the fiction of competent adulthood. Whatever differences there are among the different founders of that tradition, all accept the basic Lockean conception of a contract among parties who, in the state of nature, are 'free, equal and independent'.[10] Thus for Kant persons are characterised by both freedom and equality, and the social contract is defined as an agreement among persons so characterised. Contemporary contractarians explicitly adopt this hypothesis. For David Gauthier, people of unusual need are 'not party to the moral relationships grounded by a contractarian theory'.[11] Similarly, the citizens in Rawls's Well Ordered Society are 'fully cooperating members of society over a complete life'.[12]

Life, of course, is not like that. Real people begin their lives as helpless infants, and remain in a state of extreme, asymmetrical dependency, both physical and mental, for anywhere from ten to twenty years. At the other end of life, those who are lucky enough to live on into old age are likely to encounter another period of extreme dependency, either physical or mental or both, which may itself continue in some form for as much as twenty years. During the middle years of life, many of us encounter periods of extreme dependency, some of which involve our mental powers and some our bodily powers only, but all of which may put us in need of daily, even hourly, care by others. Finally, and centrally, there are many citizens who never have the physical and/or mental powers requisite for independence. These citizens are dependent in different ways. Some have high intellectual capabilities but are unable to give and receive love and friendship; some are capable of love, but unable to learn basic intellectual skills. Some have substantial emotional and intellectual capabilities, but in a form or at a level that requires special care. These lifelong states of asymmetrical dependency are in many respects isomorphic to the states of infants and the elderly.

In short, any real society is a care-giving and care-receiving society, and must therefore discover ways of coping with these facts of human neediness and dependency that are compatible with the self-respect of the recipients and do not exploit the care givers. This is a central issue for feminism since, in every part of the world, women do a large part of this work, usually without pay, and often without recognition that it is work. They are often thereby handicapped in other functions of life.

Kant's version of the social contract tradition, followed and extended by Rawls,[13] is in many ways the most appealing, because it is the most deeply grounded in moral intuitions about respect and reciprocity that seem crucial to any good account of political principles for contemporary society. And yet we must pause to observe that in this particular area a Kantian ethical starting point is likely to give bad guidance. For Kant, human dignity and our moral capacity, dignity's source, are radically separate from the natural world. Morality certainly has the task of providing for human neediness, but the idea that we are at bottom split beings, both rational persons and animal dwellers in the world of nature, never ceases to influence Kant's way of thinking about how these deliberations about our needs will go.

What's wrong with the split? Quite a lot. First, it ignores the fact that our dignity just is the dignity of a certain sort of animal. It is the animal sort of dignity, and that very sort of dignity could not be possessed by a being who was not mortal and vulnerable, just as the beauty of a cherry tree in bloom could not be possessed by a diamond. If it makes sense to think of God as having dignity (I'm not sure – magnificence and awe-inspiringness seem more appropriate attributes), it is emphatically not dignity of that type.[14] Second, the split wrongly denies that animality can itself have a dignity; thus it leads us to slight aspects of our own lives that have worth, and to distort our relation to the other animals.[15] Third, it makes us think of the core of ourselves as self-sufficient, not in need of

the gifts of fortune; in so thinking we greatly distort the nature of our
own morality and rationality, which are thoroughly material and animal
themselves; we learn to ignore the fact that disease, old age, and accident
can impede the moral and rational functions, just as much as the other
animal functions. Fourth, it makes us think of ourselves as a-temporal.
We forget that the usual human life cycle brings with it periods of
extreme dependency, in which our functioning is very similar to that
enjoyed by the mentally or physically handicapped throughout their
lives.

It is important to notice that the split goes wrong in both directions:
it suggests, as I have said, that our rationality is independent of our
vulnerable animality; and it also suggests that animality, and non-human
animals, lack intelligence, are just brutish and 'dumb'. Both implications
of the split should, of course, be called into question: in nature we find a
rich continuum of types of intelligence, and of practical capacities of
many types; we cannot understand ourselves well without situating
ourselves within that continuum.[16]

Political thought in the Kantian social-contract tradition (to stick
with the part of the tradition I find deepest and most appealing) suffers
from the conception of the person with which it begins. Rawls's contracting parties are fully aware of their need for material goods. Here
Rawls diverges from Kant, building need into the foundations of the
theory.[17] But he does so only to a degree: for the parties are imagined
throughout as competent contracting adults, roughly similar in need,
and capable of a level of social cooperation that makes them able to
make a contract with others. Such a hypothesis seems required by the
very idea of a contract for mutual advantage.

In so conceiving of persons, Rawls explicitly omits from the situation
of basic political choice the more extreme forms of need and dependency human beings may experience. His very concept of social cooperation is based on the idea of reciprocity between rough equals, and
has no explicit place for relations of extreme dependency. Thus, for
example, Rawls refuses to grant that we have any duties of justice to
animals, on the grounds that they are not capable of reciprocity (Rawls
1971: 17, 504–5); they are owed 'compassion and humanity,' but '[t]hey
are outside the scope of the theory of justice, and it does not seem
possible to extend the contract doctrine so as to include them in a
natural way' (Rawls 1971). This makes a large difference to his theory of
political distribution. For his account of the primary goods, introduced,
as it is, as an account of the needs of citizens who are characterised by the
two moral powers and by the capacity to be 'fully cooperating', has no
place for the need of many real people for the kind of care we give to
people who are not independent.[18]

Now of course Rawls is perfectly aware that his theory focuses on some cases and leaves others to one side. He insists that, although the need for care for people who are not independent is 'a pressing practical question,' it may reasonably be postponed to the legislative stage, after basic political institutions are designed:

> So let's add that all citizens are fully cooperating members of society over the course of a complete life. This means that everyone has sufficient intellectual powers to play a normal part in society, and no one suffers from unusual needs that are especially difficult to fulfill, for example, unusual and costly medical requirements. Of course, care for those with such requirements is a pressing practical question. But at this initial stage, the fundamental problem of social justice arises between those who are full and active and morally conscientious participants in society, and directly or indirectly associated together throughout a complete life. Therefore, it is sensible to lay aside certain difficult complications. If we can work out a theory that covers the fundamental case, we can try to extend it to other cases later (Rawls 1980: 546).

This reply seems inadequate. Care for children, the elderly, and the mentally and physically handicapped is a major part of the work that needs to be done in any society, and in most societies it is a source of great injustice. Any theory of justice needs to think about the problem from the beginning, in the design of the most basic level of institutions, and particularly in its theory of the primary goods.[19]

More generally, variations and asymmetries in physical need are simply not isolated or easily isolable cases: they are a pervasive fact of human life: pregnant or lactating women need more nutrients than non-pregnant persons, children need more protein than adults; and the very young and very old need more care than others in most areas of their lives. Even within the clearly recognised terrain of the 'fully cooperating', then, the theory of primary goods seems flawed if it does not take such variations into account in measuring who is and is not the least well off, rather than, as the theory recommends, determining that status by income and wealth alone.[20] Amartya Sen has used the example of a person in a wheelchair, who will certainly need more resources to be fully mobile than will a person whose limbs work well.[21] With the same amount of income and wealth, this person will actually be much worse off than someone whose limbs work well.[22] Rawls can't consistently exclude this person, who surely has the mental and moral powers. But even if he should exclude these physical disabilities, as some of his remarks suggest,[23] the problem of variation in need is pervasive. So even in order to take account of the physical needs of non–disabled citizens – which the theory seems bound, even on its own terms, to take account of [24] – Rawls will need a way of measuring wellbeing that does not rely on income and wealth alone, but looks at the abilities of citizens to engage in a wide range of human activities.

Thomas Scanlon confronts these problems facing a Kantian contract doctrine much more directly than does Rawls. I am unable here to discuss the subtleties of his view, which in any case is a moral and not a political contract doctrine, and which does not employ a hypothetical initial contract situation as does Rawls's theory. But, taking cognisance of the problem posed for such a theory by people with various handicaps, and by non-human animals, he concludes that we may recognise facts of extreme dependency in such a doctrine in one of two ways. Either we may persist in our pursuit of the contract doctrine, and say that the contracting parties are also trustees for those who are incapable of participating in that process; or we may say that the contract doctrine offers an account of only one part of morality: we will need a different account to cope with the facts of extreme dependency.[25] Applied to the Rawlsian project of selecting principles of justice that will form the basic structure of society,[26] this would mean that we either take the parties in the Original Position to be trustees for the interests of all dependent members of society, as they currently are trustees for future generations – or else we should grant that the Original Position is not a complete device for designing political justice, and that other approaches are also required.

The first solution seems unsatisfactory. To make the 'fully co-operating' into trustees in a hypothetical original situation slights the dignity of physically and mentally handicapped people, suggesting that they are worthy of respect in the design of basic political institutions only on account of some relationship in which they stand to so-called 'fully cooperating' people. The bargain, after all, is a bargain for mutual advantage, and it assumes a rough equality among its participants; the dependants enter the bargain not because they are equipped to participate in such a bargain, but only because a contracting party cares about their interests. Furthermore, the move also means making the 'fully cooperating' trustees for their own infancy and senility, and perhaps other stages of their own lives. Gauthier puts the problem most starkly, when he says that the elderly have paid for their care by earlier periods of productive activity, but the handicapped have not.[27] In other words, for the contractarian only productivity justifies, ultimately, a claim to support, and the elderly get support only because at one time they were not elderly. Animality and human neediness all on their own cannot justify a claim to support. Rawls's theory, though more subtle than Gauthier's, still suffers from something like this problem. To require of the parties that they split their thinking in this way, conceiving of themselves as made up of two parts, the rational and the animal, is to force into their thinking a Kantian splitting that may well prejudice their thinking about the dignity of animality in themselves. Are we not in effect saying that animality gets support only in virtue of its contingent link to 'fully cooperating' adulthood? And doesn't this slight the dignity and worth that needy human animals surely possess even when they are not fully cooperating? Surely, if it is not necessary to require such split thinking, we should avoid it.

Thus I prefer the second solution: the contract doctrine, while an excellent model for many aspects of our moral relations, does not provide a complete ethical theory. But this reply, which would be fine for Scanlon, because he is doing ethical theory, employs no hypothetical initial situation, and makes no claims to completeness, creates large problems for the contract doctrine in the area of political theory. Any approach to the design of basic political institutions must aim at a certain degree of completeness and finality, as Rawls's doctrine explicitly does.[28] We are designing the basic structure of society, those institutions that influence all citizens' life chances pervasively and from the start. So it is not open to us to say: we have done one part of that task, but of course other parts, equally basic, based on completely different principles, will come along later. If we leave for another day not only our relations to the non-human animals, but also the needs entailed by our own animality, that would leave huge areas of political justice up for grabs and would entail the recognition of much indeterminacy in the account of basic justice as so far worked out.

What, then, can be done to give the problem of care and dependency sufficient prominence in a theory of justice? The first thing we might try, one that has been suggested by Eva Kittay in her fine book, is to add the need for care during periods of extreme and asymmetrical dependency to the Rawlsian list of primary goods, thinking of care as among the basic needs of citizens (Kittay 1999: 102–3). In making this modification, citizens would be recognising that these periods of dependency are part of the facts of human life, against which they would wish to insure themselves. There is no barrier in contract doctrine as such to making such a modification. Notice, however, that in order to make it we would need to make a sharp split between two cases that I have suggested actually lie on a continuum: the case of the childhood and old age of the 'normal' 'independent' human adult, and the case of lifelong mentally or physically disabled human beings.[29] This sharp division of two closely related cases is most unfortunate. It is the basis for much social prejudice, which typically proceeds from a sharp division between the 'normal' and various people who are taken to be somehow 'spoiled', and encourages the stigmatisation of the latter.[30]

If we add care to the list of primary goods, we would be led to make another modification in the Rawlsian theory: for care is hardly a commodity, like income and wealth, to be measured by the sheer amount of it citizens have. Thus adding care to the list would cause us to notice that Rawls's list of primary goods is already quite heterogeneous in its structure. Some of its members are thing-like items such as income and wealth; but some are already more like human capabilities to function in various ways: the liberties, opportunities, and powers, and also the social basis of self-respect. Along with this suggestion, we might propose understanding the entire list of primary goods as a list not of things but of basic capabilities.[31] This change would not only enable us to deal better with people's needs for various types of love and care as elements of the list, but would also answer the point that Sen has repeatedly made all along about the unreliability of income and wealth as indices of well-being. The wellbeing of citizens will now be measured not by the sheer amount of income and wealth they have, but by the degree to which they have the various capabilities on the list. One may be well-off in terms of income and wealth, and yet unable to function well in the workplace, because of burdens of care giving at home.[32]

If we accepted these two changes, we would surely add a third, highly relevant to our thoughts about infancy and old age. We would add other capability-like items to the list of basic goods: for example the social basis of health, and the social basis of imagination and emotional wellbeing.[33]

Suppose, then, we do make these three changes in the list of primary goods: we add care in times of extreme dependency to the list of primary goods; we reconfigure the list as a list of capabilities; and we add other pertinent items to the list as well. Have we done enough to salvage the contract doctrine as a way of generating basic political principles? I believe that there is still room for doubt. Consider the role of primary goods in Rawls's theory. The account of primary goods is introduced in connection with the Kantian political conception of the person, as an account of what citizens characterised by the two moral powers need.[34] Thus, we have attributed basic importance to care only from the point of view of our own current independence. It is good to be cared for only because care subserves moral personality, understood in a Kantian way as conceptually quite distinct from need and animality. This seems like another more subtle way of making our animality subserve our humanity, where humanity is understood to exclude animality. The idea is that because we are dignified beings capable of political reciprocity, therefore we had better provide for times when we are not that, so we can get back to being that as quickly as possible. I think that this is a dubious enough way to think about illnesses in the prime of life; but it surely leads us in the direction of a contemptuous attitude toward infancy and childhood, and, a particular danger in our society, toward elderly disability. Next, it leads us strongly in the direction of not fully valuing those with lifelong mental disabilities: somehow or other, care for them is supposed to be valuable only for the sake of what it does for the 'fully cooperating.' They are, it would seem, being used as means for someone else's ends, and their full humanity is still being denied. Finally, as I have mentioned, the very positing of a sharp split between 'normals' and people with a 'spoiled identity' is central to the operations of much pernicious social prejudice, particular prejudice directed against the disabled.

So I believe that we need to delve deeper, redesigning the political conception of the person, bringing the rational and the animal into a more intimate relation with one another, and acknowledging that there are many types of dignity in the world, including the dignity of mentally disabled children and adults, the dignity of the senile demented elderly, and the dignity of babies at the breast. We want the picture of the parties who design political institutions to build these facts in from the start. The kind of reciprocity in which we humanly engage has its periods of symmetry, but also, of necessity, its periods of more or less extreme asymmetry – and this is part of our lives that we bring into our situation as parties who design just institutions. And this may well mean that the theory cannot be a contractarian theory at all.

Such a conclusion should be reached with caution. Rawls's theory, as I mentioned at the opening of this section, has often been wrongly criticised, because critics have not noticed that his model of the person in the Original Position is complex. His account of the person is not simply the account of the rationality of the parties, but that account *combined with* the account of the Veil of Ignorance, which is a complex way of modelling benevolence. Thus it is incorrect to say that he has not included concern for others in the conception of the person that forms the foundation of his theory – as he has noted, discussing Schopenhauer's similar critique of Kant.[35] What this mistake shows us is that the contract doctrine has many ways of modelling the person; so we should not rule out the possibility that some device may be found through which a doctrine basically contractarian in spirit could model need and animality, just as it has modelled benevolence.[36] There is, however, some reason to doubt that this can be done. For any such model would still involve a split of just the sort to which I have objected, one that makes our rationality trustee, in effect, for our animality. And that, as I've argued, is inadequate for the kind of dignity and centrality we want to give to the problems of asymmetrical need.

Thus, while not denying that some determined contractarian might possibly solve this problem, I think it best to proceed as if it has not been solved. When we add to our worries the fact that Rawls's contract doctrine uses a political concept of the person at a number of different points, most of them not in association with the complex model of the Original Position, we have even more reason to want the political concept of the person to be one that does justice to temporality and need.

Beyond the social contract

The social contract tradition has, I have argued, some grave problems. On the other hand, it also has some important virtues that we must not lose sight of in trying to reform it. In particular, the ideas of reciprocity and equality it contains are deeply attractive ideas for a modern society. The idea that political principles express mutual respect for human dignity, agency, and inviolability is another idea to which we should cling. Let us see, then, where the gravest problems in the tradition seem to lie, and let us see whether we can propose a reform of it that would not lose hold of these highly attractive insights.

In order to place the problems of care and dependency in the right political perspective, giving them adequate salience and recognising their importance for political justice, we need, then, to make three modifications in the dominant tradition. We need, first, a richer account of the 'primary goods' a just society distributes, goods that can be expected to be of value in any life plan that citizens choose to pursue.[37] This list should include a number of items that Rawls currently omits, including health care and education; but it must prominently include care in times of acute dependency. Because the Rawlsian list of primary goods (and my own list of capabilities) also includes the social basis of self-respect as a primary good, we will understand that the care citizens have a right to, as a basic entitlement, is care that is compatible with the self-respect of the recipient. Because the list I favour will also include the entitlement to leisure for play and the cultivation of one's faculties, political participation, and employment opportunities, we will under-stand that this care must be such as to protect the care givers against exploitation that cripples their access to these other primary goods.

The second modification that we need to make is to conceive of the whole project of distributing primary goods not in terms of resources simply, but in terms of fostering a wide range of (interlocking and mutually supportive) human capabilities. Both Sen and I argue that, particularly when we are addressing entrenched privilege and hierarchy, the perspective supplied by the capabilities approach is superior to those supplied by the more traditional focus on resources and on utility. We have not satisfied the demands of this approach unless and until we have brought all citizens up to a specified level of ability actually to choose to perform the functioning in question, and we easily see that citizens differently placed may need differing amounts of resources in order to arrive at the desired level of capability.

A shift to the capabilities perspective delivers several further dividends, which can only be briefly discussed here. First of all, such an approach dovetails nicely with the emphasis on empowerment and opportunity in many constitutional traditions of the world; it provides a nice way of thinking about what basic constitutional entitlements are all about.[38] Second, the focus on capabilities assists us greatly in thinking about the entitlements of non–human animals. Indeed, I would argue that the capabilities approach ultimately provides a basis for approaching this difficult question that is superior to the bases supplied by Utilitarianism, the social contract tradition, and even rights–based approaches.[39] Finally, and crucially, the capabilities approach is not restricted to the nation state, as the social contract approach traditionally has been. It supplies a helpful way of thinking about the need for redistribution of wealth from richer to poorer nations, something that the social contract doctrine has had great difficulty conceptualising.[40]

Finally, we need a new conception of the person for purposes of institutional design, one that does not sharply split off human dignity from human need and animality. Why should this be so very important, one might ask? What do economic and political arrangements have to do with something so abstract as a 'conception of the person'? Here, I believe, we must grant that many factors shape the way citizens see their political project, and themselves as actors in it. But the tradition of theorising in the social contract tradition, which has been very widely disseminated in Western politics, law, and economics, has surely had a very deep influence on the way people see one another as political actors. Even when people have no awareness of the particular texts of the tradition, the idea of the citizen as an independent bargainer, who pays for the benefits he gets by his own productive contributions, is a daily part of our lives.

So I believe we need to adopt a political conception of the person that is more Aristotelian than Kantian,[41] one that sees the person from the start as both capable and needy – 'in need of a rich plurality of life activities,' to use Marx's phrase, whose availability will be the measure of wellbeing. Such a conception of the person, which builds growth and decline into the trajectory of human life, will put us on the road to thinking well about what society should design. We don't have to contract for what we need by producing; we have a claim to support in the dignity of our human need itself. Since this is not just an Aristotelian idea, but one that corresponds to human experience, there is good reason to think that it can command a political consensus in a pluralistic society. If we begin with this conception of the person and with a suitable list of the central capabilities as primary goods, we can begin designing institutions by asking what it would take to get citizens up to an acceptable level on all these capabilities.

In *Women and Human Development* (Nussbaum, 2000b) I therefore proposed that the idea of central human capabilities be used as the analogue of Rawlsian primary goods, and that the guiding political conception of the person should be an Aristotelian/Marxian conception of the human being as in need of a rich plurality of life activities, to be shaped by both practical reason and affiliation, I argue that these interlocking conceptions can form the core of a political conception that is a form of political liberalism, close to Rawls's in many ways. The core of the political conception is endorsed for political purposes only, giving citizens a great deal of space to pursue their own comprehensive conceptions of value, whether secular or religious. Yet more room for a reasonable pluralism in conceptions of the good is secured by insisting that the appropriate political goal is capability only: citizens should be given the option, in each area, of functioning in accordance with a given capability or not so functioning. To secure a capability to a citizen it is not enough to create a sphere of non-interference: the public conception must design the material and institutional environment so that it provides the requisite affirmative support for all the relevant capabilities.[42] Thus care for physical and mental dependency needs will enter into the conception at many points, as part of what is required to secure to citizens one of the capabilities on the list.[43]

In most cases, we can think well about the needs of mentally disabled children and adults by adopting a specification of a general capability that is appropriate for their needs: thus, as the Individuals With Disabilities Education Act urges, we would think of the relevant educational development as a 'suitable education' for each child with a disability, one suited to develop that child's particular powers of mind and thought. At times, we may need to qualify the capability goal with reference to the particular type of disability in question. Thus for many children with Down's Syndrome, it will be reasonable to expect that they can participate in political society and learn to express their political convictions.[44] For Kittay's daughter, by contrast, who will never speak and whose cognitive level will remain at a 'low' level, political capabilities will need to be mediated through appropriate guardianship. In general, however, the aim ought to be to deliver all of the capabilities to all citizens, at some appropriate level and in some way.

My solution to these problems focuses on the importance of giving each and every citizen a set of capabilities that they can use to fashion lives for themselves. It thus lies, squarely within the liberal tradition, albeit a type of materialist liberalism more associated with T. H. Green than with neo-Lockeanism. Ideas of respect for human dignity are as central to my approach as they are for Kant, although I conceive of dignity in a subtly different, and more 'embodied' way. But Kittay suggests that we should go further, departing from all forms of the liberal tradition. She holds that Western political theory must be radically reconfigured to put the fact of dependency at its heart. The fact, she says, that we are all 'some mother's child,' existing in intertwined relations of dependency, should be the guiding image for political thought.[45] Such a care-based theory, she thinks, will be likely to be very different from any liberal theory, since the liberal tradition is deeply committed to goals of independence and liberty. Although Kittay supplies few details to clarify the practical meaning of the difference, I think her idea is that the care-based theory would support a type of politics that provides comprehensive support for need throughout all citizens' lives, as in some familiar ideals of the welfare state – but a welfare state in which liberty is far less important than security and wellbeing.

Kittay is not altogether consistent on this point. At times she herself uses classic liberal arguments, saying that we need to remember that care givers have their own lives to lead, and to support policies that give them more choices.[46] But on the whole she rejects, in the abstract, solutions that emphasise freedom as a central political goal. The concrete measures she favours do not seem to have such sweeping anti-liberal implications. The restoration and expansion of Aid to Families with Dependent Children; expansion of the Family and Medical Leave Act of 1993; various educational measures promoting the dignity of the disabled, through a judicious combination of 'mainstreaming' and separate education (Kittay 1999, Chapter 5) – all these are familiar liberal policies, which can be combined with an emphasis on choice and liberty as important social goals. Kittay's most controversial proposal, that of a direct non-means-tested payment to those who care for family dependants at home – clearly has, or could have, a liberal rationale: that of ensuring that these people are seen as active, dignified workers rather than passive non-contributors.

Indeed, if we adopt all the changes I have proposed, we will still have a theory that is basically liberal. For theories that take their start from an idea of human capability and functioning emphasise the importance of giving all citizens the chance to develop the full range of human powers, at whatever level their condition allows, and to enjoy the sort of liberty and independence their condition allows. Would we do better to reject this theory in favor of Kittay's idea, rejecting independence as a major social goal and conceiving of the state as a universal mother? To be sure, nobody is ever self-sufficient; the independence we enjoy is always both temporary and partial, and it is good to be reminded of that fact by a theory that also stresses the importance of care in times of dependency. But is being 'some mother's child' a sufficient image for the citizen in a just society? I think we need a lot more: liberty and opportunity, the chance to form a plan of life, the chance to learn and imagine on one's own.

These goals are as important for the mentally handicapped as they are for others, though much more difficult to achieve. Although Kittay's daughter Sesha will never live on her own (and although Kittay is right to say that independence should not be seen as a necessary condition of dignity for all mentally disabled people),[47] many others do aspire to hold a job, and vote, and tell their own story. Michael Bérubé ends his compelling account of his son's life with the hope that Jamie, too, will write a book about himself, as two adults with Down's Syndrome recently have.[48] One day Jamie's kindergarten class went round the room, asking the children what they wanted to be when they grew up. They said the usual things: basketball star, ballet dancer, fireman. The teacher wasn't sure Jamie would understand the question, so she asked it very clearly. Jamie just said, 'Big.' And his literal answer, said the teacher, taught them all something about the question. Bérubé too wants, simply, a society in which his son will be able to be 'big': healthy, educated, loving, active, seen as a particular person with something distinctive to contribute, rather than as 'a retarded child.'

For that to happen, his dependencies must be understood and supported. But so too must his need to be distinct and an individual: and at this point Bérubé refers sympathetically to Rawls. He argues that the idea at the heart of the Individuals With Disabilities Education Act (IDEA) – the idea that every child has the right to an 'appropriate education' in the 'least restrictive environment' possible, based on an 'Individualized Education Plan' (IEP) – is a profoundly liberal idea, an idea about individuality and freedom. One of the most important kinds of support mentally disabled children need is the support required to be free choosing adults, each in his or her own way. In so far as Kittay suggests that we downplay or marginalise such liberal notions in favour of a conception of the state that makes it the parental supporter of its 'children''s needs, I think she goes too far, misconceiving what justice would be for both the disabled and the elderly. Even for Sesha, who will never vote or write, doesn't a full human life involve a kind of freedom and individuality, namely, a space in which to exchange love and enjoy light and sound, free from confinement and mockery?

So I believe that the problem we have investigated shows us that liberal theory needs to question some of its most traditional starting points – questioning, in the process, the Kantian notion of the person. But that does not disable liberalism: it just challenges us all to produce a new form of liberalism, more attentive to need and its material and institutional conditions. The liberal ideas of freedom and of the human need for various types of liberty of action are precious ideas that feminist philosophers, it seems to me, should cherish and further develop, creating theories that make it possible for all citizens to have the support they need for the full development of their human capabilities.

If we choose the capabilities approach rather than the social contract approach, we have no difficult developing political principles that show respect for the disabled as fully equal citizens. At the same time, such an approach, as I have argued, does a superior job of conceptualising claims of justice that arise in connection with the care of children and elderly people. Their asymmetrical needs are treated as part of their human dignity, rather than as large social costs to be borne.

Although in both theory and practice the nations of the world have moved beyond earlier versions of the social contract tradition, by insisting on human dignity as a central social value in international human rights instruments and many national constitutions, we have not yet altogether shaken off a dark implication inherent in the very idea of a social bargain for mutual advantage, namely that those who are dependent and 'unproductive' are not full participants.[49] 'A more capacious and supple sense of what it is to be human'[50] is crucial, if we are to deliberate well about these problems of justice.

One reason for optimism, as Bérubé says, is that we know that human beings are able to imagine, and to communicate what they imagine, even to someone who did not have that image before. If we were able to form the old picture that divided society into the 'independent' and 'productive' and the helpless 'unproductive,' it ought to be possible to learn to think of ourselves as beings both capable and disabled, in need of support for a rich plurality of life activities.

NOTES

1 See TenBroek (1966).
2 To take just one example: According to the US Department of Labor, Women's Bureau (May 1998), an estimated 22.4 million households – nearly one in four – are providing home care for family members or friends over the age of fifty. For these and other data I am grateful to Mona Harrington (1999). This is a major theme in recent feminist work: see especially Eva Kittay (1999); Nancy Folbre (1999) and, based largely on Folbre (1999), Chapter 3 of *Human Development Report 1999*; Folbre (2001); Joan Williams (2000); Harrington (1999). Earlier influential work in this area includes Martha A. Fineman (1991, 1995); Sarah Ruddick (1989); Joan Tronto (1993); Virginia Held (1993); Robin West (1997). For an excellent collection of articles from diverse feminist perspectives, see Held (1995).

3 For just one typical example, see *Bradwell v. Illinois*, 83 US (16 Wall.) 130 (1873), in which the US Supreme Court, upholding an Illinois law that made it illegal for a woman to practise law, declared that woman's role in the family 'evidently unfits' her for 'many of the occupations of civil life'.
4 See Folbre (1999).
5 See Williams (2000).
6 Some of the material in this section is drawn from my April 2000 Presidential Address to the Central Division of the American Philosophical Association, 'The Future of Feminist Liberalism' (Nussbaum 2000a).
7 See Nussbaum (2002a).
8 See references in Nussbaum (2002a).
9 David Hume, *A Treatise of Human Nature*, Book III, Part II, Section Ii.
10 Locke, *Second Treatise on Government*, Chapter 8.
11 David Gauthier (1986: 18), speaking of all 'persons who decrease th[e] average level' of wellbeing in a society.
12 References to citizens as 'fully cooperating' occur frequently in Rawls (1980, 1996), for example Rawls (1980: 546), Rawls (1996: 183).
13 This is not precisely the right way of putting it, because Rawls takes his departure from Kant's *ethical* writings, and develops a politics based on the core ideas of these, whereas Kant himself does not so clearly do that. His political doctrines have a more Hobbesian character than one might wish, despite his strong criticism of Hobbes.
14 This problem is exacerbated, of course, by Kant's focus on some aspects of our humanity and not others as what particularly constitutes its worth and dignity.
15 For one particularly valuable treatment of this theme, see James Rachels (1990). Two wonderful pictures of the animal sort of dignity: Barbara Smuts (1999), and, my favourite, George Pitcher (1995). I discuss the implications of recognising the dignity of non-human animals in a review article about Steven M. Wise's *Rattling the Cage: Toward Legal Rights for Animals* (Cambridge, MA: Perseus Books, 2000), forthcoming in *The Harvard Law Review*. See also Alasdair MacIntyre (1999).
16 See especially Rachels (1990) and MacIntyre (1999).
17 I do not mean to deny that Kant gives need an important role in his theory: for just one good treatment of this aspect of Kant's thought, see Allen Wood (1999). What I mean is that whereas for Kant personality and animality are conceptually independent, and personality is not itself understood in terms of need, for Rawls these two elements are more thoroughly integrated, and the person is understood from the first as in need of material and other goods. Rawls draws attention to this shift by calling his view an empirical type of Kantianism.
18 As Eva Kittay has argued in an excellent discussion (Kittay 1999: 88–99), and see also Kittay (1997), there are five places in Rawls's theory where he fails to confront facts of asymmetrical neediness that might naturally have been confronted. (1) His account of the 'circumstances of justice' assumes a rough equality between persons, such that none could dominate all the others; thus we are not invited to consider relations of justice that might obtain between an adult and her infants, or her senile demented parents. (2) Rawls's idealisation of citizens as 'fully cooperating', etcetera, puts to one side the large facts about extreme neediness I have just mentioned. (3) His conception of social cooperation, again, is based on the idea of reciprocity between equals, and has no explicit place for relations of extreme dependency. (4) His account of the primary goods, introduced, as it is, as an account of the needs of citizens who are characterised by the two moral powers and by the capacity to be 'fully cooperating,' has no place for the need of many real people for the kind of care we give to people who are not independent. And (5) his account of citizens' freedom as involving the concept of being a self-authenticating source of valid claims (for example, Rawls, 1996: 32) fails to make a place for any freedom that might be enjoyed by someone who is not independent in that sense.

19 See Kittay (1999: 77): 'Dependency must be faced from the beginning of any project in egalitarian theory that hopes to include all persons within its scope.' For a remarkable narrative of a particular life that shows exactly how many social structures play a part in the life of a mentally handicapped child from the very beginning, see Michael Bérubé (1996).

20 This point has been repeatedly made by Amartya Sen in recommending an approach based on capability and functioning over the Rawlsian approach to primary goods; for the classic original statement, see Sen (1982); other good accounts of the approach are in Sen (1993, 1995); and Sen (1992), especially chapters 1, 3 and 5.

21 Sen (1982).

22 Two further problems not raised by Sen: first, even if we were to give more income and wealth to the person in a wheelchair, this would not solve the problem: for making this person mobile requires public action (construction of wheelchair ramps, accessible buses, etc.) that individuals cannot achieve on their own. Second, even if the person in the wheelchair were equally well off with regard to economic well-being, there is a separate issue of dignity and self-respect. By measuring relative social positions by income and wealth alone, Rawls ignores the possibility that a group may be reasonably well-off economically, but suffer grave disabilities with regard to the social bases of self-respect. One might argue that gays and lesbians in our society are in precisely that position; but certainly the physically and mentally handicapped will be in that position, unless society makes a major and fundamental commitment to inclusion and respect.

23 At times, as in the passage (from Rawls 1980) cited in the text above, Rawls suggests leaving aside all severe or expensive physical illness, as well as mental disability: see also Rawls (1996: 272, n.10). At other times (for example, Rawls, 1996: 302) he treats possession of the two moral powers as a sufficient, as well as a necessary, condition of fully cooperating status.

24 Rawls proposes taking account of it at the legislative stage: see Rawls (1996: 183–6); but given the pervasive role of political institutions in shaping the life chances of such citizens from the very beginning of a human life, this seems an inadequate reply. The concrete stratagems adopted to address issues of disability (laws mandating wheel-chair ramps, laws such as the Individuals with Disabilities Education Act) could well be left until this stage; but the fact that citizens experience such needs for care must be recognised from the start, and a commitment made to address these concerns.

25 See Scanlon (1999: 177–87). I am very grateful to Scanlon for correspondence that makes the complexity of his approach to these cases clear. Because this chapter is about the basic structure of a political conception, I shall hope to take up his views elsewhere.

26 Once again, it is very important to stress the fact that this is Rawls's project, not Scanlon's, and that Scanlon does not recommend applying it in this way.

27 Gauthier (1986: 18, n. 30).

28 See for example Rawls (1971: 135), where finality is a formal condition on political principles, and (1971: 175–8), in the argument for the two principles where it is made clear that the agreement 'is final and made in perpetuity' and that 'there is no second chance' (1971: 176). Rawls's opposition to intuitionism focuses on this issue: see for example Rawls (1971: 35–6).

29 For more discussion of this continuum and a critique of the idea of the 'normal', see Nussbaum (2003: Chapter 5).

30 See Erving Goffman's classic work (1963) and the discussion of his ideas in Nussbaum (2003: chapters 4 and 5).

31 Like Sen, I defend this idea (in Nussbaum 2000b: Chapter 1); unlike Sen, I propose an actual list of the central capabilities, analogous to primary goods. Nussbaum (2000b) Chapter 1 discusses in detail the relationship of my approach to Rawls's.

32 On this point see especially Williams (2000).

33 See my discussion of this point in Nussbaum (2000b), Chapter 1.

34 In Rawls (1971) primary goods were characterised as all-purpose means to the pursuit of one's own conception of the good, whatever it is; in Rawls (1980, 1996), the interpretation shifts, and Rawls acknowledges that they are means with regard to the Kantian political conception of the person: see Rawls (1996: 187–90).

35 I discuss this issue in detail in Nussbaum (2002a), with respect to both Rawls's text and the most prominent feminist critiques. See, for example, Seyla Benhabib (1992); Marilyn Friedman (1993).

36 I owe this point to Geoffrey Sayre-McCord, who pointed out that I myself have criticised feminists who don't see the Veil of Ignorance as part of the model of the person: see Nussbaum (2002a).

37 Rawls has interpreted the idea of primary goods differently over time: in Rawls (1971) he understands them as all-purpose means to whatever ends they may have; in Rawls (1980, 1996), he argues, instead, that they are to be understood in close connection with the Kantian constructivist conception of the person, as things people endowed with the 'two moral powers' would reasonably believe they need to have. I discuss my own approach to the issue of primary goods in Nussbaum (2000b), Chapter 1.

38 See Nussbaum (2003).

39 See Nussbaum (2001a).

40 See my 'Women and the Law of Peoples,' forthcoming in *Philosophy, Politics, and Economics*, and my Tanner Lectures (Nussbaum, 2002b).

41 As the late Peter Cicchino eloquently put this point, Aristotle's conception is not deductive or *a priori*: it respects widely held views about human reality, but takes experience as its source and guide. Second, it takes seriously the materiality of human beings – their need for food, shelter, friendship, care, what might be called their basic dependency. Third, it is epistemologically modest – it does not claim to have the exactitude of mathematics, but rather is content to look for 'such precision as accords with the subject-matter" (Cicchino, 1999).

42 In that way my view is close to the type of liberalism defended (against Lockean contractarianism) by T. H. Green, though my form is not perfectionistic, but is, rather, a form of political liberalism. I have found very illuminating the discussion of the liberal tradition in John Deigh (2001).

43 I attach the current version of the capabilities list as an Appendix. The view is further debated in a symposium on my political philosophy in Nussbaum (2000c); see in particular the paper by Richard Arneson, which takes me up on the question of capability and functioning, arguing that a more robust perfectionism that makes actual functioning the goal is required in areas such as health. I dispute this, defending my form of political liberalism, in Nussbaum (2000c).

44 See Mitchell Levitz and Jason Kingsley (1994), and Bérubé (1996). I discuss these cases in Nussbaum (2001b). I discuss the Individuals With Disabilities Education Act in Nussbaum (2003, forthcoming), Chapter 5.

45 Kittay (1999), Chapter 1, Part III, on political strategies, is entitled 'Some Mother's Child'.

46 For passages that focus on the need of the individual for choice and independence, see for example Kittay (1999: 34–5, 53, 98, 192 n.32).

47 See Kittay (1999), Chapter 6, a beautiful and lucid account of her daughter's life.

48 Bérubé (1996: 264): 'For I have no sweeter dream than to imagine – aesthetically and ethically and parentally – that Jamie will someday be his own advocate, his own author, his own best representative'.

49 Thus Gauthier says that while the elderly have paid for the care they receive by earlier periods of productivity, the handicapped have not (1986: 18 n. 30).

50 This phrase is Bérubé's, from a paper published after the book, entitled 'Disability and the "Difference" It Makes', delivered at the Smithsonian National Museum conference on 'Disability and the Practice of Public History', May 1999.

REFERENCES

Benhabib, Seyla (1992) 'The Generalized and the Concrete Other', in *Situating the Self: Gender, Community and Postmodernism in Contemporary Ethics*. Polity, Cambridge.

Bérubé, Michael (1996) *Life As We Know It: A Father, A Family, and An Exceptional Child*, Vintage, New York.

Cicchino, Peter M. (1999) 'Building on Foundational Myths: Feminism and the Recovery of 'Human Nature': A Response to Martha Fineman', *Journal of Gender, Social Policy and the Law*, 8 (1): 73–84.

Deigh, John (2001) 'Liberalism and Freedom' in James P. Sterba (ed.), *Social and Political Philosophy*, Routledge, London and New York.

Fineman, Martha A. (1991) *The Illusion of Equality*, University of Chicago Press, Chicago.

—— (1995) *The Neutered Mother, the Sexual Family and Other Twentieth Century Tragedies*, Routledge, New York.

Folbre, Nancy (1999) 'Care and the Global Economy', background paper prepared for the *Human Development Report 1999*, United Nations Development Programme, Oxford University Press, New York.

—— (2001) *The Invisible Heart: Economics and Family Values*, The New Press, New York.

Friedman, Marilyn (1993) *What Are Friends For? Feminist Perspectives on Personal Relationships and Moral Theory*, Cornell University Press, Ithaca.

Gauthier, David (1986) *Morals By Agreement*, Oxford University Press, New York.

Goffman, Erving (1963) *Stigma: Notes on the Management of Spoiled Identity*, Simon & Schuster, New York.

Harrington, Mona (1999) *Care and Equality*, Knopf, New York.

Held, Virginia (1993) *Feminist Morality: Transforming Culture, Society, and Politics*, University of Chicago Press, Chicago.

—— (ed.) (1995) *Justice and Care: Essential Readings in Feminist Ethics*, Westview Press, Boulder, CO.

Kittay, Eva (1997) 'Human Dependency and Rawlsian Equality', in Diana T. Meyers (ed.) *Feminists Rethink the Self*, Westview, Boulder, CO.

—— (1999) *Love's Labor: Essays on Women, Equality, and Dependency*, Routledge, New York.

Levitz, Mitchell and Jason Kingsley (1994) *Count Us In: Growing Up With Down Syndrome*, Harcourt Brace, New York.

MacIntyre, Alasdair (1999) *Dependent Rational Animals: Why Human Beings Need the Virtues*, Open Court Publishing, Peru, IL.

Nussbaum, Martha C. (2000a) 'The Future of Feminist Liberalism', *Proceedings and Addresses of The American Philosophical Association*, 74(2): 47–79.

—— (2000b) *Women and Human Development: The Capabilities Approach*, Cambridge University Press, Cambridge and New York.

—— (2000c) 'Aristotle, Politics, and Human Capabilities: A Response to Antony, Arneson, Charlesworth, and Mulgan', *Ethics*, 111: 102–40.

—— (2001) 'Animal Rights: The Need for a Theoretical Basis', *Harvard Law Review*, 114: 1506–49.

—— (2001b) 'Disabled Lives: Who Cares?', *The New York Review of Books*, January 11, pp. 34–37.

—— (2002a) 'Rawls and feminism', in Samuel Freeman (ed.) *The Cambridge Companion to Rawls*, Cambridge University Press, Cambridge.

—— (2002b) *Beyond the Social Contract: Toward Global Justice*, Tanner Lectures in Human Values, Australian National University, 12–13 November.

—— (2003, forthcoming) *Hiding From Humanity: Disgust, Shame, and the Law*, Princeton University Press, Princeton.

—— (forthcoming) 'Capabilities as fundamental entitlements: Sen and social justice', in

Deen Chatterjee, Rowman and Littlefield (eds.) *Feminist Economics and 'Constitutions and Capabilities'*.

Pitcher, George (1995) *The Dogs Who Came to Stay*, G. Putnam, New York.

Rachels, James (1990) *Created From Animals: The Moral Implications of Darwinism*, Oxford University Press, New York.

Rawls, John (1971) *A Theory of Justice*, Harvard University Press, Cambridge, MA.

—— (1980) 'Kantian constructivism in moral theory: the Dewey Lectures', *The Journal of Philosophy*, 77: 515–71.

Rawls, John (1996) *Political Liberalism*, expanded paperback edition, Columbia University Press, New York.

Ruddick, Sarah (1989) *Maternal Thinking*, Beacon Press, New York.

Scanlon, Thomas (1999) *What We Owe to Each Other*, Harvard University Press, Cambridge, MA.

Sen, A. (1982) 'Equality of what?', in A. Sen, *Choice, Welfare, and Measurement*, Basil Blackwell, Oxford.

—— (1992) *Inequality Reexamined*, Russell Sage, New York.

—— (1993) 'Capability and well-being', in M. Nussbaum and A. Sen (eds.), *The Quality of Life*, Clarendon Press, Oxford.

—— (1995) 'Gender inequality and theories of justice', in M. Nussbaum and J. Glover (eds.), *Women, Culture and Development*, Clarendon Press, Oxford.

Smuts, Barbara (1999) untitled reply to J. M. Coetzee, in Amy Gutmann (ed.), *The Lives of Animals*, Princeton University Press, Princeton.

TenBroek, J. (1966) 'The right to be in the world: the disabled in the Law of Torts', *California Law Review*, 54: 841–919.

Tronto, Joan (1993) *Moral Boundaries: A Political Argument for an Ethic of Care*, Routledge, New York.

West, Robert (1997) *Caring for Justice*, New York University Press, New York.

Williams, Joan (2000) *Unbending Gender: Why Family and Work Conflict and What to Do About It*, Oxford University Press, New York.

Wood, Allen (1999) *Kant's Ethical Theory*, Cambridge University Press, Cambridge.

Appendix: The Central Human Capabilities

1 **Life.** Being able to live to the end of a human life of normal length; not dying prematurely, or before one's life is so reduced as to be not worth living.

2 **Bodily health.** Being able to have good health, including reproductive health; to be adequately nourished; to have adequate shelter.

3 **Bodily integrity.** Being able to move freely from place to place; to be secure against violent assault, including sexual assault and domestic violence; having opportunities for sexual satisfaction and for choice in matters of reproduction.

4 **Senses, imagination and thought.** Being able to use the senses, to imagine, think, and reason – and to do these things in a 'truly human' way, a way informed and cultivated by an adequate education, including, but by no means limited to, literacy and basic mathematical and scientific training. Being able to use imagination and thought in connection with experiencing and producing works and events of one's own choice, religious, literary, musical, and so forth. Being able to use one's mind in ways protected by guarantees of freedom of expression with respect to both political and artistic speech, and freedom of religious exercise. Being able to have pleasurable experiences and to avoid non-beneficial pain.

5 **Emotions.** Being able to have attachments to things and people outside ourselves; to love those who love and care for us, to grieve at their absence; in general, to love, to grieve, to experience longing, gratitude, and justified anger. Not having one's emotional development blighted by fear and anxiety. (Supporting this capability means

supporting forms of human association that can be shown to be crucial in their development.)

6 **Practical reason**. Being able to form a conception of the good and to engage in critical reflection about the planning of one's life. (This entails protection for the liberty of conscience and religious observance.)

7 **Affiliation**.

A. Being able to live with and toward others, to recognise and show concern for other human beings, to engage in various forms of social interaction; to be able to imagine the situation of another. (Protecting this capability means protecting institutions that constitute and nourish such forms of affiliation, and also protecting the freedom of assembly and political speech.)

B. Having the social bases of self-respect and non-humiliation; being able to be treated as a dignified being whose worth is equal to that of others. This entails provisions of non-discrimination on the basis of race, sex, sexual orientation, ethnicity, caste, religion, national origin.

8 **Other species**. Being able to live with concern for and in relation to animals, plants and the world of nature.

9 **Play**. Being able to laugh, to play, to enjoy recreational activities.

10 **Control over one's environment.**

A. Political. Being able to participate effectively in political choices that govern one's life; having the right of political participation, protections of free speech and association.

B. Material. Being able to hold property (both land and movable goods), and having property rights on an equal basis with others; having the right to seek employment on an equal basis with others; having the freedom from unwarranted search and seizure. In work, being able to work as a human being, exercising practical reason and entering into meaningful relationships of mutual recognition with other workers.

NOTES ON CONTRIBUTORS

Isabella Aboderin holds an MSc in Health Promotion Sciences from the London School of Hygiene and Medicine, and a PhD from the School for Policy Studies, University of Bristol. After working as a Research Associate at the International Institute on Health and Ageing, University of Bristol, she spent a year at the World Health Organisation, where she coordinated the ageing and life course programme's initiative on life course and health. Currently she is affiliated to the Institute for Development Policy and Management (IDPM), University of Manchester, UK, where she is developing further research on intergenerational family support, poverty and economic security for the elderly in West Africa.

Armando Barrientos is Senior Lecturer in Public Economics and Development at the Institute for Development Policy and Management at the University of Manchester, UK. His research focuses on welfare and social protection, and he has published a number of papers on pension and health reforms in Latin America, and on the wellbeing and vulnerability of older workers and their households.

Vladislav Bezrukov has been Director of the Institute of Gerontology in Kiev, Ukraine, since 1989. He is also a Corresponding Member of Ukraine's Academy of Medical Science, an Honoured Scientist of Ukraine, President of the Ukrainian Gerontology and Geriatrics Society, a recipient of the N. D. Strazhesko prize of the Ukrainian National Academy of Sciences, and the Director of the WHO Collaborating Center on Ageing in Kiev. He is the Editor-in-Chief of the Ukrainian journal *Problems of Aging and Longevity*, a member of the editorial boards of several national and international journals, and the author of more than 370 publications on a variety of subjects related to ageing.

Ana Amélia Camarano is a Brazilian government economist who coordinates a research group on Family and Population within the Planning Ministry. She is also a lecturer at the National School of Statistics and at the Cândido Mendes University. She has worked on the topic of ageing since 1999 and edited the volume *Muito além dos 60: Os novos idosos brasileiros (Beyond the Sixties: The New Brazilian Elderly)* (1999). Some of her recent publications include 'O idoso no mercado de trabalho' (*IPEA, Textos para Discussão*, No. 830, 2001), 'Envelhecimento, condições de vida e política previdenciária: Como ficam as mulheres?' (presented at the Inter-American Conference on Social Security, Fortaleza, November 2001), 'Envelhecimento da população brasileira: Uma contribuição demográfica' (in *Tratado de Geriatria e Gerontologia*, organised by the Sociedade Brasileirade Geriatria and Gerontologia in 2002), and 'Familia com Idosos: Nonhos Vazios?' (*IPEA, Textos para Discussão*, No. 950, 2003).

Natalia Foigt, who holds a PhD in Economics, was appointed Head of the Laboratory of Medical Demography at the Kiev Institute of Gerontology in Ukraine in February 2003. Her research interests include population ageing, mortality and life expectancy. She is the author of 25 scientific publications, including the monograph *Life Expectancy in Old Age: Evolution, Current Status and Perspectives* (2002, in Ukrainian).

Maria Cristina Gomes da Conceição is Professor-Researcher at the Latin American Faculty of Social Sciences (FLACSO-Mexico). Previously, she was Research Associate at the National School of Public Health of Fundação Oswaldo Cruz in Rio de Janeiro. Currently she is working at the National Council of Population in Mexico. Her most recent publications include 'Household and Income: Ageing and Gender Inequalities in Urban Brazil and Colombia' (*Journal of Developing Societies*, 2002); 'Households, Income Structure and Social Policy in Brazil, Mexico and Colombia', in *Exclusion and Engagement: Social Policy in Latin America* (2002); 'México: un país de jóvenes, en rápido proceso de envejecimiento; participación laboral, pensiones, discapacidad y uso de servicios de salud' in the volume *Políticas Públicas en América Latina* (2002), 'Life Course, Households and Institutions' (*Journal of Comparative Family Studies*, 2002); and 'Households and Income; Ageing and Gender Inequalities in Urban Brazil and Colombia' (*Journal of Developing Societies*, 2002).

Paul Johnson is Professor of Economic History at the London School of Economics (LSE), UK. He has written widely on the economics and history of old age and pensions, and on the development of welfare states. His publications include *Workers versus Pensioners* (1989); *Ageing and Economic Welfare* (1992); *Labour Markets in an Ageing Europe* (1993); *Old Age: From Antiquity to Post-Modernity* (1998). He has been a consultant to the UK government and the World Bank on pension system and social sector reform. He is currently working with colleagues at LSE on the construction of a micro-simulation model of the ageing of the UK population to 2050.

John Knodel is Professor of Sociology at the Population Studies Center, University of Michigan, USA. He specialises in the areas of population dynamics and ageing in developing countries, with an emphasis on Thailand, and on European historical demography. He has also conducted several studies related to the social demography of education, especially in Thailand and Vietnam. At present, his areas of research include the socio-demographic impact of AIDS on the older persons, with a focus on Thailand; the relationship between gender and older-age well-being and intergenerational support exchanges; sexual behaviour; and the social demography of South-east Asia. He currently has grants to examine the impact of the AIDS epidemic on older persons and to conduct a comparative study of gender and ageing in eight Asian countries.

Peter Lloyd-Sherlock is Senior Lecturer in Social Development at the School of Development Studies, University of East Anglia, UK. Previously he has held posts at the London School of Hygiene and Tropical Medicine and at the University of Glasgow. He has been involved in ageing and development research for 12 years, and has led research projects in Argentina, Brazil, Thailand and South Africa. His major publications include *Old Age and Poverty in the Developing World. The Shantytowns of Buenos Aires* (1997), 'Old Age and Poverty in Developing Countries: New Policy Challenges' (*World Development*, 18, 12 2000), and 'Formal Social Protection for Older People in Developing Countries; Three Different Approaches' (*Journal of Social Policy*, 31,4, 2002).

Di McIntyre is Associate Professor at the School of Public Health of the University of Cape Town, South Africa, where she has worked since 1988. She founded the Health Economics Unit in 1990 and served as its Director for 13 years. She has nearly 20 years of experience in health economics and health policy, and has worked primarily in Southern and East Africa. Her main research interests are the evaluation of health equity issues, and the analysis of health sector reform initiatives. She is involved in a wide range of training and technical support activities. She has also served on a number of governmental policy advisory committees and is involved in a range of health economics and policy capacity development initiatives within the African region.

Verónica Montes de Oca Zavala is Research Associate at the Instituto de Investigaciones Sociales (IIS-UNAM) in Mexico, and teaches demography and sociology at the Social and Political Sciences Faculty of the National University of Mexico (UNAM) and Colegio de México. She currently conducts research on the impact of structural adjustment programmes on systems of social support for the elderly, families and households; and on formal and informal social protection and public policies. Some of her recent publications include 'Discourses, Voices and Visions on the Aged in Mexico City''' (*Indian Journal of Gerontology*, special issue, 15, 1–2, 2001), and 'Desigualdad estructural entre la población anciana en México: Factores que han condicionado el apoyo institucional entre la población con 60 años y más en México' (*Estudios Demográficos y Urbanos*, El Colegio de México, 2001). Recently, she coordinated research on community networks in Mexico City with the financial support of the Centro Latinoamericano de Demografía (CELADE, División de Población de la CEPAL) and the Italian government. In 2003 she acted as adviser on issues affecting the elderly to both the Mexico City authorities and the Older Persons National Institute (Instituto Nacional de Personas Adultas Mayores) of the Federal Government.

Martha Nussbaum is Ernst Freund Distinguished Service Professor of Law and Ethics at the University of Chicago, with appointments in the Law School, the Philosophy Department, and the Divinity School. She is an Associate Member of the Department of Political Science and the Department of Classics, a Board Member of the Human Rights Program, an Affiliate of the

Committee on Southern Asian Studies, and the founder and coordinator of the Center for Comparative Constitutionalism. From 1999 to 2002 she was a Board Member of the Center for Gender Studies. Her books include *Cultivating Humanity: a Classical Defense of Reform in Liberal Education* (1997), *Sex and Social Justice* (1999), *Women and Human Development: the Capabilities Approach* (2000), and *Upheavals of Thought: the Intelligence of Emotions* (2001).

Tetsuo Ogawa is Research Associate at the Oxford Institute of Ageing, and Senior Associate Member at St Antony's College, University of Oxford, UK. He is currently serving as Board Member for Research Committee 11: Sociology of Ageing, the International Sociological Association (ISA, 2002–6). In 1994–5 he was a British Council Fellow from Japan. His main research interest is in social policy and administration, with particular emphasis on citizens' rights, social exclusion, community development, social solidarity, and social policy development in ageing societies, in European and Asian countries. In 1996, he contributed to the BBC TV programme *The Coming of Age*. In 2003, he was a speaker at a conference convened by the Ageing Populations: Policy Lessons from the East (APPLE) project under the European Commission's 5th Framework Programme. He recently contributed to the book *Social Protection in Asia* (forthcoming).

Du Peng is Professor and Deputy Director at the Population and Development Studies Center, and Deputy Director of the Gerontology Institute at Renmin University of China. Previously, he was Visiting Scholar at the Center for Ageing Studies, Flinders University in Australia for two years. He is the author of *Ageing Issues and Policies in the European Union* (2000), *Who Will Provide for the Chinese Elderly?* (2000), *Chinese Elderly in the Ageing Process* (1996), *The Process of Population Ageing in China* (1994), and the co-author of *Social Gerontology* (1999) and *The Ageing of Population in China* (1991).

David R. Phillips is Professor of Social Policy and Associate Director of the Asia-Pacific Institute of Ageing Studies (APIAS) at Lingnan University, Hong Kong, where he is also Head of the Department of Politics and Sociology. His research and teaching interests are in health, health care and social epidemiology, with a particular focus on social gerontology and long-term care issues. He is Coordinator of the Asian Ageing Research Network and has acted as an adviser on ageing issues to the United Nations Economic and Social Commission for Asia and the Pacific, among other organisations. He is an advisory editor to *Social Science and Medicine* and a co-editor of the *Hong Kong Journal of Gerontology*. He has published over one hundred papers and some of his books since 1990 include: *Ageing in East and Southeast Asia* (1992); *Environment and Ageing* (1999); *Ageing in the Asia–Pacific Region* (2000); and *National Policies on Ageing and Long-term Care in the Asia–Pacific* (2002).

Nélida Redondo is Senior Researcher on the programme "La Deuda Social Argentina" (The Argentinean Social Debt) at the Argentinean Catholic University, Argentina. She was formerly Director of Studies and Research at the National Institute of Public Administration (1994–2001) and Planning Chief Executive at the National Institute of Social Services for Retired and Pensioners. Some of her recent publications include *Aspectos metodológicos del diseño de un sistema de información para servicios de salud a ancianos* (2001), 'El colapso de las políticas sociales dirigidas a la vejez en la Argentina' (*Revista Argentina de Gerontología y Geriatría*, 21, 4/4, 2001), 'Impacto social del envejecimiento: Radiografía de una población' (*Encrucijadas UBA*, Revista de la Universidad de Buenos Aires, 1,3, 2001), 'El riesgo vejez es argentino: Los ancianos, como inversores cautivos del mercado local, son los que más padecen las fallas del sistema' (*Diario Clarín*, 21 July 2001) and 'Mujeres: por la igualdad: Mejor, no jubilarse antes' (*Diario Clarín*, 8 March 2001).

Chanpen Saegtienchai is former Senior Researcher at the College of Population Studies, Chulalongkorn University, Thailand. She is currently an independent researcher collaborating with the Faculty of Nursing at Chulalongkorn University. She has worked in the area of ageing since 1986, and started her interest in HIV/AIDS-related issues in 1993. Her current research focuses on the impacts of AIDS on older people in Thailand.

INDEX

accountability/transparency 170, 197-8, 201-3, 223
Accra 216-17, 224
active ageing, accommodation provided to family 6; continuing economic activity 6-7, 15, 20, 44, 83; decision making 6; and International Year of Older Persons (1999) 40; leisure 29-31, 36; and pension reform 123; social participation 23, 25-30, 36, 111-12, 114-15, 148; transmission of cultural values/wisdom 6, 92
activity centres 113
Africa, 160-79, 270; sub-Saharan 4, 118, 207; East 160; Southern 160; West 160
age discrimination 5, 27, 71, 84, 89, 93, 161, 174, 299
agriculture 26, 46, 66, 88, 100-1, 104, 109-10, 132
alarmism 5, 7-8
alcoholism 85-6, 173
Anhui province 100, 102-3
Argentina 3-4, 119, 184-203; Comprehensive Health Care Programme (PAMI) 189-90, 194, 197, 201; GDP 191; Medical Federation of the Province of Buenos Aires (FEMEBA) 190; Ministry of Health 187; Ministry of Social Security 187; National Institute of Social Services for Retirees and Pensioners (INSSJP) 184-5, 188-203; National Pension System 192; Peronism 187; Welfare Programme for Older People 194, 198
Aristotle 289-90
Asia, 9, 254; South 5, 123; Asian economic crisis 254
Asian-Pacific region 114
Australia 39; GDP 39

baby boomer generation 97-8, 199
Baltic states 76
basic needs 8, 77, 82, 108, 211, 259, 275, 285
Beijing 101-3, 106, 112
Beijing Ageing Studies Centre 112
Belarus 72-4; GDP 72
Belgium 22
Belo Horizonte 46
Bérubé, Michael 292-3
Beveridge, William 34-5
Bevin, Ernest 27
birthrates 71, 74; see also fertility
Botswana 212-13
Bradford 35
Brazil 3-4, 19-21, 44-68, 117, 123-4, 128, 130-8, 206, 231-2; constitution 48, 50, 60, 123, 130-1; economic crisis (1980s) 48; GDP 3, 46, 128, 130-1; General Household Survey 54; Mid-west 45; National Housing

Bank 46; National Housing Programme 54; National Policy for Older People 52, 62; North 45; North-east 45-6, 57-9, 62-6; Plan Gerador de Benefícios Livres 131; Real Plan 47; pensions in 48, 52-3, 55, 57, 59-62 65-8, 124, 128, 130-8; South 45, 66; South-east 45-6, 49, 57-8, 64; stabilisation plans 47
bureaucracy 46
Burkina Faso 3; GDP 3
Burundi 170
Bush, George W. 199

Cambodia 253
Cameroon 167
Canada 39; GDP 39
Cape Verde 160
capitalism 32, 91
Cardoso, Fernando Henrique 131
care by elders 6, 12-13, 30, 44, 77, 89-90, 113, 162-3, 177, 206-7, 236, 239, 246, 249-72, 275; by younger older people 113; for HIV/AIDS sufferers 162-3, 177, 206-7, 249-72; see also grandparenthood
care economy 205-8
centralisation/decentralisation 10, 71, 94, 100, 169-71, 188, 200
charity 22, 143; organisations 143
child care xi, 12, 239-40
Chile 10, 117 122-4, 127-9, 132-8; GDP 128; pensions in 122-4, 127-9, 132-8
China 4, 19-20, 97-115; All China Federation of Trade Unions 107; Basic Scheme for Rural Social Security for Old Age Support at the Country Level 108; central 103; China National Committee On Ageing (CNCOA) 114; Cultural Revolution 107; eastern coastal 103, 105; economic reform 100-1, 107; GDP 101; 'Five Guarantees' 108-9, 114; Human Development Index (HDI) 101-2; Law of Elderly Care 111; Law of the Social Participation of the Elderly 111-12; Law of the People's Republic of China on Protection of the Rights and Interests of the Elderly 104, 111; local labour bureaux 107; Ministry of Civil Affairs 108; Ninth National People's Congress (NPC) 108; north-western 103; one-child policy 97-100; Regulation of the Management of the Elderly Welfare Facilities 112; southern 103; State Council 99; state-owned enterprises 107, 109; Tenth Five Year Plan (2001-5) 108; western 103; *White Paper on Population in China* 99
Chongqing 102-3
citizenship 30-2, 36, 46, 50, 59, 62, 189, 201-2, 208, 276-93

303